Speaker's *Quick Start Guide*

The Quick Start Guide is designed to help you find the specific public speaking information you're looking for as quickly as possible.

Basic Content Information, Color-Coded

This guide provides only the most basic information about the **handbook's contents**:

▶ Part numbers and titles

▶ Chapter numbers and titles within each part

▶ Page range for each part (identifying first and last pages)

The handiest feature of this guide is that it is **color-coded**: The color applied to each part in the guide corresponds to the color used for the actual part's tabbed section divider and introductory pages as well as the thumb tabs you'll find at the top of each page.

Where You'll Find More Detailed Content Information

The handbook's **full table of contents** begins on page v. Additionally, each part's **tabbed section divider** includes a detailed listing of each chapter and the chapter's subsections within the part. At the back of the book, on its last pages and inside back cover, you'll find **listings of the handbook's boxes, tables, and figures**. A detailed **index** begins on page 481.

Mapping Your Skill-Development Plan

To help orient you so that this book is as useful as possible, we offer these key suggestions:

▶ **Read Chapter 1**. This chapter introduces the five steps of public speaking that will help you prepare and deliver an effective speech. It will also help you diagnose your skill level and give you an approach to mapping out a skill-development plan for yourself.

▶ **Prepare a skill-development plan.** There are many steps to preparing an effective speech, but if you try to master every step simultaneously, you'll become frustrated and find it harder to build skills. That's why the secret of public speaking success lies in having a clear idea of what your priorities are and in deciding on a limited number of goals to pursue at any one time. This text's handbook format lets you pick one or two important skills to work on and once mastered, you can move on to other skills. Take the time to write down a skill-development plan and refer to it. Even if you revise it as you go, we guarantee that it will help you succeed.

Online Resources for *The Speaker's Handbook,* Twelfth Edition

MindTap is a personalized teaching experience with relevant assignments that guide students to analyze, apply, and improve thinking, allowing you to measure skills and outcomes with ease.

▶ **Personalized Teaching:** Becomes yours with a Learning Path that is built with key student objectives. Control what students see and when they see it. Use it as-is or match to your syllabus exactly—hide, rearrange, add, and create your own content.

▶ **Guide Students:** A unique Learning Path of relevant readings, activities such as collaborative and interactive video activities, outlining and preparation activities, and Practice and Present speech activities that move students up the learning taxonomy from basic knowledge and comprehension to analysis and application.

▶ **Promote Better Outcomes:** Empower instructors and motivate students with analytics and reports that provide a snapshot of class progress, time in course, and engagement and completion rates.

12e

the
Speaker's
Handbook

Jo Sprague
San José State University

Douglas Stuart
VMware, Incorporated

David Bodary
Sinclair Community College

Australia • Brazil • Mexico • Singapore • United Kingdom • United States

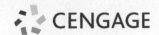

The Speaker's Handbook,
Twelfth Edition
Jo Sprague, Douglas Stuart,
David Bodary

Product Manager: Kelli Strieby

Project Manager: Julia Giannotti

Vendor Content Project Manager:
Chrystie Hopkins, Lumina
Datamatics, Inc.

Product Assistant: Camille Beckman

Marketing Manager: Allison
Moghaddasi

Content Project Manager: Dan
Saabye

Manufacturing Planner: Doug Bertke

IP Analyst: Ann Hoffman

IP Project Manager: Betsy Hathaway

Production Service: Lumina
Datamatics

Compositor: Lumina Datamatics

Art Director: Marissa Falco

Text Designer: C Miller Design

Cover Designer: C Miller Design

Cover Image: C Miller Design

For product information and technology assistance, contact us at
Cengage Customer & Sales Support, 1-800-354-9706.

For permission to use material from this text or product, submit all requests online at **www.cengage.com/permissions.**
Further permissions questions can be emailed to
permissionrequest@cengage.com.

Library of Congress Control Number: 2017950547

Student Edition:
ISBN: 978-1-337-55861-7

Loose-leaf Edition:
ISBN: 978-1-337-55862-4

Cengage
20 Channel Center Street
Boston, MA 02210
USA

Cengage is a leading provider of customized learning solutions with employees residing in nearly 40 different countries and sales in more than 125 countries around the world. Find your local representative at **www.cengage.com.**

Cengage Learning products are represented in Canada by Nelson Education, Ltd.

To learn more about Cengage platforms and services, visit **www.cengage.com.**

To register or access your online learning solution or purchase materials for your course, visit **www.cengagebrain.com.**

Printed in the United States of America
Print Number: 03   Print Year: 2019

Contents

6   Topic Selection and Analysis   67

7   Audience Analysis   86

3   Organization

4   Development

7   Sample Speeches

Preface

The Speaker's Handbook is, like its earlier editions, both a reference guide for individual speakers and a textbook for use in public speaking courses. What distinguishes *The Speaker's Handbook* from other books on public speaking, though, is not just that it was the first handbook of public speaking, but that it was originally conceived and written as one, too. From the start, each of its chapters was designed by Jo Sprague and Doug Stuart to stand by itself so that speakers may directly consult only those sections of the book that present the specific help they need. In coauthor David Bodary's last four revisions this text's origins are still evident, offering flexibility and ease of use for all kinds of public speakers.

Why *The Speaker's Handbook* Was Written

Public speaking is a lived, performed, embodied event that draws its special qualities from the immediate context, the personality of a particular speaker, the response of a certain audience and delivered in a time and place that will not be the same again. Is there really any useful general advice about so specific an act?

Apparently so. For as long as people have felt the need to speak in public, they have turned to others for advice on how to do so more effectively. Early evidence from Egyptian tombs shows that leaders gave serious thought to the choices they faced in speaking to their followers. The oral tradition captured in Homeric legend hints that the giving and taking of this advice predated the written word. The increasing supply of information about the ancient cultures of China, India, and the Americas shows that these peoples had culturally distinctive ways of speaking, which some analyzed and discussed. These observers then formulated advice for others in their culture. Such advice usually came in two forms: Those who had vast experience as speakers told stories about what worked for them; others looked beyond what worked and theorized about why it worked.

Both forms of guidance are still present. The popularity of such books year after year suggests that people find benefits in the personal and experiential approach. At the same time, university libraries continue to accumulate academic works on rhetoric and communication. Here, too, the vitality of these lines of research after thousands of years suggests that much is left to be said and investigated.

There is a third form of guidance, one that we differentiate from both those kinds of books and place within another venerable tradition that is over 2,000 years old. It is the handbook. In any field, a handbook represents a particular blending of theory and practice displayed in a concise format. The first written handbooks for speakers were probably produced by the Sophists in the Greece of 200 BCE. There are scouting handbooks, birding handbooks, management handbooks, and meditation handbooks. In all these cases, a handbook is a distillation of the experience and theory of many people and many eras. The particular usefulness of handbooks can be found in their distinctive characteristics, and the value of this handbook can be found in its unique features.

Handbooks Are Brief

The Speaker's Handbook attempts to distill the most meaningful advice and provide the most useful examples without expanding the size of the book. However, sample speeches abound: This edition, like those before it, includes annotated sample speeches by both student speakers and public figures in Part 7. Many are accompanied by speech videos and interactive activities available among the book's online resources. We refer to these sample outlines, transcripts, manuscripts, and videos throughout the text in both examples and exercises. Interspersing sample speeches throughout the body of the book, as is usual in standard textbooks, would defeat the advantages offered by the handbook format. Cartoons and multiple photographs would likewise have taken up needless space.

Handbooks Are Reference Books

The Speaker's Handbook proceeds from the premise that people like to focus first on the area of greatest concern and then design their own learning experience outward from that point. I believe that there are and ought to be many "right ways" to approach a course in public speaking. As such, the contents of a handbook are meant to be used in any order. The progression of this handbook's chapters is not random, but a reader or a teacher does not necessarily have to follow that order. The chapters are intended to be as self-contained as possible so that the book is adaptable to the differing needs of its various users.

As a reference, this book seeks to meet the needs of adult learners who have their own learning preferences, whether they are playing with their new smartphone or understanding a new job. People don't desire a course in how to use their smartphone. Instead, they try a few things, glance at the manual, ask a friend, and work until they get into trouble. Then they seek assistance again but only for the specific information they need to get beyond the current problem. In effect, they don't worry about the things they don't need yet, and they often don't know that a thing to worry about exists until it becomes a problem for them. Public speaking is like that. Until people start speaking, they cannot be sure of all the areas in which they may need improvement.

Therefore, students and individual users should take what they need from this book in the order they need it.

Likewise, teachers—who bring to the classroom different experience and an understanding of the values, needs, and capabilities of their specific students—may choose to assign chapters in any order that fits their perceptions of the best way to increase the skills of their students. There's some benefit for everyone in every chapter of this handbook; by using it you will find the order that suits you best.

Handbooks Are Handy

When people open the documentation that comes with their smartphone, they want to find the section on storing phone numbers, not read about taking photographs or how to clear the screen. We have included aids to help users get to where they want to be as quickly as possible, from elements such as the Quick Start Guide on the inside front cover to the tabbed part openers that include directories of each part's content, and from the checklists to the tables, figures, and straightforward cross-references provided throughout the book.

With this compartmentalization, users do not have to read everything at once. A student may be preparing to give an informative speech for a class and is thinking of including some humor. The student is encouraged to jump ahead and read the section in Chapter **18** on using appropriate humor. A businessperson may be giving a presentation to the board on the introduction of a new product but may feel uncertain about whether he or she has covered everything and in the most effective order. That person could read Chapter **9** on transforming ideas into speech points and Chapters **21** and **22** on informative and persuasive strategies.

About the Twelfth Edition

I have been gratified to be invited to work on the last three revisions of *The Speaker's Handbook* and am pleased that the handbook format has worked for so many students and their instructors, as well as for people who give presentations in their business or community. In this edition, I have worked once again to respond to user suggestions on how to make the information even more timely and accessible.

▶ I have focused my revisions in this latest edition on preserving the tradition and strength of *The Speaker's Handbook* originated by Jo Sprague and Douglas Stuart, while infusing it with examples and connections to the challenges and questions that I encounter with students in the classroom. I enjoy teaching immensely and have used my experience teaching community college students of all ages to improve the usefulness of this resource by including many practical tips and advice for students. In addition, I believe deeply in civic engagement and hope that comes through in the focus on effective public speaking skills in many contexts, including the workplace and the community.

▶ Graphics help to illustrate important concepts, including public speaking anxiety, audience analysis, and generational culture.

▶ New full speech examples from students and public figures provide speech models and opportunities for analysis. Videos for all *student* speeches are provided in your MindTap for *The Speaker's Handbook* along with critical-thinking questions, transcripts, and full-sentence and keyword outlines. New speeches from students and public figures include a new invitational speech addressing the use of memory drugs to treat post-traumatic stress disorder (PTSD), President George W. Bush's commemorative speech at the dedication of the National Museum of African American History and Culture, a similar speech by "Freedom Fighter" and Congressman John Lewis at that same dedication, and Eboo Patel's address on "The Only Shame Is in Stagnation," his address to the graduates of Wake Forest University. I spent considerable time selecting speeches that provide examples on topics of significance, which are both timely and timeless, and authentic in substance and style. Speeches by public figures reflect the diversity of voices that define the current age. Included in this edition are heads of state, popular artists, environmentalists, and interfaith leaders.

▶ The For Your Benefit boxes provide practical speech advice while also offering insights for speaking in the classroom and in the boardroom. Updated content provides students with tips for

▶ learning the listening stance.

▶ listening takes work.

▶ selecting a speech title.

▶ limitations of demographic generalizations.

▶ being aware of urban legends.

▶ conducting interviews.

▶ standpoint and bias.

▶ using clickers and cell phones.

▶ avoiding common attention pitfalls.

▶ being your own personal brand.

▶ placing strongest points first or last.

▶ impromptu speaking.

▶ when to use a manuscript.

▶ your voice; your brand.

▶ smiling.

▶ deciding whether to use video clips.

▶ More Checklists throughout the text provide students with frequent opportunities to check their knowledge. New and/or updated content includes:

▶ Questions for Assessing a Speaker's Claims

▶ Finding a Balance in Ethical Decisions

▶ Reducing Your Anxiety

▶ Describing Your Audiences

▶ Attention-Getting Techniques

▶ Assessing Your Speaking Image

▶ Helpful Strategies for Informative Speaking

▶ Checklist for a Positive, Neutral, and Negative Audience

▶ Assessing and Modifying Vocal Behavior

The revised **MindTap for *The Speaker's Handbook*** is a personalized teaching experience with relevant assignments that guide students to analyze, apply, and improve thinking, allowing you to measure skills and outcomes with ease. Activities, powered by MindApps developed specifically for this discipline, guide students through the process of analyzing sample speeches, topic creation, outline building, and practicing and presenting their speech.

Hallmarks of *The Speaker's Handbook*

The great strength of oral communication is that its many dimensions offer people ways to seek out connections in the midst of differences; its immediacy allows for on-the-spot adjustments. The following features of the text have therefore been retained.

▶ **Skill-building pedagogy and study tools.** Checklist boxes help readers better understand—and apply—chapter concepts. Speaker's Workshop boxes provide activities that help students prepare effective, well-structured speeches. In addition, Part **7** provides resources that speakers and users of the handbook will find practical and helpful: a guide to common pronunciation and usage errors for native and nonnative speakers of English, and a glossary of key terms.

▶ **Communicative approach.** Public speaking is consistently presented as a blend of communicative resources: writing, performance, and conversation.

▶ **Distinctive coverage of audience analysis.** Not just audience members' traits and characteristics are analyzed but also the processes by which they make sense of messages (Chapter **7**).

▶ **Consistent attention paid to social and cultural diversity.** We strive to continue attuning the handbook to the diversity of contemporary life. In our treatment of language, reasoning, and vocal and physical delivery, we attempt to show how social forces shape—and are shaped by—speech. What is appropriate or clear or persuasive constantly changes as society changes, and we emphasize that effective speakers are open to the subtle cultural variations in speech situations. If there were no differences between people, communication would be unnecessary. If there were no similarities, it would be impossible.

▶ **Extensive coverage of reasoning.** Reasoning (Chapter **16**) is discussed through an examination of the links people draw between data and conclusions. The text discusses how people can logically reach opposite conclusions from the same evidence, emphasizing the need to spell out and justify the links in one's reasoning.

▶ **Emphasis on language.** Language (Chapter **17**) is presented as a powerful communicative element (rather than an adornment or frill) in order to emphasize the need for thoughtful, sensitive, and appropriate use of words and symbols.

▶ **Full chapter on ethics.** "Speaking Ethics" (Chapter **3**) draws together key points and provides guidelines for responsible speaking. The ethical decisions speakers make are treated as a series of careful compromises, not as clear-cut do's and don'ts.

▶ **Full chapter on practicing speeches.** Chapter **24** provides detailed guidelines for practicing speech presentations, including concrete suggestions and timetables for this important dimension of speech preparation.

Resources for Students and Instructors

Accompanying this book is an integrated suite of resources to support both students and instructors.

MindTap

MindTap represents a new approach to a customizable, online, user-focused learning platform. MindTap combines all of a user's learning tools—readings, multimedia, activities, and assessments—into a singular learning unit that guides students through the curriculum based on learning objectives and outcomes. Instructors personalize the experience by customizing the presentation of these learning tools to their students, even seamlessly introducing their own content into the learning unit via "apps" that integrate into the MindTap platform.

Students and other individuals have the option of utilizing a rich array of resources to enhance and extend their learning while using *The Speaker's Handbook*. **Note to instructors:** If you want your students to have access to MindTap for *The Speaker's Handbook*, please be sure to order them for your course—if you do not order them, your students will not have access to them on the first day of class. These resources can be bundled with every new copy of the text or ordered separately. Students whose instructors do not order these resources as a package with the text may purchase them or access them at **www.cengagebrain.com**. *Contact your local Cengage Learning consultant for more details.*

Through the use of assignable and gradable interactive video activities, polling assignments, and study and exam preparation tools, MindTap brings the printed textbook to life. Students respond enthusiastically to the readspeak, highlighting, search, and dictionary features available on MindTap. Student comprehension is enhanced with the integrated e-Book and the interactive teaching and learning tools that include:

YouSeeU

With *YouSeeU*, students can upload video files of practice speeches or final performances, comment on their peers' speeches, and review their grades and instructor feedback. Instructors create courses and assignments, comment on and grade student speeches, and allow peer review. Grades flow into a gradebook that allows instructors to easily manage their course from within MindTap. Grades also can be exported for use in learning-management systems. YouSeeU's flexibility lends itself to use in traditional, hybrid, and online courses.

Outline Builder

Outline Builder breaks down the speech preparation process into manageable steps and can help alleviate speech-related anxiety. The "wizard format" provides relevant prompts and resources to guide students through the outlining process. Students are guided through topic definition, research and source citation, organizational structure outlining, and drafting note cards for speech day. The outline is assignable and gradable through MindTap.

Speech Video Library

Speech Video Library gives students a chance to watch videos of real speeches that correspond to the topics in *The Speaker's Handbook*. Each video is accompanied by a speech activity that provides a full transcript so viewers can read along the speech outline—many in note card and full sentence form, and evaluation questions so students are guided through their assessment. While viewing each clip, students evaluate the speech or scenario by completing short-answer questions and submitting their results directly to their instructor.

Additional Student Resources

▶ **CengageBrain Online Store.** CengageBrain.com is a single destination for more than 15,000 new print textbooks, textbook rentals, e-Books, single eChapters, and print, digital, and audio study tools. CengageBrain.com provides the freedom to purchase Cengage Learning products à-la-carte—exactly what you need, when you need it. Visit **www.cengagebrain.com** for details.

▶ *The Art and Strategy of Service-Learning Presentations,* **Fourth Edition.** Written by Rick Isaacson and Jeff Saperstein of San Francisco State University, this handbook provides guidelines for connecting service-learning work with classroom concepts and advice for working effectively with agencies and organizations.

▶ **A Guide to the Basic Course for ESL Students.** Specifically for communicators whose first language is not English, it features FAQs, helpful URLs, and strategies for managing communication anxiety.

Instructor Resources

Instructors who adopt this book may request a number of resources to support their teaching. These resources are available to qualified adopters, and ordering options for supplements are flexible. Please consult your local Cengage Learning consultant for more information, to evaluate examination copies of any of these instructor or student resources, or to request product demonstrations.

▶ **Instructor's Resource Manual.** Written by Tina Lim of San José State University, this manual offers guidelines for setting up your course, sample syllabi, chapter-by-chapter outlines of content, suggested topics for lectures and discussion, and a wealth of class-tested exercises and assignments. It also includes a test bank with questions marked according to varying levels of difficulty.

▶ **Instructor's Website.** Computerized testing via Cognero®, ready-to-use Power-Point® presentations (with text and images that can also be customized to suit your course needs), and an electronic version of the Instructor's Manual. Visit the Instructor's Website by accessing http://login.cengage.com or by contacting your local learning consultant.

▶ **The Teaching Assistant's Guide to the Basic Course.** Katherine G. Hendrix, who is on the faculty at the University of Memphis, prepared this resource specifically for new instructors. Based on leading communication teacher training programs, this guide discusses some of the general issues that accompany a teaching role and offers specific strategies for managing the first week of classes, leading productive discussions, managing sensitive topics in the classroom, and grading students' written and oral work.

▶ **Instructor Workbooks.** *Public Speaking: An Online Approach, Public Speaking: A Problem Based Learning Approach,* and *Public Speaking: A Service-Learning Approach for Instructors.* Written by Deanna Sellnow, University of Kentucky, these instructor workbooks include a course syllabus and icebreakers; public speaking basics such as coping with anxiety, learning cycle, and learning styles; outlining; ethics; and informative, persuasive, and ceremonial (special occasion) speeches.

▶ **Guide to Teaching Public Speaking Online.** Written by Todd Brand of Meridian Community College, this helpful online guide provides instructors who teach public speaking online with tips for establishing "classroom" norms with students, utilizing course management software and other eResources, managing logistics such as delivering and submitting speeches and making up work, discussing how peer feedback is different online, strategies for assessment, and tools such as sample syllabi and critique and evaluation forms tailored to the online course.

▶ **Service Learning in Communication Studies: A Handbook.** Written by Rick Isaacson and Jeff Saperstein, this is an invaluable resource for students in the basic course that integrates or will soon integrate a service-learning component. This handbook provides guidelines for connecting service-learning work with classroom concepts and advice for working effectively with agencies and organizations. It also provides model forms and reports and a directory of online resources.

▶ **Digital Course Support.** Get trained, get connected, and get the support you need for the seamless integration of digital resources into your course. This unparalleled technology service and training program provide robust online resources, peer-to-peer instruction, personalized training, and a customizable program you can count on. Visit **http://www .cengage.com/dcs** to sign up for online seminars, first days of class services, technical support, or personalized, face-to-face training. Our online and onsite trainings are frequently led by one of our lead teachers, faculty members who are experts in using Cengage Learning technology and can provide best practices and teaching tips.

Acknowledgments

Many thanks to the team at Cengage who accommodated, challenged, and ultimately made this book better—true synergy. Instrumental in the transition from eleventh to twelfth were Monica Eckman, product director; Kelli Strieby, product manager; Chrystie Hopkins, content developer; Camille Beckman, product assistant—they have been huge supporters of the handbook approach and invaluable partners in this project. As always, thanks to Peter Dougherty, who initially approached the original authors with the idea for *The Speaker's Handbook*. Likewise, I owe special thanks to the students who have granted us permission to use their speeches as examples—particularly my students Nathanael Dunlavy, Brian Sharkey, Kayla Strickland, and Stephen Garrett—for speeches they share in this edition.

I am indebted to Jo Sprague and Douglas Stuart, whose foundational text remains the bedrock of this edition, as well as the many loyal users of *The Speaker's Handbook* who have generously shared their comments with me and who, along with our reviewers, ensure that I continually consider how the text is best used in classrooms and conference rooms alike. I am grateful to the reviewers who took the time to help us further improve this edition: Dawn Bartlett, SUNY Jefferson Community College; Nathan Carroll, College of St. Scholastica; Diana M. Cooley, Lone Star College—North Harris; Jamie Matson, Winona State University; Shellie Michael, Volunteer State Community College; Robert Schwing, Benedictine University; and Clayton Whitson, Fort Scott Community College. In addition, I remain appreciative of reviewers of previous editions who have also helped to shape this text throughout the years.

Family and friends provide the love and support that serve as the foundation necessary to complete a writing project. That they have continued with that support through each revision leaves me thankful and appreciative. I greatly appreciate my daughter, Annelise, for her artistic insight, son Samuel for his willingness to brainstorm with me, and daughter Lily for understanding that I am "that Dad." I am most thankful for my fantastic wife Susan, without her guidance I would be lost.

David Bodary

The Value of Public Speaking Skills

Whether you desire to improve your situation at work, school, or community, chances are good that doing so will require that you speak up for yourself, your colleagues, classmates, family members, or community. That may mean that you need to speak publicly. Whatever the context, this *is* an opportunity and this *is* a good thing.

For some, the idea of having "an opportunity to give a public speech" may sound a bit ominous. Most people we've met acknowledge some nervousness about speaking up publicly. Your feelings might range from mild apprehension to severe panic. But there is one thing worse than being called on to give a public speech when you *don't* want to—that is not being *able* to give a public speech when you *do* want to.

Do any of the following scenarios sound familiar?

▶ You listen to your acquaintances telling stories of funny things that have happened to them, and you would like to share your own experiences, but you are too shy to speak up.

▶ You sit in class, knowing the answer to the instructor's question, but you lack the confidence to raise your hand.

▶ You begin a presentation on a topic you know well, but you soon forget your key ideas and hastily finish your speech.

▶ You attend a business meeting to discuss a problem. You think you have some insights that could be part of the solution, but others don't seem to hear or understand what you are trying to say.

▶ You would like to take on a leadership role in a work or social group, but hesitate to share your views or struggle to persuade others to follow you.

▶ You are being interviewed for a job you really want and think you are qualified for, but your ideas come out jumbled and lack clarity, confidence, and detail.

▶ You attend a public meeting on an issue crucial to your family. You believe you have a valid concern that is being overlooked, but aren't sure how to phrase your opposition.

Social and Societal Benefits of Public Speaking

A democratic society requires the free exchange of ideas so people can listen to each other's views, understand the implications of policies, and select the best courses of collective action. In the words of historian Daniel J. Boorstin, "Disagreement is the life blood of democracy."[1] Likewise, U.S. Senator J. William Fulbright noted, "The citizen who criticizes his country is paying it an implied tribute."[2] All citizens must be willing to contribute positively to their democracy and be able to speak up to protect their own rights as well as the rights of others.

Not only are communication skills important to our democracy, but they are also important to business. Warren Buffett, famed investor and billionaire, says it this way, "If you can't communicate and talk to other people and get across your ideas, you're giving up your potential. You have to learn to communicate in life—it's enormously important."[3] Perhaps most of all, our families and communities need people who are sensitive to and skilled in communication, because it is through storytelling and personal sharing that we are able to form healthy family and community bonds.

Personal and Professional Benefits of Public Speaking

Experience with analyzing information and expressing your opinions through public speaking not only will increase your confidence in day-to-day activities, but will also help you get more out of your classes. Participating constructively in class discussions and applying the skills of preparation, organization, development, and presentation will enhance your learning experience.

Regarding professional benefits, a quick glance at job descriptions at websites such as indeed.com, LinkedIn.com, and SimplyHired.com reveals regular and frequent use of phrases like "strong communication skills," "excellent verbal and written skills," and "ability to motivate others." Clearly, the skills you develop as a public speaker not only will help you land a job, but will also help you succeed and advance in your profession. In a job interview, the candidate who offers concise responses, who expresses ideas in memorable ways, and who remains calm under pressure will make a stronger impression. Once you get the job, you can use these communication skills to improve your workplace and product, influence those around you, and gain personal satisfaction while being an effective and valued professional resource.

Improving Your Public Speaking Skills

For the most part, the factors that inhibit people from speaking in public can be overcome through education, practice, and coaching. Effective speaking is a skill you can learn.

Although it may seem that a great speaker was born that way, in truth great speakers are made. While Dr. Martin Luther King, Jr., certainly was helped by being born into the family of a preacher, he also went to school where he learned both content and confidence, prepared himself through study, practiced extensively, and presented before audiences many times. Each of us can improve our speaking skills, regardless of our prior experiences.

As with any other skill (such as writing, playing guitar, meditation, or brain surgery), there are principles to be mastered with public speaking; there is a need for concentration and practice; and there are benefits to working with a skilled teacher and supportive co-learners. As classroom faculty and speech coaches, we have seen reticent speakers gain confidence and poise. We have observed people develop the ability to effectively analyze and create mutual understanding with their audience. We have watched people, who initially detested speech outlines, admit the improved clarity and structure afforded by outlining and the resulting improvement of their messages. Believe it or not, some of the most reluctant speakers have discovered that making a presentation can even be fun. They find it exhilarating to be heard, to be understood, and possibly even persuade their audience. More importantly, lives are improved and opportunities are expanded by our willingness and ability to speak.

Effective speaking and listening go hand in hand. If you master the techniques in this handbook, it's inevitable you will be more appreciative of good speaking when you hear it, recognizing the art and craft that come into play to create a satisfying and successful speaking event. You will also be a more critical listener of the speeches and reasoning you hear.

We all like to receive compliments and applause when our ideas resound with others. We enjoy a sense of satisfaction when our ideas are taken seriously and can contribute to improving understanding or advancing the public dialogue. In short, there is power and personal fulfillment in finding our voices in the public sphere.

Critical Thinking Questions

▶ What dollar value would you put on the ability to speak publicly with confidence?

▶ What will it take to improve your public speaking skills?

▶ How will you commit to the work of improving your public speaking skills?

1

Understanding Speaking

Understand that public speaking is the act of creating meaning with your listeners and that, by consciously combining communicative resources you already possess, you can speak successfully.

In the process of preparing a public speech, we make dozens of decisions. Delivering a speech involves a complex process coordinating mind, body, and voice from moment to moment. Giving a speech can never be made simple, but thinking about it can be greatly *simplified* if we understand the basics of communicating and speaking. Understanding some fundamental communication principles and the theoretical framework of public speaking can reduce complexity, bring clarity, and guide the choices we make in planning and presenting a speech.

1-1 Understand What It Means to Be a Public Speaker

When most people hear the words *public speaking*, they imagine a podium, a stage, and an auditorium with a large audience—the components of a classic "capital S" Speech. This handbook offers a broader picture of public speaking. We are speakers not only when we stand behind the podium at an awards banquet or when we approach the microphone at a planning commission meeting but also when we sit at a table with a few members of our work group and present a problem. We are speakers in class, at work, and among friends and family. In each of these situations, we are the same speakers working with the same set of communication skills, but we will apply those skills differently in each situation.

But let's not broaden the context too much. Not all oral communication in a group setting is public speaking. **Public speaking** is an event in which a group of people

PHOTO 1.1
Communication is similar to the give-and-take between dancers.

Dmitry Morgan/Shutterstock.com

agree that one person, the speaker, will direct the event. Because the speaker directs the event, it would be easy to assume that speakers and listeners are vastly different in the public speaking situation. However, there are probably more similarities than differences between these roles. In essence, speakers create **meaning** with listeners. Communication theorists stress that meaning is socially constructed in a mutual transaction between speakers and listeners. In a sense then, the speaker and listener are involved in what might be termed *co-creation*, a sort of dance, a give-and-take that unfolds over time into a meaningful exchange (Photo 1.1). Continuing with this meta-phor, the more experience two dance partners have together, the more effectively each is able to anticipate the moves (intended meaning) of the other and respond appro-priately. This **mutuality of concern** is central to the effective communication of any message.

This view of speaking as a mutual transaction does not relieve the speaker of cer-tain basic responsibilities; nor does it mean every speaking situation is an improvisa-tion. To uphold their end of the agreement, speakers are obliged to lead their audience partners and create an effective, efficient, perhaps even enjoyable event. To achieve this sort of event, speakers must follow certain guidelines, but like good dancers, they must also be creative and bring something that is uniquely theirs to the interaction. Just as we want our dance partner to know the basics but not follow the same pattern for every dance, each new speech situation calls for certain basic elements but allows for those elements to be arranged into countless combinations.

MindTap°   Visit the MindTap for *The Speaker's Handbook* and click on **Additional Resources** to visit a site that discusses the sender's and receiver's different realities, perceptions, and experiences as communicators. How will your audience member's perceptions of your or your topic impact your ability to communicate your intended message?

1-1a Common Public Speaking Misconceptions

There are many approaches to teaching public speaking and much folk wisdom about how speakers become effective. Mastery of speaking will come more quickly if you can avoid being affected by the four common misconceptions: (1) Good speakers are born, not made; (2) good speaking should be easy right away; (3) speaking will always be as difficult as it is when you are first learning it; and (4) there are simple formulas for effective speaking.

Misconception 1: Good Speakers Are Born, Not Made Though it may seem that some people are born better speakers, in fact they are people who have already learned a number of speech skills or who happen to learn speech-related skills quickly. No one is born an effective speaker any more than one is born a good dancer, an accomplished writer, or an expert guitar player. Although predispositions and early learning mean some people learn faster and move more smoothly, anyone who is moderately coordinated, is adequately motivated, and receives sound instruction can learn to dance, develop a short story, or play a tune on the guitar. Similarly, virtually anyone can learn to give a clear, effective public speech.

Misconception 2: Good Speaking Should Be Easy Right Away When we watch world-class figure skaters, we are fascinated by the apparent ease with which they perform what we know are extremely difficult moves. We appreciate the years of training, dedication, and discipline that have gone into making their movements seem so effortless. Not everyone figure skates—but everyone communicates. Skillful communicators can make public speaking look easy, but it takes work—and lots of it. While many of us have communicated for years, there's a difference between just communicating and communicating effectively. Effective communication takes regular practice, constant reflection, and improvement.

Misconception 3: Speaking Will Always Be as Difficult as It Is When You Are First Learning It Preparing an oral message on a substantial topic for a live audience is demanding. When, at least initially, you must spend hours preparing for a short presentation, there is a real temptation to say, "Forget this. I can't invest this much time and effort every time I give a speech." Remind yourself that learning a skill requires effort and attention, but it becomes easier once mastered. Recall the concentration required when you learned to drive a car. Now that you have mastered the skill, you simply think of the goal you want to achieve—the actions necessary to reach the

MindTap® **SPEAKER'S WORKSHOP 1.1**

Which misconceptions about public speaking do you personally hold? Which do you think are most widespread? Are there other misconceptions that have not been mentioned here?

goal happen largely on their own. When you get discouraged with a speech outline that just won't come together or with phrasing that just won't flow, remember: It *will* get easier.

Misconception 4: There Are Simple Formulas for Effective Speaking

Communicating with an audience is an incredibly complex and sophisticated act. Every public speaking event is unique. Each speaker has a distinctive style and personality, the audience has idiosyncratic needs and preferences, and the situation differs from case to case. How these three factors interact creates the meaning in any speaking event. No one can give an all-purpose formula for preparing or delivering a speech. Be wary of programs that promise instant speaking success. When you want to learn a skill well enough for it to become habitual, you need time to develop good habits. The advice in this handbook is based not on what is easiest or fastest but on what has proved to be effective based on years of application. It takes longer to develop a full-sentence outline than to jot down points in the order they occur to you. It is harder to sound conversational and look poised standing and speaking from notes than it is to read while leaning on a table. But once you master these proven techniques, you will be flexible and effective and ready for any speaking situation.

MindTap® **SPEAKER'S WORKSHOP 1.2**

Assess the resources you already have as a public speaker by thinking about your strengths and weaknesses as a conversationalist, a writer, and a performer. Which of these resources

- Will be the most transferable to your public speaking?
- Will be difficult for you to transfer to public speaking?
- Might you tend to draw too much from as a speaker?
- Offers you the most room for improvement?

1-2 Theoretical Foundations of Effective Public Speaking

Although this handbook emphasizes practical advice for speakers, its recommendations are distilled from a number of communication theories and traditions. Table 1.1 summarizes the many insights of four prominent theoretical foundations of public speaking: oral cultures, classical rhetoric, communication studies, and dialogic perspectives.

1-2a Oral Cultures

Just as children speak before they write, humans developed systems of communal speech long before they created the first systems of writing. Scholars of preliterate societies remind us that speech is the most fundamental tool of social organization. Oral cultures relied on the spoken word to draw them together, affirm their connectedness, and preserve their traditions.

TABLE 1.1

Insights from theoretical foundations of public speaking

THEORETICAL FOUNDATION	INSIGHTS AND WHERE THIS BOOK DISCUSSES THEM
Our ancient oral traditions	▶ Public speaking existed in preliterate societies. It is a form of communal experience that bonds people together.
	▶ Public speaking, despite the visual, textual, and electronic aids that enhance it today, still finds its essence in the sounds made by the human voice.
	▶ Speech is a medium characterized by immediacy and concreteness. Rhythm, repetition, participation, conflict, and vivid details make it powerful and memorable.
	▶ Human beings are innate storytellers. The narrative form is the most natural way to engage an audience.
	You will encounter some of these principles in Chapters **1, 18, 26, 27,** and **33.**
Our rhetorical heritage	▶ Public speakers are, above all, decision makers. They choose among many possible ways to speak their truth, seeking the one that is most effective for the situation.
	▶ Speech influences people by appealing to their rationality, but effective speakers view rationality as more than logic. They integrate appeals of motivation and credibility into their speeches.
	▶ Speech is complex and it is helpful to analyze its various components and the demands of various speech situations.
	▶ Because speech is used to influence others and shape common decisions, it always has an ethical dimension.
	You will encounter some of these principles in Chapters **1, 3, 6, 7, 16, 19, 20, 22,** and **34.**

THEORETICAL FOUNDATION	INSIGHTS AND WHERE THIS BOOK DISCUSSES THEM
Information transmission theories	▶ Speech is a process and can be studied scientifically.
	▶ Public speakers are information managers. They need to control the flow of information to keep it from flooding the listeners, and they need to minimize and compensate for the noise present in every encounter.
	▶ Communication is impossible without a shared code. Using words and language to convey meaning is crucial, but so is an understanding of the nonverbal, social, and cultural codes that shape the interpretation of meaning.
	▶ Receivers are not passive recipients of speech; they bring their own filters to the decoding process.
	▶ Communication is never complete until feedback has been received and interpreted.
	You will encounter some of these principles in Chapters **15, 17, 21, 27,** and **31.**
Dialogic perspectives on communication	Though what we say is important, the ways we speak can change society for better or worse.
	▶ Speakers are not always trying to change other people; they may use communication to advance mutual understanding.
	▶ Even when someone seems to be presenting a monologue, it can be done with a dialogic perspective of humility, openness, and respect.
	▶ Empathy and consensus are built over time and start with finding common ground, which then expands to authentic speaking and listening.
	▶ It is possible to stand your ground about important principles and be receptive to other perspectives at the same time.
	You will encounter some of these principles in Chapters **1, 2, 3,** and **29.**

Walter Ong is one of the scholars who have identified a special feature of oral cultures: When the spoken word was the only form of preserving culture, speech had to be memorable.[4] Memorable speech took the form of dramatic stories of intense conflicts between powerful villains and heroes. These early stories were concrete and close to the "lifeworld" of the community. To aid memory and be sure the stories were passed on, the storytellers used repetition and rhyme to create songlike inflections.

After centuries of literacy based on books and printing presses, Marshall McLuhan[5] and other media scholars observed that the electronic media, especially television, had transformed communication into a sort of global village. They coined the term **secondary orality** to describe the rekindling of a preference for intense, visceral, immediate kinds of communication. The Internet, e-mail, and presentation software have brought the written word back into the speech act in ways that differ radically from the textualized orations found in anthologies of great speeches. It is difficult to imagine what exciting combinations of speaking, writing, images, videos, and sound will evolve in the future. But recognizing the features of orality that characterized speech in the earliest human societies will always help us understand what makes public speaking so powerful.

1-2b Classical Rhetoric

The genesis of formal theorizing about speech is usually placed in the thousand years that straddled the beginning of the Common Era. The most influential texts were produced in Greece between the fifth and fourth centuries BCE and in Rome during the 200 years following that period. In truth, these texts share commonalities with teachings associated with the Egyptian philosopher Ptahhotep years earlier.

Classical rhetorical theories emerged in the context of expanding political participation. In the early forms of democracy, citizens of the Greek city-states were allowed to speak in the public assembly and were required to defend themselves in courtroom struggles over property. Traveling teachers known as *sophists* served as speaking coaches and speechwriters. *Sophist* translates generally as "wise one" or "one who makes a business out of wisdom." Undoubtedly, the useful tips of these well-paid teachers empowered a people who might have lacked political voice. But the sophists were severely criticized by philosophers such as Plato, who claimed that the sophists' emphasis on **rhetoric** encouraged people to employ tricks of persuasion instead of searching for the truth.

Aristotle, a student of Plato and a scholar in many disciplines, tried to resolve this controversy in *The Rhetoric*, a comprehensive treatment of public speaking that was the basis of communication theory for centuries. Aristotle's definition of *rhetoric* as "the ability to find in any situation the available means of persuasion" differed sharply from the sophists' definition in that it made the speaker a decision maker, not just a technician. Aristotle's discussion of rhetoric also differed from Plato's philosophical notion of seeking one absolute, all-encompassing truth: Aristotle emphasized that what counts as truth varies with each situation. In other words, although speakers should not tell lies in order to persuade an audience, they are wise to recognize the many truths about each topic and to select the one that is most appropriate to the specific audience and situation.

Thus, much of Aristotle's *Rhetoric* deals with how a speaker analyzes situations, audiences, and issues in order to make wise choices. For example, Aristotle differentiates among three genres of speaking:

▶ *Forensic* speaking, as in a courtroom, where a speaker needs to convince a judge or jury that a certain claim is true or untrue;

▶ *Deliberative* speaking, as in a legislature or any decision-making setting, where a speaker is persuading others to make a certain decision or take a course of action; and

▶ *Epideictic* or *ceremonial* speaking, where the speaker is praising, blaming, or otherwise appealing to common values.

Each genre of speech requires different skills of the speaker. Audiences have different expectations and demands in these situations. Most notably, Aristotle identifies three categories of persuasive appeals. The most fundamental of these, *logos*, refers not just to logic as its name might hint but to all the intellectual substance of a speech—its arguments, reasons, and evidence. In addition to logos, speakers can draw on *pathos*, or motivational appeals to the values, needs, passions, and emotions of listeners. Finally, Aristotle recognized a third kind of persuasive appeal—one that goes beyond the content of the message and the feelings it evokes, and springs from the *ethos* of the speaker. *Ethos* refers to the personal power or credibility that comes from a speaker's force of personality or depth of character.

Effective speaking is too complex to understand as a single skill. Instead, it is made up of five areas of study, sometimes called *canons* of rhetoric, each requiring instruction and practice.

▶ *Invention*: The process of creating something that did not exist before.

▶ *Organization*: The grouping of ideas with supporting evidence and arranging the parts of the speech in a way that makes sense and affects the audience in a particular way.

▶ *Style*: The selection of words to make the points clear and engaging.

▶ *Delivery*: The use of body and voice, unobtrusively but gracefully, to convey a compelling message.

▶ *Memory*: The ways of focusing one's mind during a speech so that all of the speech's elements are coordinated with ease.

1-2c Communication Studies

In more recent times, attention has shifted from persuasive speaking to informative speaking. In the mid-twentieth century, some new perspectives emerged that treated communication more as science than as art, even examining features of machine systems to see what they might share with human communication. The model of human communication developed by Shannon and Weaver[6] in this period was a mechanistic view that emphasized one-way transmission from a sender to a receiver. From this line of thinking came the interactional and transactional perspectives. These two-way perspectives are represented in models of human communication such as the one in Figure 1.1.

Messages originate inside senders, or *sources*, who formulate their mental images into words or other symbols in a process of *encoding*. The sender then *transmits* the message through one or more *channels*, where it may encounter resistance or static known as *noise*. If the message gets past the noise, it is received at its *destination*. The signal must then be turned back into meaningful symbols through a process of *decoding*. If the resulting mental image generally corresponds to the mental image of the sender, there is *fidelity* of communication. If the two images are significantly different,

FIGURE 1.1
A two-way communication model

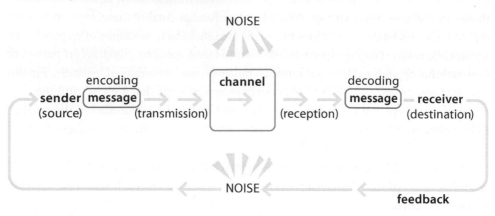

there has been a *communication breakdown*. The comparison of the intended message with the received message is accomplished through the process of *feedback*.

Feedback entails reversing the roles of sender and receiver. Feedback can be formal, as in a critique, but more often it is less formal, taking the form of instantaneous nonverbal communication as a listener makes eye contact, smiles, frowns, or perhaps nods off with boredom. The speaker notices, reacts, and adapts to these micromessages. The shifts back and forth between sender and receiver are nearly simultaneous, with each participant sending–receiving–encoding–decoding constantly. The distinction between sender and receiver almost disappears as their interaction becomes more fluid.

These information-based approaches showed that even the simplest exchange is packed with dozens of opportunities for communication to break down. Applied to public speaking, the information transmission models reminded speakers that it is never sufficient just to say what they mean and assume communication follows. Speakers must learn to pay close attention to the way they phrase messages to ensure shared understanding, just as good dancers respond to music and to their partners while dancing. By including feedback in the communication model, scholars realized that in a situation where interference (visual and psychological as well as acoustic) was likely, communicators could clarify their messages through repetition and redundancy. And, perhaps most importantly, they learned that no communication is complete without feedback to confirm what has been received.

1-2d Dialogic Perspectives

A fourth important way to look at communication is through the lens of dialogic theories. Dialogue, associated with give-and-take, may at first seem incompatible with our definition of public speaking. But dialogic theories are less about the *format* of a communicative event—whether one person is leading the event, for instance—than they are about the *attitude* of the speaker. In a dialogue, the speaker is not setting out to change the listeners according to some blueprint but engages in a much more open and collaborative event. Participants accept that points of view other than their own have validity and are open to changing their views; they avoid inflammatory language and statements of dogmatic certainty. In interacting with their audience, dialogic speakers show respect for different opinions and seek out areas of common understanding. Participation in a public discussion or invitational speech might be examples of this dialogic speech.

Some of the central ideas of dialogic theories can be traced to mid-twentieth-century philosophers such as Martin Buber. Buber envisioned a kind of communication in which the primary goal is mutual understanding. Speakers recognize their differences and hold to their beliefs, but they seek out the "between" as the place where communication must start. Dialogue is possible to the extent that participants speak and listen with authenticity, and that they establish what Buber called I–Thou relationships, in which people recognize one another's unique humanness, rather than I–It relationships, in which people treat one another as means to an end. Perhaps you have experienced this sort of communication where you live or work, from effective leaders as they moved organizational members through a difficult change.

Consistent with the nonexploitative approach of dialogic theory is a contemporary notion called *invitational rhetoric*. Foss and Griffin[7] urge speakers to pay less attention to trying to change their audiences and instead to invite listeners to explore ideas together and discover common interests. This orientation is particularly relevant for discussions of controversial issues where people's positions reflect deeply held values. At the most practical level, the invitational approach is often the only way to begin discussion among people who strongly disagree. People are more likely to hear a speaker out if they know the speech will be followed by a genuine give-and-take of ideas. A group of communication scholars known as the Public Dialogue Consortium is committed to applying these principles to speech in the public sphere. Their goal is to promote ways of speaking that will lead to an inclusive society that handles conflict constructively and respectfully. In such a world, they say, people would speak so others are able to listen and listen so others are able to speak.

MindTap°   Visit the MindTap for *The Speaker's Handbook* and click on **Additional Resources** to visit the Public Dialogue Consortium's website. There, review the seven principles for developing public dialogue in communities.

1-3 The Social Construction of Meaning

As different as the theoretical foundations of communication scholarship are, it is evident there are some common strands. People make meaning together, not alone, and what is effective varies from situation to situation. In recent decades, ideas like these have converged into a perspective that focuses on the *social construction of meaning*. This perspective provides the primary framework for the rest of this book.

As we've discussed, for decades after the dawn of the Information Age, *communication* was defined in terms of the clear transmission of information from a sender to a receiver. For some kinds of speaking and some aspects of speech preparation, this notion is useful. (See Chapter **21**.) But comparing speaking with delivering a package has severe limitations. This metaphor tends to convey the image of discrete, sender-controlled steps. "Giving a speech" becomes a matter of selecting ideas, packaging them, shipping them, and verifying their receipt. Of course, this simplistic approach is inadequate. A more collaborative and complex model of communication is needed.

1-3a Collaborative Creation of Meaning

The metaphor of collaborative creation evokes a different set of images. Think about a group of friends hanging out after school or a patient care team in a nursing home. At any given time, one individual may put forth ideas while the others listen and react. The product is a composite that emerges from the interaction; it did not exist in any one person's mind at the outset. The shift in emphasis from messages (speaker controlled) to meanings (jointly created) has important implications.

An example of this joint creation of meaning is exemplified by dynamic content in Web design so common in our virtual world. The ability for users to post content to others' pages (e.g., Pinterest and Facebook), to change content on shared pages (wikis and Google Documents), and to influence the types of content received are all wonderful examples of the way we jointly create meaning in our virtual world. It's useful to be able to upload a page of content that can be accessed by others on the Web, but it is much more useful to be able to collaboratively create Web content, change it, and be changed by it for mutual benefit.

Meaning Is Social No individual, sender or receiver, can control the "true meaning" of a statement. A speaker who has violated a social norm cannot get off the hook by saying, "I did not intend that statement to be offensive, so it wasn't." But neither can a single receiver unilaterally control what a statement or an action really means to others. A thin-skinned listener is not justified in overreacting to a rather innocent comment by declaring, "I felt offended, so that statement was offensive." Similarly, saying you didn't mean something the way it was taken doesn't take it back.

Meaning Is Contextual Words or messages alone cannot tell us the "true meaning" of the communication. Words take their meanings not just from a dictionary but from all that surrounds them as they are uttered. The *context*, that which surrounds a text (*con-text*), must be considered to understand its meaning. This approach to meaning considers when and where a statement was made, who was present, what happened previously, and what tone of voice and expression accompanied the utterance. Perhaps the importance of context is demonstrated by an incident involving Shirley Sherrod in 2010. Her videotaped comments were edited out of context and posted to the Web by commentator Andrew Breitbart.[8] In this case, Sherrod, a U.S. Department of Agriculture (USDA) employee, was forced to resign her job before the full context of her comments was brought to light and she was allowed to defend her comments as appropriate within the context of their original form. Her subsequent defamation lawsuit against the estate of deceased Andrew Breitbart was settled confidentially. The USDA offered to restore her to her job, which she declined.

Meaning Is Negotiated When the "true meaning" of a message is contested, appeals to the words themselves, to the speaker's intentions, or to the listeners' response have all been shown to be inadequate. Instead, groups work out meanings over time. For example, one court case does not settle what counts as sexual harassment in the workplace. The meaning of sexual harassment has been worked out in speeches, op-ed columns, letters to the editor, and countless personal conversations. Groups whose definition of *sexual harassment* included even friendly comments found their definition rejected. So did those whose definition excluded everything except physical assault. Gradually, a range of meanings of the term within contemporary U.S. culture came into general understanding. However, because these meanings are social, contextual, and contingent, they will continue to change.

FOR YOUR BENEFIT

No Simple Dos and Don'ts for Every Situation

We often joke with students that the answer to each question on our exams is the same: "It depends." This applies outside of school, too. The key to becoming an effective speaker is to understand what it depends on. Although the chapters of this handbook are written as prescriptions, there are no dos and don'ts to apply automatically to every situation. The fundamentals of speaking are stated simply, but the application and combination of these principles depend on your good judgment according to the speaking situation.

1-4 Balance Communication Resources

Public speakers should seek to create meaning with their audiences. Think of all the times you have successfully created meaning with different groups of people, in different contexts, and on different topics. When you enter the agreement that designates you as a speaker, you are not required to master a new skill. Rather, your challenge is to adapt several communication skills you already have in your repertoire: conversation, composition, and performance, as Figure 1.2 shows.

1-4a Conversation Skills

In everyday conversations, you do certain things to be effective. You probably are relaxed, spontaneous, and responsive to the situation, and you express your changing feelings naturally. Your attention is centered on the person or people to whom you are speaking and on the ideas you want to convey. You don't worry about your exact words because the event is interactive, with meaning clarified in the give-and-take.

Conversation is a form of risk taking in that you are not sure of the outcome at any point. This uncertainty does not usually prevent you from conversing, even if you know disagreements may occur. Apprehension about public speaking can be dissipated if you carry this aspect of conversation into the speaking event. One of the highest compliments a speaker can receive is to be called "conversational." The conversation

FIGURE 1.2
Three communication resources

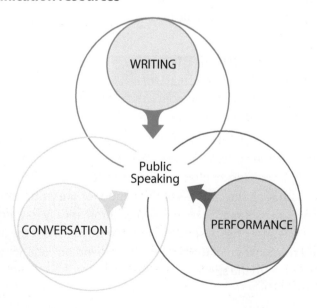

skills that are useful to a public speaker include speaking in a comfortable and confident manner, listening to and considering the perspectives of others, and adapting constantly to feedback.

1-4b Composition Skills

Composing a written or oral work enables you to distance yourself from your ideas and to freeze them on paper. This distancing allows you to craft and tinker—to experiment with alternative forms and play them out in your imagination. This tinkering takes much longer than a conversational exploration of ideas, in which the vague "you know what I mean" to a friend can substitute for a few paragraphs of content.

When composing, you pay close attention to word choices and organization. Vocabulary in a speech is more precise than in conversation. By taking the time to enjoy wordplay, explore nuance, and create elegant phrasing, you make memorable, meaningful messages. Composing can create the distance you need to view your ideas objectively, test them logically, and see how well they fit together. When composing, you can also incorporate additional authoritative sources with your own. Good composition requires time to polish your words to achieve the most economical and forceful way of conveying your message. When composing, then, a speaker draws on the attention to language, the order of ideas, and the internal unity of the speech.

1-4c Performance Skills

We are all performers, even if we have never appeared on *Dancing with the Stars*, acted in a Broadway show, or sung karaoke. In one sense, performance occurs whenever we do something rather than merely think about doing it. When you tell a story to your family, you are performing. Even the process of telling a joke requires performance skills in order to know how long to pause before delivering the punch line. Performance skills refer to your use of physical qualities—tone of voice, gestures, and movement—in the process of delivering a message.

To many, performance also connotes drama and talent: the flash of a track star or the passion of an actor in a dramatic scene. In context and in appropriate forms, drama and talent are good things for a speaker to exhibit. A message might be more fully heard and understood if your delivery is energetic and your movement intentional.

A speaker must learn to strike an appropriate balance between being too dramatic (acting) and not being dramatic enough (stiff or boring). But to downplay the performance-related aspects of public speech is to deny the essential power that makes a speech more than conversation, a PowerPoint presentation, or a transcript. *Performance* refers not to display or phoniness but to the enactment of an event between speaker and listeners that transcends the exchange of information, that makes people say, "You had to be there."

Performance skills that are useful to speakers include the ability to pay attention to the entire effect, the knowledge of how to use setting and timing, and the capacity to turn a collection of individuals into a cohesive group. Performers tie together visual effects, lighting, sound, music, humor, and drama. Performance skills that are useful to speakers include a sense of timing and an understanding of how to direct emotional buildup and choose the right moment for the climax.

To be successful, public speaking requires the ability to balance all three qualities of conversation, composition, and performance. A speaker needs to command the flexibility of conversation, the organization of composition, and the engagement of performance to earn the undivided attention of an audience. This is not to say that each resource merits equal emphasis in all situations for all speakers. Instead, effective speakers understand that any speaking situation requires a delicate dance in order to maximize impact and audience response. Similarly, giving too much priority to one element over the others can be dangerous. A speaker who spends too much time composing and too little time practicing may develop a great speech but falter during delivery; one who counts on stellar performance skills at the expense of organizing ideas could also face disaster. The "Balancing Communicative Resources" checklist describes some of the perils of leaning too much or too little on any one resource.

How you combine these resources depends on your level of consciousness of your competence (discussed later in this chapter) and on the kinds of feedback you receive in your practice sessions (see Chapters 2 and 25). Next, let's look at some things to consider as you decide how to combine your communicative resources to create an effective speech.

Consider the Situation and Expectations of the Audience Most of us understand that how we act on Friday night with friends is much different from how we behave on Monday morning at work. We consider the situation and respond accordingly. As speakers we must do the same. The type of speech and the situation determine how you blend the skills of communication in various speeches. A formal occasion and a large audience often require a speaker to give a writer's attention to word choice and overall unity. Moderating a discussion with a smaller audience entails tapping the listening skills involved in conversation. A festive occasion in front of a larger audience may require a larger-than-life performance.

Chapter 7 gives some suggestions on how to learn more about the people to whom you will speak. Chapters 17 and 28 present guidelines about occasions and situations.

Consider Your Personality and Distinctive Speaking Style Speakers differ even when speaking on the same occasion and topic. Each of us approaches every situation with a slightly different perspective and style. If you are a great storyteller or have

CHECKLIST ~ Balancing Communicative Resources

Do you use conversational skills effectively?

☐ Speech is conversational in tone with minimal vocal pauses or filler words.

☐ Speech appears spontaneous and personal.

☐ Speech is easy for listeners to follow.

Composition—Do you take time to compose speech content carefully?

☐ Ideas appear thoughtfully developed.

☐ Claims are supported with credible evidence.

☐ Speech is well organized.

Performance—Is your delivery lively without being overly theatrical?

☐ Delivery is energized and draws listeners' interest.

☐ Delivery is natural for the speaker with minimal distractions.

Dusit/Shutterstock.com

a dramatic flair, you should use that resource to the appropriate extent. If you know you have trouble being spontaneous, let alone dramatic, in front of a group, you should focus on developing the content of your speech so that your words and message bond you to your listeners. The choices you make depend on your strengths and weaknesses as a speaker, as well as on the context and situation of the speech event. Again, each dance and dancer is unique.

1-5 The Role of Consciousness in Learning

We learn complex skills differently from the way we learn simple facts. A complex skill like public speaking involves combining a number of intellectual and physical operations. You know how to breathe, how to raise and lower your voice, how to move your hands, how to define a new term, and how to group ideas into categories. What you may not know is how to put all of these skills together to make an effective public speech.

The learning of skills is said to progress through four stages: unconscious incompetence, conscious incompetence, conscious competence, and unconscious competence (Figure 1.3).

▶ *Stage 1: Unconscious incompetence.* In this stage, people are not aware that they are making errors, and they may even be unaware that some particular skill needs to be learned.

▶ *Stage 2: Conscious incompetence.* People in this stage have come to the realization that they are doing something ineptly and need to improve. In many cases, this awareness creates anxiety, which then magnifies incompetence.

FIGURE 1.3
Four stages of skill learning

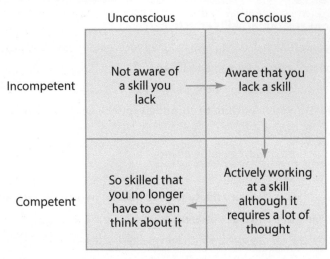

	Unconscious	Conscious
Incompetent	Not aware of a skill you lack →	Aware that you lack a skill
Competent	So skilled that you no longer have to even think about it ←	Actively working at a skill although it requires a lot of thought

▶ *Stage 3: Conscious competence.* In this stage, people have worked to improve in an area in which they felt incompetent but must now consciously try to perform competently. If they do not make a conscious effort, they are likely to regress to more comfortable but less competent patterns. However, if they persevere, the awkwardness of the new behavior and the need for self-monitoring diminish.

▶ *Stage 4: Unconscious competence.* People in this stage have integrated the learned skills to the extent that competence comes naturally—there is no longer a need for conscious attention. Performing the skill becomes relatively effortless and may even be fun. Speakers at this level can do more than merely talk; they are free to pay attention to audience response and to make spontaneous adjustments that enhance the quality of the communication.

A great deal of communication behavior is unconscious. You don't think about how you move your lips to make sounds or why you speak one way with your friends and another with your boss. These are areas of unconscious competence. At the same time, you may not be aware that you say "you know," mispronounce "library" and "February," scratch your head when you are nervous, or often commit the fallacy of hasty generalization. These are examples of unconscious incompetence.

When do your communication behaviors receive your conscious attention? Usually when you are learning new skills or when you run into difficulties in communicating. As soon as a skill is mastered or a communication problem is solved, your behavior becomes unconscious again. This is an efficient system. You are constantly freeing yourself to direct your conscious attention to something more challenging.

As a developing speaker, you can set priorities for learning and decide where to focus your attention. Several of the misconceptions listed in the next section can be understood in terms of this approach to skill development. The person who thinks speaking should be effortless (Misconception 2) usually wants to jump straight to Stage 4, unconscious competence, without going through the process of discovering weaknesses and practicing new ways of communicating. The person who thinks speaking is impossibly hard (Misconception 3) does not trust that Stage 3, conscious competence, will eventually lead to unconscious competence (Stage 4). As we attempt to become conscious of what is usually an unconscious act, things may even seem to get worse before they get better. But if increased competence is the goal, the process is necessary, and it does pay off. Before you know it, the new, formerly awkward, behaviors are as habitual as the old ones—but they work better.

The person relying too heavily on the performance model is overly conscious of the physical and vocal delivery of ideas at the expense of the ideas themselves. Speakers holding this view who also see themselves as consciously incompetent can become paralyzed by self-consciousness and anxiety. At the other extreme are speakers who are overly conscious of what they see as competence in delivering a speech. They are so enamored with their own gestures and voice that the result is an affected and showy style. Their attention is on the presentation of self rather than on the presentation of ideas. For the audience, this can translate into a speaker so distracting that the message is entirely lost.

Speakers who rely too much on composition skills misdirect awareness in the opposite direction. They may think too much about what they are saying and too little about how they are saying it. Or they may go on talking to the formulas on the board while the audience snoozes, or become incoherent when someone asks a question that derails them from their complex train of thought.

Speakers who think little of composition and performance skills while concentrating on conversation can end up being personable in a speaking event but delivering little substance. If a speaker, however, has been able to use composition and performing skills to develop the speech, the person's conversation strengths will further enhance the well-planned and well-practiced speech.

MindTap® SPEAKER'S WORKSHOP 1.3

1. Compare the speeches by Brian Sharkey, Nathanael Dunlavy, and Kayla Strickland that are available through the MindTap for *The Speaker's Handbook*. Can you find specific examples of how each speaker uses the three resources of conversation, composition, and performance? Next, contrast the speakers in their use of these resources. Which resource did each rely on the most? Which did each use most effectively? Do you attribute the differences to individual style or to the nature of the occasion on which they spoke?

2. What are some of your areas of conscious competence as a public speaker? Conscious incompetence? Unconscious competence? Can you speculate about some areas of unconscious incompetence or remember examples from the past?

Recognizing that a speech really is an extension of interpersonal communication should keep you from being overly conscious of either your manner of speaking or the exact language of your message. In day-to-day interactions, you are usually conscious of a few basic things: your reason for speaking, the message you want to get across, your relationship with the other communicator, and the response you are receiving. These are the same things you should be aware of when you speak in public.

1-5a Follow Five Steps of Public Speaking

Preparing and delivering a speech are complex and can be daunting processes. However, the essentials of preparing any speech, even the most basic one, can be distilled into five steps: plan, investigate, compose, practice, and present. This list will help you get started. Later, you will add variations to these steps, master specialized formats, and incorporate specific strategies. Table 1.2 summarizes these steps.

For simplicity, the five steps are presented in a linear fashion, but in practice, a speaker may move through the steps in a different order. For a major speech, you might return to topic analysis in order to refine it after you have done some research. Or, when composing the speech, you may discover you need to return for further research. For any speech, it's critical to think through each step!

TABLE 1.2
The five steps of public speaking

STEP	PRIMARY TASKS	CHAPTER WHERE YOU'LL FIND HELP
Plan	Initial decisions and analysis	Prepare plan **5**
		Select and narrow topic **6**
		Consider occasion **7**
		Clarify purpose **6**
		Determine mode of delivery **23**
		Frame thesis statement **6**
		Analyze topic **6**
		Analyze audience **7**
		Counter anxiety **4**
Investigate	Research for resources and materials	Locate credible resources **8**
		Investigate articles, books, and websites **8**
		Conduct interviews **8**
		Keep research notes **8**

STEP	PRIMARY TASKS	CHAPTER WHERE YOU'LL FIND HELP
Compose	Development of speech materials	Develop rough working outline **9, 10**
		Develop full-sentence outline **11**
		Add supporting materials **15, 16**
		Add attention factors **18**
		Prepare transitions **12**
		Prepare introduction and conclusion **13, 14**
		Prepare presentation aids **27**
		Prepare speech notes **17, 24**
Practice	Preparation for oral performance	Give the speech aloud **17, 24, 25, 26**
		Practice with presentation aids **27**
		Work on vocal delivery **25**
		Work on physical delivery **26**
		Get feedback **24**
Present	The culmination of all your work—relax, enjoy, connect with your audience, and debrief to learn something for next time	Adapting to the speech situation **28**
		Answering questions **29**

Summary

1-1 Understand what it means to be a public speaker.

▶ Public speaking requires understanding mutuality of concern.

▶ It also requires that we understand the common public speaking misconceptions.

1-2 Explain the theoretical foundations of effective public speaking.

▶ The roots of the study of communication begin with the development of human society through an oral culture.

▶ Aristotle advanced our understanding with the introduction of rhetorical studies including recommendations for persuasion and canons of speech.

▶ Various models of communication including the conception of feedback highlighted an era of communication studies.

▶ Most recently a dialogic perspective suggested that communication is a collaborative process, a creation of shared meaning.

1-3 Recognize communication as a social construction of meaning.

▶ Meaning is created through social interaction with others.

▶ Meaning is tied to the context of time and space.

▶ Meaning is negotiated by participants.

1-4 Determine how to balance communication resources to speak effectively.

▶ The three communicative resources we can draw on as we prepare public speeches are conversational skills, composition skills, and performance skills.

▶ Balancing these skills requires the flexibility of conversation, the organization of composition, and the engagement of performance to earn the undivided attention of an audience.

▶ Finding the right balance appropriate to the speaker, audience, and situation becomes the delicate dance.

1-5 Discover the role of consciousness in skill learning.

▶ Skill learning involves varying degrees of conscious and unconscious awareness: We might start out unconscious of our incompetence (skill deficient), and move to becoming conscious of our incompetence until we are able to be consciously competent and to perform a skill if we concentrate on it. Eventually we may achieve unconscious competence at the skill or task, no longer having to concentrate to perform a skill or task.

Critical Thinking Questions

▶ How does a meaning-centered perspective differ from a message-centered perspective?

▶ What impact does a meaning-centered perspective of communication have on your ability to speak publicly?

▶ What are your communicative resources, and how can you maximize their impact?

▶ What are the four stages of skill learning, and how might they help you improve your speaking skills?

▶ Which of the five steps of the public speaking process do you find most challenging and why?

Putting It into Practice

MindTap® Visit the MindTap for *The Speaker's Handbook* and click on **Additional Resources** to visit the Public Dialogue Consortium's website and view some of their projects.

1. What are the community benefits of public dialogue?

2. How might your community benefit by addressing an issue publicly?

3. What issue would you have your community address?

4. What topic would motivate you to speak publicly?

2

Listening

Develop your skills as a listener to enhance your own critical thinking and speaking and to meet your obligations as an audience member.

MindTap® Read, highlight, and take notes online.

istening and speaking are closely tied. An effective speaker must learn to listen to his or her audience prior to and during each presentation. To be able to speak effectively, a person must listen to understand the needs and wants of the audience. Although we spend more hours of our day listening than speaking, that doesn't make listening easy or guarantee we are good at it. Doing something often is not the same as doing it well. Only by understanding how we listen effectively and learning to provide constructive feedback based on that listening can speakers prepare a speech that will be heard, understood, and remembered by an audience.

2-1 Practice Effective Listening Skills

Throughout this handbook, listeners are cast as coauthors of every speech. A message does not really exist until it is received and shaped by a listener. The act of **listening** is defined as a complex and active process of receiving, processing, and evaluating an oral message. It includes the reception of stimuli, their organization into usable chunks of sound, the identification of comprehensible words or phrases, and the interpretation of meanings. From this, it follows that listening is not passive but an active process, involving specific skills that require preparation, explicit attention, and practice.

MindTap® Visit the MindTap for *The Speaker's Handbook* and click on **Additional Resources** to visit the International Listening Association website, which provides some short articles on the value of listening, a compendium of irritating listening habits, and some inspiring and entertaining quotations about listening.

2-1a Prepare Yourself to Listen

It may seem silly to talk about "preparing to listen," but it is necessary if we are to become effective listeners. Athletic teams spend considerable time and effort preparing for competitive events. In the same way, it makes sense to prepare to listen because it can quickly improve our ability.

1. Remove Distractions

In our multitasking society, we listen to the podcasts or music while driving, watch television while texting or talking on a cell phone, or make to-do lists while listening to a lecture. When listening demands your full attention, you should not be doing anything else. In many situations, this means sitting up straight, looking at the speaker, and clearing away all materials except those needed for note-taking.

2. Stop Talking

As obvious as this advice sounds, many people enter situations, such as interviews, in which they need to gain information from others, and then proceed to do most of the talking. Even when they stop talking, many listeners continue to be distracted from genuine listening as they plan what to say next. Stop talking, avoid your cell phone, look at the person who is talking, and listen.

3. Decide on Your Purpose as a Listener

Are you listening to learn? To understand a new point of view? To solve a problem? To evaluate a controversial argument? To enjoy a narrative by a talented storyteller? These are just four of many possible listening objectives—and to achieve any one of them requires different subsets of listening skills and approaches. Your empathy, your curiosity, your critical analysis, your concentration—all come into play in different ways in different situations. As listeners, if we understand the purpose for our listening, we are more likely to match the situation with the appropriate listening intensity to meet our listening goals.

2-1b Balance Open Curiosity with Critical Analysis

When participating as an audience member, it is unfair to the speaker if you are so resistant to a message that you close yourself off from new ideas or different opinions. You also do yourself a disservice if you accept the ideas and information you encounter without a critical eye. Effective listeners navigate between these two extremes. You will want to balance a charitable and open receptiveness to what the speaker is saying with a careful assessment based on your knowledge, experiences, and common sense.

1. Show Respect

Even if you disagree with a viewpoint or find a topic to be dull, recognize that speaking in public takes courage and effort. Give the speaker your full attention, and adhere to the courtesies of a public situation. This is important whether you are an audience member or the next speaker. Listeners show courtesy by minimizing distractions, looking at the speaker, asking questions or responding to questions if that is appropriate, and avoiding any verbal or nonverbal behavior that would distract either the speaker or other listeners. This basic norm of politeness is broken when audience members arrive late or leave early; distracting behavior also includes reviewing your own note cards, talking to others, checking your phone for messages, and any other activity that might diminish even the perception of paying attention.

2. Be Open to the Speaker's Point of View

It is not really possible to suspend judgment until a speaker has finished. People cannot help evaluating everything they hear as they hear it. But instead of criticizing, be curious. While listening, ask yourself, "What, exactly, is this person saying? What led this person to that position? What assumptions underlie the speaker's position?"

The discussion of reasoning (see Chapter **16**) suggests that people can start with the same data but end up with different interpretations. Get inside the speaker's world with this analytic approach, and one of two things will happen: You will be able to put your finger on the exact points you want to question or refute, or you will find your opinion changing to accommodate part of the speaker's view.

3. Follow the Structure of the Speech

Try to identify the speech's thesis, main points, supporting materials, and crucial links, whether these are explicitly stated or not. Discerning the structure helps you retain content and evaluate its validity.

Unfortunately, not every speaker will be skilled at highlighting important points and providing clear transitions to signal relationships. To get the most out of a speech, you may need to create a mental outline to structure the points you hear. Listen for the speaker's thesis. Can you discern the main point of the speech?

FOR YOUR BENEFIT

Learn the Listening Stance

Listening requires considerable effort and is made easier when listeners assume a listening stance to maximize focus and attention. Seat yourself comfortably facing the speaker, with your feet on the ground and shoulders square with the speaker. Avoid slouching and crossing your legs to maximize blood flow. Breathe deeply to reduce stress and increase oxygen in your system. Make eye contact so as to see the speaker's facial expressions and gestures. Assume a comfortable stance allowing you to focus your attention and take notes as needed to remember key information.

4. Carefully Assess the Speaker's Claims

As you listen to any speaker who makes a controversial claim, engage your critical thinking skills to test the validity of the argument. Does the speaker rely on rational or emotional appeals? Use the "Questions for Assessing a Speaker's Claims" checklist to ask yourself the necessary questions.

5. Ask Questions at the Designated Time

Jot down any points you want to return to during the question-and-answer period. Be sure to ask genuine questions: Do not turn your opportunity to ask a question into your own speech or an argument with the speaker, and avoid attempts to trap the speaker. Again, the spirit of curiosity and ethics should help you frame questions whose answers will lead yourself and others to an understanding of what the speaker is trying to communicate.

2-1c Listen Holistically

Chapter **8** covers seeking information from other people as you research your speech. Effective listening in these situations will enable you to reach a deeper understanding of your topic and use your time more efficiently. Listening to understand the whole person—in context, in the moment—is called **holistic listening**. It requires open and receptive attitudes that characterize caring friends and helping professionals when establishing empathy is a major goal of communicating. We listen holistically as audience members whether in a business meeting or in a classroom. A speaker might listen holistically when conducting audience analysis (see Chapter 7) to get a general sense of how audience members see the world.

CHECKLIST ~ Questions for Assessing a Speaker's Claims

- Do the main points, taken together, justify the thesis? (See Chapter **9**.)
- Is each claim stated clearly as a proposition that can be validated or rejected? (See Chapter **22**.)
- Is this claim a proposition of fact, value, or policy? (See Chapter **22**.)
- Is the support offered for each claim relevant to the point? (See Chapter **15**.)
- Does each piece of evidence pass the appropriate tests for examples, testimony, or statistics? (See Chapter **15**.)
- Are the links between the points logically drawn? (See Chapter **16**.)
- What premises are taken for granted without being stated? Are these assumptions valid? (See Chapter **16**.)
- Are any fallacies present? (See Chapter **16**.)
- Does the speaker misuse emotional appeals or substitute them for intellectual argument? (See Chapter **20**.)

1. Listen at Multiple Levels

All utterances have a surface message, but there are other deeper meanings that reveal how a person feels. The full richness of meaning can be discovered by being alert to word choices, metaphors, and tone of voice.

2. Listen between the Lines

Another implication of holistic listening is that the full meaning of an utterance is embedded in the nonverbal cues that surround the words. We listen not just with our ears but with our eyes and hearts. You can observe when a person's vocal tones or body language is emphasizing or contradicting some of the words. Practice noticing variations in emotional intensity, which can be revealing. It is in these nonverbal messages that Netflix shows like *Lie to Me* and *The Mentalist* have focused.

3. Listen to the Silences

Sometimes, it is not the utterance that communicates. Form the habit of noticing what a speaker does *not* say. What topics are omitted or rushed through? When do long pauses occur? If a job applicant has a two-year gap in a résumé or a salesperson talks about every feature of a product except price, these omissions may be important.

In formal interviews of experts or in more informal conversations on your topic, use the following listening response techniques.

4. Paraphrase

Check your understanding of the points being made by paraphrasing and clarifying. This involves restating what you think you heard so that the speaker can confirm or correct your interpretations: "In other words, what you are saying is…" or "Would [give example] be an example of what you are talking about?" or "Are you using the term *current* with the denotation of *in present time*?"

5. Ask Follow-Up Questions

In Chapter **8**'s discussion about interviewing people, it is suggested that you devise a list of specific, open-ended questions, which not only keep the interview focused on the person's expertise but also allow the person to go in a fruitful direction you might not have anticipated. Careful listening will enable you to capitalize on this, as well as to focus on following up. As the expert answers the open-ended questions, follow up with more specific questions in response to those answers: "You said a minute ago that the global impact of biofuels may be more harmful than the environmental impact of burning fossil fuels. Why do you say that?"

6. Take Notes

Be sure to take notes as you listen to a speaker. At first, having to write as well as listen may seem to get in the way of actually hearing what is being said. However, because taking notes forces you to think about what is said, it will actually help you listen better. As you take notes, realize that it isn't necessary to capture the speaker's words verbatim. Instead, make notes of the key ideas offered by the speaker in order to help you comprehend and critically consider what the speaker is saying.

2-2 Provide Constructive Feedback

In one special situation, when you act as a critic or consultant, you agree to listen as more than an audience member and to provide feedback on the decisions a speaker has made and the effectiveness of the presentation. This may occur during a practice session of a speech that is still in preparation, or it may take place after a speech has been given, with the goal of helping the speaker improve future presentations. (See Chapter **24.**) In either case, the role of critic–consultant requires a special blend of honesty and tact. The supportive critic bears in mind the fragility of partially formed ideas and the close connection between a person's speaking personality and that person's self-image. The following guidelines are for listeners who have been asked to give feedback.

1. Assume Positive Intent
Acknowledge the positive intent of what the speaker has tried to do. By focusing on the positive, you help reduce defensiveness and maintain openness for the constructive feedback to follow. For example, "I tell you've put a great deal of effort into developing your introduction."

2. Make Important Comments First
Begin your feedback with the most significant issues. Think first about whether the message makes sense and whether the overall strategy is effective. Resolve issues regarding main points before addressing lesser concerns.

3. Be Descriptive about Strengths and Weaknesses
It is more helpful to say, "You were discussing causes of the problem in Point 1 and then again in Point 3, which confused me," rather than "This speech was disorganized." With positive comments as well, it is better to describe what was effective by saying, "Comparing the greenhouse effect to the atmosphere inside a closed car really helped me understand," rather than "The speech is great."

4. Offer Suggestions, Not Orders
Acknowledge in your comments that your reactions are those of just one listener and others may differ. Also, recognize that some wonderful ideas can and should be rejected by a speaker because they simply do not fit that person's style. Bearing these things in mind, you might suggest something along the lines of "I have never cared for a heavily dramatic delivery, though I know it works for some people. Have you thought about…?"

5. Consider the Speaker's Feelings

Always consider the speaker's feelings when deciding what to say and how to phrase it. There is no need to comment on aspects of a person's speech style that are tied to cultural identity. Also, some delivery problems are so obvious that encouraging the speaker to review his or her own video recording may be more effective than confronting the speaker about the problem. Other problems might be so complex that it would be better for a speech professional to address them.

6. Match Feedback to Preparation Phase

Be aware of the time constraints a speaker faces. If you are giving feedback early in the development of the speech, you can make some larger suggestions for revision. However, if the speech is in final rehearsal, it is probably too late to suggest going back to substantially change main points. Try to offer a few suggestions that can improve the speech, rather than make the speaker wish for time to prepare a different one.

7. Use the 90/10 Principle

This principle, developed by one of the authors in teaching interpersonal communication, states that people's weaknesses are rarely the *opposite* of their strengths. More often, they are the *excesses*. This awareness suggests a way of phrasing feedback: "The first 90 percent of (quality A) is a positive addition to your speech, but the last 10 percent of (quality A) begins to work in the opposite way." You are not suggesting that speakers eliminate a characteristic behavior, but that they hold it in check. Actual feedback phrased this way might sound like this: "Generally, the use of evidence made this speech especially compelling. Sometimes, though, the statistics were so complicated I found them hard to comprehend, and wonder if you might be more effective if you insert an example or a brief illustration in place of some of the statistics."

CHECKLIST ~ Constructive Feedback

Think about the last time you had to offer constructive feedback to someone.
Did you

- [ ] initiate the feedback with something positive?
- [ ] offer the most important comments first?
- [ ] share specific information with examples from the speech?
- [ ] offer your observations with suggestions, as opposed to orders?
- [ ] consider the speaker's feelings?
- [ ] match feedback to be appropriate to the preparation phase of the speaker?
- [ ] use the 90/10 principle?

1. The following statements might have been directed at a speaker during a feedback session. Place yourself in these situations and revise the criticism so that they better adhere to the principles of constructive feedback.

   ▶ I can't understand you because of your accent.

   ▶ Your voice is too soft.

   ▶ Your speech was interesting.

   ▶ Stop playing with your hair; use more humor; your points don't prove your thesis.

2. Visit the MindTap for *The Speaker's Handbook* and select one student speech from the book's interactive videos. As you watch it, prepare constructive comments and feedback you would give this speaker to help improve the speech.

3. Or watch one of your classmate's first speeches. Prepare constructive comments and feedback you would give this speaker to help improve the speech.

FOR YOUR BENEFIT

Benefits

Listening Takes Work

Little attention is given in academic settings to the importance or process of effective listening. Many people assume if you don't have a hearing disability, you can listen; but just because people can hear doesn't mean they are good listeners. Listening requires energy and attention. Even the best listener will benefit from recognizing and avoiding the following listening pitfalls.

2-3 Common Listening Pitfalls

1. Daydreaming, Doodling, and Disengaging

It is easy for your mind to wander during a speech, in part because it takes a speaker longer to state an idea than for a listener to think the same thing. Listening experts recommend using that time differential constructively. As you listen, use your extra processing time to think of questions to ask later, consider the implications of what is being proposed, or consider how your own speech might benefit from some of the strategies used by the speaker. Stay mentally active in ways that connect to the speech topic.

2. Becoming Distracted by Superficial Qualities of the Speaker

You may notice that a speaker mispronounces a word, makes a grammatical error, sways back and forth, or makes every statement sound like a question. Or you may notice that another speaker has a charming accent, sounds like a radio announcer, or looks wonderful in that shade of blue. In either case, letting yourself become distracted with these traits hinders your ability to listen to the speech. As a listener, your job is to overcome superficial distractions and focus on the message.

3. Uncritically Accepting a Message

Do not automatically assume that if a speaker makes a statement, it must be true. Listeners share an ethical responsibility for the meanings that come out of speeches. Passivity in listening abandons this responsibility. Give a speaker's ideas the scrutiny they require.

4. Prematurely or Totally Rejecting a Message

Hear the speaker out. For instance, you may totally oppose capital punishment, but don't be quick to assume this speaker is the same as all other proponents. Listen attentively, and you may hear a new argument or find an intriguing point you hadn't considered.

5. Planning Your Response or Rebuttal to a Speech instead of Listening to It

You can certainly be critical and analytical, but unless you are in a debate that requires on-the-spot **refutation**, don't divert your attention to the extent of composing your own messages.

FOR YOUR BENEFIT

Listening to Non-Native English Speakers

American businesses and classrooms have grown increasingly diverse. Developing sensitivity for various accents, expressions, and perspectives will serve you well in our increasingly multicultural society. Practice listening to non-native speakers and consider studying a second language yourself. Remember that to communicate with you, the speaker has worked to learn American English vocabulary, grammar, and syntax, and then has risked speaking publicly in that new language. Remember that some non-native speakers will have difficulty making certain English sounds such as R and TH because these sounds may not be part of the person's native language. With a small amount of effort, most listeners can adjust to non-native speakers' inflection and unusual pronunciation or pauses, and understand effectively. When possible, check your understanding with the speaker by paraphrasing the message.

ESB Professional/Shutterstock.com

MindTap®   SPEAKER'S WORKSHOP 2.2

Visit the MindTap for *The Speaker's Handbook* and access the book's video activities. First read the transcript of and then watch the video of Harriet Kamakil's speech "The Maasai Initiation Ceremony."

▶ Are you distracted from listening by any aspects of the speaker's topic, content, or delivery?

▶ What steps do you take to help focus your attention to the message? What more could you do?

6. Failing to Monitor Your Nonverbal Behaviors as a Listener

Even when you disagree or are confused, don't grimace or roll your eyes. For that matter, don't look bored or allow your eyes to glaze over. At times it may prove politically savvy to mask your initial reaction, whether you are listening to a classmate in school or a colleague in a business meeting. Out of courtesy and respect, assume a supportive and responsive listening demeanor.

Summary

In this chapter, we discussed the listening skills that are important when you are either an audience member or a speaker. Following is a summary of the chapter broken down by the chapter's learning objectives, which are found on the tabbed page for Part 1.

2-1 Practice effective listening skills.

▶ Prepare yourself to listen.

▶ Balance open curiosity with critical analysis.

▶ Listen holistically.

2-2 Summarize the guidelines for providing constructive feedback.

▶ Assume positive intent.

▶ Make important comments first.

▶ Be descriptive about strengths and weaknesses.

▶ Offer suggestions, not orders.

▶ Consider the speaker's feelings.

▶ Match feedback to preparation phase.

2-3 Recognize listening pitfalls.

▶ Daydreaming, doodling, and disengaging

▶ Becoming distracted by superficial qualities of the speaker

▶ Uncritically accepting a message

▶ Prematurely or totally rejecting a message

▶ Planning your response or rebuttal to a speech instead of listening to it

▶ Failing to monitor your nonverbal behaviors as a listener

Critical Thinking Questions

▶ How does listening relate to the process of effective speech making?

▶ What can you do to improve your listening effectiveness?

▶ What advice would you offer a friend required to give feedback to coworkers?

▶ Which listening pitfall do you find most challenging, and what could you do to overcome this difficulty?

Putting It into Practice

MindTap° Visit the MindTap for *The Speaker's Handbook* and click on **Additional Resources**. There, read Tanya Glaser's summary of the article "Dialogic Listening: Sculpting Mutual Meanings."

1. What listening techniques are suggested in the summary?

2. Pick two of the listening techniques suggested and use them as you listen to others at home, work, or school.

3. What differences do you notice in how others respond to you when you practice dialogic listening?

4. How could these listening strategies be useful to you?

Speaking Ethics

Commit yourself to a set of ethical principles that will guide you as a public speaker.

MindTap®   Read, highlight, and take notes online.

This handbook serves primarily to help you plan and present effective public speeches—that is, speeches that allow you to achieve your goals in speaking. But there is something more to consider. Sometimes, a speaker succeeds in getting a point across or in persuading an audience but does so in a manner that is manipulative, exploitative, dishonest, or otherwise offensive. These cases raise questions about the ethical obligations of all speakers. Ethical questions do not merely ask, "What works?" but rather, ask, "What is appropriate?" As a speaker we must consider the ethics of our choices.

Fortunately, effective speaking and ethical speaking work together. The speaker who plays games with statistics or quotes authorities out of context frequently commits fallacies of reasoning in the process, and heavy-handed use of emotional appeals or shocking visual aids may backfire, if not immediately then eventually. Credibility suffers when listeners perceive a speaker to be manipulative or insincere. There are no guarantees, though, that audiences will always respond positively to those speakers who take the moral high ground. Ultimately, the question transcends the simple yes/no choice of "Can I get away with it?" and moves to the more complex realm of personal values, where each speaker has to decide what is ethically justifiable.

Your approach to the ethical choices in public speaking grows out of your beliefs about matters such as how people should treat one another and what counts as honesty. In one sense, ethical beliefs are so individual they seem almost to be a matter of each person's own conscience. Yet other people influence our beliefs about right and wrong. Professional groups such as health and business professionals have formalized codes of ethics. Other less formal codes of ethical conduct come to us through family, religious traditions, and culture.

3-1 Be Aware of Ethical Choices in Public Speaking

We make choices based on values and ethics every day. Sometimes these choices are clear-cut and easy, but often they are less clear or perhaps a choice between the lesser of two evils. Our choices as speakers have significant ethical dimensions and are rarely clear-cut, and the best choice may depend on the contextual issues relating to the context of our circumstance, or audience.

3-1a Every Decision Has an Ethical Dimension

No decision a speaker makes is morally neutral. We speak because we believe that what we say will make a difference. And it does. The results of a speech can be as serious as persuading others to follow a dangerous course of action or as apparently harmless as wasting their time with an unprepared and unfocused message. Every time you speak, you exercise power, and assume responsibility for the consequences of what you do or don't say.

3-1b Ethical Decisions Are Rarely Clear-Cut

Often, the answer to questions about what works in public speaking is, "It depends." Questions about what is the right or ethical course of action are just as complex. Ethics grow from our values, and values sometimes conflict. Classic communication dilemmas in everyday life deal with choices about whether to be honest and hurt someone's feelings or to be tactful and less than fully truthful. Rarely are there black-and-white choices. The best we can do most of the time is to select among various shades of gray. As communicators, we are obligated to consider each case and to make a judgment based on experience and reflection. As time goes by, we will likely be more discerning about the nuances of situations and more skilled in using language and nonverbal communication in sensitive and responsible ways.

3-1c Ethical Decisions Vary with Context

In a speech tournament, a debater might argue for recreational marijuana at 9 A.M. and argue against it at 10:30. In this context, it is understood that the rules of the game are to defend the assigned side of a topic as vigorously and skillfully as possible. This is considered no more unethical than the case of the football team that defends the north goal in the first and third quarters and just as vigorously defends the south goal in the second and fourth. However, if a political candidate gets caught taking one position when speaking to voters in Colorado and the opposite position in Indiana, we judge that to be unethical because we view such public speeches not as part of a game but as sincere statements of the speaker's true beliefs.

What you can pass off as your own words varies as well. We would expect the governor of our state to employ a speechwriter because the demands on public servants make it impossible to personally prepare each speech he or she gives. However, in an academic environment, it is understood that students must create and deliver their own speeches. So, for the student it would be unethical to buy a speech online or use a speech written by a friend, just as it would be unethical for one employee to take credit for another employee's work.

3-2 Respect the Integrity of Your Core Values, Audience, and Ideas

1. Your Core Values

As a public speaker, you are not simply a transmitter of messages; you also put yourself in contact with an audience. Although you may adapt, adjust, and accommodate to meet your goals, you have an ethical obligation to be true to yourself. When you've finished a speech, regardless of how anyone else responds, you should always feel good about what you said and how you said it. Never be reluctant to speak from your heart, to express your passion and conviction on a topic. Yet, as the speaker, you must also respect your audience.

2. Your Audience

Public speakers have a special kind of power. When audience members entrust you with their time and attention, you take on an obligation to treat them fairly. In a democracy that means we must recognize that each human being is an autonomous being with free will. We must ensure our own actions to impinge on the rights of others to make decisions for themselves as adults. Within this value system, those who have power over others do not have the right to use people as a means to their selfish ends. We must treat our audience members responsibly.

You have every right to pursue your own reasons for speaking, but not at the expense of your listeners' welfare. As an ethical speaker, do not underestimate audience members' intelligence or try to trick them into making decisions that endanger their health, safety, financial security, or other interests. And at the end of each speech, you should feel confident that your listeners are better off than they were before the speech. Whether or not they agree with your points, you have given them a chance to consider ideas without coercion or manipulation so that they can make informed decisions.

3. Ideas

Because the "victim" of unethical behavior is not immediately obvious, speakers find the responsibility to honor the integrity of ideas the most difficult to understand, and thus, the easiest to overlook. To live and work together, people have to trust that overall, communication proceeds honestly and reliably. Imagine the impact of one piece of misinformation shared with twenty people, who each share that information with three other people. The result is the misinformation of eighty people. We need look no further than social media feeds to see the impact of this misinformation.

As speakers we are entrusted with a huge responsibility, which requires that we act with the best interest of our audience and community when we speak. This trust requires that we avoid plagiarism, lies, and oversimplification, and strive toward balanced use of language, emotion, and strategy.

3-2a Don't Plagiarize

In addition to yourself and your audience, there are others, not present, to whom you have some ethical obligations. These are the people whose ideas and words you draw into the speech situation. The ethics of public speaking generally prohibit the use of another's major ideas or exact words—even paraphrasing them—without giving credit to the source. Anything short of that is essentially theft. See Table 3.1 for a comparison of appropriate paraphrasing and bad paraphrasing that would be considered plagiarism.

TABLE 3.1
Avoiding plagiarism through bad paraphrasing

PASSAGE FROM ORIGINAL SOURCE	BAD PARAPHRASE RESULTING IN PLAGIARISM	GOOD PARAPHRASE RESULTING IN AN APPROPRIATE CITATION
"Of the four phases of the creative process, most speech training emphasizes the logical, rule-bound processes of preparation and refinement. The middle two phases of incubation and illumination are rarely mentioned because they do not lend themselves to systematization. These middle steps touch the emotions."	"Most speech training emphasizes the preparation and refinement phases of the creative process. This is because they are systematic, logical processes. The middle two phases, incubation and illumination, aren't mentioned because they are less systematic and more emotional."	"The two middle phases of the creative process don't get the attention in speech training that the other two do. According to Sprague, Stuart, and Bodary, incubation and illumination get less attention because they deal with less logical aspects of creativity than preparation and refinement, which are more logically ordered."
Sprague, Stuart, and Bodary, *The Speaker's Handbook*	Condensing, changing the order of some words, and substituting synonyms do not make this an honest paraphrase.	Attributing the ideas discussed to the original authors makes this an honest paraphrase.

Most institutions are clear about having a specific policy for addressing issues of plagiarism and academic dishonesty—it is not adequate to claim you did not know that plagiarism was unacceptable. It is incumbent upon you as a speaker to give credit to the sources that inform you. Careers have been ruined when students, journalists, and public figures have been exposed as plagiarists. To avoid even the appearance of unethical use of speech content, form the habit of taking careful notes of the sources of all your ideas, statistics, and evidence. It is your obligation to explain the source of your information as you use it in your speech. And when you hear a wonderful anecdote, story, or turn of phrase you might like to quote some-day, make a note right then so you will remember to give credit to the source. (See Chapter **8**.)

MindTap°   A useful tool for gathering, organizing, and tracking your sources online is Zotero. Visit the MindTap for *The Speaker's Handbook* and click on **Additional Resources** to learn more about this free resource. In addition, there are links to several resources available through Northwestern University and Purdue University that will guide you in avoiding even the appearance of plagiarism.

3-2b Don't Lie

Nothing written here will stop the pathological liar or the ill-intentioned person. For the majority of us, the issues surrounding honesty are much subtler. Our courts require an oath to tell "the truth, the whole truth, and nothing but the truth," although rarely do we live up to that standard in everyday interactions. For example, out of kind-ness, someone compliments a friend's new outfit although they don't find it attractive. Acting on the best information available, a presidential candidate promises "to bring home the troops." A nurse tells a child that the shot "will only sting a little bit." You exaggerate a funny story to better entertain your listeners. The phrase "it depends" always crops up in conversations about what counts as a lie, a white lie, a fib, or tactful avoidance of an issue, or intentional deception.

In public speaking, most people would consider that at least the following catego-ries of behavior cross the line between honest and dishonest speech.

Making Statements That Are Completely Counterfactual "I have no finan-cial interest in this fitness center. I just care about your health." [when you receive a commission for every new member you enroll]

Playing Word Games to Create a False Impression Sometimes a speaker can use words with great precision of definition, being technically correct but totally mis-leading: "In response to allegations of illegal drug use, let me say that I have never broken the laws of this country." [when the drug use was in another country]

Don't Mislead the Listener "None of the studies in the dozens I reviewed show that smoking causes lung cancer." [But many show a strong link.]

3-2c Don't Oversimplify

Another dimension of the integrity of ideas has to do with faithfulness to the facts and realities of your subject matter. Although there is rarely one "real truth" on any complex issue, some accounts are so shallow or oversimplified as to provide a false picture. Before you speak in public, thus contributing to and shaping the public discourse on a topic, you have an ethical obligation to do your homework, to look beneath the surface, to weigh evidence carefully, and to explore a variety of viewpoints.

3-3 Balance Language, Emotional Appeals, and Persuasive Strategy

As a speaker, you perform a delicate balancing act in many of the decisions you make. Be especially aware of the ethical impact of choices you make about language, facts, emotional appeals, and persuasive strategies. Use the "Finding a Balance in Ethical Decisions" checklist to ask yourself the necessary questions.

1. Avoid Offensive Language
When occupying a public platform, speakers can cause pain by using words that some find demeaning, racist, sexist, or obscene. This is not to say that a speaker must rely on weak or feeble phrasing. The wonderful richness of vocabulary, metaphor, and style provides many ways to be colorful, precise, and sensitive.

2. Avoid Sharing Opinions as Facts
Newspapers have editorial sections that clearly distinguish the opinions of the newspaper staff from articles about issues of news. Advertisements in magazines and newspapers are expected to be clearly marked. Online content should similarly clarify what is fact from opinion or paid advertising although this line has blurred in recent years. Similarly, public speakers have a responsibility to support their claims with evidence and should avoid presenting opinions or rumors as facts.

3. Avoid an Overreliance on Emotional Appeals
When your argument is logically sound and well documented, appeals to your listeners' feelings are legitimate ways to support and emphasize your points. And it is common for a speaker with a deeply held belief to use strong emotional language. However, an overreliance on appeals to needs, emotions, or values is distrustful when:

▶ A need is created that listeners had not perceived before causes considerable pain or discomfort, leading to direct benefits for the speaker;

▶ Extreme emotional appeals are made to listeners at a time of great emotional susceptibility or are related to an area of their lives in which they are particularly vulnerable;

▶ Emotional appeals are part of a sustained, systematic effort to make listeners feel more confused, dependent, insecure, fearful, or helpless; and

▶ The basic logical argument would not be validated by dispassionate and informed observers without the underlying the emotional appeal.

3-3a Avoid Simplistic Persuasive Techniques

By definition, persuasion is not neutral. If you have decided to persuade, you have decided that a point of view is worth advocating. (See the persuasive strategies outlined in Chapter **22**.) But in your zeal to get across your point of view, remember that a good speaker never shortchanges the role of logical arguments supported by sound evidence. The classic list of propaganda devices identified by a group of journalists some decades ago sets forth the techniques unethical speakers can use to short-circuit an audience's rational processes.[1]

▶ *Name-calling.* By attaching a negative label to an idea or a person, a speaker can provoke fear or hatred in an audience. For instance, charged words such as *traitor, sexist, terrorist*, or *anti-American* can be used to short-circuit a listener's critical thinking. Such speakers hope this tide of emotion will gloss over the lack of substance in their positions. (See Chapter **16**.)

▶ *Glittering generalities.* At the other extreme is the speaker who generates a positive response to a statement by using words or phrases that represent some vague virtue. This technique attempts to convert listeners not on the merits of a position but because adoption of the position would be, for example, the patriotic thing to do.

▶ *Testimonials.* Another way to generate positive emotions is to link a popular figure with some cause or product. Here, the speaker replaces sound argument with inappropriate extension of the person's credibility. Thus, an actor may be admired in his role as a doctor, but when he endorses a headache remedy, he is way beyond his qualifications. In this case, the testimonial is based on a misleading impression.

▶ *"Just plain folks."* It is fine to build identification with an audience so that members are receptive to the ideas presented. This process goes too far, though, when the speaker implies, "You should believe me, not because of the inherent validity of what I say, but because I'm just like you." Examples of the "we are all just plain folks here" technique include politicians who roll up their flannel shirt sleeves on the campaign trail in numerous states throughout the Midwest.

▶ *Card stacking.* In this method, a speaker carefully uses only facts or examples that bolster his or her position, and the biased selection is passed off as representative. An opponent of hiring more police officers might stress accounts of police sexual misconduct and reports of pilferage of confiscated drugs and ask, "Do we want to spend money to put more of that kind of person in positions of authority?"

▶ *The bandwagon.* This technique is useful to a speaker who wishes to discourage independent thinking. The "everyone is doing it" approach appeals to the need for security and plays on fears of being different or left out. Speakers frequently cite public opinion polls to support their positions. However, the fact that many people are in favor of some proposal does not necessarily make it right. A proposition should be sold on its merits, not on its popularity.

▶ *Transference.* To make some unfamiliar thing more (or less) acceptable to an audience, many speakers will ascribe to it characteristics of something familiar. Often, there is no true relationship between the two. For example, characterizing video games as a "cancer spreading through our society" would inappropriately equate video games with losing someone you love to cancer.

CHECKLIST ~ Finding a Balance in Ethical Decisions

- ☐ Have you used lively language that doesn't inflict pain or offend your audience?
- ☐ Have you appealed to your audience on an emotional level without abusing emotional appeals?
- ☐ Have you clarified the source of your information?
- ☐ Have you avoided introducing opinions as facts?
- ☐ Have you used compelling persuasive appeals but avoided oversimplifying your argument or the associated facts?

Dusit/Shutterstock.com

MindTap   SPEAKER'S WORKSHOP 3.1

1. The following ethical principles might be useful to guide a public speaker's choices. As you develop your speech, consider each principle as it relates to your topic and audience.

   A. *Principle of beneficence*—The desire to bring about good in the world. Does your speech promote actions that will improve others' lives? Does your speech waste the audience time either because it is too trivial or lacks substance?

   B. *Principle of nonmaleficence*—Speakers must above all else, do no harm. Does your speech mislead or misinform audience members?

   C. *Principle of respect for autonomy*—The idea that we must respect others' right to decide what is best for them in their own lives. Does your speech make assumptions about what actions others must take or include language that limits others' perceived choices?

   D. *Principle of justice*—The idea that we must work to ensure others are treated with a sense of equity and impartiality. Does your speech in anyway demean or diminish the dignity of others?

2. What can a listener reasonably expect from a public speaker? Write an "Audience's Bill of Rights" you would like to see adopted.

3. Evaluate these uses of emotional appeals according to the principles suggested in this chapter.

    A. I saw a vision and knew that if I didn't raise $1 million by April 1, I would surely die. Please send in your contributions.

    B. I know how shocked you are by the deaths of your two classmates last week. They would certainly want you to write your senator today, demanding stricter penalties for drug dealers. You can show your love for them and save others from going through the pain you are experiencing.

    C. You can make $50,000 a year in your spare time by becoming a distributor for our organization. But you must do exactly as I say. Put yourself in my hands, and I will make you rich.

    D. If you can pinch an inch of flesh at your midriff, you are disgustingly fat and should buy a membership in my health club.

This list is far from comprehensive. Effective modern persuaders also use such techniques as snob appeal (the opposite of "just plain folks") and stand-out-from-the-crowd (the opposite of the bandwagon). Such persuasive appeals are questionable whenever they serve to:

▶ Distract listeners from important issues;

▶ Cloud important distinctions;

▶ Introduce irrelevant factors in the decision-making process; and

▶ Use emotional appeals inappropriately or excessively.

Summary

Ethics are involved in every aspect of developing a speech.

3-1 Recognize the ethical implications of our choices throughout the speech-making process.

▶ Every decision has an ethical dimension.

▶ Ethical decisions are rarely clear-cut.

▶ Ethical decisions vary with context.

3-2 Demonstrate how public speakers respect the integrity of their core values, the audience, and ideas.

▶ Respect the integrity of your core values.

▶ Respect the integrity of your audience.

▶ Respect the integrity of ideas.

3-3 Describe the benefit of a balanced use of language, emotional appeals, and persuasive strategy in public speaking.

▶ Speakers benefit by learning how to properly cite credible information sources avoiding plagiarism, lies, and oversimplification.

Critical Thinking Questions

▶ Make a list of the ethical issues speakers face.

▶ Explain what balance has to do with managing any ethical speaking situation.

▶ Address what makes plagiarism so heinous. How should a person who commits plagiarism be treated?

▶ Describe the propaganda devices listed in this chapter that you have used. Was it ethical to do so?

Putting It into Practice

Make a list of three to five well-known people who have made errors in ethical judgment. Creating the list is easy: Think of examples such as Monica Crowley, candidate for the National Security Council; Melania Trump's speech at the Republican National Convention; Robin Thicke and Pharrell Williams' use of Marvin Gaye's music without permission; or Kenny Florian, the Mixed Martial artist turned analyst, plagiarism of boxing analyst Lee Wylie.

1. What may have contributed to their choice to plagiarize?

2. Were specific ethical or legal codes violated?

3. What short- or long-term effects did the choice have on an individual's professional and personal lives?

4. How might these ethical errors have been avoided?

4

Lynne Nicholson/Shutterstock.com

Addressing Speech Anxiety

Understand, analyze, and accept your fear of speaking. Combine thorough preparation with relaxation and visualization techniques to increase your confidence.

MindTap® Read, highlight, and take notes online.

Stage fright, communication apprehension, speech anxiety, reticence, and shyness are among the most researched and analyzed variables in the literature on communication, precisely because so many people experience public speaking anxiety. Although there are no simple ways to eliminate the associated feelings entirely, experts do offer some tips that can help you become more comfortable and confident when you speak in public. Tips you can use to work toward this goal include putting fear into perspective, building confidence through preparation and practice, managing the physical effects of fear, and using positive self-suggestion to combat the anxiety.

4-1 Understand Public Speaking Anxiety

Anticipating a speech as well as giving the presentation can trigger the body's natural defense mechanisms intended to keep us safe. The brain's "fight or flight" response involves a series of triggers to the hypothalamus and pituitary gland resulting in a release of cortisol from the adrenal gland. This cortisol triggers a series of responses throughout the body, as described in Figure 4.1.

For some people, simply thinking about giving a speech activates the body's fear response. For others, the feelings may not hit them until they are standing in front of their audience. Too often we give public speaking fear more power than it warrants. The more we avoid our fears rather than face them, the more power they hold over us. Fortunately, there are several techniques you can use to help you put your fear into perspective and even make it work for you.

FIGURE 4.1
The body's response to speech anxiety

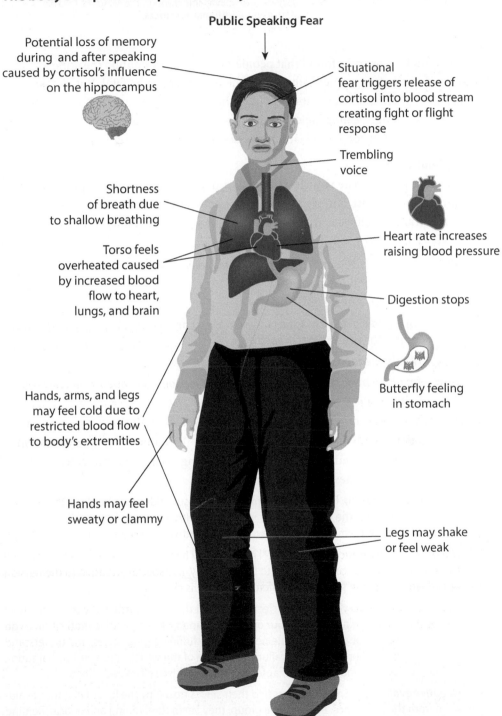

Public Speaking Fear

Potential loss of memory during and after speaking caused by cortisol's influence on the hippocampus

Situational fear triggers release of cortisol into blood stream creating fight or flight response

Trembling voice

Shortness of breath due to shallow breathing

Heart rate increases raising blood pressure

Torso feels overheated caused by increased blood flow to heart, lungs, and brain

Digestion stops

Butterfly feeling in stomach

Hands, arms, and legs may feel cold due to restricted blood flow to body's extremities

Hands may feel sweaty or clammy

Legs may shake or feel weak

MindTap One way to test your level of communication apprehension is to take the PRCA-24, a self-report inventory, available through the MindTap for *The Speaker's Handbook*. Click on **Additional Resources**.

Although one survey found that people rank the fear of public speaking ahead of the fear of death, few people really believe the experience to be fatal. But just what are we afraid of? Perhaps we are more afraid of the feelings associated with our fear then the actual speaking. Dealing logically with this fear requires examining its components so you can isolate issues, understand them, and prepare accordingly.

1. List Your Fears

It may be helpful to write your fears down on paper. Be as specific as possible, using this format for your list, and try to identify the actual outcome you find troubling:

I am afraid [specific event] will occur and then [specific result] will follow.

Not: *I'm afraid I'll make a fool of myself.*

But: *I'm afraid I'll forget my points, and the audience will think I don't know what I'm talking about.*

Not: *I'm afraid I'll freeze up.*

But: *I'm afraid my heart will start pounding, and my mouth will get dry, and I'll feel terrible the whole time I'm speaking.*

Not: *I'm afraid they won't like me.*

But: *I'm afraid my listeners will see through my facade of confidence and feel contempt for me.*

2. Classify Your Fears

The mere act of writing the fears down should make them more manageable and often reveals a solution. The additional step of classifying your fears into categories will show you common themes, as shown here.

▶ *Seeming incompetent.* For items like "I'm afraid my visual aids won't be clear," the solution is simple. Check out the clarity of your visual aids with a few people, and if there is any problem, redesign them. Many fears have roots in inadequate preparation.

▶ *Uncomfortable physical responses.* "I'm afraid my hands will shake and my voice will crack." If many of your concerns fall into this category, pay special attention to the tension release and relaxation suggestions offered later in this chapter.

▶ *Not measuring up to your ideal.* Perfectionists find this issue particularly troubling. Recognize the fear of failing to meet your own high standards as a positive motivation to do the best you can. But also realize the power of self-fulfilling prophesies, and understand that focusing on failure can create failure. Use some of the visualization and verbalization techniques recommended in this chapter to create positive self-expectations.

▶ *Negative evaluation.* Some speakers find themselves frozen by the fear of negative evaluation from their audience. Perhaps as a group, they seem threatening and critical. Remind yourself that an audience is merely a group of individuals and a speech is merely an enlarged conversation. If it would not be frightening to speak to any three or four of them, then what makes speaking to the larger group more threatening? Remember, audience members would much rather listen to you speak than speak themselves. They want you to succeed. This final, and probably most pervasive, category taps into widely held assumptions about speakers' vulnerability before an audience, the topic of the next section.

4-1a Keep Fear in Perspective

Many speakers believe they must be completely calm in every speech situation. This is unrealistic; all speakers feel some nervousness. One out of five people experiences rather serious fear, enough to adversely affect performance. One out of twenty suffers such serious fear that he or she is essentially unable to get through a public speech. For most of us, though, the fear can be managed and sometimes even turned to positive effect, in much the same way athletes benefit from the rush of adrenaline generated from competition.

The more speeches you give, the more confident you will become. You will recognize that fear is usually worst just prior to the speech and during the introduction. Once your speech is under way and the audience responds to you, negative emotions are often replaced by exhilaration.

4-1b The Role of the Audience

If one technique in particular has helped people cope with their fears, it is reconceptualizing the role of the audience.

▶ *Change the audience from "critic" to "recipient."* Remind yourself that you are there not to *perform* but to *share*. Think about how you might benefit your audience—even enrich their lives.

▶ *Realize that the listeners want you to succeed.* Most listeners are caring and supportive. They want to hear a good speech given by a confident speaker. Recall a time when you listened to a nervous speaker: Your discomfort and embarrassment were probably almost as great as the speaker's. This is testimony to the empathy of most audiences and quite possibly a biological response of mirror neurons in listeners.[1]

▶ *"Talk with" your listeners; don't perform for them.* All of this advice comes back to the importance of the conversational resource at the time of speaking. (See Chapter **1**.) It comes down to this: If you can think of yourself as "talking with" the listeners rather than "performing for" them, you will feel more comfortable.

4-2 Manage Public Speaking Anxiety

In our experience, people don't rid themselves of public speaking anxiety; instead, they learn to manage their fear and use it to their advantage. Effective speakers learn to control their fears rather than be controlled by them. By preparing thoroughly, practicing in advance, and learning to manage the anxiety, speakers can learn to control their public speaking anxiety and present messages quite successfully.

4-2a Practice and Prepare

The fact that good speakers make speech making look effortless does not mean that it is easy. Their seeming lack of effort is based on extensive preparation over time. The confidence they exude is also a result of preparation, not genes, fate, or dumb luck. Speakers who have prepared thoroughly can be as confident as skydivers who know they will reach the ground in one piece because they have trained exhaustively.

If you feel uneasy about getting your speech started, perhaps your introduction needs more work. If you are fearful of losing the continuity of the speech, you may need to practice it aloud several more times to internalize the flow of ideas. If you find yourself becoming generally anxious, use this as a stimulus to go over your preparation yet again. Drill yourself on the particulars of your supporting material. Go over your outline a number of times. Whatever else you do, remember that time spent fretting about the outcome could be better used taking positive action to ensure a positive outcome.

4-2b Manage the Physical Effects of Fear by Releasing Tension and Relaxing

You can better manage the body's fear reaction by learning tension release and relaxation techniques, and by practicing positive self-talk.

Tension Release The physical symptoms you experience, such as those described in Figure 4.1, will probably diminish with time as your successful speaking experiences help counter the unfounded fears you imagined. But some degree of physical discomfort is likely to persist. Fortunately, you can master techniques to help you feel more comfortable.

When too much adrenaline makes you jumpy, physical activity usually helps. Of course, heavy exercise before a speech is impractical. But a brisk walk around the block, a few push-ups, or a little pacing in the hall can be enough to bring your body back to normal. If you have a few moments of privacy, light exercise will feel good—just a few knee bends, arm swings, and neck rolls. If you remain in sight of your audience before the speech, clench and unclench your hands or toes unobtrusively. Once the speech begins, take advantage of the extra energy that the adrenaline provides to make your delivery more energetic. Appropriate, dynamic gestures will also help you release your nervousness.

Relaxation Techniques You can also manage nervousness by learning relaxation techniques. Relaxation, like any other skill, is achieved through practice. Using audio books or podcasts on stress, tension, and relaxation, you can learn first to isolate the areas of your body that are tense and then to relax them. Try meditation, biofeedback, or self-hypnosis. Explore such methods as tightening and then relaxing your hands, torso, and leg muscles; breathing deeply; visualizing serene settings; or imagining sensations such as warmth or heaviness in parts of your body. Experiment until you find a technique that is effective for you.

Self-medication through alcohol, drugs, and sedatives is inadvisable for public speakers. Most have side effects that impair your mental and physical performance during a speech, not to mention fabricating a false sense of security. Mastering your fear is preferred to masking your fear whenever possible.

4-2c Use Positive Self-Suggestion

Self-fulfilling prophecies can either hold you back or support your success. Through the power of the mind, we can increase or decrease our fear. Learning the power of positive thinking can help you diminish the effect of your fears.

Visualize Success Psychologists have discovered the tremendous power of visualization in influencing performance. When we experience fear, we often visualize the most negative outcome for our speech. Unfortunately, if we avoid something out of fear, we are never able to replace the imagined danger with a real lived experience. It is possible, however, to turn these fearful visions around. Many athletes have found it helpful to visualize what they are striving for in order to excel in their sport.

When you detect negative thoughts, try to replace them with a more positive scenario. For instance, "I will approach the lectern calmly, smile at the audience, and begin. My voice will sound strong and confident." Do not set unrealistic standards of perfection. Build some contingencies into your fantasy: "If I forget a point, I will use my notes to remember and focus on communicating each main idea." Run through these positive visualizations a few times a day before you speak. As you practice, picture the audience responding favorably to the speech. And just before you get up to speak, remind yourself of the general tone and image you wish to project: "When I get up there, I am going to communicate my sincerity and concern in a warm, natural, confident manner."

Replace Negative Internal Statements with Positive Ones One technique for reducing fears is **cognitive restructuring**. In essence, it is used to probe the internal voices that cause us to lack confidence, identify the unrealistic or irrational statements that compound our fears, and replace them with more positive, realistic beliefs. We all have constant narrations running through our minds. These internal voices are so familiar we are barely conscious of them. With some reflection, we can bring them to the mental forefront and examine the effect they have on our behavior. Remember, these are not statements of fact but statements of belief we have created that can be replaced if necessary. Become aware of your public speaking beliefs and replace the unproductive beliefs with positive ones. Table 4.1 gives some examples.

Your mental commentaries are habitual and will not change easily. At first, you will have to repeat the replacement sentences mechanically, as you might in memorizing

TABLE 4.1
Replacement belief statements

INITIAL BELIEF	REPLACEMENT BELIEF
My speech will be a failure unless everyone in the audience likes it.	I will be successful if most people respond favorably.
A good speaker never says "uh" or "er."	A few nonfluencies aren't even noticed unless attention is called to them.
My mind always goes blank.	I've practiced several times, and I know the basic structure of this speech. I can use brief notes to help me remember.
I will make a mistake and ruin everything.	My speech doesn't have to be perfect to be worthwhile.
No one will be able to understand me because of my accent.	My listeners will want to hear what I have to say, not how I say it.
Someone will ask me a question that exposes my ignorance.	I've researched this topic, and I'm prepared for any reasonable question. I am not ignorant.

a phone number. The reassuring nature of repeating the words may help you become physically calmer, and this more comfortable sensation acts to reinforce the new beliefs.

Practice Systematic Desensitization   A common strategy used to help people overcome all manner of fears involves systematic exposure of the subject to the stressor over time. For instance, a person who is arachnophobic (afraid of spiders) might systematically be exposed to pictures of spiders and then perhaps to spiders inside closed containers or at a safe distance. In addition, the person would be educated about spiders and trained in relaxation and visualization techniques. Over time, this systematic exposure can lead to a reduced apprehension of spiders. The same idea holds true for public speaking. By accepting minor speaking opportunities such as introducing yourself to a stranger or answering a question in front of classmates, a person can systematically reduce the apprehensions associated with speaking in public.

MindTap°   **SPEAKER'S WORKSHOP 4.1**

The power of positive thinking has long been recognized as helpful but recent research is challenging the usefulness of positive thinking alone. According to Gabriele Oettingen writing in the Harvard Business Review, "What does help [more than mere positive thinking] is mental contrasting, an exercise that brings together our positive fantasy about the future with a visualization of the obstacle standing in the way. Even more beneficial is adding if-then planning that allows you to address the obstacle when it arises."[2]

Other Approaches Many colleges and universities offer special sections of speech classes for fearful students. Others offer ungraded workshops to supplement regular classes. These programs use systematic desensitization, cognitive restructuring, skills training, or a combination of these and other methods. Psychologists and speech consultants also offer programs to help reduce fear of speaking. Such programs may be publicized under the names of *stage fright, communication apprehension, speech anxiety, reticence,* or *shyness.*

Some deeply rooted public speaking fears cannot be remedied by the methods suggested here. If your fear of speaking is almost paralyzing, you may need additional help. Research shows that even severe fear of speaking can be reduced to a manageable level when treated by a qualified professional. In some cases, medications have been found to successfully reduce unproductive fear responses in individuals, allowing even the most fearful person to speak in front of others.

CHECKLIST ~ Reducing Your Anxiety

- [ ] Did you list your fears? Example: "I am afraid people will laugh at me if I make a mistake."

- [ ] Have you classified your fears? Are your concerns related to fears of appearing incompetent, uncomfortable physical responses, perceptions of not measuring up?

- [ ] Did you reconceptualize your audience? Example: "My audience want me to succeed; they want me to talk to them; they aren't expecting a perfect performance." Or "I should be excited; some nervousness is normal."

- [ ] Did you recognize that past beliefs, while reasonable then, may not be the only plausible interpretations in your current situation? Example: "My audience will not be insensitive like my fifth-grade classmates."

- [ ] Did you thoroughly practice and prepare for your speech? Example: "Did you complete a thorough outline of your speech enough in advance that you can practice it three to five times a few days before the presentation?"

- [ ] Did you use techniques for managing the physical effects of anxiety? Example: "Try muscle tension release and meditative relaxation techniques."

- [ ] Did you practice visualization techniques? Example: "Visualizing success helps people in all walks of life. See yourself speaking successfully."

- [ ] Did you try to replace negative internal statements with positive ones? Example: "My speech doesn't have to be flawless to be worthwhile."

- [ ] Did you try systematic desensitization if other techniques didn't work? Example: "Seeking minor opportunities to speak regularly may help you feel more confident."

- [ ] Did you seek help from a professional if your anxiety is severe? Example: "Professional speech coaches, psychologists, and other counseling or medical professionals can help if extreme anxiety is your challenge."

Summary

Doing something for the first time—whether dancing, golfing, or giving a speech—can be scary and difficult. The more we practice the behavior, the less our nervousness impairs our ability to succeed. This chapter has focused on two learning objectives to help you reduce the negative effects of speech apprehension:

4-1 Demonstrate an understanding of your public speaking anxiety, what happens inside your body, and how reconceptualizing your audience will help you in managing your anxiety.

▶ Put fear into perspective; some public speaking fear is normal.

▶ Reconceptualize the audience as recipient, not critic, understanding that a speech is not a performance but a conversation with the audience.

4-2 Develop a plan to manage public speaking anxiety.

▶ Physical effects of speech apprehension can be managed through techniques of tension release and relaxation.

▶ Psychological effects of speech apprehension can be managed through visualization, cognitive restructuring, systematic desensitization, and, in extreme cases, professional intervention.

Critical Thinking Questions

▶ What are your greatest fears about speaking in public?

▶ How might you restructure your beliefs to break free of old fears?

▶ Which of the relaxation and tension reduction techniques do you find useful?

▶ How will you prepare your next speech to better manage your apprehension?

Putting It into Practice

1. What past experiences have you had that frame your feelings about public speaking?

2. How did Stephen Eggleston reframe his negative experience to overcome his apprehensions?

3. What false beliefs about public speaking do you need to replace?

4. Create positive replacement statements to counter your false beliefs.

The First Stage of the Public Speaking Process

The ability to float doesn't make a person a proficient swimmer. Likewise, knowing how to talk doesn't make a person an effective public speaker. Floating and speaking are feasible enough if we are relaxed, but tension and anxiety, which sometimes result from inexperience or poor preparation, cause many of us to sink. When we are preparing to speak, tension can also arise if we focus on the final *product* of the speech, rather than on the creative *process*, and we experience a sense of urgency to produce something. That urgency can lead to poor choices, such as accepting the first topic that enters our minds or the first resource we encounter on that topic. Experienced speakers save time and avoid wasted effort by organizing their preparation. They understand that the creative process progresses unevenly and that if they persist through all its steps, a respectable product will result. Part 2 of this handbook will help you develop a positive routine for preparing your speech, incorporating planning, topic selection, audience analysis, and research.

Planning

Make a schedule for the preparation of your speech so that you will have time to progress through the four phases of creativity.

MindTap® Read, highlight, and take notes online.

Preparing a substantial public speech is not a mechanical act like assembling a toy. It is a creative act in which you bring into existence something that has never been before, and that no one but you would have designed in exactly this form. Speech preparation is more like painting a picture, creating a dance, or inventing a product. Once you recognize the importance of creativity, you can strategically manage your preparation to allow time for each phase of the creative process.

5-1 Allow Time for the Four Phases of Creativity

The creative process has four phases: preparation, incubation, illumination, and refinement.[1] For speakers, the preparation phase includes gathering the materials, analyzing the topic and audience, and making the first attempts at putting the parts together. Incubation is a phase marked by frustration, even despair, when the problems seem insoluble and the speech is often set aside. During this phase, the unconscious mind and peripheral awareness work on the problems. Suddenly, in a moment of illumination, the pieces fit together or there is a dawning awareness that grows in intensity. Illumination may occur while working on the project, but it is just as likely to occur when driving on the freeway, taking a shower, or just before waking. Exhilaration and relief accompany this phase. After the creative burst, there follows a comparatively long period of refinement that includes checking details, fine-tuning, and polishing. Like the preparation phase, this phase is largely cognitive and requires concentration and discipline.

FIGURE 5.1
The four phases of creativity

1. Preparation	2. Incubation	3. Illumination	4. Refinement
• Gather materials	• Set the speech aside	• You see how the pieces fit together	• Check the details
• Analyze topic and audience	• Let your unconscious mind work on its problems	• You see solutions to the problems	• Fine-tune and polish your speech
• Start putting pieces together			

It is essential that adequate time be planned for *each* phase of the creative process. Too often, first-rate ideas fall short because they are not properly refined. Figure 5.1 summarizes the phases. The rest of this chapter supplies guidance for optimizing your planning so that none of the creative phases is slighted.

5-1a Make a Realistic Timetable

At one university, a group of public speaking instructors survey their students informally at the end of each term, asking what advice they would pass on to the next group of students. Consistently, the students' suggest "start early." They regret underestimating the time necessary to prepare a good-quality speech.

When professionals plan a major project—whether it is organizing an event, designing a public relations campaign, or tooling up to manufacture a new product—they use a number of structured time-management techniques. Valuable project management tools include program evaluation and review technique (**PERT**) and **Gantt** charts.

MindTap Visit the MindTap for *The Speaker's Handbook* to create a schedule for preparing your speech based on how much time you have available. It can also help you manage your time as your work progresses.

5-1b List Tasks, Estimate Time

Speech making involves many time-consuming intellectual tasks, such as analyzing your topic, and physical tasks, such as going to the library or making visual aids. Effective planning involves identifying the most and least optimistic estimates of the time needed to complete each task. Certain parts of the creative process should not be rushed, and it's wise to allow extra time for emergencies. Speech research and rehearsal can go on when you have a headache or are in an emotional funk, but the creative

FIGURE 5.2
Speech planning and practice

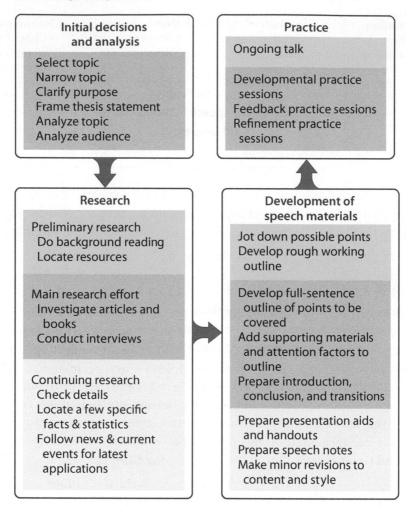

aspects of speech organization require physical and psychological alertness. Establishing an honest estimate of the time needed for each task is a good first step in the speech-making process. Figure 5.2 clarifies the many tasks associated with the four stages of speech planning and practice.

5-1c Determine the Order for Completing Tasks

Professional project managers call this step *determining the critical path*. It is not enough to schedule three hours for speech practice and call that *planning*. Those three hours must occur after the speech outline is completed. The outline cannot

FOR YOUR BENEFIT

Estimating Preparation Time

Novice speakers and professionals alike often underestimate the time needed to research, compose, practice, and deliver a speech. A general rule of thumb is to plan to spend approximately one hour of preparation time for each minute of a speech. Although this may seem extreme, it is better to overestimate and have extra time than to underestimate and be inadequately prepared.

ESB Professional/Shutterstock.com

be completed until you have articulated your speech's purpose and carefully considered the audience for the speech. When you lay out the entire project in this linear fashion and add up the time estimates for each task, you will determine the critical path.

Suppose your speech is due in three weeks, and the critical path adds up to five weeks. It is better to discover now that the plans are unrealistic rather than two days before the speech is due. In rare cases, a speech can be rescheduled for a later time, but more frequently, plans can be scaled back. Perhaps this means conducting two or three interviews by phone instead of five in person. Perhaps it requires minimizing development of PowerPoint slides. Ultimately, what's the most important is that you decide on and stick to your schedule, or else you will end up skipping the crucial later steps of practice and refinement.

5-1d Set Intermediate Deadlines for Major Stages

The process of speech planning and practice are divided into four stages: initial decisions and analysis, research, development of speech materials, and practice (see Figure 5.2). The chart will help you to see how the central tasks of one stage cannot really be started until the central tasks of the previous stage are completed. At some point, you must make preliminary decisions regarding a narrowed and focused topic, purpose, and thesis, and then get into your serious research.

Eventually, you must stop gathering material and start putting the speech together because you'll need adequate time to develop and practice your speech. There is no point in scheduling your feedback practice sessions so late that adjustments cannot be made based on the feedback.

Occasionally, you might retrace your steps. Maybe important new evidence presents itself, or a feedback session suggests more visual aids are needed. Such backward steps should be minimal; under almost no circumstances should you be returning to significant tasks, such as topic selection. Nor should you make any substantive changes to the speech at the last minute. During the final practice sessions, you should have complete mastery of the organization and basic content so you can concentrate on refining your phrasing, delivery, and timing, and on attaining the desired outcome.

5-2 Plan for Preparation and Presentation Phases

Because a speech is delivered orally, it must be composed orally. And because the meaning of a speech depends on the interaction between speaker and listeners, it should be created collaboratively. Keep the speech conversational, even during those parts of preparation that require you to draw on your skills as a writer or performer.

Although you cannot practice the speech until your basic outline exists, one form of oral preparation begins with your first idea. This is the ongoing talk suggested by the large orange section in the practice column of Figure 5.2. Talk to yourself about your topic. Talk to other people. Try out your ideas and words to see if they make sense. Work your ideas into conversations over lunch and chats with colleagues and friends. After talking to a number of people, you will find you have begun to work out the wording of the speech. Continue to incorporate feedback throughout your preparation and practice phases as suggested in Chapter **24**.

5-2a Focus on Different Resources

As speakers, most of you already have substantial resources at your disposal. You are conversationalists, writers, and presenters. These resources should be present throughout the planning and practice stages of a speech, but they may be utilized in different amounts at different times to achieve a successful final presentation. Figure 5.3 illustrates these changing priorities.

FIGURE 5.3
Key communicative resources for different phases

Generally, during the preparation stage, writing skills come to the fore. *This does not mean that you write out your speech!* Rather, it means that you consciously begin selecting points, arranging them, choosing your support, and thinking of appropriate examples. Focus your attention on transitions between ideas and refine the language of the speech.

Once the speech exists in some form, you move into a practice phase, in which the importance of performance-related elements increases. Through oral practice, you can experiment with vocal and physical dynamics to emphasize certain points and create certain effects. Here, you also introduce visual aids, props, and movements to begin to envision how the entire presentation will engage your audience.

If these resources are fully explored during preparation and practice, the writer and performer sides of you will recede during the actual speech, and the conversationalist will come forth. By using **enhanced conversation**, the speaking style effective for almost all speech situations, and emphasizing a relaxed, informal delivery despite following a well-planned, carefully organized outline, you will seem conversational and natural, and your conscious attention will be centered on the give-and-take with the audience. When proper time is devoted to the planning stages, speakers are able to develop a natural conversational style. That is because the writing and performance elements emphasized during the preparation and practice phases are revealed as areas of unconscious competence during the presentation phase. The nature of these changes is detailed in various chapters of the handbook. (See Chapters **17, 23, 25,** and **26.**)

CHECKLIST ~ Avoid Common Planning Pitfalls

- Did you allow enough time for incubation? Try to live with your topic for awhile before you start composing your speech. Plan an hour of preparation for each minute of speech.

- Did you build in time for unexpected emergencies? Don't overrate your efficiency and cut your preparation time too close. As insurance, put some breathing room in your schedule.

- Did you keep working through writer's block? Don't give in to the temptation to do "a little more time" research or planning. For your speech to succeed, you must stop getting ready to create and start creating well before the final deadline.

- Start early to practice orally. You will need to practice a speech aloud several times to be successful. Plan to orally practice for three days before your actual speech date. The first time you give the speech aloud should never be in front of an audience.

Summary

This section of the handbook emphasizes the planning stage of the preparation process. Above all, we learned that effective planning takes time to allow for creativity to develop.

5-1 Summarize the four phases of creativity.

▶ The four phases include preparation, incubation, illumination, and refinement.

▶ Allow yourself adequate time for this process to emerge.

▶ Create a schedule that identifies the time you'll need for each task, prioritizes the order of tasks, and sets deadlines throughout the process.

5-2 Prepare speech orally and collaboratively through preparation and presentation phases.

▶ The preparation process is an oral and collaborative process, and relies on different communicative resources during each phase: writing during the preparation phase, performance during the practice phase, and conversation during the presentation phase.

▶ The process can be accomplished successfully if you plan effectively and avoid common planning pitfalls.

Critical Thinking Questions

▶ Why is it important to allow time for creativity in the speech development process?

▶ How is practicing "in your head" not really practicing at all?

▶ What are your personal planning pitfalls and how can you overcome them?

Putting It into Practice

1. Why does the author suggest that canceling a speech is sometimes the best thing to do?

2. What is the author's view on public speaking?

3. How would preparation be different for an audience that disagreed with you rather than one that agreed with your major points?

Topic Selection and Analysis

Select a topic that is interesting, manageable, and likely to evoke the desired response. When you have chosen a promising topic, create a thesis statement to help you stay focused as you develop your speech.

MindTap®   Read, highlight, and take notes online.

Topic selection can be a difficult process. However, many speakers' topics are determined by their roles and responsibilities. Students in a speech class may have more freedom in choosing a topic than most speakers after college. It is important to consider a variety of different topics, as well as how they might be perceived by your audience, early in the planning process. When you believe you have identified a promising topic, clarify your speaking goal, narrow your topic, and crystallize your reasons for speaking to your specific audience about that particular subject into a concise thesis statement.

MindTap®   Visit the MindTap for *The Speaker's Handbook* and click on **Additional Resources** to read a good article about how to narrow your speech topics. Also check out the other links for good advice about how to choose good topics for informative and persuasive speeches.

6-1 Identify Your Speech Topic

As a speaker, you have varying degrees of freedom in topic choice, depending on the situation. In some instances, respected speakers will be given free rein to speak on the topic of their choice. But it's more common to be given a specific subject matter. For example, an assistant manager might be told to give an oral report on the effectiveness of the current employee scheduling system or a student is told, "Two weeks from Friday, you will speak third and give a persuasive speech on the dangers of social networking."

Most speaking situations fall between these extremes. You may be asked to welcome delegates to a conference or to speak to the Rotary Club about a service project. In these cases, you still have to select a theme for your talk. Even when the general topic is set, you need to zero in on an approach that will fit you, the audience, and the situation.

6-1a Draw from Your Experience, Expertise, and Interests

You bring a body of knowledge to the speech situation. Perhaps you have been asked to speak about your experiences in the Marines or with Habitat for Humanity. Your background will be the springboard for narrowing in on a topic, which can be developed into a compelling and substantial speech.

Brainstorming is a great way to generate possible topic ideas based on your experiences. This can be done alone or with others. The principle behind brainstorming is that even an unworkable idea may trigger one or more workable ideas, or a group of mediocre ideas may combine to make a great one. Therefore, don't judge any one idea until you have generated many. Later, you will select your best topic for the audience and the occasion. Consider the following questions to help you to identify a meaningful and manageable topic.

What Unusual Experiences Have You Had? Consider places you have traveled, jobs you have held, and events you have experienced. Perhaps you have met a celebrity or traveled to a foreign country. Do not overlook aspects of your life that you take for granted but that might be interesting to others. If you are adopted, have always been self-employed, or grew up speaking one language at home and another at school, you can introduce your audience to novel life experiences.

What Special Knowledge or Expertise Do You Have? Each of us has developed mastery in certain areas. How do you make your living? If your work in real estate has provided you with a good income, you can be certain there will be people eager to hear about your techniques. Yet a job need not be high paying or prestigious to generate speech topics. People like to know how things work. They are often quite interested in hearing about procedures, even ones the people performing them consider mundane. For instance, you might share how a person's credit score is determined or what goes on backstage at a concert.

Your course of study in school or your hobbies may have given you knowledge about topics that are obscure to your potential audience. Could you build a speech on the risks and benefits of tanning salons, the benefits of playing a musical instrument as relaxation therapy, or the health benefits of proper posture? Or you may have researched a topic simply because it interests you: David Fincher films, radio ID technology, craft beer, the country of Azerbaijan, the health effects of energy drinks, and so on.

What Strong Opinions and Beliefs Do You Hold? Have you ever overheard someone arguing fervently about the importance of free speech? What topics stir your passions in this way? Issues that touch on your core values (see Chapter **20**) frequently make excellent speech topics. You will be less self-conscious if you are speaking from a sense of deep conviction. And the audience will be more generous in spirit, even when they are in opposition, if they see you are passionate and sincere about your topic. You may also be motivated to investigate your topic more thoroughly than one assigned to you arbitrarily.

Besides issues that can provoke you into heated debate, others may fascinate you intellectually. Do you have a theory as to why successful marriages have declined, what makes a good teacher, or the impact of driverless vehicles? Explaining and exploring the basis of your beliefs can make an excellent speech.

What Would You Like to Know More About? Perhaps you are curious about recent research suggesting scientists might be able to improve the flavor of supermarket tomatoes. Or after reading about shifting alliances in the Middle East, you have become interested in the history of the U.S. role there. Perhaps after developing a headache, you decide to investigate the types and causes of this common ailment. Use the occasion of giving a speech as an opportunity to research a topic that has piqued your curiosity.

How Are You Uniquely Prepared to Assist Your Audience? Perhaps your role at work or in an organization affords you unique knowledge or insights that others need. Organizations often require people to share knowledge, perspectives, and priorities with coworkers. Perhaps your topic could come from your work role expertise.

6-1b Select a Topic Appropriate to the Audience and the Occasion

By brainstorming, you have created a possible subject list of great variety. To choose the one topic you will speak about, think about the audience and the occasion (see also Chapter **7**). There are two more questions you can ask yourself at this point:

▶ What does the audience expect? (audience)

▶ What might the audience expect on the day you speak? (occasion)

Knowing who your audience is and why its members are gathered together can help you narrow your topic list. A speech on the fluctuating gold market could be interesting, but not to a class of seventh graders at an assembly just before summer vacation.

When you have removed the inappropriate subjects from your list, find the *most* appropriate of the remainder. Place yourself in the audience's shoes. What topic do you think the audience would find worth hearing? Don't be the speaker who wastes an audience's time with a speech that doesn't meet their needs and interests or is beyond their understanding.

6-1c Select a Topic That Is Timely and Timeless

After considering your audience and the occasion, you may still have more than one possible topic on your list. Other things being equal, the best topics are those that are both timely and timeless. Certain issues have always been and always will be part of human discourse. People have been discussing the rights of the individual versus the rights of the state and the need for security versus the need for adventure for centuries and will continue to do so into the future. When you tie a contemporary event to one of these enduring human dialogues, you link the timely and the timeless.

Neither one of these conditions by itself is an indication the topic will be a good one. Consider the criterion of timeliness. If an event has been front page news for two weeks, a speech on that topic may be timely. But unless you can tell your audience what it all means in more universal terms, you will probably give them little they do not know already. The reverse is true as well: Your audience can miss or fail to be interested in the depth of your topic if you do not tie it into the fabric of their current existence. A profound, timeless topic needs a timely application.

Table 6.1 shows how topics that are too narrowly contemporary or too broadly universal may be altered to meet these criteria. Notice the different kinds of speeches to which the timely–timeless standard can apply.

6-1d Select a Topic That Is Meaningful and Manageable

Perhaps the most difficult aspect of topic selection is finding a topic that is both meaningful, in the sense that it is timely and timeless, *and* manageable. A manageable topic is one that can be discussed in the time allotted for your speech. For example, if you

TABLE 6.1
Timely and timeless topics

TIMELY (BUT POTENTIALLY TRIVIAL)	TIMELESS (BUT POTENTIALLY DIFFUSE)	TIMELY AND TIMELESS
There was a major confrontation last week when the Ku Klux Klan held a rally downtown.	Freedom of assembly must be protected for everyone.	Last week's confrontation over the Ku Klux Klan rally raised important questions about what restrictions, if any, should be placed on freedom of assembly.
I took a trip to Québec.	Travel helps people understand diversity of human cultures.	My trip to Québec helped me understand my own culture by contrasting it with another.
Our company has adopted a new profit-sharing plan.	The best management philosophy is one that treats employees like partners.	Our new profit-sharing plan will benefit the employees directly and reflects an enlightened philosophy of management.

MindTap® SPEAKER'S WORKSHOP 6.1

Suppose each of the following topics is of great interest to you, and you are qualified to speak about all of them:

1. Martial arts
2. Mediation before litigation
3. Problems of our health care system
4. The way television commercials are made
5. Western misconceptions about Islam

   Which of these topics would be best for each of the following audiences? Select more than one if you wish, but justify your answers.

A. A speech class in which the assignment is to support a thesis with factual and statistical evidence from several different sources
B. A community service club luncheon
C. A neighborhood youth group
D. A current-events study group
E. A keynote address at a business conference

have only ten minutes in which to explain your main points, can you cover *all* the aspects of Sudanese culture? Focusing on just one or two key aspects of the culture will make your topic more manageable.

6-1e Narrow Your Topic

To get into a topic, to get under the surface, you have to limit yourself to the number of points that can be adequately developed in the time available. You can expedite your research and preparation by narrowing your topic from the beginning. Thus, instead of looking up all the books and articles about the impact of the Internet on the society, you can focus on those related to the influence of social network sites in higher education.

Determine the Number of Ideas Time Will Allow The average speaker utters 100–150 words per minute. If you speak very rapidly or very slowly, you may fall outside this range. Chances are, though, your rate of speaking is somewhere near 125 words per minute. If you want to check your rate, see Chapter **25**.

A typical journalistic paragraph of simple sentences runs about 125 words. Thus, a general rule of thumb is that an average speaker speaks about one short paragraph per minute. If your material is technical or interspersed with statistics, dialogue, and dramatic pauses, or if you speak slowly, you had better allot two minutes per paragraph. This system, though rough, might help you to realistically adjust your topic to the time allotted.

For instance, if you plan on speaking informatively for eight to ten minutes on the U.S. Electoral College system, you need to set aside at least one to two minutes for the introduction and one minute for the conclusion. This leaves six to seven minutes for the body of your speech. If you plan to talk about the history of the Electoral College system, the cause for its inception, the way Electoral College votes are determined, and the influences of an Electoral College process on the 2012 and 2016 elections, you can spend about one to one and a half minutes on each subject. That would hardly be adequate. By narrowing the topic to one of these areas, you can develop two subpoints for three minutes each or three subpoints for two minutes each—a more realistic plan. The same principle can be applied to longer speeches, business presentations, and lectures. A twenty-minute speech can be thought of as twenty short, simple paragraphs or ten longer, more developed paragraphs. Table 6.2 shows how the speech about the Electoral College might be broken down.

Select a Few Main Ideas to Cover   Knowing that the Electoral College system speech in the preceding section should be cut to one or two main points does not tell you *which* one or two to select. To develop your ability to narrow a topic effectively, consider the following questions.

TABLE 6.2
Time allotment of speech elements

SPEECH PART	MINUTES
Introduction	
Welcome audience	1
Share startling statistic about the 2016 U.S. election	1
State topic and preview main points	1
First main point	
Explain and define	1
Subpoint	2
Subpoint	2
Second main point (including subpoints)	5
Third main point (including subpoints)	5
Conclusion	2
TOTAL	20

MindTap®   SPEAKER'S WORKSHOP 6.2

1. A speech has 2,900 words. Roughly how long would it take for the average person to deliver it?

2. Go to your MindTap for *The Speaker's Handbook* and select a transcript from the sample speeches available in the interactive video activities. Suppose you were allotted one third of the time needed to give that speech. How would you limit the topic?

3. Look at the outline on comic books in Chapter **10**. If you were to present that speech to avid comics collectors, how would you limit the topic? Look at the outline on women in the labor force in Chapter **11**. How would you limit that topic if you were given fifteen minutes to speak to a high school social studies class?

▶ *Which aspects of your topic are best covered in the public, oral mode?* Is it wise to spend five minutes reading a list of numbers? Might this data be included in a handout for further study and the *meaning* of the key numbers discussed instead? Ask yourself: Is this an important topic to discuss in a public speech? A speech should not be used to transmit routine information, to discuss specialized problems of a small portion of the audience, or to indulge the speaker's ego.

▶ *Which aspects of your topic are best suited to this audience and occasion?* Let audience analysis direct the emphasis of your speech. Select those points that relate most directly to the needs, attitudes, knowledge, and expectations of your listeners. (See Chapter **7**.) Will it give the audience "more for their money"? *Which aspects of your topic can you present most effectively?* Select those points on which you have the most knowledge and in which you have the most interest. Do you excel at explaining complex material? At making abstract ideas personal? Are you better with human interest stories than statistics or vice versa? *Select those points that best fit your speaking style.*

6-2 Identify the Purpose of Your Speech

Imagine you've decided to go on vacation with your friends or family. It will be important to begin the process by thinking about the goal of the vacation. Are you trying to get to the mountains or the ocean? Are you looking to escape the cold or get away from the heat? Once you decide where you are going, you will need to make additional decisions about where you might stay or what you might like to do while there. Similarly, developing a speech involves numerous decisions that impact subsequent choices. Deciding what direction to take with a speech requires considerable thought and attention to the audience, circumstances, and intended outcomes of the speech. It is important as the speaker to think through the primary reason for speaking in order to ensure accomplishment of that goal. It is helpful to consider the general purpose, a specific purpose, and a set of desired outcomes of a speech as we set out to develop our ideas, understanding that each choice will impact future options.

6-2a Identify the General Purpose

The general purpose of a speech is the overall intention you hope to accomplish. Typically, the general purpose is one of four intentions: to inform, to persuade, to invite, or to commemorate.

For instance, depending on your general purpose, a speech about "Lead rock and roll guitarists" could take many different forms. Do you want to explain the feedback-manipulating guitar work of Jimi Hendrix to your audience? Or do you want to convince them that Mark Knopfler has not been given the attention he is due? Or perhaps you want to inspire your audience by telling of the amazing abilities of B.B. King. The general purpose of a speech can be classified in one of four ways:

▶ *Inform*: A speech designed to explain, instruct, define, clarify, demonstrate, or teach.

▶ *Invite*: A speech designed to explore a topic with an audience or invite the audience to respond.

▶ *Persuade*: A speech designed to influence, convince, motivate, sell, preach, or stimulate action.

▶ *Evoke*: A speech designed to entertain, inspire, celebrate, commemorate, or bond, or to help listeners relive a significant event.

The speech to evoke is often called the "speech to entertain," but this is too narrow a definition. An evocative speech elicits a certain feeling or emotional response. The emotion or feeling can be one of fun, escape, and diversion—entertainment, if you will—but it can also be solemn and serious, as in a eulogy, in which a sense of community and an appreciation of individual worth may be evoked.

You will quickly discover that no speech has only one purpose. Most have a combination, but one purpose is usually dominant. For instance, a classroom lecture is used primarily to teach, but at the same time, it can be found entertaining. The purpose of a campaign speech is to drum up support for the candidate, but the speech can also inform. An excellent sermon might do all four: inform, invite, persuade, and evoke.

6-2b Decide on the Specific Purpose

Knowing which one of the four purposes—to inform, invite, persuade, or evoke—is predominant in your speech will help you in the next step: deciding what you really want to accomplish with your topic. In phrasing this purpose, isolate your central reason for speaking. You will have many incidental goals, but you cannot select and organize your materials without a clear set of priorities. Be both specific and realistic about the purpose you set for yourself. Do you want to teach your listeners all about chess in a ten-minute speech? Or do you simply want to give them the basic principles of the game? Do you want the audience members to buy your social media consulting services? Or do you want them to learn about social media strategies? Do not go any further until you can complete this sentence:

If there is one goal I want to achieve in this speech, it is to…. At this point, your topic should have a clear focus:

Not: *My specific purpose is to inform the audience about politics.*

But: *My specific purpose is to inform the audience about the role of the two-party system in American politics.*

Not: *My specific purpose is to invite the audience to discuss traffic safety.*

But: *My specific purpose is to invite the audience to understand red-light-camera laws and share their perspectives about the use of the laws in our community.*

Not: *My specific purpose is to persuade the audience against illegal immigration.*

But: *My specific purpose is to persuade the audience of the need for stronger enforcement of existing illegal immigration laws.*

MindTap·   SPEAKER'S WORKSHOP 6.3

Describe how each of the following topics could be made into a speech to inform, a speech to invite, a speech to persuade, and a speech to evoke.

Topics

International travel

Driverless vehicles

Hydroponic gardening

Rugby

Drone package delivery

6-2c Specify the Desired Outcomes

Once your goal is phrased in the terms of what you want to do, turn it around and phrase it in terms of what you want your *audience* to do: **If there is one action I want my listeners to take after my speech, it is to....**

In other words, if your speech is a success, what will your audience do? This is called the **primary audience outcome**.

> **Not:** *My desired outcome is to sell this product.*
>
> **But:** *My desired outcome is to <u>have you buy</u> this product.*
>
> **Not:** *My desired outcome is to explain hydroponics.*
>
> **But:** *My desired outcome is to <u>have you understand</u> the techniques of hydroponics.*

After you have identified the single most important audience outcome you are looking for, you can clarify your speech goals even further. Implicit in every general goal statement are many contributing subgoals that may also be phrased in terms of concrete audience behaviors. If your overall goal is to persuade members to take up the guitar, you want them first to *decide* that this is a good idea, second to *purchase* a guitar, third to *sign up* for lessons, and last to *continue* to practice. Notice the significance of the verbs in each case. The emphasis is on the behavior you want the audience to adopt.

The same procedures will help you plan your speech. Break the primary audience outcome into components. Pay particular attention to using phrases with verbs that describe overt actions rather than general states of mind. "I want my audience to *appreciate* art" is fine for a primary audience outcome, but you must go further and ask yourself how you will know if you have succeeded. What, exactly, are people doing when they are appreciating art? If you think about the specific behaviors or operations that contribute to appreciating art, you will come up with a list like this:

▶ *Go* to galleries.

▶ *Read* books on art.

▶ *Create* pieces of art themselves.

Observe how speech purposes and outcomes can be crystallized for each type of speech: informative, invitational, persuasive, and evocative.

Informative Speech

General purpose: To inform.

Specific purpose: To inform the audience of the uses for radio frequency identification (RFID).

Primary audience outcome: I want my audience to know how RFID can be used.

Contributing audience outcomes: I want my audience to

▶ *differentiate* RFID from other forms of identification systems
▶ *understand* what RFID is
▶ *recognize* some current uses of radio ID
▶ *contemplate* some future uses of RFID

Invitational Speech

General purpose: To invite.

Specific purpose: To invite my audience to explore the impact of a tobacco ban on campus.

Primary audience outcome: I want my audience to become familiar with the impact of the tobacco ban.

Contributing audience outcomes: I want my audience to

▶ *consider* the negative impacts of the tobacco ban on local businesses
▶ *recognize* the benefits of the tobacco ban on overall campus health
▶ *discuss* additional impacts of the tobacco ban on the cleanliness of campus walkways

Persuasive Speech

General purpose: To persuade.

Specific purpose: To convince the audience to change their eating habits.

Primary audience outcome: I want my audience members to start eating locally grown, organic foods.

Contributing audience outcomes: I want my audience to

▶ *minimize* consumption of fast food
▶ *shop* at local farm markets when in season
▶ *buy* organic food when possible
▶ *eat* organically grown foods when possible

Evocative Speech

General purpose: To evoke.

Specific purpose: To celebrate the successful conclusion of a veteran's memorial project and honor the individuals responsible for the success.

Primary audience outcome: I want my audience to experience a sense of community with all those who participated in the Veteran's memorial.

Contributing audience outcomes: I want my audience to

▶ *recognize* the contribution and achievement of each group: builders, fundraisers, donors, and support staff

▶ *feel* pride in their individual contribution

▶ *relive* some of the accomplishments

▶ *identify* with each other by telling a story common to those involved with the project

▶ *share in* the warmth felt for Mia, the "spark plug" of the organization

6-3 Develop a Clear Thesis Statement

Many organizations devise a short mission statement to focus the energy of its staff, to guide their choices. In a similar vein, your topic analysis needs a thesis statement that gives you something concrete against which to test ideas. In contrast to your "purpose" and "outcomes," your thesis sentence states your topic as a proposition to be proved or a theme to be developed. This sentence, sometimes referred to as the **central idea**, gives your speech focus. It helps you make the transition from thinking about where you want to end up (your goal) to how you will get there.

6-3a Formulate a Single Declarative Sentence

A thesis statement should not merely announce your topic. It should encapsulate what you plan to say about the topic. By writing your thesis as a complete sentence, you ensure the clarity of thought that comes from delineating both what you are talking

MindTap°   **SPEAKER'S WORKSHOP 6.4**

▶ Go to your MindTap for *The Speaker's Handbook* and watch the speech videos by Harriet Kamakil and Brian Sharkey. Identify these speeches by their type—informative, invitational, persuasive, or evocative. State the one-sentence specific purpose you think each speaker had.

▶ List at least four contributing audience outcomes that might be developed for each of the following primary outcomes. Use specific, concrete verbs to describe the behaviors.

   A. I want my audience to learn about genetic engineering.

   B. I want my audience to experience the thrills of visiting the Galápagos Islands.

   C. I want my audience to drive more safely.

about (the subject of the sentence) and what you are saying about it (the predicate of the sentence). A thesis statement whose single declarative sentence is "Today I will talk about cell phone plans" makes *you* the subject and makes the fact that you *are talking* the predicate—hardly the essence of your speech's content. However, "Cell phone plans are confusing and need to be simplified" makes the topic (cell phone plans) serve as subject and the point being made about it (they are confusing and need to be simplified) the predicate. See Chapter **11** for further discussion of the role of propositional phrasing in testing the relevance and completeness of ideas.

Be sure your thesis statement includes enough information to differentiate your approach from other possibilities.

Informative Speech

Not: *My speech is on gangs.*

Or even: *Young people find gangs attractive.*

But: *There are a number of sociological and developmental reasons why young people find gangs attractive.*

Invitational Speech

Not: *Exploring credit promises and pitfalls.*

Or even: *There are many credit promises and pitfalls.*

But: *Today, we will explore the promises and pitfalls associated with credit card use.*

Persuasive Speech

Not: *Something must be done about human papillomavirus (HPV).*

Or even: *HPV is on the increase and should be combatted.*

But: *The threat of human papillomavirus requires a program of education and treatment.*

Evocative Speech

Not: *We are here to dedicate the new hospital wing.*

Or even: *The opening of this wing is a great day for Memorial Hospital and the community.*

But: *This new surgical wing reflects the efforts of many dedicated fundraisers and increases the quality and quantity of medical care available in our community.*

6-3b Break Your Thesis Statement into a List of Questions

When chemists analyze a substance, they identify its components. As a speaker, you analyze the topic to find all the subtopics within it. All types of speeches require this type of analysis, and in persuasive speeches, this takes the form of a structured issue analysis. (See Chapter **22**.) To perform this analysis, consider the set of questions your thesis statement brings to mind. These questions are the ones your listeners will expect to be answered before they accept your thesis. Thus, they are the ones you should identify before proceeding with your research. The analysis will help anticipate your audience's reaction to your speech, direct your research, help you develop your main points and subpoints, and prevent you from committing any glaring oversights. You'll find the answers to these questions as you research your topic.

Consider this thesis for a persuasive speech:

Today I will demonstrate the problem of homelessness in our community, share a solution being offered by St. Vincent Hotel and Booth House, and help you to recognize the benefits of supporting this local organization.

Embedded in this thesis are three questions your audience will be asking as they listen:

▶ Is homelessness a problem that needs to be addressed?

▶ Does the St. Vincent Hotel and Booth House effectively address this problem?

▶ Do the benefits outweigh the costs necessary to move listeners to action?

MindTap   SPEAKER'S WORKSHOP 6.5

1. Read one or more of the speech transcripts available among the book's online resources, and formulate a single declarative sentence that best sums up the content. You may find the actual sentence in the speech itself or you may, in the case of an implicit thesis, have to draft a sentence of your own.

2. Evaluate the following as thesis statements for a speech. If they are not effective, rewrite them.

    A. What shall we do about the problem of racism?

    B. Syria—its history, its people, its problems—will be the topic I will cover today.

    C. To explore the need for mandatory drug testing of athletes!

    D. Taxpayers should not have to subsidize art that is pornographic or unpatriotic.

    E. How to make a Caesar salad.

    F. There are three forces impacting the gerrymandering of congressional districts.

For a speech about comic books, you might develop the following thesis sentence:

With their scope, history, and influence, comic books are an interesting component of American popular culture. For this informative speech, four questions present themselves:

▶ What is the scope of comic book themes?

▶ What is the history of the comic book?

▶ What influence have comic books had?

▶ Are comic books an interesting component of American popular culture?

Even in an invitational speech to a classroom audience, you might encapsulate your message into this thesis sentence:

We will explore the advantages and disadvantages of a motorcycle helmet law in our state and I will invite you to share your perspective.

This thesis brings to mind several questions you ought to investigate:

▶ What would a new motorcycle helmet law entail?

▶ What are the possible advantages of a motorcycle helmet law in the state?

▶ What possible disadvantages of a helmet law could be identified and for whom?

▶ How might the audience members' perspective be invited?

To answer these questions, you can investigate the impact of helmet laws in other states, perhaps interview some motorcycle owners you know to learn their perspective, speak to a police officer or your insurance provider about the possible impact of a law, and plan to invite your audience's perspective as part of your speech's main points.

MindTap   SPEAKER'S WORKSHOP 6.6

1. Look at each of the thesis statements you have identified or written for Speaker's Workshop 6.5. Identify the questions implicit in each. Do the speakers address each issue?

2. Identify the questions embedded in each of these thesis statements:

    A. The conceal carry law has been in effect for one year with both positive and negative effects.

    B. Together we will explore the promise and pitfalls of credit card use.

    C. Because the property tax is essentially regressive, it is an uncertain and inequitable source of revenue for the city and therefore must be changed.

FOR YOUR BENEFIT

Select a Speech Title If Necessary

Although every speech needs a thesis and a purpose, not every speech needs a title. A title is necessary when there is to be advance publicity, when there is a printed program, and, usually, when the speaker is going to be formally introduced. Unless there is a definite deadline to announce your title, you can defer selecting one until after the speech has been composed.

▶ A title can take any grammatical form. It can be a declarative sentence, question, phrase, or fragment. Consider the following:

- ○ "Freedom of Speech Is in Jeopardy"
- ○ "Is Free Speech Really Free?"
- ○ "Threats to Free Speech"
- ○ "Free Speech: An Endangered Species"

▶ An effective title should stimulate interest in your subject and make the audience eager to listen. Sometimes, a metaphor, quotation, or allusion that is central to the speech can be part of the title:

- ○ "Who Will Be David to This Modern Goliath?"
- ○ "The Quiet Revolution"[1]
- ○ "Women's Progress Is Human Progress"[2]
- ○ Are We Ready for Tomorrow, Today?"[3]
- ○ "Educated Citizens in a Changing World"[4]
- ○ "From Tentative Twig to Mighty Branch"[5]

In an effort to be clever or profound, do not devise a title that will mystify your audience, like "Whoot, Whoot!" or "The Heraclitus of Sycamore High." Nor should you select a title that promises more than you can deliver. That is false advertising. Do not announce "How to Double Your Income While Working Two Days a Week" and then give a speech on how to make one's first investment in income property. This may sell tabloids at the supermarket, but it is not considered good speaking technique.

MindTap® SPEAKER'S WORKSHOP 6.7

1. Go to your MindTap for *The Speaker's Handbook* and evaluate the titles of the speeches by Harriet Kamakil and Brian Sharkey. Are they effective?

2. Select titles for the comic book speech outlined in Chapter **10** and the speech on women in the labor force outlined in Chapter **11**.

3. Match each of the numbered categories to a lettered example.

Categories

1. General topic
2. Narrowed topic
3. General purpose
4. Specific purpose
5. Primary audience outcome
6. Contributing audience outcome
7. Thesis statement
8. Analysis question
9. Title

Examples

A. Have more lives been saved when a cardiopulmonary resuscitation (CPR)-trained person has been present?

B. To convince the audience that the greater the number of people who know CPR, the better the chance of more lives being saved every day.

C. Encourage friends to take a class in CPR.

D. Cardiopulmonary resuscitation.

E. I want my audience to actively work toward increasing the number of people who know CPR.

F. Learn CPR and make the world a safer place.

G. As many people as possible should learn CPR to increase the probability that a person trained in this life-saving technique will be available in the event of a heart attack or similar medical emergency.

H. To persuade.

I. The value of learning CPR.

Summary

Selecting a speech topic is your first step in developing an effective speech. In this chapter, we have focused on the following learning outcomes.

6-1 Identify a speech topic that is appropriate to your audience and the situation.

▶ Topic selection can come from your life experience, expertise, and interests.

▶ Considering what topic expectation or needs the audience and occasion might create will help you select an appropriate topic.

▶ A timely and timeless topic will help to ensure audience interest and avoid topics that may be perceived as too narrow (trivial) or too broad.

6-2 Discuss the general purpose and specific purpose of your speech, and the desired outcomes.

▶ Your general purpose will help determine the direction of your speech and establish it as informative, invitational, persuasive, or evocative.

▶ Your specific purpose will clarify your central reason for speaking; it is the one goal you want to achieve in the speech for that particular audience.

▶ Your primary audience outcome establishes what you want your audience to do as a result of your speech. This might include both primary and secondary outcomes you hope to accomplish as a result of speaking.

6-3 Explain how to develop a clear thesis statement.

▶ The thesis statement should be written as a single declarative sentence encapsulating your main points.

▶ Often the thesis establishes for the listener a list of questions to be answered by the speech.

Critical Thinking Questions

▶ Explain the process and benefit of selecting a topic appropriate to the audience and occasion.

▶ How might one's audience influence topic selection?

▶ Brainstorm a list of possible speech topics, choose the topic you're most interested in speaking about, and create a general purpose, specific purpose, primary audience outcome, and contributing audience outcome for this speech.

Putting It into Practice

Brainstorm and then select a topic that would be appropriate to deliver where you work. Identify a general purpose and specific purpose for this speech.

1. What topics would be appropriate for your workplace? What would be inappropriate?

2. Who would attend your speech? Why would they attend?

3. Would the speech be informative, invitational, persuasive, or evocative?

4. What audience outcomes would you desire? What outcomes would your direct supervisor desire?

Audience Analysis

Base your speech preparation on thorough audience analysis.

MindTap® Read, highlight, and take notes online.

I f communication is a collaborative creation of meaning between interactions, as explained in Chapter 1, then speakers do not just give speeches *to* audiences; they jointly create meaning *with* audiences. Audience analysis, then, is much more than a step in planning a speech; it requires constant speaker awareness of those intended as the "coauthors" of your speech—the listeners.

If you do not know the composition of your audience, you cannot make intelligent decisions about what to include, what to emphasize, and how best to arrange and frame your ideas. A thorough understanding of your audience, their age, sex, beliefs, attitudes, values, and expectations are all essential to your organization, development, and speech presentation (see Figure 7.1).

The composition of audiences varies. The members of one audience may have many similarities; the members of another, little in common. Within a given audience, the degree of homogeneity (similarity) or heterogeneity (diversity) can vary for each of the characteristics discussed in this chapter. For instance, an audience can be fairly homogeneous in terms of sex—predominantly female, say—and heterogeneous in its composition of people who agree or disagree with your position.

Thinking through audience analysis requires careful consideration and critical thinking. In this text, we approach each of these audience characteristics as a discrete factor and describe the techniques to be used with various kinds of homogeneous audiences. You will need to carefully mix and match these techniques as you uncover the actual composition of your potential audience, even if that audience includes your classmates. Later in the process of preparing your speech, you can use the audience information to tailor your presentation to your situation and audience.

FIGURE 7.1
Impact of audience analysis on speech development, organization, and presentation

7-1 Seek Audience Information

When you ask an audience to listen to your ideas, you are asking them to come partway into your experience. It is your obligation, in turn, to go partway into theirs. Every person is also a member of multiple discourse communities that are tied to specific cultural heritages, geographical locations, occupational groups, and many other factors. Each of these communities has its own set of norms and specialized vocabulary. By observing and reflecting on your audience from different perspectives, you can discover what communication links are already present between you and them—and what gaps need to be bridged.

The following are valuable ways to gain information about your audience. But it's important not to limit yourself to any one of them; these techniques work regardless of whether your audience includes attendees at a business luncheon or classmates in a marketing or public speaking class.

7-1a Use Direct Observation

When you have a lot in common with an audience, it can be easy to think you will know what will interest and engage them. Observing a less familiar audience may require you to think a bit harder about what they know or might need to know about your topic. With a well-known or lesser-known group, it is important to take time to reflect on the group's demographics. Notice the group's demographics such as age, gender, and ethnicity. Consider what they might already know or need to know about your topic in order to develop shared understanding. What examples or evidence might resonate with them? Try to determine any attitudes, beliefs, and/or values that might influence the audience member's ability to share your message. Observing a group, be it at a meeting or during class, can help you tailor you message to be most easily understood.

7-1b Do Systematic Data Collection

One excellent way to become informed about your audience is to ask them directly. Politicians and advertisers spend millions on public opinion and market surveys. Such research reveals who their audiences are and how they think. Business professionals routinely research the backgrounds of key audience members to understand attitudes, beliefs, and values associated with a product or service. You might gather information from your audience through a three- or four-item questionnaire prior to speaking. The survey will both arouse interest and allow you to gain valuable information.

7-1c Conduct Selected Interviews or Focus Groups

When you cannot get information on the whole audience, arrange to talk to one or two members of the group. If that is not possible, talk to someone who shares characteristics with your potential listeners. For a speech to a group of Young Libertarians, talking to one libertarian—even if she or he will not be a member of that audience—can provide you with useful information. The same applies to interviewing someone who manages a nonprofit organization if nonprofit managers will be in your audience. Similarly, you will benefit from conversing with a friend who is active in the local chapter of the American Red Cross, at whose regional conference you will speak. In each of these instances some information is better than none.

In these interviews, try to find out not just *what* people think but also *how* they think. Ask open-ended questions and encourage respondents to expand on their answers by probing with follow-up questions. Listen to the language they use. You can gain insight into what is most meaningful to people by tuning in to the words and metaphors they use. (See Chapter **17**.)

7-1d Talk with the Contact Person

The person who asked you to speak has certain expectations about the interaction between you and the audience; otherwise, you would not have been invited. Ask the contact person to elaborate on his or her perceptions of the audience. Ask about previous speakers, both best and worst, to better understand what to do and what to avoid.

Learn all you can about this group's collective history. What projects have they undertaken? What have they shared or accomplished? What other speakers have they heard? You may find possible connections to your speech topic.

7-1e Use Intelligent Inference and Empathy

When you have no specific information about an audience, draw on your general knowledge of human behavior and groups. What are reasonable assumptions about a college audience at 9:00 A.M. on your campus, or at a Rotary Club monthly luncheon meeting? It probably isn't too much of a leap to realize that a 9:00 A.M. speech will require some extra attention to awaken the audience and the Rotary luncheon meeting may have some predictable distractions.

Let empathy lead your understanding. Get outside yourself and think like your audience members. Recall a similar situation in your life: Ask yourself, "When have I felt as they likely feel?" and "What would be my main concerns?" Plan to address the resulting feelings and concerns through your speech. Use that empathy to plan appropriate responses to your audience's concerns.

7-2 Analyze Audience Demographics

Each and every audience is different. Obtaining each audience's vital statistics enables you to make general predictions about their responses. The "Describe Your Audience" checklist provides questions you can use to analyze the demographics of your audience.

Obviously, all demographic characteristics are not equally important for any given speech. For example, knowledge of your audience members' faith traditions will be important in preparing a speech on issues such as euthanasia or whether prayer speeds healing. But a person's faith tradition might have no bearing whatsoever on a topic of distracted driving. Although audience demographics may not always impact every topic, it is important for the speaker to note an audience's demographic characteristics, if only to improve the speaker's ability to empathize with an audience's perspective.

Holding a generalized image of your audience in mind as you prepare and practice your speech will impact dozens of minor decisions affecting your speech success. On the basis of your audience awareness, you will tailor your language, humor, appearance, visual aids, and style of delivery to match your audience and situation. In addition, Chapters **22** and **23** will help you plan more specific adaptations.

7-2a Generational Culture

It is likely that your classroom or workplace has at least five different generational groups, including Traditionalists, Boomers, Gen Xs, Gen Ys, and Millennials.[1] These groups have been influenced by very different environmental, political, and sociological circumstances leading to quite different perspectives (see Figure 7.2).[2] Of course, not every person in a particular generation will espouse the values of that generation, but some tendencies are worth consideration.

▶ Traditionalists have been shaped directly or indirectly by the Great Depression and World War II. They tend to value privacy, hard work, trustworthiness, formal communication authority, and social order. They tend to be fiscally conservative.

▶ Boomers have been shaped by the post-World War II economic boom. They tend to value competition, change, hard work, and inclusion, and take a more collaborative approach to work.

▶ Generation X has been shaped by greater independence at a younger age than previous generations and raised with instant access (latchkey kids). They tend to be highly independent, creative, entrepreneurial, and comfortable with change. They tend to value feedback, balance, fun, informality, information, and instant access to information.

▶ Generation Y and Millenials have been shaped by technology and instant access to information. They tend to value positive reinforcement, autonomy, flexibility, diversity, technology, multitasking, and constant access to information available through their extensive social network.

7-2b Sex and Gender

Sex is the demographic category that relates to biological status determined by a pair of chromosomes. A mammal with an XX chromosome pair is female and one with an XY chromosome pair is male. *Gender* refers to the socialized roles we have learned as appropriate for our sex. There may be a few experiences that are directly linked to sex;

FIGURE 7.2
Generational values

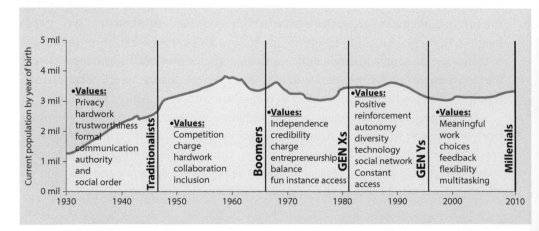

CHECKLIST ~ Describe Your Audience

- [ ] What is the average age of the audience members?
- [ ] What is the age range?
- [ ] With which generational group would audience members most closely associate?
- [ ] What is the proportion of males and females in the audience?
- [ ] What relational arrangements are represented (married, single, divorced, in a civil union or domestic partnership)?
- [ ] What cultural groups are represented, in about what proportions?
- [ ] What is the socioeconomic composition of the group?
- [ ] What occupations are represented?
- [ ] What religious groups are represented?
- [ ] What is the political orientation of the group?
- [ ] How homogeneous or heterogeneous are the audience members for each of these characteristics?

Dusit/Shutterstock.com

a speech on breastfeeding or circumcision might take the actual male–female composition of an audience into account. Far more commonly, however, gender issues enter into audience analysis. The issue is not how many males and females are present, but how audience members of either sex think about masculinity and femininity. These gender expectations are culture bound and have changed dramatically in recent years. The failure to recognize this change could seriously harm a speaker's credibility.

▶ As a speaker, you are well advised to avoid statements that may offend a sizable portion of your audience. Women, especially as they become aware of past oppression, are naturally sensitive to slights to their dignity and their roles as autonomous adults. Avoid referring to women as "girls," "gals," or "ladies"—all of which tend to trivialize their status. Many women believe that references to their clothes and appearance, however complimentary and well-meant, focus on them as sex objects or decorative accessories.

7-2c Race and Ethnicity

Ethnicity refers to a person's "identity with or membership in a particular racial, national, or cultural group and observance of that group's customs, beliefs, and language."[3] The term *race* is more problematic. Although it has historically been used to group people along lines of physical appearance, particularly skin color, biologists think of race as an arbitrary social construction that does not align with genetic and biological boundaries. Regardless of the biological reality, people do self-identify as members of a particular "race," and that identification and the perception of racial differences has great sociological and political force.

Because a single community or organization may be composed of dozens of cultures, it is not a reasonable goal to become an expert on the cultural values and symbols of each group. But you can familiarize yourself with their experiences. We all have a responsibility to become informed about one another if only to ensure our increased ability to communicate effectively with one another in an increasingly diverse world. For example, the common experience of nonwhite racial groups and most other ethnic minorities in the United States has included discrimination and oppression. Members of these groups, similar to women, are justifiably sensitive to any communication that reduces their status or limits them to stereotypes. In all cases, use an individual's proper title and don't address one group any more or less favorably than another. Work to remove all language that can be construed as sexist, ageist, racist, or otherwise limiting people's ability, such as the following:

▶ "I was chatting at dinner with your lovely vice president, Professor Ruhly."

▶ "To Pat Davis's left, the charming young man in the wheelchair is our sales manager, Myron."

▶ "If you had a son about to take over your business, you would probably tell him …. " [Why not a daughter?]

▶ "I saw a father babysitting his daughter at the mall the other day." [Should we think of fathers as "babysitters" when we think of mothers as "parents" or "caregivers"?]

FOR YOUR BENEFIT

Limitations of Demographic Generalizations

Few generalizations can be made on the basis of demographic factors. The studies from which generalizations are drawn are often flawed. Also, social change occurs so rapidly that by the time research is reported, the situation may have changed. Social science research, even when carefully controlled and well designed, tells us how one group differs from another group *on average*. With respect to almost any trait, the differences among all women or among all men are far greater than the differences between the average man and the average woman.

Still, demographic data let us make some *probability statements*. That is, we can say many people in an audience *are likely* to respond in a certain way even though we cannot say any individual in that audience definitely *will* respond in a given way. Knowing that an audience is all female or all over 65 years of age or all Mexican American is more helpful than having no information about the audience at all, but by no means does this data tell us everything we need to know.

Beyond showing sensitivity to the relationships between members of dominant and nondominant cultural groups, a speaker can also demonstrate an appreciation of cultural diversity. People of any ethnic group can tend to look at things from the standpoint of the group's own history and culture. Taking the time to investigate other cultural views can open up a number of refreshingly different avenues to good communication. Making the effort to pronounce unfamiliar names and phrases correctly, and avoiding stereotypical cultural generalizations, show your goodwill and openness.

This kind of investigation is worthwhile only if it is put to appropriate use. The superficial approach, equivalent to the politician who is filmed eating her way through every ethnic restaurant in her constituency, results in a speech that rings false. The focus should be on the factors that influence communication: What constitutes a credible image? What level of eye contact is appropriate? How much controversy or intensity becomes discomforting? What is an appropriate greeting or social distance?

7-3 Identify What Is Meaningful to Your Audience

Because speakers are not transmitting information, but rather are jointly constructing meanings with listeners, no part of audience analysis is as important as learning *how a particular group of people makes meaning*. The demographic data you collect can be useful, but only if treated within the context of this complex process. Age, race, and sex all contribute to a person's interpretation of the world. But so, too, do religious and spiritual traditions, social class, educational level, economic status, sexual orientation, health, physical ability, and many other factors. As the incredible diversity and constantly changing profile of the U.S. society have made clear, no formula can tell a speaker how each of these variables relates to a particular topic, let alone how they all interact. In a sense, as a speaker, you have been freed from the unrealistic goal of making predictions based on static traits of your listeners. Instead, your task is to consider thoughtfully how they engage in a constant process of constructing, and reconstructing, the world. Table 7.1 lists ways to relate to an audience.

This third and most useful way of understanding audiences requires both empathy and intellect. From this perspective, you can begin to grasp how different people can observe the same events but interpret them "logically" to come to opposite conclusions. (See Chapter **16**.) In this sort of audience analysis, you are trying to glimpse what some describe as *core values* (or *worldviews, personal construct systems, frames of reference, informal theories,* or *master narratives*). (See the discussion of listeners' values in Chapter **20**.) What do your listeners draw on to organize their experience and make sense of it?

TABLE 7.1
Relating to an audience

LEVEL OF UNDERSTANDING	ANALYSIS
Being oblivious to the audience (poor understanding).	Here is how I see this issue. You should see it the same way.
Adapting to the audience's traits (better understanding; although be cautious to avoid hasty generalizations).	Because you are male, you probably like sports and will enjoy my speech about basketball. Because you are older, you may be conservative and will be skeptical about dramatic change.
Understanding and respecting how the audience interprets the topic (best understanding).	Because of your experiences, you will value certain things. I can see how your worldview makes sense to you, and here is how my position overlaps and resonates with what you value.

There are two sources of such information. You can learn about cultural and group differences by reading, traveling, and exposing yourself to literature and art forms that shake up your own worldviews. You can also learn by listening openly to and participating in dialogues with the people you want to understand. Some people can tell you explicitly about their beliefs and attitudes, but often, the processes by which they make meaning are taken for granted and difficult to articulate. You may not get the insights you want through questionnaires or traditional interviews, so you need to rely on extended observation and careful attention to the ways their talk reveals their values, priorities, and conflicts. (See Chapter **17.**)

7-3a Determine the Audience's Attitudes toward Your Topic

Theoretically, you could spread every possible reaction a person might have to the thesis of your speech across a continuum that ranges from extreme disagreement to extreme agreement. Much social science research is based on asking people to clarify their attitudes on scales like this one:

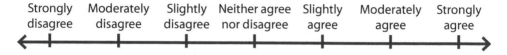

If your goal is to bring about some specific act, your listeners' responses will range across these categories:

If the majority of your audience falls to the left on either continuum, that audience should be considered *unfavorable*, and if it falls to the right, it is *favorable*. If it is in the middle, it is *neutral*.

MindTap°   SPEAKER'S WORKSHOP 7.1

Imagine you are planning to make a presentation in a public forum in your community. Use an online resource such as **www.census.gov** or **www.indexmundi. com** to learn about the general demographic makeup of your state, county, or city (if available). What information confirms your assumptions? What surprises you? How might this information be useful to a speaker? What is missing from this information that you would need to seek out prior to a speaking engagement?

Most speakers agree that knowing the audience's predisposition toward the topic is the single most important bit of information in planning their speech strategy. If your speech deals with a controversial topic, it is crucial that you interview people who differ from you in terms of attitude and experience. Listen carefully and respectfully to their perspective on the topic. At the information-gathering stage, your goal is not to plan a strategy for changing them, but rather to see how their views and yours might be connected. Once you determine whether your audience is favorable, neutral, or unfavorable, you can follow the specific suggestions offered in Chapter **22** to tailor your message. Although attitudes toward your topic are most obviously relevant to persuasive speaking, they can influence the speech to inform, invite, or evoke as well.

7-3b Gather Details about the Specific Speech Situation

We have stressed the importance of knowing your purpose in speaking, but what is your audience's purpose in listening? Why should they sit there and give you their valuable attention? Knowing your audience expectation for a speech is vital to the preparation of your speech. An expertly delivered speech can fail miserably if the audience expected something different than the speech you gave.

Think about the situation of your audience. Did your listeners just arrive from home, or have they been sitting in session since 8:00 this morning? What length of speech do they expect? Have they just finished a big meal or do they need one? The overly relaxed audience can be a challenge to a speaker, but so can the impatient or hungry one. Is your speech the keynote, or are they anticipating someone to follow you? This is not to say you must be bound by the audience's expectations. You can lead them to a new mind-set, but to do that, you need to discover what they know and expect. Start with the questions in the "Audience Expectations" checklist.

You obviously cannot control all the conditions surrounding your speech, but this makes it all the more important to find out as much as possible about audience expectations beforehand. Then you can direct your time to preparing a speech ideally suited to the occasion.

MindTap®   SPEAKER'S WORKSHOP 7.2

Go to your MindTap for *The Speaker's Handbook* and watch the videos of Brian Sharkey's and Kayla Strickland's speeches. Both speeches were prepared for college-age audiences. After watching the speeches, what assumptions do you think they made about their audiences? Imagine a situation where either of these student speakers had the opportunity to address an older "public audience" on the same topic. Identify the characteristics of the audience and suggest several specific adaptations that could be made in these speeches.

CHECKLIST ~ Audience Expectations

- *What does my audience know about my topic?*
- *Did I avoid making blanket assumptions about the sophistication of my audience?*
- *Did I use the techniques of audience analysis to determine accurately audience information needs?*
- *Did I determine how my audience members feel about my topic?* What an audience knows and what they feel can often be very different. Understanding and showing your understanding to an audience is a good way to help your audience listen to your ideas.
- *What do they think about me?* Learn what your audience has heard, read, or assumed about you. If they believe you are an unquestioned expert, a misguided fanatic, or funny, it will surely influence how they listen to you. Knowing what your credibility is prior to the speech helps you decide how much you need to bolster it during the speech. (See Chapter **19**.)
- *Have I tried to determine the history of my audience as a group?* Audiences come in many different forms, with varied levels of group cohesion. Most audiences have some common history, but that may range from a long association at work to a few weeks together in a classroom. *What is the program surrounding my speech?* You should know where in the program your speech falls, who will introduce you, and what happens immediately after you speak.
- *Do I understand my speech's place in the context of the immediate situation?* Whether you are part of a three-day professional conference or a high school assembly, familiarize yourself with the agenda and where you fit into it.

FOR YOUR BENEFIT

Multiple Identities of Audience Members

Audiences are not only culturally diverse, but they are also composed of individuals who themselves are multicultural. This is evident in the case of President Barack Obama, whose father is from Kenya, whose mother is an American from Kansas, and who lived in Hawaii and in Indonesia as a young person.[4] It is increasingly rare to find someone whose heritage is monocultural in any real sense. One person may have one European parent and one South American parent and have lived on four continents. Another individual may be part of an ethnic group that has largely been oppressed but may personally have had a privileged upper middle class lifestyle and education. A third-generation Korean American will share most of the cultural experiences of other native-born U.S. citizens but may have had different experiences or treatment based on having a Korean name or "Asian" features. Because people's experiences, not their traits, shape them as listeners, there are no simple prescriptions for analyzing an audience's cultural background.

Summary

In this chapter, we focused on the following:

7-1 Seek audience information.

▶ Gathering audience information might include the use of direct observation, systematic data collection, selected interviews or focus groups, conversations with a contact person, and intelligent inferences.

7-2 Analyze demographic information to determine audience values, beliefs, and attitudes.

▶ Generational culture can provide insight into the possible values that may influence your audience's thinking.

▶ Consideration of the audience demographics can include such information as the audience size, age, makeup, and cultural groups, among other things, that can lead to insights to audience attitudes.

7-3 Identify what is meaningful to your audience.

▶ Determining your audience's attitude can be used to develop a speech strategy.

▶ Determining details about the speech situation can offer insight into the audience's purpose for listening. Important details might include the length of the speech, the time of day it will be conducted, what will be happening before or after the speech, and the audience's attitudes toward the topic, speaker, and situation.

Critical Thinking Questions

▶ What demographic information would you want in the event you couldn't gather the information directly?

▶ How might you best determine your audience's attitude and expectations toward you and your topic?

▶ How might social media help you gather demographic and attitudinal information about your audience?

▶ What does audience analysis affect in the process of speech preparation, practice, and delivery?

Putting It into Practice

Prepare a speech for a club or organization that you belong to or can easily access—perhaps a student club on campus or a service organization such as Lions Club, Rotary Club, or Sertoma in your community.

1. What do you know about the organization's membership?
2. What do the members expect of speakers presenting at their meeting?
3. What situational elements might make speaking to this group a challenge?
4. What topics would be appropriate?

8

Research

Research your topic. Plan to gather information from a broad range of sources.

Y ou know you have a speech to prepare, but you just aren't sure where to begin. You've chosen a topic, understand your purpose, thought about your audience, and what they expect for the situation. What's next? You might decide to browse around the Web using your favorite search engine for information on your topic. While you are there, you decide to check your Twitter or Snapchat. An hour later you've connected with three friends, responded to a few friends, but you still haven't found what you need and may recognize the need to fact-check what information you did find. On the other hand, a better plan is to develop a research plan including a brief list of what statistics you need to support your ideas and who you might be able to contact for some information, and determine which information your local librarian can best help you access to avoid meandering around aimlessly for information.

8-1 Use a Research Strategy

A well-researched topic doesn't happen accidentally. A well-planned research strategy optimizes your effort in the time allotted. A research strategy requires you to reflect upon your topic broadly before pouring into the details. How much time do you have? What key terms may need definition? What might your audience already know? What might they need to know? What can you find online? What might require the help of a librarian? What information might best come from an interview?

Your approach to research can vary widely according to the time you have to prepare and the nature of your topic. Chapter 5 advises having a realistic timetable for preparation. With one day's notice, you cannot make an exhaustive study of the literature, but you can draw from general references found online. With more time, a broader effort is possible, starting with the information gleaned from general online resources, some more specific text, or online resources and perhaps a few specific sources, such as interviews with local experts.

MindTap°   The Web Search Guide is an excellent place to find information on various search engines and subject directories and strategies for using them. Visit this site by going to the MindTap for *The Speaker's Handbook* and click on **Additional Resources**. See especially its tutorials for Web searches and its comparisons of search engines. Another extremely valuable site is UC Berkeley Library's "Finding Information on the Internet: A Tutorial," which you can also find on the **Additional Resources** page.

8-1a Work from General to Specific

Start with an investigation of the "big picture." As you move further into your research, you can become more focused. Knowing from a broad standpoint what you can afford to ignore and what areas are essential will allow you to conduct your research strategically.

As the planning chart in Chapter **5** indicates, a round of preliminary or exploratory research precedes your main research effort. Many people turn to broad research tools Google and Wikipedia for initial information, but research can't stop there. There are two other basic sources to tap for research: published information and people. By starting first with published information, you will be better able to consider what questions to ask of a peer or an expert later.

8-1b Search Efficiently

One of the most useful research strategies for early research is the ability to skim. Even if you have unlimited time to prepare, it makes little sense to grab all the available books and articles on a topic and read them cover to cover. Before checking out any text resources from the library (or buying them, for that matter), look through a number of them quickly. Because you will not have time to read everything, try to get a feel for the most important approaches and theories. Use the table of contents or quickly skim key paragraphs of an article or the first and last chapters of the book. Jot down the names of the frequently cited scholars and public figures, as well as recurring concepts and studies. Do not feel obligated to read every single sentence.

Develop an efficient search technique as you search online, too. It is easy to be seduced by a long set of online links that are fun and interesting but may not lead to useful information. One way to sidestep this problem is to start with subject directories such as About, the Best of the Web (**botw.org/**), or the Librarian's Internet Index (**ipl.org/div/subject**) rather than search engines such as Google or Bing. If you do use search engines, you should be able to develop, after a time, a sense for the ranking algorithm used by each engine, and skip some highly ranked hits that really don't match your criteria. Be aware that, often, the top few links returned by a search engine have paid for prominent placement and may be less relevant to your search than those further down the list.

Some search engines and subject directories let you focus your search with *Boolean operators* ("this AND that," "this OR that," "this NOT that"). For example, if you search for "Finland" in hopes of finding some information on Finnish exports in 2010, you may have to wade through websites extolling Grandmother Kovanen's cookie recipes, Bob and Diane's trip to Helsinki, and so on, before finding anything useful. With Boolean operators, you can specify "Finland AND exports" or "Finland NOT recipes." Many engines permit users to specify that one word in the search should be near another and offer other tools (such as wildcards and required terms) to be as precise as possible; check the Help feature of your favorite search tools to learn their searching shortcuts. Most search engines also have an advanced features option with additional tools. For example, you can limit your search to a specific domain (such as .edu, or educational sites) or to pages that were updated recently. Figure 8.1 shows Google's Advanced Search page.

FIGURE 8.1
A Google search

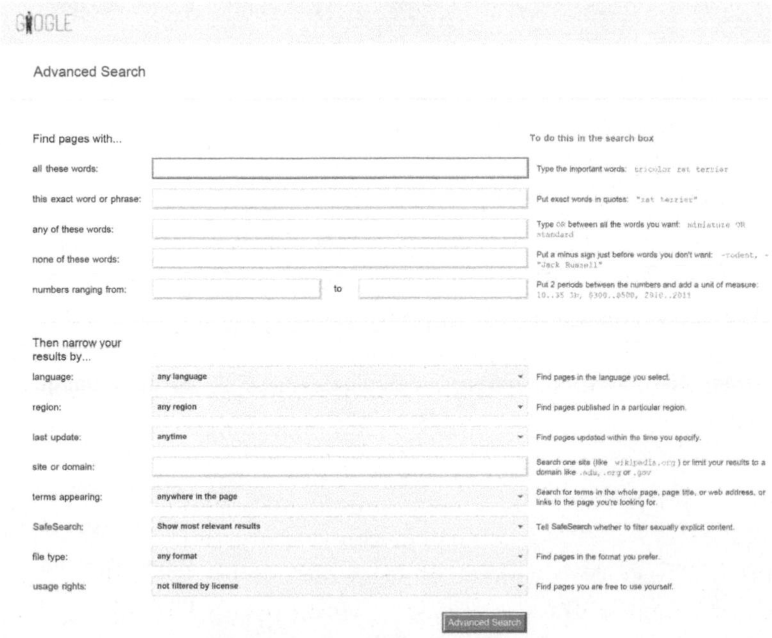

Courtesy of Google

For the most efficient use of any electronic resource, create a research strategy by narrowing your topic after considering different avenues of approach. Then you can decide on the most likely categories and keywords related to your topic. Being prepared for your search will help you avoid going down too many blind alleys.

If you need to fill in the holes in your background knowledge about a topic, you can go to online versions of basic reference books, such as encyclopedias, dictionaries, and almanacs. Table 8.1 lists some useful references that could be the starting point for your Internet research. You can also use them to double-check facts.

TABLE 8.1
Useful references on the Web

Dictionaries and pronunciation guides	
Merriam-Webster Online Dictionary and Thesaurus—includes audio pronunciations	**merriam webster.com**
VOA Pronunciation Guide—audio guide for names in the news	**names.voa.gov**
Encyclopedias and other reference works	
Encyclopedia Britannica—free condensed articles; full articles available to subscribers	**britannica.com**
Bartleby—reference collection with *Columbia Encyclopedia, Encyclopedia of World History, Columbia Gazetteer,* and *World Factbook* (Note that many of the references posted on this site are in the public domain, so they were published at least 75 years ago. Nonetheless, this is still a useful resource.)	**bartleby.com/reference**
LibrarySpot—multipurpose resource center	**libraryspot.com**
Quotations	
Quotations at Bartleby—search *Bartlett's Familiar Quotations, Grocott's Familiar Quotations,* and *Respectfully Quoted*	**bartleby.com/quotations**
Statistics	
FedStats—links to statistics collected by the U.S. government	**fedstats.sites.usa.gov**
NationMaster—creates graphs for comparisons among countries	**nationmaster.com**
StateMaster—creates graphs from comparisons among U.S. states	**statemaster.com**
Population Reference Bureau—worldwide data about population trends, health, and the environment	**prb.org**

Media links	
OnlineNewspapers—links to newspapers around the world	**onlinenewspapers.com**
Center for Communication—exposes readers to the issues, the ethics, the people, and the creative products that define the media business	**centerforcommunication .org/**
U.S. history and government	
Library of Congress—U.S. history resources	**loc.gov**
U.S. Congress—searchable database of federal legislation	**congress.gov**
U.S. National Archives and Records Administration—historically important U.S. government documents and records	**archives.gov**
Science	
Eric Weisstein's World of Science—links about math, chemistry, physics, and astronomy	**scienceworld.wolfram.com**
BrightSurf—science news stories	**brightsurf.com**
How Stuff Works—brief articles and Web links about how all sorts of things work	**howstuffworks.com**

As you begin your research, look for summary or state-of-the-art articles, books, and sites that synthesize current thinking on your subject. Articles that trace the history of your topic are also useful. Often, these sources are readily identifiable by their titles:

▶ Gregory, Sean. "It's Time to Pay College Athletes." *Time.* p. 36. Sept. 15, 2013.

▶ Emmert, Mark. "Paying College Athletes Is a Terrible Idea." *Wall Street Journal–Eastern Edition* Jan. 11, 2012: A11. *Business Source Complete.* Web. Oct. 12, 2013.

▶ Cohen, Ben. "The Case for Paying College Athletes." *Wall Street Journal–Eastern Edition* Sept. 16, 2011: D10. *Newspaper Source.* Web. Oct. 12, 2013.

▶ Smith, Chris. "Plans to Pay College Athletes Are Laughable While the NCAA Still Rules." *Forbes.Com* (2013): 14. *Business Source Complete.* Web. Oct. 12, 2013.

▶ "Let's Start Paying College Athletes." *New York Times Magazine* (2012): 8. *Newspaper Source.* Web. Oct. 12, 2013.

▶ "College Students' Perceptions on the Payment of Intercollegiate Student Athletes." [Raymond G. Schneider. 2001.]

Skimming several sources and reading a few general ones will give you a good overview of your topic. You can then further narrow your topic and focus the remainder of your research.

8-1c Develop a List of Key Terms

Beginning to study a new topic is almost like learning a new language. As you start exploring your topic, make a list of key terms that come up. In researching paying college athletes, for example, you will find you need to understand the distinctions made

FOR YOUR BENEFIT

Beware of Spreading Urban Legends

Because electronic information travels so fast, rumors and hoaxes can be shared as "facts." If a friend tells you about a barely believable story that happened to "a friend of a friend," check it out before you pass it along. Here are several searchable websites where you can "Fact check" a story. You can find these links on your MindTap for *The Speaker's Handbook* in **Additional Resources**.

FactCheck.Org http://www.factcheck.org/ Describe themselves as a nonpartisan, nonprofit "consumer advocate" for voters that aims to reduce the level of deception and confusion in U.S. politics funded by public contributions and the Annenberg Public Policy Center. Snopes.com, a popular site for verifying online rumors and hoaxes and RationalWiki, which has been described as a conspiracy theory debunking website.

between *college scholarships, monetized value, student sponsorship,* and *team revenue.* You will notice certain phrases such as *amateur myth* and *student athlete* that have been coined by earlier writers and that are widely used in the discourse on this topic. Familiarity with the language of your topic is essential as you continue your research because you need to identify keywords as you search through the literature. This is particularly useful in searches for electronic information—using precise language is one way to obtain a manageable number of hits with your Internet search.

8-1d Use Your Audience Analysis Questions

When you've made one pass through for background research, but before you launch a more extensive effort, go back and analyze your topic. Consider whether you want to narrow your topic, adjust your speech objectives, or fine-tune the wording of your thesis statement. Carefully follow the suggestions in Chapter **6** to list the questions about your topic your audience will want answers to. These questions become the basis of your research objectives.

Suppose this is your thesis:

The NCAA has exploited student athletes for their talents by cashing in on their amateur status.

Your audience may want to hear the answers to questions like these: Are student athletes being exploited? Do student athletes add value to the NCAA? Does student amateur status make them vulnerable to exploitation? Do student athletes profit from their talents? Clearly then, your list of research objectives will include goals like these: Find out how much money the NCAA gains from college athletics. Find specific examples of college athletes being exploited. Find an expert definition of *exploitation*. Find out how revenues related to college athletics have changed over time, and so on.

Like a shopping list you take to the grocery, this set of questions can provide focus and direction. Equipped with this list of research objectives, you are ready to make the best use of your research time and to ask appropriate experts for the help you need.

8-2 Gather Credible Content Using a Variety of Sources

Electronically accessible information ranges from Web pages to online editions of encyclopedias and news magazines, to stock market reports, to government statistics, to sports and entertainment news and weblogs (blogs). Apps for portable devices such as tablets and smartphones have become widely available, creating easy access to information from anywhere.

Search engines and metasearch engines are comparable to the index of a book except they catalogue the World Wide Web. Metasearch engines combine the results from several search engines. Here are some examples of both:

> Google **google.com**
> Bing **bing.com**
> DuckDuckGo—**duckduckgo.com**
> Wolfram Alpha—**wolframalpha.com**
> Dogpile (metasearch engine) **dogpile.com**

If a search engine is like the index of a book, a subject directory is like the library's book catalog. You find the general subject and then browse around in it to see what may be related and useful. Subject directories consist of links organized by topic. Most of the original subject directories like the Open Directory Project and Yahoo directory have closed. Some subject experts and librarians have created several smaller, but more select, subject guides. Here is a sampling:

> About (summaries and links from experts in 500 subjects) **about.com**
> Internet Public Library (subject directory and online reference books) **ipl.org**
> The Scout Report Archives (searchable virtual library of more than 20,000 selected websites) **scout.wisc.edu/Archives**
> Internet Archive—https://archive.org/index.php (searchable nonprofit library of millions of free books, movies, software, music, websites, and more).

In addition, a few search engines look for information on the *invisible* Web or databases (such as Census Bureau statistics and reports from government agencies) that may not be accessible via standard search engines.

▶ FirstGov (search or browse U.S. government websites) **usa.gov**

▶ Federal Digital System (search information databases produced by the U.S. government) **gpo.gov/fdsys**

▶ Congress (search engine for legislative information from the Library of Congress, including U.S. Congress bills, treaties, votes, and more) **congress.gov**

Also invisible to standard search engines are the messages and articles on Listserv e-mail discussion groups, Usenet newsgroups, and blogs. If you know your subject well and want a special piece of information, these may be worth checking out. Some search engines do special searches of groups and blogs. Here are a few:

▶ CataList (browsable catalog of public Listserv lists) **lsoft.com/catalist.html**

▶ Google Groups **groups.google.com**

▶ Yahoo! Groups **groups.yahoo.com**

▶ Google Blog Search **google.com**

▶ Technorati (blog search engine) **technorati.com**

MindTap®   A useful resource for making contact with such groups is the Encyclopedia of Associations, available at the library, or you can find a partial listing of societies and associations on the **Additional Resources** page at the MindTap for *The Speaker's Handbook*.

Scrutinize Web-based materials with special care. Although *any* information you gather in the course of research should be subjected to tests of credibility and reliability as described in Chapters **15** and **19**, the wide-open nature of the World Wide Web requires a particularly critical eye. The amplification of "fake news" stories has made online research more difficult. In contrast to the review processes applied to peer-reviewed content, it takes only a few dollars to post content to a commercial Internet website. Many websites are the equivalent of an opinion forcefully stated at a party: the authority resides in the volume, not the merit. With this in mind, consider the "Questions for Evaluating Internet Sources" checklist as you review a site.

8-2a Use the Library

Although the Internet can offer us access to many resources, the library is still the place to find the widest variety of research tools (including free access to the Internet) and, most importantly, the place to find professional researchers who can quickly help you avoid the pitfalls of fake news and locate valuable content. Mostly every college or public library has a lending relationship with a larger library system through which

CHECKLIST ~ Questions for Evaluating Internet Sources

- *Who created it*? Is it a personal page? If so, what are the person's credentials and how compelling are they? If it is an organization's page, does it provide enough background information (e.g., an "About Us" page) for you to make a judgment about its credibility? Who is funding the development of this page?

- *What is its bias*? Why was this site created? Was it to provide information, advocate a position, or just rant? If it's providing information, how is that information influenced by the underlying assumptions of the site's creator or funding by its sponsors?

- *Is it up to date*? Does the site have regular maintenance that keeps it on top of developments?

- *What company does it keep*? That is, who does it link to? Are those sites credible and competent?

- *How does it compare to other online or print sources*? Does the information square with what you know about the topic and with information from other sources?

  Especially if something on a Web page seems questionable, be sure to check it against a reliable source. For specific techniques on evaluating websites, see UC Berkeley Library's tutorial and the guidelines from Johns Hopkins University's Sheridan Library, "Practical Steps in Evaluating Internet Resources". You can find

MindTap these links under **Additional Resources** in the MindTap for *The Speaker's Handbook*.

members can request books and other resources. If your library offers tours of their facility, be sure you take advantage of this introduction either in person or in online as it will save you a great deal of time and energy.

Talk to a Librarian Librarians are service-oriented information specialists there to help you find the materials you need. Do not hesitate to ask your librarian questions. He or she will welcome the challenge of trying to understand your needs and direct you to the answers you seek—whether you have questions about key terms, general resources for a particular topic, the best databases, Internet search strategies, and any other part of your research.

Locate Books and Articles on Your Topic In addition to the librarian, important library resources include the online book catalog, periodical indexes and databases, and specialized dictionaries and encyclopedias.

The book catalog In most libraries, the book catalog is an online resource. These database systems let you search for entries in a number of ways. For instance, you may choose to search by some combination of subject, author, and title. Or you can focus on topics as they are grouped in the Dewey decimal system or the Library of Congress classifications. Or you can search by keywords or *descriptors*—words or short phrases that the database uses to identify entries on related topics. (In our example of paying college athletes, some keywords might be *NCAA, college athlete, student athlete, sports scholarship, Manziel,* and *sports law.*) Or, in some cases, you may make a *free text search,* in which the computer does not limit itself to defined descriptors, but rather looks for words and combinations of words you have chosen within the titles and content summaries of the books in the database. If you encounter difficulty, do not hesitate to ask for assistance from a library staff member.

Utilize periodical indexes and databases   You can locate magazine, journal, and newspaper articles on your topic by using the periodical indexes and databases available at the library. This may entail searching a computer database or perusing bound volumes. Some of the indexes and databases are general in their coverage; others are about a specific field. Whether your topic is art, criminal justice, religion, engineering, business, music, tax law, or any one of a multitude of topics, there is a good chance a specialized index or database exists for it. Once again, do not hesitate to approach the librarian for guidance in finding these sources.

Your library probably provides access to one or more electronic databases. LexisNexis, Gale (AccessMyLibrary), Dialog, EBSCOHost Research Databases, BRS (Bibliographic Retrieval Service), and Wilson OmniFile are some of the services that provide information retrieval. A service can have hundreds of databases to choose from, each of which can cover hundreds of thousands of articles and papers. Many times the information available through these services is not accessible through the public Internet resources available through search tools like Google or Bing. Many public libraries subscribe to at least one service. Public college and university libraries are likely to have a search service, available to the general public as well as students, staff, and faculty.

Use specialized dictionaries, encyclopedias, and other resources   Special dictionaries and encyclopedias are useful tools, especially for clarifying terms and concepts in fields in which you may have little knowledge. Many such reference works cover world history, finance, law, medicine, science, philosophy, music, literature, and other subjects of significance.

Depending on its size, the library may have many other sources of information available, including atlases, photographs, art collections, video recordings, compact discs, and all nature of digital media.

Talk to People   Research is more than delving into piles of Web pages, books, and papers. You are surrounded by potential sources of information in the form of other people. These sources can supplement and complement your online and library research. Human resources are all around you—at home, at school and work, in the community, and often as close as your phone. As you consider your topic and the information needed to support your thesis, ask yourself who you could talk to help bring insight to your effort.

Acquaintances, family, and coworkers   Share your developing speech ideas with the people you come in contact with every day. You may encounter surprising sources of expertise. Your neighbor who's always walking her dog the same time you are may turn out to know quite a bit about long-haul trucking, or your dentist may have gone to China last summer. On many topics, what these people can offer you is not so much expertise as a lay perspective you will not find in any book. What are your closest friends' most amazing technology mistakes? What do they think is the most urgent economic problem the country faces? (You might turn this into an informal survey, or even go a step further and develop a brief questionnaire.) Do not stop your research at this point, but use these contacts as a springboard to other, more specialized resources.

Expert   In every community, there are people with specialized expertise in your topic. They can make a significant contribution to your research, perhaps by telling you of unpublished data, local applications, or local examples of your subject, or by directing you to obscure sources. The information provided by local experts will likely be seen as more interesting and more credible than information obtained through less familiar online resources. Isn't it far more interesting to say, "According to Officer Jeff Burian of the local police department" than to say, "According to the stuff I read in a book about crime"?

FOR YOUR BENEFIT

Information Everywhere

Finding information is easy these days. Unfortunately, finding factual, accurate, timely, relevant information is not always easy. Learning to utilize your information resources will be one of the smartest and most important things you can do. Regularly ask for an update as to what might be new and improved at your library. New e-books, databases, and online journals may not be immediately evident but will be highly useful to you. Approach your information search strategically, keeping in mind what information you need and how you wish to use it. The skills you develop researching your speech will prove equally valuable as you research a possible employer, treatment alternatives for a medical condition, or the impact of some new technology on your family members.

▶ ***Educators.***   At whatever level—high school, trade school, college, or university—educators are usually approachable experts. Dissemination of information is their business. If you do not already have a specific person in mind after your research to this point, call the appropriate department or check with your local librarian for a referral. They will direct you to someone knowledgeable.

▶ ***Public officials and agencies.***   People elected to public office consider it one of their duties to make information available to their constituents. Most have staffs whose job it is to locate and send out government documents, copies of bills pending, and so on. In addition, scores of public agencies are staffed by experts who are ready to help you. If you do not know where to start, call the main phone number for the local or regional government offices and explain the direction of your research. The operator can tell you the department with which to begin.

▶ ***Independent agencies and special-interest groups.***   Groups such as the American Cancer Society, Planned Parenthood, and the local Lions Club can be excellent sources of information. Be aware, however, that such groups often represent a limited perspective. Talk to a spokesperson from, say, the National Rifle Association or the Sierra Club, but consider your source's biases. (See Chapter **15**.) When possible, interview experts who have differing orientations toward your subject, especially if the subject is controversial.

MindTap   Links to Usenet FAQs of all kinds can be found at the Internet FAQ Archives, which you can access by going to your MindTap for *The Speaker's Handbook* and clicking on **Additional Resources**.

▶ ***Potpourri.***   Judges, athletes, businesspeople, police officers, doctors, merchants, and accountants can all be experts. If you do not know a person in the particular field, see if you have a one-step link to one through a colleague or friend. Failing that, be alert to people mentioned in the newspapers. Chances are, if they were interviewed once, they will be willing to answer other questions. If you have no contacts in a large organization, start with the public relations officer. However, when you know who you want to talk to, there is no harm in calling that person's office and explaining your request. Maybe you will not get an appointment with the mayor, the chief of police, or the head football coach, but you may be able to meet with a top aide or assistant.

Look also for experts who may have credentials of a less formal sort. A homeless person, for instance, is an expert on certain dimensions of homelessness. In short, do not skip a potential source of useful information and possibly a fresh viewpoint by limiting your definition of "expert."

Experts are also accessible by computer. Newsgroups and Web conferences available online can introduce you to knowledgeable people around the country and even around the world. Thousands of forums exist, covering just about every topic—from Celtic music to calculus, to corporate law, and from bicycling to boycotts, to Barbie dolls. In these groups and on message boards, people carry on extended dialogue on many issues. Questions are asked and answered, challenged and rebutted. Join in by asking your own questions and engage in the multifaceted discussion that can result.

FOR YOUR BENEFIT

Conducting Interviews

As with all aspects of public speaking, in interviewing, preparation is just as important as the process itself. Prior to any interview, think about who the person is, and ask yourself how she or he can best contribute to your research. If the person has written an article or a book on the subject, read it. Prepare open-ended questions rather than yes/no questions or simple factual queries, but at the same time, don't be so vague that you give the person no starting place.

For instance, suppose you are interested in the issue of paying college students for their performance as athletes in the NCAA, and you are directing your questions to athletic director at the local university.

Not: *How many scholarship athletes are there at the university? [You could have looked up the figure before.]*

Not: *What are the problems that student athletes encounter? [This would be more appropriate for a student athlete.]*

But: *What impact would paying players to play have on our sports programs at the University?*

Spend the first few minutes of your interview establishing rapport and setting a context for the interview. Explain who you are, why you need the information, and how far you have gotten. Also, confirm your understanding of the time available, even if you did this when setting up the meeting. If you wish to record the interview on tape or with a digital voice recorder, ask permission at this point. Remember, technology can fail, so plan to take a few notes as well.

Also, use questions to summarize and direct the interview: "So far you've talked about four problem issues of paying students to play— who gets paid, how pay might be regulated, how this might impact competitiveness among schools, and the issue of sponsorship for pay. Are there others?" You can also use what's known as a **clearinghouse question**, such as "Is there anything else you can share that might be useful to me?"

Allow for a closing phase for the interview. Respect the interviewee's time limit, and if you are approaching it, stop—even if you have gone through only half of your questions. Summarize your perspective of the interview. Ask if they might be contacted in the future and, of course, convey your thanks.

Before asking a specific question, check to see if it is one that has come up many times before. Questions of this sort, along with their answers, are usually posted in a frequently asked questions (FAQ) file. If there is such a posting in your area of interest, read it first—you may find many answers immediately, and you may also find answers to questions you had not yet thought to ask.

> MindTap® Go to your MindTap for *The Speaker's Handbook* for help developing a record of your sources and a list of references.

8-3 Capture Information for Later Use

It is imperative to keep track of your research as you progress. Form the habit of identifying the source for every piece of information you use and of recording complete bibliographic information for each source. Your credibility will be crushed if you are questioned about a bit of evidence and your only reply is, "I found this on the Internet." That would be like saying you found it on the sidewalk. With electronic catalogs your task often will be easier—most now allow you establish an account that allows you to save search results you find helpful; certainly, you can save or e-mail yourself useful article or links. Should you print pages from the Internet, be certain that your printed page includes the headers and footers from your browser, which contain the page title and the page's Uniform Resource Locator (URL). Some people use an online tool called Zotero (see **Additional Resources** in MindTap) to collect, manage, and cite research sources. Other tools such as Evernote (see Figure 8.2) make the process of storing, sorting, categorizing, and retrieving search results easy and efficient. In some situations, you will need to track the vital information physically. Writing down volume numbers of journals, or the cities of publication of books, or the telephone numbers of interviewees—details you will never mention in your speech—may seem unnecessary, but routinely recording all such information will help you retrieve sources if you need to check them again. And if you later develop your speech into a written report or article, your research notes will be priceless.

> MindTap® Go to your MindTap for *The Speaker's Handbook* for help developing the categories you use to group your ideas.

8-3a Simplify Organization of Ideas

In the process of doing your research, gather and record your information and ideas in a way that makes it as easy as possible to find things later on and to work with them creatively. The ability to download pages and pages of text from the Web does not make it any easier to review the information you have. Smaller, more manageable units will promote creative flexibility as you arrange and rearrange, and structure and

FIGURE 8.2
Evernote is a tool for gathering and storing content electronically

EVERNOTE
Search
+ New Note
All Notes
Communication Teacher
Vol. 18, No. 3, July 2004, pp. 91–93
Any Questions?

Courtesy of Evernote

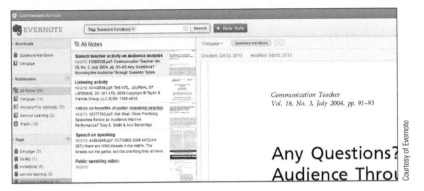

restructure, your thoughts and data. We talk about index cards in this chapter, but the important thing is not the media or the cardstock but the activity. If you use an outlining tool or idea development software on a tablet or computer, these suggestions are just as pertinent. That said, traditional 4-by-6-inch index cards are easy to manipulate and don't require a power source nearby.

8-3b Index Cards from Print and Electronic Sources

As you read the book or article, jot down each discrete idea or bit of information onto a separate card, being sure you add the identifying code (discussed shortly) and page number. Use only one side of each card. There are three kinds of data you might record: direct quotations or citations (Figure 8.3), paraphrased ideas (Figure 8.4), and

FIGURE 8.3
Direct quotations or citations

Gregory, p. 38
On History of Not Paying Student Athletes
"The historic justification for not paying players is that they are amateur student-athletes and the value of their scholarships -- often worth in excess of $100,000 over four years -- is payment enough."

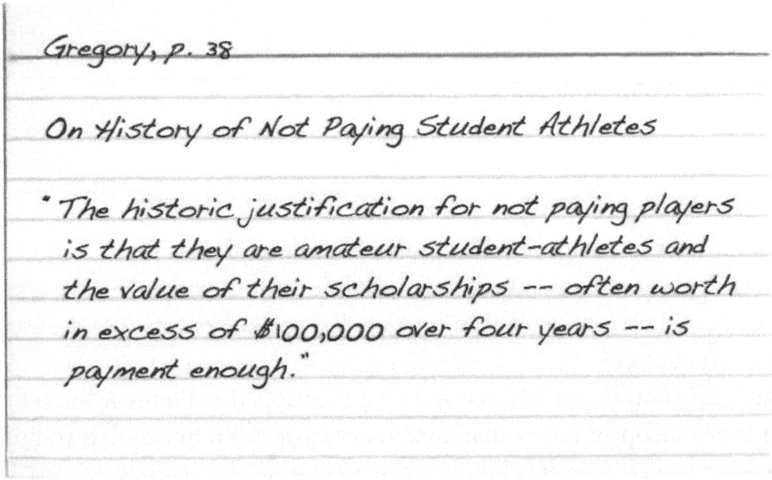

© Annelise Bodary

FIGURE 8.4
Paraphrased ideas

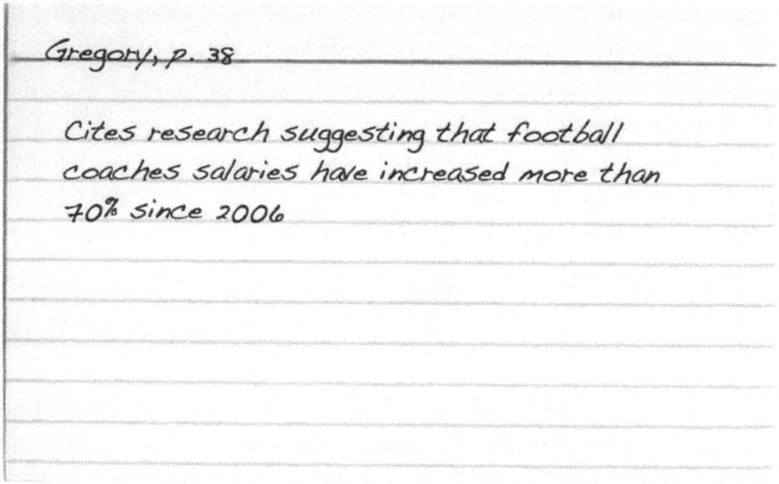

Gregory, p. 38

Cites research suggesting that football
coaches salaries have increased more than
70% since 2006

© Annelise Bodary

FIGURE 8.5
References for later use

Gregory, 40–41

Graphic on football team revenue for top 5
teams 2011–12 ranging from 104 million to 75
million dollars suggests 1.4 billion total revenue
for 25 richest college football teams.

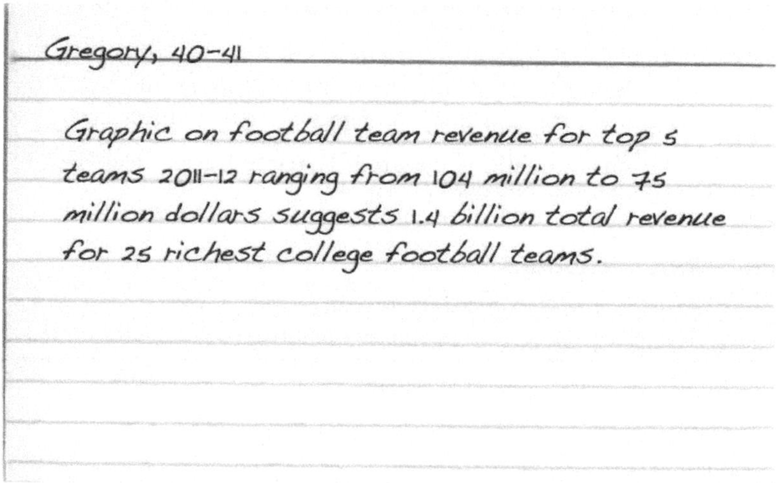

© Annelise Bodary

references for later use (Figure 8.5). Do not neglect to do this for materials obtained online. Even if you have a printout, it is valuable to go through the process of paraphrasing or quoting so you isolate and internalize the key points that drew you to the source in the first place.

If you decide now or later that the graphic mentioned in Figure 8.5 is valuable, you may want to photocopy it rather than tediously transcribe it by hand. If you photocopy lists, diagrams, tables, and other technical material, immediately head the sheet as you would an index card. Be certain to keep track of the bibliographic information for each and every source you utilize.

For each source, select a one- or two-word identification code that refers to that source and no other. Usually, the author's last name is sufficient: "Gregory." If there is another book by Gregory among your references, you may need to use "Gregory, 2010" and "Gregory, 2013." Or, if there are two sources from that author and year, you could use "Gregory, *It's Time to Pay*" and "Gregory, *Play to Pay*." Or, of course, if you have different authors with the same last name, then "Gregory, B." and "Gregory, F."

If you copy entire articles or chapters, be sure to make a bibliography card for each. Many people find it helpful to photocopy the title page and copyright page of the book or periodical to make sure they have the title and year accurately recorded.

8-3c Index Cards from Interviews and Surveys

Make a bibliography card or some other notation for each interview, citing the person interviewed, his or her qualifications, the date of the interview, and the person's telephone number or address. As you listen to the voice recording or review your notes, consider transcribing the information onto cards.

8-3d Grouping Your Ideas

When you have gathered your information or index cards, you may want to organize them under categories such as "History," "Causes," and "Solutions." As you will see in Part **3** on organization, this grouping of ideas and naming of categories usually occurs later in the process of preparing your speech.

MindTap°   Go to your MindTap for *The Speaker's Handbook* to see how other students cited sources in their speeches. Or record a speech you're working on, upload it, and ask your peers for their feedback. What feedback could you use to fine-tune your source citations before you give your speech in class?

8-4 Cite Your Sources Using a Standard Format

Because you are recording all the details about your sources anyway, we recommend you master one of the standard formats for citing references. Then, if you need to append a reference list to an outline or decide to produce a handout for your audience, the sources of your research will be appropriately laid out. Three of the most popular formats for the humanities and social sciences are found in *The Chicago Manual of Style* (CMS), 16th edition (2010), usually referred to simply as *Chicago* style; the Modern Language Association's *MLA Handbook for Writers of Research Papers*,

8th edition (2016), referred to as MLA style; and the *Publication Manual of the American Psychological Association,* 6th edition (2013), or referred to as APA style. For the sciences, two other popular formats are found in the 2014 *IEEE Standards Style Manual* (Institute of Electrical and Electronics Engineers) and *The CSE Manual for Authors, Editors, and Publishers,* 8th edition (2014), a publication of the Council of Science Editors.

MLA and APA styles are the ones most likely to be used in the context of a speech class. Individual variations notwithstanding, all five styles require an alphabetical listing of research sources that includes author, title, date, and publication details. An easy way to remember these categories is to include who, what, when, and where information for every source possible. In addition to the conventions for citing books, articles, chapters, and abstracts, there are established ways to cite nearly every known type of source, including interviews, TV shows, websites, and e-mail. Table 8.2 shows the APA and MLA styles for thirteen types of reference citations. Note the different sequence of information required by each, and also the differences in capitalization, punctuation, order of names, and so on. Again, keep in mind this list is just a sampling of the types of publications and communications that can end up in a reference list.

TABLE 8.2
Selected reference list entries in APA and MLA styles

	PUBLICATION MANUAL OF THE APA	**MLA HANDBOOK**
Book, two authors	Lastname, A. A., & Lastname, B. B. (date). *Title of work.* City: Publisher.	Lastname, Firstname, and Firstname Lastname. *Title of Work.* City: Publisher, date.
	Crossan, J. D., & Reed, J. L. (2001). *Excavating Jesus: Beneath the stones, behind the texts.* San Francisco: HarperSanFrancisco.	Crossan, John Dominic, and Jonathan L. Reed. *Excavating Jesus: Beneath the Stones, Behind the Texts.* San Francisco: HarperSanFrancisco, 2001.
Periodical, journal	Lastname, A. A. (date). Title of article. *Periodical,* volume, pages.	Lastname, Firstname. "Title of Article." *Periodical* volume (date): pages.
	Hughes, M. (2002). Moving from information transfer to knowledge creation: A new value proposition for technical communicators. *Technical Communication,* 49, 257–285.	Hughes, Michael. "Moving from Information Transfer to Knowledge Creation: A New Value Proposition for Communicators." *Technical Communication* 49 (2002): 257–285.

	PUBLICATION MANUAL OF THE APA	MLA HANDBOOK
Periodical, magazine	Lastname, A. A. (date). Title of article. *Periodical,* volume, pages. Schoenfeld, S. (1997, May/June). An experience in culture. *Timeline,* 33, 3–4.	Lastname, Firstname. "Title of Article." *Periodical,* date: pages. Schoenfeld, Samantha. "An Experience in Culture." *Timeline,* May–June 1997: 3–4.
Newspaper	Lastname, A. A. (date). Title of article. *Newspaper* [add city in brackets if necessary], pages. Guido, M. (2003, September 11). Lawmakers seek to plug loophole: Chipmakers got refunds but paid no tax to state. *San Jose Mercury News,* C1–2.	Lastname, Firstname. "Title of Article." *Newspaper* date [edition, if named]: pages. Guido, Michelle. "Lawmakers Seek to Plug Loophole: Chipmakers Got Refunds but Paid No Tax to State." *San Jose Mercury News* 11 Sep. 2003, [Peninsula/SF ed.]: C1–2.
Internet document (nonperiodical, no author)	Organization publishing website. (date). *Document title.* Retrieved date from address League of American Bicyclists. (2003). *How to commute by bicycle.* Retrieved August 4, 2008, from **www.bikeleague.org/ resources/better/commuters .php**	"Document Title." Site. Date. Organization publishing site. Date of retrieval "How to Commute by Bicycle." League of American Bicyclists. 2008. League of American Bicyclists. 08 Aug. 2008 **www .bikeleague.org/resources/ better/commuters.php**
E-mail	[Personal communication not included in reference list.]	Lastname, Firstname. "Subject Line/Description." E-mail to Firstname Lastname. Date. Thor, Leifur. "Info on the Design Science Initiative Project." E-mail to Doug Stuart. 2 May 2003.
Interview conducted by the speaker	[Personal communication not included in the reference list.]	Lastname, Firstname. Personal/ Telephone/E-mail interview. Date. Thor, Leifur. Telephone interview. 5 May 2003.

8-4a Cite Your Sources Smoothly in Your Speech

In the discussion on supporting materials in Chapter **15**, we talk about weaving them smoothly into the speech while citing the source. The form this citation takes is, like many choices in speaking, dependent on the context. In some cases, there is a rigid and stylized form; in others, there is a lot more flexibility available to the speaker.

The college debate or speech contest may have a strict form, developed by tradition. Otherwise, you can choose the *density* level of your citation—how much information you need to include about the source as you speak—according to how much you think your audience has to hear to accept the source as legitimate (although they may not agree with it).

One context is your listeners' attitude toward you and your topic: Chapter **22** discusses the adjustments you may have to make, depending on whether your audience is *favorable, neutral,* or *unfavorable.* As you might imagine, the more unfavorably your listeners regard your position, the more useful it may be to include denser citations as you introduce your supporting material (and to have a complete reference list printed up and ready to hand out). Another determinant in the density of your citations is your judgment on projecting credibility. (See Chapter **19**.) You may find in some cases that citing your sources more fully would be to your advantage, especially if a goal is to impress upon your listeners your competence and trustworthiness.

Here are three examples along the continuum of citation density. The first introduces the information with no citation at all. This is inappropriate as it lacks credibility and smacks of plagiarism. The second presents the name of the source, which indicates you are not picking numbers out of the air. The third example is fairly dense, giving your listeners enough information that they can jot down and use it to check your source if they so wish.

No Citation

The football program at the University of Texas showed a $77.9 million dollar profit in the 2011–12 season.

Light Citation

According to Sports Illustrated author Sean Gregory, the University of Texas football program showed a $77.9 million profit for the 2011–12 season.

Dense Citation

In his September 13, 2013, TIME magazine cover story titled, "It's time to pay college athletes," sports writer Sean Gregory notes that the football program at the University of Texas posted a net profit of $77.9 million for the 2011–12 season.

If you must be dense in your citing, make it as conversational as possible.

Writers are encouraged to keep source information inside of parentheses something like this: "Sports writer Sean Gregory ("It's time to pay college athletes," *Time Magazine,* September, 2013) notes that...." But notice how this creates a "parenthetical speed bump" in the sentence. It may take a few more words to come up with a smooth way to cite your sources, but the results, whether light or dense, will be more natural to the ears.

Summary

8-1 Develop a research strategy to gather credible information from a variety of sources.

▶ Start with a clear and efficient research strategy.

▶ Consider how to achieve a broad scope of the topic and a thorough understanding of the material within the time allotted.

8-2 Demonstrate how to gather credible content from a variety of sources.

▶ Recognize the importance of credible content and know where you can access it through the Internet, your library, and possibly personal interviews.

8-3 Explain how to capture your information for later use.

▶ Capture your information electronically or physically in a way that will allow for the creative process to flow.

8-4 Cite your sources using a standard format.

▶ Citing your sources aloud is required both to avoid plagiarism and to build credibility with your audience. Whether your citation is light or dense, it is imperative to phrase citations naturally and avoid the parenthetical interruptions common in written works.

Critical Thinking Questions

▶ What are the advantages and disadvantages of using Google in the early stages of research?

▶ What advantages might using note cards have to your research process? What might be the drawbacks?

▶ What are the advantages and disadvantages of local interviews as a source of information on a topic?

▶ Why technology will you use to track your sources in the preparation stage of speech development?

Putting It into Practice

Think of a topic for a speech that you could give.

1. What are the most effective sources of content for your topic and audience situation?

2. Would experts, educators, public officials, or special-interest groups be well received by your audience?

3. What level of citation within your speech is customary for this audience?

4. What would be the advantages of increasing the specificity of your source citations for this group?

Bringing Order to Your Ideas

Of the four phases of the creative process (described in Chapter **5**), most speech training emphasizes the logical, rule-bound processes of preparation and refinement. The middle phases of incubation and illumination are more difficult to explain as they are not rule-bound but instead touch the emotions. The process of creating a rap, story, painting, melody, or speech can produce intense feelings of excitement and at times discouragement. This process is rarely straightforward and systematic. Even with adequate preparation, you can find yourself pacing the floor, staring into space, and frustrated by false starts. Rest assured you are not alone when this happens to you.

In writing this book, we did not sit down at the computer, type the title *The Speaker's Handbook*, and then proceed unerringly through to the last page. The naming and arranging of categories took hours: Should practice be dealt with as an aspect of preparation? Can style be separated from content? Does the motivated sequence fit under patterns of organization or under motivational appeals? Even when we had settled on a general outline, we altered the details of that outline again and again as the actual writing progressed. At times, the topics seemed so interconnected that we felt we were trying to untangle headphone cords. Would it ever come untangled?

This frustration is an inherent part of the creative process. When you have read only one article on a topic, it is easy to write a summary of it. But when you have researched and analyzed a topic more thoroughly, your brain begins to be overloaded. You are challenged first by the amount of information and second by the number of connections the topic presents. This frustration is a sign you have gone beyond the "book report" stage and are imposing your own creative structure on the topic. Keep in mind that by experiencing this frustration and struggling until you have developed conceptual clarity, you are saving your audience from the agony of information overload.

The analysis and synthesis of information have appropriately been called *invention*. *Analysis* is the taking apart of a topic, a process that follows specified rules. *Synthesis* is the remolding of the parts into a new whole—truly creating or inventing an interpretation that did not exist before. There are no set rules for synthesis.

Although many people can collect the same information and divide a topic into certain logical parts, no two people will prepare the same speech. The synthesis you create reflects your own personality, values, and perspective.

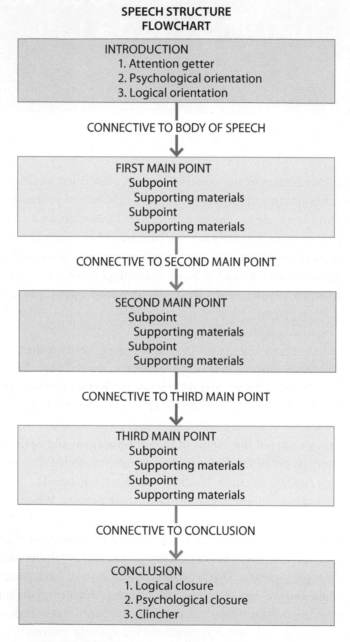

**SPEECH STRUCTURE
FLOWCHART**

INTRODUCTION
1. Attention getter
2. Psychological orientation
3. Logical orientation

CONNECTIVE TO BODY OF SPEECH

FIRST MAIN POINT
Subpoint
Supporting materials
Subpoint
Supporting materials

CONNECTIVE TO SECOND MAIN POINT

SECOND MAIN POINT
Subpoint
Supporting materials
Subpoint
Supporting materials

CONNECTIVE TO THIRD MAIN POINT

THIRD MAIN POINT
Subpoint
Supporting materials
Subpoint
Supporting materials

CONNECTIVE TO CONCLUSION

CONCLUSION
1. Logical closure
2. Psychological closure
3. Clincher

Once you've done all this work, you can put the pieces together in an organization that connects the information and presents it in a coherent and compelling flow. (See the Speech Structure Flowchart.)

9

Transforming Ideas into Speech Points

TFoxFoto/Shutterstock.com

Look for logical groupings of ideas that could be developed as main points and subpoints of your speech.

MindTap®   Read, highlight, and take notes online.

Y ou may have a lot of good ideas, but prioritizing them can be difficult. The process of sifting through all the ideas and establishing a satisfactory pattern must be done carefully and thoughtfully. The process of organizing has four basic stages:

1. Generating many ideas
2. Grouping them
3. Labeling each group of ideas
4. Reworking and trimming the ideas until you have two to five major groups that encompass the most important ideas and that can be developed in your allotted time

MindTap®   Go to your MindTap for *The Speaker's Handbook* for help developing, limiting, and organizing the main ideas related to your thesis.

9-1 Gather Promising Ideas and Information

Like topic selection, the process of assembling ideas begins with brainstorming. Start to prepare your ideas by jotting down every item you might possibly cover in your speech. Do not judge or dismiss any idea, but instead write them all down. There is no need yet to impose any order on what you are writing. Work quickly, following the techniques of brainstorming or mind-mapping and develop quantity rather than quality at this point.

Review the brainstorming list you made and consider how you might organize or cluster the entries. Are there any that stand out as main points? Are there any that seem to fit together? Are there any that are naturally subordinate to others?

There is no one correct way to group these ideas. Some ideas won't be included and others may fit into another idea. You may notice that not all the points in one group are of equal importance. Sometimes, one or more of the ideas from your brainstorming list can serve as a category around which to group lesser points. Other times, you will group several minor ideas and then determine the category.

9-1a Draft a Topic Outline

Perhaps the most traditional technique of speech organization is to arrange ideas in the hierarchical, indented outline format. At this early stage of development, however, you do not want to be constrained yet by the requirements of the formal *full-sentence outline*. (See Chapter 11.) The full-sentence outline will be important later in helping you elaborate points and subpoints, but a less rigid form, the topic outline, is more useful now. A **topic outline** uses words or phrases to identify the essential points a speech will cover. Complete examples of both types of outlines are shown in Chapter 11; however, an excerpt from that topic outline is shown here to provide an immediate example.

Sample Topic Outline

Topic: The History of Working Women in the United States

I. Preindustrial
  A. Colonial women
    1. Soap
    2. Clothing
  B. Frontier women
    1. Indian attacks
    2. Farmwork
II. Increased industrialization to Civil War

  A. Women in factories
    1. Smaller hands suited to weaving
    2. One dollar per week, less lodging
  B. First union attempts
    1. 1824
    2. Lady Shoe Binders, Lynn, Massachusetts

Because you are likely to experiment with several different groupings of ideas, don't spend time on phrasing or format. Just try to fit ideas under one another, nesting them in various ways until you discover the pattern that seems to make the most sense.

If the topic outline is a comfortable method for you, you will have a head start on developing the full-sentence outline. However, even this loose form of outlining may be premature if it blocks your thought processes. Next, we describe other, more spatially oriented ways you can collect your thoughts.

9-1b Use Concept Mapping

Concept mapping is a visual method of showing how your ideas relate to each other. In its most basic form, you quickly draw a simple diagram made of labeled shapes, connecting them with lines.

Starting with your central idea—your topic—write it in a box or circle in the center of a sheet of paper. Based on your brainstorm, jot some major ideas around the topic, leaving enough room to add more subpoints. As you write down each new idea, draw a line to connect it to its related point. This doesn't have to be done hierarchically, however. Subpoints might come to you before a broader point does. You can redraw as relationships become clear.

A variety of styles exists for doing this, under the names of *clustering, mind-mapping, branching,* and *ballooning.* Figure 9.1 shows a simple concept map. (This led to the comic book outline you'll find in Chapter **10**.)

FIGURE 9.1
Simple concept map

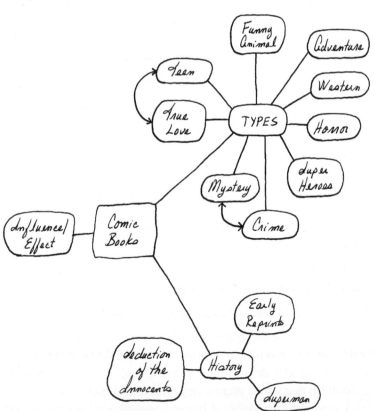

9-1c Manipulate Movable Notes

You can manipulate notes spatially or linearly. For example, you can jot down your ideas on sticky notes and stick them to a wall or desktop. Cluster the ideas according to themes, moving items from group to group until you are happy with the organization. (You can also group your research note cards under subject cover cards, which was suggested in Chapter **8**.) You can write ideas, connectives, and syntheses on additional sticky notes or cards and plug them in where you think they fit. These two paper-based approaches can also be accomplished using word processing software or specialized idea development software. Software to assist you in idea development is widely available, including MindMeister.com or Vue from vue.tufts.edu. By beginning with a brainstorm, you will have a set of potential points for your speech. The next step is to choose the points that work best for your audience and purpose.

9-2 Develop Main Points That Correspond to Your Thesis

Main points are primary ideas, those that are central and indispensable to the development of the thesis. To decide which main points to include in your speech, first look at your general purpose, specific purpose, and thesis statement. Follow the steps discussed in Chapter **6** to identify the essential questions you must answer for your thesis. For persuasive speeches that develop propositions of fact, value, or policy, consult Chapter **22** for information on how to identify the essential questions with more precision.

9-2a Correspond Main Points to Your Thesis

Once you know what a complete development of your topic requires, use the thesis statement to develop your main points. Ask yourself these two questions:

1. Is there any part of my thesis that is not developed in the speech?
2. Is there any main idea of the speech that is not reflected in my thesis?

To see how this works, look at the following thesis and main points:

Thesis statement: The jojoba plant is an effective energy source capable of eliminating U.S. dependence on foreign oil.

A. The jojoba plant is a virtually untapped source of energy.
B. Energy can be produced from the jojoba plant efficiently and safely.
C. Given an adequate educational program, the public would come to accept jojoba plant energy.

Obviously, something is missing. Either the thesis should be changed by deleting "capable of eliminating U.S. dependence on foreign oil," or another main point should be added to establish that jojoba plant energy has that ability.

The following set of main points corresponds better to the thesis statement; nothing essential is missing, and nothing superfluous is included:

Thesis statement: The jojoba plant is an effective energy source capable of eliminating U.S. dependence on foreign oil.

A. The jojoba plant is a virtually untapped source of energy.

B. The jojoba plant is a safe, efficient, and marketable source of energy.

C. The jojoba plant could create sufficient energy to eliminate U.S. dependence on foreign oil.

Sometimes, you may need to adjust your thesis to reflect the refinement of your ideas that resulted from the organizing process. Such changes are acceptable so long as your resulting thesis still fulfills the purpose and other requirements established for the situation.

9-2b Ensure Main Points Are Mutually Exclusive

Sometimes, when you are grouping ideas under potential main points, you will find that many fit into two or more categories. When this overlapping occurs, you know you have not yet found an effective system for classifying your ideas. For maximum clarity, the ideas in your main points should be mutually exclusive. Settling on a single organizational pattern is essential. If you do not know where an idea fits, your

---

MindTap®   **SPEAKER'S WORKSHOP 9.1**

Do the main points correspond to their thesis statements in the following two examples? If not, rewrite the main points or the thesis so that they correspond.

Thesis statement: A four-day workweek would be beneficial to our company, our employees, and our community.

I.   The company will benefit from increased productivity.

II. Employees will enjoy longer weekends.

III. The community will benefit from reduced carbon emissions and rush-hour traffic.

Thesis statement: Skateboarders are discriminated against wherever they ride.

I.   Public facilities have "No Skateboarding" signs.

II. Skateboarders are needlessly harassed by private property owners.

III. Skateboarding is a difficult sport that encourages agility and physical fitness.

audience certainly will not. If you were unsure of your pattern, the result might be an outline like this:

Topic: Great Films

I. Action

    A. *Saving Private Ryan* (1998)

    B. *The Lord of the Rings: The Return of the King* (2003)

    C. *The Magnificent Seven* (2016)

II. Science fiction

    A. *The Matrix* (1999)

    B. *Marvel's The Avengers* (2012)

    C. *Resident Evil: The Final Chapter* (2016)

III. Black-and-white

    A. *Citizen Kane* (1941)

    B. *To Kill a Mockingbird* (1962)

    C. *Raging Bull* (1980)

    A quick look shows that this speaker began to lay out the structure of the speech before thinking through the topic completely. Apparently, the speaker was unable to decide whether the discussion on film should be by dramatic category or by color or the lack of it. Whether a movie was shot on color or black-and-white stock has no intrinsic relationship to genre. These three main points—action, science fiction, and black-and-white—are not parallel categories.

    Ideally, if you have mutually exclusive main points, you will know how to classify any film and list it under one point only. If we put the sample outline to the test, however, we encounter uncertainty. *Resident Evil: The Final Chapter* (2016) could fit not only under "Action" but also under "Science fiction." So, although each main point by itself seems a plausible way to classify movies, the three main points taken together do not constitute a sensible way to look at the topic.

    Here is another example of an outline on the same topic:

Topic: Great Films

I. Black-and-white

    A. Drama

        1. *Citizen Kane* (1941)

        2. *To Kill a Mockingbird* (1962)

        3. *Raging Bull* (1980)

II. Comedy

        1. *The General* (1927)

     2. *Bringing Up Baby* (1938)

     3. *Some Like It Hot* (1959)

     4. *A Hard Day's Night* (1964)

III. Color

    A. Drama

       1. *Rear Window* (1954)

       2. *The Shawshank Redemption* (1994)

       3. *Fight Club* (1999)

       4. *Manchester by the Sea* (2016)

    B. Comedy

       1. *Monty Python and the Holy Grail* (1975)

       2. *The Princess Bride* (1987)

       3. *Anchorman 2* (2004)

       4. *La La Land* (2016)

Here, the topic is divided into main points along a single dimension: color or lack of it. These two main points are each divided into the same two subpoints.

This same topic could be organized in many other ways. For example, the main points might be organized chronologically, topically, or spatially. (Additional organization patterns are discussed in Chapter 10.) For instance, a speech about award-winning movies could be organized by when they were made, who directed them, or where they were filmed.

FOR YOUR BENEFIT

Tailor Main Points for Your Audience and Situation

When you are faced with decisions about which point(s) to cover in a speech, remember to consider your audience. Exclude points that have limited interest to your audience. Focus on main points that are essential issues for the people you will be addressing. That means you may need to make adjustments when giving a speech on the same topic to different audiences. For instance, if your job requires you to inform plant employees about upcoming health care changes, the issues of importance to members of the day shift might be very different from the issues of the night shift members. So, your choice of main points should be adjusted accordingly.

9-2c Include Two to Five Main Points That Reflect Relationships

Although this rule sounds arbitrary, it is not as unreasonable as you might think. As a speaker, you should be able to cluster your ideas around a few main themes. Your audience is unlikely to remember more than few main points. So, gather a few of the most relevant points (main points) and support them with examples, statistics, or testimony and avoid the perception of an unorganized barrage of information. Consider the nature of the relationship between ideas be they coordinate, subordinate, or superordinate.

Ideas of equal importance are called **coordinate points**. Points of lesser significance that support, explain, or contribute steps of logical development to other ideas are called **subordinate points**. Points of greater significance are called **superordinate points**. The relative importance of the various points must be very clear in your mind. Every point in the speech is subordinate, coordinate, or superordinate to every other.

If you were to classify methods of transporting goods, you might come up with a list like this one:

Transportation of Goods

Trains

Trucks

Airplanes

Ships

In this example, the modes of transportation (trains, trucks, airplanes, or ships) have a coordinate relationship to each other, and they all have a subordinate relationship to the larger, or superordinate, category of "Transportation of Goods."

Each mode of transportation, in turn, may have more specific divisions:

Types of Trucks

Tractors

Vans

Dump trucks

Tankers

Flatbeds

Here, each type of truck bears a subordinate relationship to the larger category of "Types of Trucks" and a coordinate relationship to each other.

Logical relationships can also be shown through subordination and coordination, as in this example:

Trucks are an efficient means of transporting goods.

[*because*] They have a wide network of destinations.

[*because*] They have great versatility of design.

[*and because*] They are relatively cheap to operate.

It is evident that the reasons are subordinate to the points they establish.

Subordinate Points Should Fit within a Larger Idea   Sometimes ideas that are too big for the points they are intended to support can slip in. As you read the following example from a speech on the role of aircraft carriers in World War II, consider the fit of the subordinate points.

I. Aircraft carriers were instrumental in winning the war in the Pacific.
   A. The successful use of aircraft carriers at the battles of the Coral Sea and Midway blunted the Japanese drive across the Pacific.
   B. Planes launched from aircraft carriers were able to inflict damage on enemy bases out of the range of land-based aircraft.
   C. Antisubmarine warfare was instrumental to winning the war in the Atlantic.

In this case, subpoint C is neither related to the major idea nor is it subordinate in importance. The use of antisubmarine warfare in the Atlantic does not belong under the use of aircraft carriers in the Pacific. The two ideas bear a coordinate relationship, and the statement in subpoint C should probably be main point II.

Coordinate Points Should Be of Equal Importance   Occasionally, an idea is too small to fit with the others at its level. In the following outline, the subpoints are not coordinate:

I. Aircraft carriers were instrumental in winning the war in the Pacific.
   A. The successful use of aircraft carriers at the battles of the Coral Sea and Midway blunted the Japanese drive across the Pacific.
   B. A number of new aircraft carriers were named after carriers sunk earlier in the war.
   C. Planes launched from aircraft carriers were able to inflict damage on enemy bases out of the range of land-based aircraft.

Notice how subpoint B stands out when compared to the other two subpoints. There may have been some initial benefit from the confusion that such naming caused among the intelligence services of the Japanese, but it was hardly "instrumental."

If you have one main idea that seems much less important than the other(s), omit it altogether, or create another main point so that this less important idea can become a subpoint, or mention the idea only as part of the introduction or conclusion. You might also occasionally consider a catchall main point, such as "There are several other factors…."

Each Subpoint Should Directly Relate to the Point It Supports Do not group unrelated subpoints, as was done here:

I. Aircraft carriers were instrumental in winning the war in the Pacific.

   A. The successful use of aircraft carriers at the battles of the Coral Sea and Midway blunted the Japanese drive across the Pacific.

   B. The F4F fighter was redesigned to have folding wings so that aircraft carriers could carry more planes.

   C. Planes launched from aircraft carriers were able to inflict damage on enemy bases out of the range of land-based aircraft.

Subpoint B is interesting and may be appropriate as a subpoint somewhere in this speech, perhaps supporting a superordinate point about steps taken to make the carrier force more efficient. Clearly, though, subpoint B has no *direct* relationship to the point about the war in the Pacific.

Summary

In this chapter, we discuss developing ideas into speech points. Several strategies can be useful including the following:

9-1 Gather promising ideas and information.

▶   Developing a topic outline, a concept map, and using movable notes are three useful tools for the early development of your speech content.

9-2 Select main points that correspond to your thesis.

▶   When selecting main points, take care to ensure that ideas fit the thesis and that they are mutually exclusive, limited in number, and worded to reveal coordinate, subordinate, or superordinate relationships.

Critical Thinking Questions

▶   What would you do if you realized your main points didn't fit your thesis?

▶   How might a speaker adjust his or her speech, understanding that audience members are unlikely to remember more than three to five main points?

▶   How might mind-mapping software or the sticky-note technique improve your process of preparing a speech?

Putting It into Practice

Write the thesis for an informative speech to be given where you work or volunteer. Brainstorm the main points for the speech thesis you have written. Review the following questions:

1. Do your main points correspond to your thesis? Adjust if necessary.
2. Are your main points clear?
3. Are the coordinate points of equal importance?
4. Are your main points ordered effectively for your particular audience and situation?

10

Organizing Points

When you organize your points, consider the traditional patterns of speech organization and select the one that is best suited to your topic and purpose.

MindTap®   Read, highlight, and take notes online.

Once the main ideas of a speech are selected, you need to arrange them in the order that will maximize effectiveness. In some cases, the decision is virtually made for you. For an argument to seem logical to an audience, the premises must unfold in a certain order, as is explained in Chapter **16**. Debate speeches or closing arguments to juries, for example, have such strict requirements that they almost always unfold according to stock issues, as shown in Chapter **22**. Many ceremonial or special-occasion speeches are so stylized that they follow a formula. (See Chapter **33**.) We can expect a commencement speaker to begin by congratulating the graduates and their family members, and then to posit a challenge for the future. We can anticipate that at a retirement dinner, the speaker will begin by summarizing the honoree's achievements and then speculate humorously about the honoree's coming leisure time. But for the usual informative, invitational, or persuasive speech, there is no required pattern. You, as a speaker, must select the best arrangement of ideas.

MindTap®   Go to your MindTap for *The Speaker's Handbook* for help with choosing an arrangement pattern that presents your main ideas effectively, is appropriate for your speech's goal and purpose, and supports your thesis.

10-1 Recognize Organizational Patterns for Main Points

There are several traditional patterns of speech organization: chronological, spatial, cause–effect, problem–solution, and topical. Organizing main points following these traditional organization schemes will help audience members understand the structure and direction of the speech.

10-1a Using Chronological Patterns

Probably the most ancient form of extended discourse is the narrative unfolding of a story. Many contemporary speeches still follow this time-ordered format. *Historical* development is the most common **chronological pattern**. If you were giving a speech on the influences of early rock music, you might arrange it this way:

I. Rhythm and blues (1940s–1950s)

II. Rockabilly (mid-1950s)

III. British Invasion (1960s)

For another example, look at the outline on women workers in Chapter **11**.

Another chronological pattern divides a topic into *past–present–future*. In a speech on automobile propulsion, you might arrange your ideas in this manner:

I. In the days of cheap oil, auto engines did not need to be energy efficient.

II. Today, fossil fuel costs have risen, creating a demand for more efficient hybrid vehicles.

III. Future projects suggest that alternative power sources may soon replace fossil fuel–burning engines altogether.

A third way to look at a subject chronologically is to analyze a process *step by step*. The topic "How to repair a hole in drywall" could generate this outline:

I. Gather materials, including a tin can lid, string, a small stick or pencil, patching compound, and tools.

II. Punch holes in the lid and place string through the holes.

III. Holding the string, place the tin can lid inside the wall and position it behind the hole; tie the string to a pencil or a small stick; and twist until solidly in place.

IV. Fill the hole with plaster and let dry.

V. Cut the string to remove the stick, add a finish coat, let dry, and sand until smooth.

10-1b Using Spatial Patterns

The **spatial pattern** of speech organization arranges points according to the relationships among physical locations, and is often based on geography. This can be global geography or the geography of the two blocks around your house:

Topic: Afghanistan occupation zones

I. Northern zone

II. Central zone

III. South central zone

IV. Southern zone

Other geographically organized speeches might look at aid relief distribution after hurricane Haiyan.

Geography is not only areas on a map, but also other spatial divisions of society:

Topic: Schools

I. Rural schools

II. Urban schools

III. Suburban schools

Spatial organization can also be applied to smaller areas, such as the floor plan of a house or the arrangement of a library. The spatial pattern example in Figure 10.1 describes a very small area indeed:

Topic: An Aircraft Instrument Panel

FIGURE 10.1
Early airplane instrument panel

Source: Ken LaRock/National Museum of the US Air Force

I. Instruments needed to maintain controlled flight are on the left side of the panel.

   A. Compass

   B. Altimeter

   C. Artificial horizon

   D. Turn and bank indicator

   B. Air speed indicator

II. Instruments providing information on the operating condition of the aircraft are on the right side.

   A. Tachometer

   B. Manifold pressure gauge

   C. Oil temperature gauge

   D. Oil pressure gauge

   E. Fuel gauge

10-1c Using Cause–Effect Patterns

This pattern is used to show that events that occur in sequence are, in fact, causally related. A **cause–effect pattern** is well suited to a speech in which the goal is to achieve understanding or agreement rather than overt action, as here:

I. The recent economic recession has decreased housing values in many communities.

II. [*This is the result.*] Real estate prices have dropped to record lows in many areas, making it a good time to buy some properties.

Occasionally, the pattern may be reversed to an effect–cause sequence:

I. Mortgage rates and housing prices are at record lows.

II. [*This is the cause.*] There has been a sharp drop in home values.

Of course, when using the cause–effect pattern, you must be sure the causal relationship you propose is a valid one. (See Chapter **16**.)

10-1d Using Problem–Solution Patterns

The **problem–solution pattern** begins with a topic of concern and then explains how that concern can best be addressed. It is often used in persuasive speeches that advocate a new policy or a specific course of action, as in the following:

I. The current system of financing health care in the United States is inadequate.

II. [*This is the solution to that problem.*] A system of national health insurance would provide medical care to all citizens.

On rare occasions, speakers choose a solution–problem pattern:

I. A system of national health insurance would provide adequate medical care to all citizens.

II. [*That is the way to solve the following problem.*] The current system of financing health care in the United States is inadequate.

This pattern tends to be weak both stylistically and psychologically because most audiences will resist accepting a proposed change before hearing why the change is needed.

10-1e Using Topical Patterns

The topical sequence is the most frequently used speech pattern. It is also the most difficult in that you must understand the range and limitations of the subject in order to select an effective **topical pattern**. This pattern consists of simply developing topical areas, with no implication that these points have a specific logical relationship or a relationship in time or space. Some topics obviously fit a time or space sequence; many subjects, however, do not lend themselves readily to any of the arrangements discussed so far. In these cases, you need to generate an original system for structuring the speech. Because a pattern intrinsic to one subject will not work with another, the application of any topical pattern you select will be unique to that one speech.

Often, the best structure for a speech is a list of the components of a whole or a list of reasons that add up to the thesis. The following is an example of a topical pattern that lists reasons for a conclusion:

Thesis statement: Students should limit their use of social media.

I. Social media can become addictive.

II. Social media influences users' perceptions of reality.

III. The risks associated with the use of social media warrant reducing its use.

Sometimes, topical patterns combine aspects of other organizational patterns. For instance, a *cause* leads to an *effect*, which is seen as a *problem* that requires a *solution*. Here's an example:

I. Children's screen time has increased.

II. [*Therefore*] The increase in screen time has led to a reduction in childhood reading and creative play.

III. [*And this is a problem; so, to remedy it*] Parents should limit children's screen time.

Other topics easily suggest their own arrangements, such as grouping the pros and cons on a controversial issue or answering questions that have been laid out checklist style by some expert on your subject.

MindTap® For more ideas about how to organize speeches, go to your MindTap for *The Speaker's Handbook* and access the **Additional Resources**. In addition to organizing speeches according to the patterns described in this book, you can organize by an acronym, by opinions, by storylines, and more.

When you are building a speech that supports a controversial thesis, as in most persuasive speeches, arranging your main points is more complex than merely choosing a pattern. Your speech will consist of an *argument* for your thesis, and the main points may be parts of that argument or may be a series of smaller arguments that add up to your overall conclusion. You have important decisions to make about how best to lead your audience through your reasoning pattern. For an unfavorable audience (see Chapter 7), this requires laying out every step of the process. Besides these logical considerations, you also may need to think about the psychological impact you are creating. See Chapters **15** and **22** for discussions of these advanced organizational patterns.

10-2 Group Subpoints According to a Pattern

After your main ideas are set, look at the subpoints under each. These, too, need to be arranged in an effective order. You do not have to repeat the pattern you used for the main points; you can choose the format that makes the most sense for each set of subpoints. Notice the different arrangements of subpoints in the following detailed outline, whose main points are organized topically.

MindTap®   SPEAKER'S WORKSHOP 10.1

1. By generating separate sets of main points, show how each of these topics could be presented in three different organizational patterns:
    ▶ Tobacco-free laws
    ▶ National parks
    ▶ Racial discrimination in the United States
    ▶ Fundamentalism in religion
    ▶ Cajun cooking
2. Which patterns are used in the speeches "The 54th Massachusetts," by Nathanael Dunlavy; and "The Four Ways Sound Affects Us," by Julian Treasure? You can find these speeches in Part **7** in *The Speaker's Handbook*.

Thesis statement: With their scope, history, and influence, comic books are an interesting component of American popular culture.

Topical

I.   Comic books are not merely "comic," but rather explore a range of subject matter.

    A.   Funny-animal comics and kid comics are parables and parodies of the human condition.

        1.   Elmer Fudd and Bugs: Tradition versus the pioneering spirit.

        2.   Barks's ducks: Epic adventure and human foibles.

        3.   Harvey's rich kids: Capitalism with a human face.

    B.   Western and adventure comics concentrate on the triumph of good over evil.

        1.   Western cattle barons learn that saviors slinging six-guns arise naturally from oppressed common folk.

        2.   Adventure stories pit virtuous types against the blind malice of uncaring Nature.

    C.   Horror and mystery comics investigate ethics and morality while titillating and scaring readers.

        1.   Eternal punishment for an unethical choice is a recurring theme of horror comics.

        2.   The tempting hedonism of wrongdoers is graphically displayed in mystery comics—until the ironic twist of fate on the last page.

    D.   Superhero comics manifest the unspoken and sometimes frightening fantasies and aspirations of the American people.

        1.   Superman is the supremely powerful spokesperson and law enforcer for the American definition of the "right way."

        2.   The jackbooted hero Blackhawk was created in World War II to fight totalitarian fire with fire.

        3.   Mar-Vell personifies the desire for total knowledge and the wisdom needed to use it.

        4.   Spider-Man is the embodiment of the perennial underdog triumphant.

II.   Comic books started as anthologies of another medium but soon grew into a separate art form developing along a path of its own.

Chronological

    A.   Early comic books were mostly reprints of Sunday newspaper comic strip sections.

        1.   "Foxy Granpa" was reprinted in a number of comic books just after the turn of the century.

        2.   The following decades saw strips like "Mutt and Jeff," "Little Orphan Annie," and "Moon Mullins" reprinted.

        3.   Reprint books in the 1930s included titles such as "Tarzan" in Tip Top Comics and "Terry and the Pirates" in Popular Comics.

B. By 1938, the majority of comic books contained original work, and, with the appearance of Superman, the golden age of comics began.

    1. Detective Comics was the first single-theme, all-original comic.

    2. Superman, the first costumed superhero, was featured in *Action* no. 1.

    3. More than 150 titles were in print by the end of 1941.

C. By the late 1950s, comic books had started to overcome their tarnished image.

    1. In creating the Comics Code Authority, publishers hoped to reassure worried parents and legislators.

    2. The silver age of comics began with the reintroduction of long-dormant golden-age characters.

D. In the early 1990s, the trend toward darker storylines grew, the effects of which were eventually felt in the other comic genres.

    1. Darkness and nihilism were manifested in DC's production of "A Death in the Family," in which Batman's sidekick Robin is murdered by the Joker.

    2. Comic books and graphic novels became accepted by a wider, more literate adult audience.

    3. Concern with ethical and even political questions became more evident in cartoons and graphic novels.

III. Comic books have an effect beyond their entertainment value.

Cause–Effect

A. Comic books are a unique and vigorous art form.

    1. Comic books have developed exciting and innovative methods for transcending the static nature of the panel format (series of distinct pictures across and down the page) to produce a sense of motion and drama.

    2. The art of comics is not confined to the work within a single panel, but also touches the arrangement of panels on a page.

B. [As a result] Comic books have influenced other media.

    1. Many filmmakers' use of split screens and quick cuts demonstrates a stylistic adaptation of the comic panel format.

    2. The movie *Hercules: The Thracian Wars* is based on the graphic novel by cartoonists Steve Moore and Admira Wijaya.

C. [Also as a result] Comic books are in demand with collectors.

    1. Some issues of rare comics can bring prices in the thousands of dollars.

    2. Every year there are many large conventions around the United States where comics can be bought, sold, and traded.

MindTap® SPEAKER'S WORKSHOP 10.2

Identify which organizational pattern Brian Sharkey uses in his speech, available through your MindTap for *The Speaker's Handbook*. Would you call this a well-organized speech? Why or why not?

FOR YOUR BENEFIT

Organizational Patterns Are Handy Devices

Many students fear impromptu speaking precisely because there is no way to prepare for it. But did you know that the organizational patterns used in planned speeches are just as useful in unplanned speeches? The same organizational schemes can be used to quickly organize impromptu speeches, policy papers, and all kinds of public and private writing. The topical pattern is highly flexible while the problem–solution works well to sell an idea. Thinking on the fly just got easier.

Summary

This chapter focuses on the arrangement of main points in a speech.

10-1 Recognize organizational patterns for main points.

▌ A speech's main points can be organized in a variety of patterns, including the topical, chronological, spatial, cause–effect, and problem–solution patterns.

10-2 Group subpoints according to a pattern.

▌ Main and subpoints need not follow the same organizational scheme.

▌ The appropriate organizational pattern depends on what will best help the speaker inform, invite, persuade, or inspire the audience regarding a particular topic.

Critical Thinking Questions

▌ How would you arrange a speech addressing the equipment used in the game of lacrosse?

▶ Why is topical organization the most frequently used pattern?

▶ When would a spatial organizational scheme work best?

▶ What type of speech is a problem–solution format best suited for? Why?

Putting It into Practice

MindTap° Read or watch Barack Obama's "Farewell Address," delivered on January 10, 2017. For easy access to this speech, go to your MindTap for *The Speaker's Handbook* and click on **Additional Resources**.

1. How does Obama organize this speech?

2. Could it be organized another way?

3. What impact does Obama's speaking situation have on his choices of main points and the organization of those points?

4. How does Obama tailor the speech for this Chicago audience and situation?

11

Outlining

Use a formal outline as an organizational tool.

The speech outline is an indispensable tool of speech organization that provides a detailed logical plan for a speech. Preparing a clear outline helps you keep track of the points you hope to cover and increases the chances that your audience will understand your message. The act of outlining—laying your ideas out in a logical order on paper—forces you to select the points that support your thesis and to demonstrate how they fit together. As the planning and practice chart in Figure 5.2 illustrates, you must develop a logical outline of your points and supporting materials before you can effectively practice your speech aloud.

Only through this outline development can you avoid falling into one of the familiar traps: either overestimating or underestimating your preparedness. In the first case, you might say, "I've researched this subject so much that I've got it down cold." But until you give the speech—or begin writing down your ideas—how can you be sure? In the second case, you might say, "I'll never understand this topic, even though I've spent weeks in the library!" An outlining session could surprise you by making evident your understanding of the subject. In short, the developed outline gives you some distance from the thoughts spinning around in your mind. By freezing your ideas on paper, you make it possible to evaluate the ideas. By sharing your outline with a teacher, colleague, or peer group, you will discover whether the ideas you've chosen are clear and compelling.

We are less concerned about including the introduction and conclusion in the outline. Rather, we think outlining is best used to order the *basic* ideas in the body of the speech. Also, be careful not to confuse the formal speech outline with informal research notes (see Chapter **8**), preliminary organizational tools (see Chapter **9**), or speaking notes (see Chapter **24**). Although any of these may take an outline form, the *outline* described in the following sections is a detailed logical plan of the speech.

Do not mistake your outline with a manuscript of the speech. (See Chapter **23**.) The outline is not intended to be the text of the speech itself, like an essay. Instead, it is the framework of your speech, built by the strategic organization of your main points and subpoints. Although you will refine your ideas in writing as you develop your outline, the point of the outline is to allow you to strategically structure the speech. Remember that a speech is an oral, not a written, form of expression.

MindTap° For more about effective outlining, visit the MindTap for *The Speaker's Handbook* and click on **Additional Resources**. Purdue University's Online Writing Lab provides some good tips.

11-1 Develop a Visual Outline Format

Help yourself visualize the relationships among the ideas of your speech by using standard rules for outlining.

1. Follow a Consistent Set of Symbols

It is conventional to use Roman numerals to label the main ideas of the speech and to alternate between letters and numbers for each successive level of subordination. This outlining system is simple, and most people find it familiar and easy to understand, simple to adjust to, and illuminating in its design. Most word processors include outlining features that simplify this process.

I. Main point
   A. First level of subordination
      1. Second level of subordination
         a. Third level of subordination
           (1) Fourth level of subordination
              (a) Fifth level of subordination

Do not skip levels. If your speech has only main points and one level of subpoints, use I., II., III., and A., B., C. If your outline includes a second level of subordination, use 1., 2., 3. for items on that level.

2. Show Logical Relationships through Indentation

Each subordinate idea should be indented several spaces to align with the first word—not the labeling numeral or letter—of the point it supports. This makes the relationship among ideas easy to see.

Wrong:

I. Bagpipes are not solely a Scottish instrument.

A. Bagpipes originated in Asia Minor.

B. There are various forms of bagpipes in Ireland and Spain, for example.

1. Spanish bagpipes are similar in construction to Scottish pipes, with the sizes of the parts being different.

2. Uilleann bagpipes in Ireland differ from Scottish pipes in that the uilleann piper uses a bellows under the arm to keep the bag full rather than blowing into the bag.

Right:

I. Bagpipes are not solely a Scottish instrument.

    A. Bagpipes originated in Asia Minor.

    B. There are various forms of bagpipes in Ireland and Spain, for example.

        1. Spanish bagpipes are similar in construction to Scottish pipes, with the sizes of the parts being different.

        2. Uilleann bagpipes in Ireland differ from Scottish pipes in that the uilleann piper uses a bellows under the arm to keep the bag full rather than blowing into the bag.

Your outline exists only to illuminate and clarify the structure of your ideas. Notice how *hanging indention* allows your eye to quickly recognize the levels of subordination even when sentences extend over several lines.

3. Develop Each Level of Subordination with Two or More Parts

English teachers are fond of saying, "Never have a 1 without a 2 or an A without a B." Generally, this is a good advice. The concept of dividing an idea into parts—subordination—becomes nonsensical if a major point is "divided" into only one subpoint. Categories are useful because they encompass several related things. Suppose you outline a main point of your speech as follows:

I. Redwood City is the best California city in which to live.

    A. It has the best climate.

II. ....

If Redwood City's climate is your only example, you are in trouble. A good climate is hardly enough to justify the conclusion you have drawn. Thus, you are guilty of hasty generalization. To avoid this type of generalization, outline your speech following the rule of having *at least* two supporting points at each level of subordination. (Hasty generalization and other common fallacies are discussed in greater detail in Chapter **16**.) It is far better to develop a few points fully than to cover many points superficially. The rule "No 1 without a 2 and no A without a B" is a good one to ensure depth of analysis.

SPEAKER'S WORKSHOP 11.1

Outline the transcript of Dianna Cohen's speech available in Part **7** in *The Speaker's Handbook*. How many levels of subordination does the speaker use? Are there cases of a 1 without a 2, or an A without a B?

4. Be Sure Each Symbol Designates Only One Point and That Every Point Has a Symbol

Do not combine two or more ideas in any point of your outline. Give each idea its own logical heading. By the same token, your outline should not contain any free-floating words or phrases. Every idea should be firmly anchored to a symbol in the hierarchy of points.

Wrong:

Causes

    A. Both economic and sociological factors contribute significantly to urban decline.

    B. Political factors are of minor importance.

Right:

I. Urban decline has a number of causes.   [Free-floating header made into a main point]

    A. Economic factors are the major cause.   [Old Point A split into two points]

    B. Sociological factors are also significant.

    C. Political factors are relatively minor.

11-2 Create a Full-Sentence Outline

In a **full-sentence outline**, the thesis statement (see Chapter **6**), the main points, and at least the first level of subpoints are stated as declarative sentences. The *declarative sentence* is, in effect, a proposition that can be proved or disproved, accepted or rejected.

Look at the following sentence:

I. Secondhand smoke harms nonsmokers.

If this sentence were presented in a true–false test, you could, with adequate knowledge, answer one way or the other. It is the black-or-white condition of the declarative sentence that makes it such a useful tool.

But what would you do if you encountered these items on a true–false test?

I. Nonsmokers' rights

or

I. What is the effect of secondhand smoke on nonsmokers?

Obviously, an answer of true or false to either of these examples is impossible. It would be equally absurd if a stranger approached you and asked, "Do you agree with me about the dangers of overspending?" Your inevitable retort would be, "Well, what *do* you think about the dangers of overspending?"

Far too many speeches are constructed around just such vague phrases, questions, and uncompleted ideas. Listeners can identify the speaker's general topic but cannot always recognize the specific points the speaker is trying to make. Consider these examples:

Wrong: I. *What are the causes of crime?* [Avoid using a question as your main point.]

Right: I. *Crime is caused by a number of factors.* [This is a declarative statement.]

Wrong: I. *The history of the feminist movement in the United States.* [What is being declared?]

Right: I. *U.S. feminism can be divided into four historical periods.* [Better.]

Wrong: I. *Buying a house will have tax advantages. You will also build equity. House ownership is fun and fosters pride.* [A single declarative statement is needed.]

Right: I. *There are multiple benefits to owning a home.*

or

I. *There are both economic and emotional benefits to owning a house.*

Besides making the speech more coherent for your audience, the use of declarative sentences in your outline makes you more conscious of the exact points you want to make and forces you to frame them explicitly. As you begin to research any topic, you will find scores of interesting details and perspectives. How do you decide which ones to include in your speech and which ones to leave out? Once the thesis and main points are stated clearly, they will provide a basis against which you can test all other speech content.

The following outline deals with the history of working women in the United States. Observe how the use of a thesis sentence and full-sentence main and secondary points provides a basis for the speaker's decisions about what to include.

11-2a Full-Sentence Outline Example

Thesis statement: Since the beginning of the Industrial Revolution, women in the United States have been exploited as a cheap and expendable source of labor.

I. In preindustrial colonial settings, the boundaries between men's and women's spheres were indistinct.

    A. Colonial women ran self-sufficient domestic factories.

        1. Women produced the major source of artificial light, candles.

        2. Clothing and bedding were manufactured by women.

        3. The making of soap was a major contribution.

    B. The rigors of frontier life decreed a more equal division of labor between women and men than was found on the rapidly industrializing Eastern Seaboard.

        1. Men and women shared long hours of joint farmwork.

        2. Women were often left alone for long periods to run the farm.

II. Between the Revolution and the Civil War, increased industrialization led to increased exploitation of women workers.

    A. Factories undercut home production.

    B. When the western migration caused shortages of male workers, women became a cheap source of labor for the factories.

        1. The percentage of women in the workforce increased.

        2. Women, in 1829, earned one quarter of what men did.

    C. Women workers' efforts to improve their lot were not successful.

        1. The first women's strike was in 1824, but poor organization made it and others ineffective.

        2. Associations of women workers failed because of the women's isolation and inexperience.

III. In spite of increasing unionization between the Civil War and World War II, women's position in the workforce remained inferior.

    A. Women were an unwelcome minority in trade organizations.

        1. Male union leaders did not believe in equal pay for equal work.

        2. Women were barred from union offices, men said, because "no conveniences were available."

    B. Attempts by women before 1900 to organize among themselves met with failure.

        1. Women's unions were not taken seriously.

        2. Women workers were usually too impoverished to strike successfully.

    C. Important gains by women workers in the first decades of the twentieth century yielded little net improvement.

        1. Women's situation had improved in some areas.

            a. Unionization of the garment industry was successful.

            b. New job classifications were opened to women during World War I.

        2. Women workers still had neither security nor equality.

            a. Men got their jobs back after the war.

            b. Women received one half of comparable men's pay.

IV. During World War II and after, women were used as a dispensable and secondary source of labor.

    A. Traditional views of femininity were conveniently set aside according to economic needs.

      1. Three million women were recruited to replace our fighting men.

      2. "Rosie the Riveter" became a mythic ideal.

  B. After the war, labor, government, and industry cooperated to push women out of their new jobs.

      1. Although most women wanted to keep working, by 1946 four million were gone from the workforce.

      2. When plants began to rehire men, women's seniority was often ignored.

      3. With the unions' tacit approval, many jobs held by women during the war were reclassified as men's jobs.

      4. Many of the laid-off women were denied unemployment insurance.

      5. Articles and pamphlets exhorted women to return to their "primary role."

         a. Women were needed to provide a haven for returning men.

         b. Women were needed to nurture the nuclear family.

The full-sentence outline is important in preparing informative, invitational, and evocative speeches, as well as argumentative and persuasive speeches. In a speech to evoke, to invite, or to inform, you do not literally *prove* a thesis or its main points, but you do have an obligation to cover topics fully. Using sentences rather than phrases will provide you with clearer criteria for deciding which points to include and which to leave out. Full-sentence outlines may take extra work, but they are a necessary tool to ensure logical relationships between ideas in the speech.

Once you think these issues through with the help of an outline, you can proceed to a more spontaneous and fluid oral form of expression, confident that the underlying structure of your speech is sound.

11-2b Phrase Main Points to Lead into Subpoints

It is not enough to have an outline with full sentences as main points. The sentences must logically encompass the main ideas of the speech. Suppose a speech outline has the following as a main point:

I. Many people are unaware of the origins of the paper they use every day. If this is really the main idea being developed in this section of the speech, the subpoints should look something like this:

  A. Ursula is utterly unaware of the origin of paper.

  B. Clint is clueless about where paper comes from.

  C. Ned never thought about paper for a minute.

  D. … and so on … .

Obviously, the speaker does not intend to spend this whole portion of the speech exposing the ignorance of the general public. More likely, she or he will talk about where paper comes from, and the main point should reflect this. The idea that "many people are unaware" does not have to be jettisoned, but it can become a transitional lead-in, not the essence of the main point.

Think of the main points of a speech as subthesis statements, and apply the tests introduced in Chapter **6** to their phrasing. Recall that a thesis statement is required to answer two simple questions about the speech: "What's it about?" and "What about it?" Each main point should be cast so that it answers these same questions about the section of the speech that is being covered.

Wrong:

Main point (subthesis sentence):	*I first would like to take a few minutes to discuss the origin of paper.*
What's it about?	*A speaker talking for a few minutes.*
What about it?	*The topic being talked about is the origin of paper.*

Right:

Main point (subthesis sentence):	*The origins of paper can be traced to the use of papyrus in ancient Egypt.*
What's it about?	*The origin of paper.*
What about it?	*It can be traced to papyrus in ancient Egypt.*

Do not include transitional phrases that might be part of your oral presentation in the outline. They make for pseudosentences. Also, do not include your supporting evidence in the phrasing of a main point.

Wrong:

Subthesis sentence:	*A study done by Dr. Wilson showed that in three major companies in our area, 148 people were diagnosed with carpal tunnel syndrome last year.*
What's it about?	*A researcher did a study.*
What about it?	*The study found that carpal tunnel syndrome affected 148 people at three companies.*

Right:

Subthesis sentence:	*Carpal tunnel syndrome is one of the most common forms of repetitive strain injuries.*
What's it about?	*Carpal tunnel syndrome.*
What about it?	*It is a very common form of repetitive strain injury.*

SPEAKER'S WORKSHOP 11.2

Using our example of Main Point I as a guide, compare the remaining main points of the two outlines, and specify which subpoints are extraneous and which need to be modified.

It is unlikely that Dr. Wilson's study would be a *main* point of a speech (unless it is for a group of carpal tunnel specialists). Keep statistics, testimony, and examples at the subordinate levels. Your main points should express more general ideas; these are supported by evidence or data.

11-3 Phrase Points in Concise, Parallel Language

Once you have framed your main ideas so that they are logically and grammatically complete, take time to recast your points in language that highlights them for your audience. In this final phase of refining the outline, you move from one aspect of composition—organizing points logically—to another, which is sometimes called "writing for the ear." This step is the bridge from completing the outline to beginning to imagine the oral performance that will ultimately occur. Of course, you will not be reading or memorizing your full-sentence outline, and you may never state the points as they are written out. But you want to phrase the key ideas, so they are similar to each other (parallel), but also stand out when you give your presentation.

Expressing your main points in parallel language means using sentences that follow the same arrangement and structure to make them more easily identifiable in your speech. This augments the techniques of signposts, previews, and reviews covered in Chapter **12**, all of which you use to make your organization clear to your listeners.

Ideas that are phrased in concise, colorful, parallel language are more likely to be remembered by both speaker and listeners. (Language is also discussed in Chapter **17**.) Look at the following main points from a speech on higher education with the thesis, "A college education offers you many opportunities for improvement."

11-3a Examples of Weak, Better, and Best Parallel Language

Weak: Wordy, Not Parallel

I. The skills you will learn in college will add to the probability of your earning more money, not only in your first job but also throughout your entire lifetime.

II. Through higher education, one can also gain a perspective on many aspects of life, to enrich the nonworking hours and provide for a more creative use of leisure time.

III. While they are in college, most students have a variety of social and interpersonal experiences and make new friends through extracurricular activities and informal exchanges.

These are declarative sentences, as they ought to be, and they do show three separate, important arguments in favor of the thesis that a college education is valuable. However, the points are too wordy, and do not stand out clearly.

Here, they are more concise, and they have maintained their basic meaning.

Better: Concise, Not Parallel

I. Your earning power will be increased by a college education.

II. One can prepare for a richer use of leisure time by attending college.

III. In college, students meet new friends and enjoy worthwhile social experiences.

However, notice how changes from active to passive voice make the main ideas seem disconnected. Because the statements are not written in the same active voice,

MindTap · SPEAKER'S WORKSHOP 11.3

1. Rephrase the main points in the following outlines so that they are concise and parallel.

   Thesis: Globalization has raised the stakes for U.S. students to be competitive in a global marketplace.

   I. Weak math and science scores have resulted in fewer U.S. students eligible for cutting-edge jobs.

   II. Market expansion in India and China has affected U.S. corporate hiring practices.

   III. There are more honors students in India than in the United States.

   Thesis: Advertisers use a variety of techniques to influence consumers.

   I. Tone and mood can be established through color.

   II. Many advertisers use music effectively to attain their goals.

   III. You can manipulate images for visual impact.

2. You'll find several sample outlines in Part **7** and through your MindTap for *The Speaker's Handbook*. After reviewing how some of these student speakers use the outline format, watch the video of Brian Sharkey's speech "Native American Code Talkers" and construct an outline of it.

the sentences lack parallelism. Listeners cannot quickly see the relationships between points when the perspective keeps changing. Strive for grammatical consistency of structure, person, number, and voice. Notice how much easier the following concise, parallel main points are to read and remember.

Best: Concise and Parallel

I.   A college education will enhance your earning power.

II. A college education will enrich your use of leisure time.

III. A college education will expose you to new social experiences.

Summary

Outlining provides a detailed, visual plan for a speech. Preparing a clear outline helps you keep track of the points you hope to cover and increases the chances your audience will understand your message.

11-1 Develop a visual outline format.

▌ An often-overlooked benefit of outlining is the quick visual reference afforded by this organizational scheme. By following a consistent symbolization, indentation, and coordination of subordination for each and every point, the framework of your speech will become easier to follow and adjust if necessary.

11-2 Create an outline using full sentences.

▌ The use of declarative sentences will improve the coherence of your speech. These statements should clearly state what the main point is about and what about the main point is important.

11-3 Demonstrate the ability to use concise language, parallel in structure for main and subpoints.

▌ Phrasing your main points to forecast subpoints so that they are concise and parallel in structure means using sentences that follow the same arrangement and structure, making the speech easier for the audience to listen to and understand. This will ensure that your points are clear and memorable to your audience.

Critical Thinking Questions

▌ Why is a full-sentence outline preferable to a topic outline at this phase in the development process?

▶ Why is an outline preferable to a manuscript of your speech at this phase?

▶ How might technology help simplify your ability to create and manipulate an outline?

▶ How will the use of main points that are concise and parallel make the speech better?

Putting It into Practice

MindTap° Visit the MindTap for *The Speaker's Handbook* and click on **Additional Resources** and pick one speech from the link.

1. Create a topic outline of the speech's main and supporting points.
2. Outline the main points of the speech by using full-sentence form.

12

Connectives

Connectives should link points to provide unity and express relationships among ideas.

MindTap Read, highlight, and take notes online.

Connective sentences, phrases, and words serve as bridges between points. Sometimes called *transitions*, connectives literally connect ideas and often signal to listeners how two ideas are related. Connective words can completely change the message. Observe the not-so-subtle differences in these three sentences:

1. He plays the piano, *and* I invited him to my party.
2. He plays the piano, *so* I invited him to my party.
3. He plays the piano, *but* I invited him to my party.

Clear and evocative connectives are more important in speaking than in writing because the spoken message is fleeting. (See Chapter **17**.) In this book, for example, we show you the relationships among ideas by indenting, capitalizing, and using different punctuation and typefaces. As a speaker, however, you do not have access to these devices. You need to use verbal *signposting* techniques to help your audience hear how your points relate. (See Chapter **21**.) You can keep your listeners informed about the overall structure of your speech by the generous use of phrases like these:

▶ The second cause of inflation is …

▶ To show you what I mean, let me tell you three stories.

▶ In summarizing this argument …

▶ The final point we should consider is …

▶ What, then, is the solution to this three-part problem I have outlined?

▶ We see that malaria is a global problem; we see a simple, proven solution to the problem; now let's consider the benefits of ending malaria.

Do not worry about using too many signposts. Your audience will appreciate them.

MindTap   Go to your MindTap for *the Speaker's Handbook* for help with transitions.

12-1 Create Connectives to Link Ideas and Express Relationships

The connectives you choose should link ideas in your speech and make clear the organizational structure of the speech. The logical structure of your speech is revealed through the connective terms used. Notice in the following examples the emphasized words used to reveal the logical structure of ideas.

Problem–solution

Thesis statement: …

Main point I. The *problem* of global warming is evident in *two ways* …

Main point II. The *solution* to the global warming problem involves *three steps,* …

Chronological organization

Thesis statement: …

Main point I. *First,* …

Main point II. *Second,* …

Main point III. *Finally,* …

Points can be related in a number of ways. Crystallizing these relationships and expressing them through appropriate transitional phrases will enhance your clarity. Try to use a variety of transitions instead of linking all your ideas with "OK, next let's look at …" or "Another thing …, and another thing …," and so on. Table 12.1 lists common connective words that can be used to tie main points to one another, main points to subpoints, subpoints to one another, supporting evidence to arguments, and introductions and conclusions to the body of the speech. Connectives improve message clarity in all these places.

MindTap   For tips on connectives that supplement Table 12.1, visit the MaidTap for *The Speaker's Handbook* and click on **Additional Resources.**

President George W. Bush used transitional words and phrases in his speech delivered at the dedication of the National Museum of African American History and Culture, Washington D.C., September 24, 2016.[1] After giving proper ceremonial recognition to sitting President and First Lady Barack and Michele Obama, his own spouse, and museum board member Laura Bush as well as numerous others dignitaries, he offered these words:

> This museum is an important addition to our country for many reasons. Here are three: *First,* it shows our commitment to truth… *Second,* this museum shows America's capacity to change… *And finally,* the museum showcases the talent of some of our finest American's.

TABLE 12.1
Connective words that signal relationships

RELATIONSHIP	CONNECTIVE WORDS
Chronological	First, second, third
	After
	Following
	Finally
Cause–effect	So, since, thus
	Therefore, hence
	Consequently, as a result
	Due to
	Because
Part-to-whole	One such
	Another
	The first (second, third) of these
	For instance, for example
	Illustrative of this
	A case in point
	Let me give you an example
Equality	Similarly, additionally
	Another
	Of equal importance
	Also, moreover
Opposition	But, though, however
	On the other hand
	Conversely, on the contrary
	Yet
	In spite of
	Nonetheless, nevertheless

Notice that the italicized words serve to tie the parts of the speech together and provide a sense of unity to President Bush's speech.

12-1a Develop Internal Previews and Summaries

An **internal preview** is a kind of connective that provides a link by forecasting the points that are yet to be developed. An **internal summary** is a kind of connective that provides a link among parts of the speech by recapping what has been covered so far. Examples of both connective types, as well as a combination internal summary and preview, follow.

Internal preview

Once your résumé is prepared, the next step in job seeking is to prepare a list of specific job openings. The three best sources here are newspaper listings, your campus placement service, and word-of-mouth recommendations. We will examine the pros and cons of each of these.

Internal summary

Because the problems in our department were affecting morale, and because we had found they were caused by poor communication, we instituted an unusual training program. Let me tell you about it.

Internal summary and preview

I've told you why we need to reduce our dependence on automobiles, and I hope I've convinced you that a light rail system is the best alternative for our city. Now, you're probably asking two questions: What will it cost? and Can it be sustained? I want to answer both these questions. First, the question of cost.

FOR YOUR BENEFIT

Premature Summaries

Beginning speakers often cause their audience to expect the end of their speech prematurely by saying "In conclusion" or "In summary" before they are really ready to conclude the speech. Be careful to qualify your internal summaries with phrases such as "So, to summarize this first idea …" and "Let me review the points so far."

MindTap° SPEAKER'S WORKSHOP 12.1

1. Write connectives for the main points of the comic book outline in Chapter **10** and the working women outline in Chapter **11**.

2. Go to Part 7 in *The Speaker's Handbook* and select one or more of the speech transcripts available. Identify the connective sentences, phrases, and words in the speeches you choose.

Summary

12-1 Create connectives to link ideas and express relationships.

▶ Connectives are words or phrases that serve as bridges between speech points. They literally connect ideas. These elements, which could be single words or phrases, can be used to show logical connection.

▶ For longer speeches, internal previews and summaries serve to guide the listener in much the same way that signposts guide travelers to their destination.

12-2 Critical Thinking Questions

▶ What is wrong with vague connectives such as "next" or "also"?

▶ How are connectives similar to bridges between ideas?

Putting It into Practice

MindTap° Locate a political or professional speech. Consider using one from *Vital Speeches of the Day* or from another online source such as the White House's Briefing Room, which can be found by visiting **Additional Resources** in the MindTap.

1. Circle the words or phrases that connect main points in the speech.

2. How effective would the speech be without them?

3. How could the connectives have been improved?

4. What can you use from this professional speech to improve your own speech development?

13

Introductions

Use an introduction to capture attention, and orient the listener both psychologically and logically to the topic.

MindTap° Read, highlight, and take notes online.

How do you go about trying to capture the attention of your audience? Knowing what you want to say doesn't mean you will always know how to begin saying it. An **introduction** should prepare your listeners to hear your ideas. It should be clear, confident, and captures your audience's interest while providing psychological and logical orientation for your speech. An effective introduction will help audience members listen more closely to your message, potentially improving your ability to communicate with them.

MindTap° Visit the MindTap for *The Speaker's Handbook* for help developing a successful introduction for your speech.

13-1 Develop an Effective Introduction to Your Speech

Sometimes starting your speech is the hardest part. Yet, how you open your speech is entirely within your ability to plan, practice, and present. Don't risk leaving your opening sentences to the inspiration of the moment. Strong opening material will capture your audience's interest and carry the speech forward.

Start with a sentence that leaves no doubt you are beginning. Avoid false starts and apologetic or tentative phrases: "Can you hear me now?" or "Before I begin... ." Tone is almost as important as content here. Your immediate purpose is to command the attention of your audience. (For more on this, see Chapter **18**.) Techniques such as suspense, novelty, humor, and conflict are effective, and you will probably use them throughout your speech; they are highly recommended in your introduction.

13-1a Capture Audience Attention Immediately

You should begin with an **attention getter**, which in a few sentences captures your audience's interest and invites them to listen to you. You could share a story, offer an appropriate quotation, tell a joke, make a startling statement, or ask a few provocative questions. Use your imagination, but make sure your attention getter relates to your topic and draws your audience's attention.

Your attention getter should be consistent with your personality and the situation. Adopting a style that doesn't fit you will not only make you uncomfortable, but your audience will also sense that you are not being yourself. Consider the following attention getter for Kayla Strickland's speech about malaria.

> *It's just a mosquito, right? To us it is but to half the world it is also fever, vomiting, aches, jaundice, and anemia. It is seizures, comas, lung inflammation, kidney failure, and paralysis. It is low birth-weight babies, still births, and maternal death. It is speech impediments. It is blindness. It is deafness. It is malaria.*[1]

As this example illustrates, attention getters need not be unduly catchy or clever. However, it is essential that you begin your speech with a few well-planned sentences that say, in effect, "I know where I'm going and I want you to come with me—it will be worth your while."

MindTap®   Visit the MindTap for *The Speaker's Handbook* and click on **Additional Resources** to visit Mesa Community College's site on speech introductions, which includes ideas for attention getters.

MindTap®   **SPEAKER'S WORKSHOP 13.1**

1. Visit the MindTap for *The Speaker's Handbook* to watch the introductions from speeches by Brian Sharkey and Kayla Strickland. What kind of attention getter does each speaker use? Are these effective? These speeches are also available in Part **7**.

2. Write an engaging attention getter for the speech on working women in Chapter **11**.

13-1b Provide Psychological Orientation

Once you've gained the audience's attention, you need to help your audience take interest in your speech. This requires orienting the audience to you and your topic by creating a bond with your listeners and generating enthusiasm about your topic. Note the two parts of this process: establishing a connection with your listeners and motivating them to consider your topic.

Create a Connection Sometimes speakers can seem remote and cold, cut off from the audience by role and status. This psychological distance can be present for keynote speakers, executives, and even students who find themselves different in age or interests from their audience. Use your introduction to create a connection with your listeners. You can do this with references to everyday, common occurrences. If your audience can visualize you going to the dentist, enjoying a movie, losing your keys, or playing Ultimate Frisbee®, they will be more conscious of you as a human being and not merely as a distant dispenser of information.

In addition to establishing a warm, friendly relationship, you want the introduction to set a tone of collaboration with your audience. For the most part, people learn better when they are active than when they are passive, and they are more committed to decisions in which they have participated. You can therefore appreciate that a collaborative tone will aid you in achieving your speech goals. Here are some ways to create a sense of dialogue, even in a speech that is primarily a monologue:

▶ *Acknowledge your audience's expertise:* "As managers, you've likely experienced social loafing in your work teams and could offer a dozen examples of it."

▶ *Admit your own fallibility:* "One issue I'm still struggling with is…"

▶ *Ask for their help:* "I hope that later during the discussion period you will share some of the solutions you've found most helpful."

The idea you are trying to project is that you recognize communication is a two-way street involving the give and take of information.

When deciding how to build a positive relationship with your audience, you should ask two questions:

1. What relationship do I have with these people now?

2. What relationship do I need to develop to accomplish my speech purpose?

In effect, you are conducting one of the phases of audience analysis described in Chapter 7. The answers to these questions will help you decide which combination of the following techniques to use in your introduction to build rapport with your listeners.

1. **Establish Credibility.** The judgments audience members make about you as a person influence the judgments they make about your speech. To gain respect and credibility, a speaker should be perceived as competent, concerned, trustworthy, and dynamic. (See Chapter **19**.) For instance, a speaker may have given previous

speeches establishing herself as a criminal justice major but with each speech she will want to remind audience members of her connection to the speech topic and her concern for the audience. Or you may be speaking to a group of friends who like and trust you but wonder what you really know about alternative power sources. In either case, you should use your introduction to gain the audience's respect for you as a knowledgeable, trustworthy speaker concerned about your audience.

2. **Establish Common Ground.** You can emphasize similar backgrounds, experience, interests, and goals to show what you and your audience share. Observe how Robert Gates, U.S. Secretary of Defense, builds a sense of common ground in his speech celebrating the sixty-fifth anniversary of the allied victory in Europe delivered at the Eisenhower Library in Abilene, Kansas, on May 8, 2010:

I'm pleased to be here for several reasons. First, it's always a treat to be someplace other than Washington, D.C. … it's even better to return to my home state of Kansas—a place of little pretense and ample common sense. And, above all, I am honored and humbled to be at this wonderful institution on this occasion, and to be associated in even a small way with the legacy of Dwight D. Eisenhower. I should note that this is actually my second visit to the Eisenhower Library and Museum. My first was with my sixth-grade class from Wichita 54 years ago.[2]

3. **Refer to the Setting or Occasion.** One way to demonstrate your personal connection to the immediate speaking situation is to refer directly to the time and place. Lisa Kudrow, actress in the popular show *Friends*, began a commencement speech at her alma mater this way:

I sat exactly where you're sitting, exactly 25 years ago. Well it was 25 years ago—I know it's hard to believe—and Governor Mario Cuomo was our speaker. I had been up all night so I was drifting in and out of consciousness—like that guy. I don't remember much, but I do remember at one point Governor Cuomo told us to look around at our classmates. The idea was to really take in these people we've just had this very meaningful experience with for four important years in our lives. So you can go ahead and do that now if you want to. Did you do it? I don't know what you all just felt, but when I did it 25 years ago.…[3]

4. **Flatter Your Audience.** Everyone likes to be complimented, as long as it is personalized and not too contrived. Audience members who perceive that you like and admire them are likely to return the favor. In a speech presented at a workshop for teachers, one of the authors used this approach:

Those of you who gave up your Saturday morning to be here are not a typical group of teachers. Study after study reveals that the teachers who show up voluntarily to in-service workshops on teaching skills are the very best teachers. Just look around you. The ones who most need this workshop aren't here today, are they? But a brush-up is always helpful. "A" teachers want to learn to be "A+" teachers. And maybe together we can find some ways to reach those "C–" teachers who didn't come.

5. ***Refer to a Person in the Audience.*** One good way to build a relationship with a group is to demonstrate that you relate successfully to one of its popular members:

Thank you, Jack, for that very flattering introduction. In the fifteen years we've known each other, there have been many opportunities for reciprocity: We've borrowed each other's tools and books, our families have house-sat for each other, and now here's a new opportunity. I hope I may be called upon some day to return the favor with a gracious introduction of you.

6. ***Use Humor.*** A sense of humor is a good basis for a relationship, both at the interpersonal level and on a larger scale. Show your audience that you and they laugh at the same things. Keep in mind that using humor can be tricky. See Chapter 18 for pitfalls and suggestions about its use. Glenn Beck used self-deprecating humor as a technique in his introduction to the Conservative Political Action Committee Conference in Washington, D.C.

I am so, I mean it is such an honor to be here, it really is. Last year, I was, uh, actually in my car, listening to Rush Limbaugh give the keynote—Rush is a hero of mine and I—I'm listening to him, and my producer—I write him a text on my e-mail and he gave it to me just this week. I wrote him last year, wow, what must that be like to give the keynote at CSPAC, at CPAC? Here I am, today, and I cannot believe it. I—I mean it's been a tough year for you, hasn't it? I mean if you're down to me, it's a tough year.[4]

13-1c Motivating Your Audience to Listen

This step is one of those most often overlooked in speech making, but it is *the* pivotal step of the introduction. Your speech, in spite of your enthusiasm for your topic, can be derailed by your audience's "what's it to me?" attitude. This attitude is not limited to the hostile audience; it is typical of all audiences. You need to reassure your listeners that there are good reasons for their listening to your informative, invitational, persuasive, or evocative speech—that the speech will be worthy of their attention. You do this by explaining how listening to your speech will benefit them. For example, it may help them understand better, make money, save time, or become more successful.

CHECKLIST ~ Connecting with Your Audience

- [ ] Do you refer to the setting or occasion if appropriate?
- [ ] Do you acknowledge the person who introduced you or some other VIPs present?
- [ ] If appropriate, do you flatter your audience?
- [ ] Have you developed common ground with the audience?
- [ ] If appropriate, do you use self-deprecating humor?
- [ ] Have you established your credibility?

Dusiy/Shutterstock.com

MindTap°   SPEAKER'S WORKSHOP 13.2

1. Go to Part **7** or visit the MindTap for *The Speaker's Handbook* and read or watch the speech by Nathanael Dunlavy. How many different techniques does this speaker use to create a psychological orientation for his speech?

2. Suppose you are speaking to the following audiences on the topics indicated. How will you go about building a positive relationship? How will you motivate them to listen further?

   A. A civic organization of businesspeople about the need to encourage awareness and proper utilization of bike lanes downtown

   B. A group of EMS/firefighters about the opioid epidemic in their county

   C. A college speech class about the dangers of binge drinking

Sometimes, a two-step link is necessary—not every speech topic can be sold to your audience on the grounds that it will help them succeed, or make them popular. When you cannot make a direct link to a basic need, motivating your audience depends on a step-by-step exposure of connections that lead from your topic to some core value. Perhaps explain how listening will make them more knowledgeable and that knowledge may come in handy in a job interview or on a blind date. (You will find more information about these topics in Chapter **18**, "Attention and Interest," and Chapter **20**, "Motivational Appeals.")

13-1d Provide a Logical Orientation

Now that your audience is *motivated* to listen, you must be sure they are *prepared* to listen. In the **logical orientation**, you show your listeners how you will approach and develop your topic—in effect, giving them an intellectual road map.

Logical is used here in its broadest sense, as a contrast to *psychological* used previously. The intent is to offer the listener clear, logical connections to aid listening. In this phase of your introduction, you preview the parts to reveal how they fit with the larger context of your speech.

Establish a Context for Your Speech Give your audience a perspective on your topic by using one or more of the following approaches to establish *context*.

1. ***Fit Your Topic into a Familiar Framework.*** Consider this statement:

   Turkey is located south of the Black Sea, east of the Aegean Sea, and north of the Mediterranean Sea. Turkey shares its southern border with Syria and Iraq, and its eastern edge borders Iran, Armenia, and Georgia.

Here, the unknown is linked to the known in a geographical sense. You can also relate your topic to some schema, chart, organizational structure, or process with which your audience is already familiar. In this case, your listeners presumably know where the Mediterranean Sea and Iraq are, so they can start to understand Turkey's general location. In the next example, the speaker clarifies the speech by putting it in the context of a known structure:

> *As you know, the federal government is divided into three branches: the legislative, the judicial, and the executive. When we think of the legislative branch, we think of the Congress. However, there are several other parts of this branch. Today I want to describe to you the workings of the Speech Writing Division of the Congressional Research Service, part of the Library of Congress.*

The speaker can also connect an unfamiliar topic to the familiar by using an analogy:

> *When the traffic lights break down on a busy corner, you see a traffic cop standing in the middle of the intersection, blowing a whistle, and telling impatient motorists where to go. In effect, that is what I do as crisis manager at the Metacom Corporation.*

2. ***Place Your Topic Historically.*** Another way to provide perspective on your topic is to describe its historical context. It helps listeners to learn about the events that led up to the situation as it stands at the time of your speech. One of the most famous speeches by an American, Abraham Lincoln's "Gettysburg Address," used this simple form of introduction:

> *Fourscore and seven years ago our fathers brought forth on this continent a new nation, conceived in liberty and dedicated to the proposition that all men are created equal. Now we are engaged in a great civil war, testing whether that nation or any nation so conceived and so dedicated can long endure. We are met on a great battlefield of that war. We have come to dedicate a portion of that field, as a final resting place for those who here gave their lives that that nation might live. It is altogether fitting and proper that we should do this.*

On far less momentous occasions, whenever an audience needs to be briefed or reminded about the background that forms the context for a particular speech, a historical recounting can be effective:

> *Last June, following the series of gang-related incidents in the Ravensbrook and Southside neighborhoods, our mayor appointed a special task force to explore the scope and causes of increasing gang violence in our city and to make recommendations to the city council. Throughout the summer, eleven of us on that task force held a series of briefings by experts and scholars. Then, between September and January, we held eight "town hall" meetings throughout the community. To complete our data analysis, we also conducted more than one hundred interviews. Tonight's meeting is the first open hearing on the preliminary draft of our recommendations.*

You might also want to place your topic in a broader historical context. For example, in the introduction of a speech dealing with some aspect of the French Revolution, you could mention what was happening in America, the rest of Europe, or the Far East at that time in history, thereby providing the listeners with the larger picture. Keep in mind, if more than a brief historic recap is necessary, it might be necessary to include that discussion as one of the main points of the speech.

3. **Place Your Topic Conceptually.** Just as you can place your topic in time or space, you can also locate it in the world of ideas. By showing your listeners how your speech fits in with certain familiar theories, concepts, and definitions, you help them prepare to listen. For example:

    You're familiar with the law of supply and demand as it relates to goods and services. Let me review this basic market mechanism with you, because I want to ask you to apply these same essential principles to our system of information exchange.

4. **Provide New Definitions and Concepts.** If you use unfamiliar terms and concepts in your speech, or use familiar terms in unfamiliar ways, prepare your audience. Related to this, if you use a term or phrase that has been co-opted as a slogan or rallying cry by some group, with all the attendant distortion of meaning, be sure early on to define exactly how you plan to use it. Here is how you might introduce an unfamiliar term:

    By logistics, I'm referring to the art and science of moving something exactly where it needs to be, exactly when it needs to be there. Logistics done well means that sellers more efficiently connect with buyers. And that means more profitability and growth opportunities.[5]

In introducing her topic, Carol W. Kinsley, executive director of the Community Service Learning Center, took care to clarify her topic:

Here is a definition: Community Service Learning is an educational process … that involves students in service experiences with two firm anchors: first, their service is directly related to academic subject matter; and second, it involves them in making positive contributions to individuals and community institutions.[6]

Orient the Audience to Your Speech Structure   Once you have shown how your speech fits into some larger context, the second step in a logical orientation is to preview the structure of your speech. In a **preview**, the speaker gives his or her listeners a reassuring road map to carry through the speech, one that will help them avoid feeling lost. By previewing your speech, you offer your listeners a framework on which to attach your main points, improving their understanding and later recall of your ideas.

Reassuring your audience of what you are going to cover will reduce audience uncertainty and confusion. Suppose you declare, "I will discuss the background of the problem and discuss my solutions to it, and then I will answer those objections most often raised against my position." Hearing this, your audience will likely be patient, not raising those arguments in their minds to block out your position before you have stated it.

In most introductions, you will explicitly state one or more of the following: your topic, thesis, title, or purpose—for example, "I would like to persuade you to change your vote on this bond issue." (The circumstances that would make this strategically *not* the thing to do are discussed in Chapter **22** on persuasive strategies.) At times, you may also want to share what you will *not* talk about—essentially explaining to your audience how you have narrowed your topic. Here is an example, derived from the comic book outline in Chapter **10**, of a speaker spelling out what the speech will not cover:

> *I am not going to tell you which comic books are currently the best investment. Nor am I going to explain how to treat and store comic books so that the acid in the paper won't turn them into yellow confetti. I am, however, going to tell you some things about comic books that will help you better understand their place in American popular culture.*

You must also decide whether to give an exact preview of the points you are going to cover or merely a much more general overview of your topic. Explicit previews are useful in the majority of speeches and essential for speeches with fairly technical or complex topics.

When should you *not* use an explicit preview? If your speech is built around a dramatic sequence, you should not ruin the effect by giving the climax away in a preview. Rather, provide a thorough summary in the conclusion. In addition, when each point builds on the audience's understanding of the previous points, a detailed preview might do more harm than good. Finally, very short, simple, or ceremonial speeches rarely need previewing.

MindTap°   SPEAKER'S WORKSHOP 13.3

1. Visit the MindTap for *The Speaker's Handbook* to watch or read the introductions to the speeches by Brian Sharkey and Kayla Strickland. What methods do they use in their speeches to provide logical orientation? Would any of these speeches be more effective if they did or did not include a specific preview?

2. Write a logical orientation for either the comic book outline in Chapter **10** or the outline on working women in the labor force in Chapter **11**. Include a specific preview of the main points. Then rewrite it, substituting a more general preview that briefly paraphrases the main points. Under what circumstances would each form be most effective?

MindTap®   Visit the MindTap for *The Speaker's Handbook* and click on **Additional Resources** to visit Hamilton College's page of basic do's and don'ts for speech introductions.

After fully understanding the steps, it is worth recognizing that not every situation calls for each discrete step. It may be appropriate to omit steps. For instance, a presidential speech can begin, "My fellow Americans, tonight I want to talk about the serious problem of international terrorism." Attention, credibility, and motivation to listen are understood due to the significance of the speaker and situation.

When attention is already riveted on you—as when you are about to announce the long-awaited results of a competition—a lengthy opening story is unnecessary and unwelcome. Likewise, if you have just been introduced by another speaker who listed your credentials, it would be unnecessary to repeat those details. Or if you are a minister speaking to your own congregation or a candidate addressing a rally of your campaign workers, you certainly do not need to waste time building a relationship. Finally, a study group that meets regularly to hear lectures on a certain topic needs very little logical orientation; rather, you can jump quite directly into the substance of your speech.

Examine your audience, the occasion, and your speech purpose to see which aspects of an introduction can be combined, which ones can be handled with a passing sentence or indirect reference, and whether any can be omitted. Just be sure that by the time you begin your first main point, you can answer yes to each of these questions:

▶ Are they listening?

▶ Do they have a reason to keep listening to me?

▶ Do they want or need to know more about this topic?

▶ Do they understand where I'm coming from?

▶ Do they understand where I'm going?

FOR YOUR BENEFIT

Tips for the Introduction

Generally, the introduction should take up 10-15 percent of your speaking time. If your introduction includes all the steps given in this chapter as discrete units, it might be longer than the speech itself. If you progress mechanically through these steps, your introduction will be choppy, disjointed, and overlong. It is better instead to organize the introduction in a natural narrative style, keeping in mind the *functions* of getting attention, and providing psychological and logical orientation. Whenever possible, select material that fulfills several of the functions discussed in this chapter.

MindTap®   SPEAKER'S WORKSHOP 13.4

1. Go to Part **7** in *The Speaker's Handbook* to read the speeches by Harriet Kamakil and George W. Bush. Are all of the steps of an introduction present in each? What steps are omitted? Do you think the omissions are justified? What functions are combined?

CHECKLIST ~ Avoid Common Introduction Pitfalls

☐ Do you avoid drawing negative attention to yourself prior to speaking by showing up organized and on time?

☐ Do you avoid starting your speech with "Before I start, I'd like to say …"? *You have started.*

☐ Do you avoid apologizing and start your speech with an attention getter?

☐ Do you maximize eye contact and keep your inflection natural and conversational?

☐ Do you act like yourself when you deliver your speech?

☐ Do keep your speech focused throughout?

☐ Do you keep your introduction to 10–15 percent of the total speech (thirty to forty-five seconds in a five-minute speech)?

☐ Do you avoid name-dropping?

☐ Do you keep your introduction clear and concise?

Dusit/Shutterstock.com

Summary

13-1 Develop an effective introduction to your speech.

▶ A clear, confident, and meaningful introduction captures audience interest and provides psychological and logical orientation for a speech. It should use no more than 10-15 percent of the time available for the speech. Done well, the introduction leaves the audience clear about the speech topic, interested in listening, and certain about the context and structure of the speech to follow.

Critical Thinking Questions

▶ How does a speaker's first five words influence the audience's attention?

▶ How might gaining the attention of classmates be different from gaining the attention of coworkers?

▶ Which is more important for an informative speech to an audience that knows the speaker well: psychological orientation or logical orientation? Why?

▶ Why should the introduction be limited to about 10 percent of the speech length?

Putting It into Practice

MindTap° Locate a political or professional speech. Consider using one from *Vital Speeches of the Day* or another online source such as AmericanRhetoric.com. Visit **Additional Resources** in the MindTap for *The Speaker's Handbook* for a link to the website.

1. How does the speaker capture the audience's attention?

2. What does the speaker do to create a positive relationship with the audience?

3. What does the speaker do to provide a logical orientation for the listener? Is it adequate?

4. Is the introduction effective? How so?

14

Conclusions

Use a conclusion to provide logical and psychological closure.

Just as we lead our audiences into our topics step-by-step in the introduction, so must we lead them out again with a conclusion. A good conclusion is like a well-wrapped gift: Crisp, clean, colorful, pleasing to the eye, and carefully prepared with a lovely bow. Like the introduction, the conclusion should be precisely planned and practiced in advance. Social scientists tell us that people are most likely to remember what they hear last, so we must choose our final words carefully. A well-constructed conclusion provides logical closure, psychological closure, and ends memorably.

14-1 Provide Logical Closure

Although you have already demonstrated the interconnectedness of your points and ideas in the body of the speech by the use of transitions and internal previews and summaries, you still need to tie it all together for your audience at the end.

With the exception of short or ceremonial speeches, such as a speech of introduction or acceptance, you should develop a logical closure—a summary that clearly restates the main ideas of the speech. Although there are sometimes good reasons not to state your thesis and main points in your introduction, it is nearly always helpful to remind your audience of your main points in the conclusion.

In a technical or argumentative speech, it can be particularly useful to restate your thesis and main points exactly, including the logical steps you ask your audience to consider. For instance, the following excerpt comes from Brian Sharkey's speech on Native American code talkers available in Part 7:

> *Hopefully now you all understand a little better the important role the Navajo had in fighting World War II. Today I shared how the Navajo came to be used as code talkers, how they developed the unbreakable code, and how they were invaluable to the U.S. Marines, specifically in the battle for Iwo Jima.*

If this kind of summary seems too mechanical, you can paraphrase rather than restate exactly, summing up the content, but not in the identical words:

> *Today, I have tried to give you a sense of the Navajo code talkers, including how they were used, how the code was developed, and the impact they had on the U.S. efforts in World War II.*

14-1a   Reestablish Your Topic's Connection to a Larger Context

In the introduction, you drew your speech topic out of some broader context. After developing your ideas, you may want to show how they tie back to the original larger picture. For instance, a speech on the training of teachers may have such a format, as shown graphically in Figure 14.1. In some cases, a conclusion serves to pull together several ideas into a pattern that has been implicit all along. This might be true of a speech organized inductively with numerous examples to support a final conclusion or

FIGURE 14.1
Relationship of the introduction, body, and conclusion to the larger picture

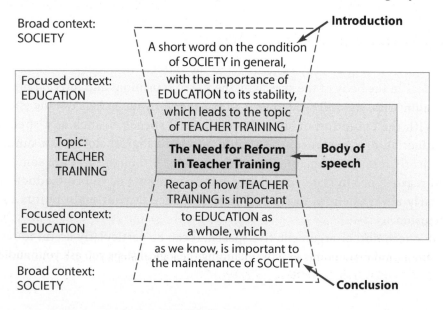

whenever the final relationship among points needs to be spelled out. (For additional information on reasoning see Chapter **16**.) In other cases, you might want to build on the points you established in order to highlight broader implications or ramifications of your topic. There may not be time to address these topics in your speech, but at least you want to raise them for your audience to think about. If you have introduced new definitions and concepts, or familiar definitions and concepts in unfamiliar ways, use the conclusion to reinforce your use of new terms. Most importantly, connect your ideas back to the larger context.

14-1b Provide Psychological Closure

Making your main points fit together logically for your audience is not enough. Your listeners should leave psychologically satisfied with your speech—you need to have touched them. When you plan your conclusion, think not only about what you want your listeners to understand and agree with, but also about what they *need* and how you want them to *feel* at the end of the speech.

1. Remind the Audience How the Topic Affects Their Lives
In the introduction, you make the topic personal to your audience. During the speech itself, you implicitly sustain that orientation by making your examples and manner of speaking appropriately personal. At the end, you bring the topic home again and show your listeners why it should be of more than academic interest to them—why they have a stake in what you have described.

2. Make an Appeal
Part of the psychological wrap-up of a speech can be a direct appeal to your audience, especially in a speech to persuade. Ask them directly to behave in a certain way (through adoption, deterrence, discontinuance, or continuance; see Chapter **22**), or ask them to change their attitudes.

MindTap®   SPEAKER'S WORKSHOP 14.1

1. Visit the MindTap for *The Speaker's Handbook* and watch the speeches by Nathanael Dunlavy or Kayla Strickland, or read the transcript of the speech by Eboo Patel in Part **7**. How do they provide logical closure in their speeches? How effective are their decisions to summarize explicitly, generally, or not at all?

2. Write a logical wrap-up for either the comic book outline in Chapter **10** or the outline on working women in Chapter **11**.

A statement of your own intent can strengthen an appeal.

In the malaria speech referred to in Chapter **13**, Kayla Strickland concludes by summarizing her main points, calling her audience to action, making a statement of intent, creating psychological closure, and ending with a clincher.

> *I've told you how malaria affects us, showed a way of fighting it and revealed the benefits that we could see by being rid of it. So what can you do to take your bite out of malaria? Buy a net. Ten dollars will provide the funds for a treated net, its distribution, and education for the happy owner. I bought one through biteback. net.... You may be saying, "One net? What will that accomplish?" Consider the African proverb: "If you think you're too small to make a difference, try sleeping in a closed room with a mosquito." Just take a look at the benefits we've been over, and you can see that a simple bed net is probably one of the best investments you could ever make. The mosquito will always be a nuisance, but it doesn't have to be a killer.*[1]

In some speeches, the appeal makes the most sense if it is partitioned. You might make one appeal for immediate action and another for long-range action. Or you might make one appeal telling people what they can do individually and another telling them what they can do collectively. With a large and diverse audience, you might direct different appeals to segments of the audience, as Peter M. Gerhart did in wrapping up his speech on the future of the legal profession:

> *In closing, I have separate messages for lawyers and the general public.*
>
> *For lawyers, my message is this. Our challenge is not public relations; it is human relations. Our challenge is not too much commercialism; it is too little attention to making legal markets work better. Our challenge is not to protect the mystery of the legal profession; it is to project its humility. ...*
>
> *Ultimately, my message is not to fight change, but to capture change, to make it work for the public in the context of professionalism. It will be good for the public, and I think that it will make practicing law more fun.*
>
> *To the nonlawyers, I add this: we lawyers are here to serve. Call on the best that is in us. You can, and should, expect a legal system that works for you. It is your legal system; ultimately, we are going to put you in control of it. It is precisely because what we do is so central to the American experience, so central to protecting individuality while building the American community, that your expectations should be high. When we fail to meet these expectations, we will try to do better. But watch us do better. We have a lot of good still to do.*[2]

MindTap SPEAKER'S WORKSHOP 14.2

Go to Part **7** or visit the MindTap for *The Speaker's Handbook* to read or watch the sample speeches by Harriet Kamakil, Brian Sharkey, and Nathanael Dunlavy. What do these speeches do to provide psychological closure? Are they effective?

14-1c End Your Speech Memorably

It is just as important to plan your last sentence as it is your first. Every speech needs a powerful, memorable closing—in a word, a **clincher**. Speakers who have not prepared one tend to keep summarizing while trying to devise a good exit line. As a result, many of them taper off in dismay and defeat with such frail endings as these:

▶ I guess that's all I wanted to say.

▶ Oops! My time is up. I'd better stop now. Thank you.

▶ Well, I'd like to say more, but I ought to take questions.

Other speakers do not taper off; they simply stop, leaving the audience to decide whether the silence is a pause or the actual ending. One type of effective clincher for a speech ties back to the attention getter used in the introduction. This involves answering definitively the provocative question you asked initially or reintroducing your opening joke or story and taking it one step further—or twisting it in the light of your thesis:

> *Frank Salacuse's syndicate spent $17,500 for its comic book, but all you need is a pocketful of change and transportation to the nearest newsstand or grocery store to rediscover a unique facet of Americana.*

Also consider clinching your speech with a proverb, aphorism, quotation, or piece of poetry. Martin Luther King, Jr., ended his historic "I Have a Dream" speech by evoking the words of an old spiritual: "Free at last, free at last, thank God almighty, we are free at last."

Do not use "thank you" as a substitute for a clincher. It is customary to thank your audience only when you have been honored by a special invitation to speak, not after a classroom speech or a business presentation. In this case, "thank you" can be the transition from the other parts of your conclusion into your clincher:

> *And so, for all these reasons, I hope you agree that government regulation must be checked.*
>
> *Thank you for inviting me to be here and for your kind attention. As you seek solutions to the complex problems of your industry, I hope that you will remember the words of Thomas Jefferson: "The price of liberty is eternal vigilance."*

The delivery of your clincher is as important as its content. Do not mumble your final sentence in a throwaway voice or spend the last few speaking moments gathering up your notes and slinking away. Be familiar enough with your clincher that you can deliver it while maintaining eye contact with your listeners. When you finish, lower your gaze briefly and then reestablish eye contact to indicate willingness to answer questions or to acknowledge applause. Inevitably, just as in the beginning, you will be self-conscious at this point. You will feel the focus changing from your message back to you. Remind yourself to project a confident image here so you do not undo the effect of your clincher.

SPEAKER'S WORKSHOP 14.3

1. Go to Part **7** in *The Speaker's Handbook* to evaluate the last few sentences of the speeches by Eboo Patel and Dianna Cohen. Does the final lines of each successfully serve the functions of a clincher?

2. Write a clincher for either the outline on comic books in Chapter **10** or the outline on working women in Chapter **11**.

CHECKLIST ~ Avoid Common Conclusion Pitfalls

- [ ] Does your speech connect back to your introduction to create closure?
- [ ] Does your conclusion summarize?
- [ ] Does your speech end memorably?
- [ ] Is your conclusion short and to the point?
- [ ] Is your conclusion consistent with the style and mood of the rest of the speech?

Dusit/Shutterstock.com

Summary

14-1 Create a conclusion that provides logical and psychological closure and allows the speaker to end memorably.

The key to an effective conclusion includes

- the ability to capture the essential elements of your speech concisely;
- a logical and psychological closure;

▶   a memorable ending with a powerful challenge, quotation, proverb, or story; and

▶   a definitive sense of completeness.

Critical Thinking Questions

▶   What are the dangers associated with a weak conclusion?

▶   How much of the total speech time should the conclusion entail?

▶   How might the conclusion of a persuasive appeal differ from that of an informative or an invitational speech?

Putting It into Practice

Use an online quotation tool to identify four to six possible quotations to use as clinchers for a speech you are planning.

1.   What makes an effective clincher?

2.   Besides the clincher, what else is needed in your conclusion to ensure logical and psychological closure?

Checklists

Shaping Your Speech

Rudyard Kipling, author of many popular story books, is quoted as saying, "Words are, of course, the most powerful drug used by mankind." The next eight chapters deal with words and our ability to use them effectively with an ethical impact on our audience. Of all the choices you make as a speaker, by far the most important is how you will craft your message.

The recent U.S. Presidential campaign has placed a spotlight on the significance of communicating in the public sphere. Effective public speaking is important. The support you select, reasoning you use, credibility you develop, language choices, strategies, and appeals matter in significant ways. Perhaps you don't believe your seven-minute speech is a big deal, but consider that an audience of twenty-five people equates to nearly three hours of collective time. Would you want to waste three hours of another's time? This view of the speaking situation dramatizes your opportunity and responsibility.

Effective speakers invest considerable time not only in gathering compelling material but also in designing an overall speech strategy. A speech strategy is only this: a master plan for combining your content with other elements of speaking to meet a certain goal.

Particularly when the goal is to inform or persuade, we believe that speakers have an ethical obligation to respect the audience's interests as well as their own. Of course, speakers always have a purpose in speaking, but they should not abuse the power of the platform. Emotional appeals, loaded language, and personal charisma may mesmerize listeners, but their misuse would be unethical. Regardless of your political proclivity, recent and historic politics have challenged our thinking on this issue. Despite these events, we believe that facts matter and ethics are important.

An effective speech can certainly be emotional, but it should never substitute emotion for reason. Supporting materials, including definitions, examples, statistics, and expert testimony, can be combined with emotional appeals, stories, and personal testimony for an effective balance of logic and emotion. When you presume to command people's time and attention, you owe it to them to know what you are talking about. Your message should be logical, factual, and coherent. Only after developing a sound, rational base should you move on to making the message personal and palatable.

15

Supporting Materials

Clarify and justify each of your points with supporting materials through the use of definitions, examples, statistics, and testimony. Be sure these materials are varied, provide sound evidence, and are smoothly integrated into the speech.

MindTap   Read, highlight, and take notes online.

After you have set up the basic structure of your speech, your next step is selecting the materials—whether from your research or from your thinking—that will make up its real substance. This process is similar to adding furniture, curtains, and wall hangings to a plain white wall of your living room or adding backup vocals and instrumentation to a musical ballad. These supporting materials are crucial to your success. They are the "stuff" it is made of. They may well determine whether your listeners characterize your statements as believable or unbelievable and interesting or boring.

You can select the forms of support only after your basic structure is in place. It is impossible to judge the appropriateness of supporting materials unless you are very clear about what you are supporting. It is extremely important, as Chapter **6** (on topic selection and analysis) and Chapter **9** (on transforming ideas) stress, that you measure every component of your speech against a logical outline. If your point is that crime is on the increase, then the story of a single crime, however compelling, is not enough. To *support* your point, you need comparative data—examples collected from at least two periods of time to establish a trend.

Supporting materials may take the form of clarification or proof and can include definitions, examples, statistics, or testimony. Often, especially in speeches to inform or evoke, supporting materials clarify or expand on ideas. Supporting materials can also be used as evidence to support the claims you make in your speech. Although it may be nearly impossible to completely *prove* a point, we speak of supporting materials as proof because they can serve to justify an idea, adding to the probability of its acceptance. Frequently, a single piece of support, such as a statistic, functions as both clarification and proof of a point. Some kinds of support, though, like hypothetical examples or definitions, can be used only as amplification; they never serve to prove anything. For a fuller discussion of methods for clarifying ideas, refer to Chapter **21** ("Informative Strategies"). For further advice on proving controversial claims, see Chapter **22** ("Persuasive Strategies").

Select the support for your ideas first on the basis of relevance; second on soundness; and third on interest value. By using a variety of supporting strategies, a speaker can avoid falling into the rut of relying exclusively on a single form of support.

15-1 Define Unfamiliar Words and Concepts

Does "regressive taxes" mean poor people pay more, or less? Does "left-brain function" refer to the logical or the creative side? What does it mean to "deglaze the pan"? Speakers must be careful not to confuse audience members with the words they choose. One way to clarify the various terms you use in your speech is by using definitions, but there are different types of definitions you can use. Depending on your situation and the needs of your speech, consider using one or more of these types to clarify the terms you use.

1. Logical Definition
Also known as dictionary definitions, **logical definitions** have two steps. It first places the concept to be defined into a category; then it explains the characteristics that distinguish the concept from all other members of the category. For example:

ANTHROPOLOGY IS A...

Step 1: Category	*... formal field of academic study that studies the human species ...*	*[not a religion or a political system or a health food]*
Step 2: Distinguishing characteristics	*... as a whole to develop a comprehensive understanding of human nature and history.*	*[which differentiates it from physics, sociology, biology, psychology]*

2. Historical and Etymological Definitions
One way you can explain a word's meaning to your audience is to explain how the word was derived, either as linked to some historical event (**historical definition**) or as drawn from root words in an older culture (**etymological definition**):

   a. **Historical**

      In 1880, Charles G. Boycott, an English land agent in Ireland, refused to reduce rents. In response, his tenants refused to pay them. The word *boycott* has

entered the language to mean the act of refusing to engage in social or economic interaction with some entity, either to coerce or to express disapproval.

   b. Etymological

   Anthropology is drawn from the Greek *anthropos*, meaning "human being," and
   ology, meaning "the study of."

3. Operational Definition

One way to explain a term is to tell how the object or concept referred to works or
operates, providing an **operational definition**. Such definitions may simply indicate
the steps that make up a process:

▸ The *arithmetic mean* is what you get when you add up all the scores and divide by the
number of scores.

▸ *Blogging* consists of writing an online journal or web-based log.

Social scientists use operational definitions to explain how conceptual terms are
measured.

Returning to the anthropology example, you might define the field by telling what
an anthropologist does:

▸ An *anthropologist* makes systematic observations about past or present human behavior
and then synthesizes these observations into generalizations about human nature and
history.

4. Definition by Negation

Socrates said, "Nobody knows what justice is, but everyone knows what injustice is." In
many cases, the best way to clarify a term is to explain what it is not, a practice known
as **definition by negation** or opposition. Abstract notions, such as fairness, clarity, and
power, can sometimes be better defined by describing actions that are unfair, relationships that are unclear, or people who are powerless. Reference to opposites can be used
to explain concrete terms, too:

▸ Hypoglycemia is something like the opposite of diabetes.

▸ Forensic anthropologists do not amass specialized data on a whim. They don't go digging
for bones because they need the exercise.

This sort of definition can be powerful and intriguing. For a well-rounded picture,
however, negation is best combined with other forms of definition.

5. Definition by Authority

This method of defining is useful for controversial or vague terms for which a choice
must be made among plausible alternatives. When you use **definition by authority**,
the arbiter of meaning becomes the person with the most credibility or the most
power:

▸ I don't know what *you* mean by "a little late," but the boss says anything more than fifteen
minutes goes on your record.

MindTap   SPEAKER'S WORKSHOP 15.1

1. Use two different methods to define each of these terms:
   A. Eco-friendly
   B. Marriage
   C. Inflation
   D. Renewable energy
   E. Autonomous vehicles

2. Read or watch the Harriet Kamakil speech on the Maasai people of Africa, available in Part **7** and in the MindTap for *The Speaker's Handbook*. Identify at least four definitions she presents. How would you classify each definition? Are they effective?

▶ Free speech cannot be suppressed unless a "clear and present danger" exists. The Supreme Court has defined it thus: "No danger flowing from speech can be deemed clear and present, unless the incidence of the evil apprehended is so imminent that it may befall before there is opportunity for full discussion …. Only an emergency can justify repression."

6. Definition by Example

Using a **definition by example** is a common and effective way to explain something by pointing at it, verbally or literally:

▶ When I talk about a charismatic leader, I mean someone like Raymond A. Kroc (founder of McDonald's), or Martin Luther King, Jr., Herb Kelleher (Founder of Southwest Airlines), Oprah Winfrey, or Eva Perón.

▶ There are two basic ways to cause the strings of the guitar to vibrate: strumming, which sounds like this [strums], and picking, which sounds like this [picks].

15-2 Use Various Types of Examples

Few sentences perk up an audience better than "Now let me give you an example." Beyond the universal appeal of a good story, examples provide audience members with a chance to check their perceptions of a speaker's message. When concepts are linked to actual cases, the listeners can see if their images coincide with those of the speaker. As a speaker, you need to decide whether to use real examples or hypothetical ones and how long these examples should be.

15-2a Use Factual Examples

Factual examples rely upon facts. A *fact* is an assertion that is universally accepted. Sometimes, it is directly verifiable, as in "Elena Kagan is a justice of the Supreme Court." Even if you were not at the swearing-in, you could find plenty of sources to help you verify that this is a factual statement. "The earth is 93 million miles from the sun" is another assertion accepted as a fact although it is not *directly* verifiable through any of the five senses. But we accept it, because we know scientists have studied it and through calculations have arrived at the same answer. When you use such examples for explanation, it is essential that they be clear, relevant, and varied. When you use examples to prove a point, though, specific logical tests must be met. These tests are the essence of *inductive reasoning* as discussed in Chapter **16**.

Are Sufficient Examples Given? To establish the point that high schools in your county are failing to teach basic literacy skills, it would not suffice to tell about one or two functionally illiterate graduates you know personally. The more examples you give, the less likely your listeners are to dismiss the phenomenon as the product of chance.

Are the Examples Representative? Even if you gave a dozen examples of local graduates who are functionally illiterate, the conclusion would be suspect if all the cases were from one remedial class in one school. To be credible, examples should represent a cross section of students in the county from a variety of schools.

Are Negative Instances Accounted For? When you reason by example, you must look into and account for dramatic negative examples. If your friend points out that her cousin was a National Merit Scholar or that test scores at Arbor Estates High School were above the national average, you might reconsider your conclusion about the failure of the schools. Perhaps the niece has an IQ of 175. Maybe Arbor Estates High School has a cadre of amazing English teachers. Your obligation, if you wish to carry your point, is to show how these examples are atypical and why they should be excluded from a consideration of the general status of most students in most schools in the county.

15-2b Use Hypothetical Examples

Sometimes, when no factual example quite suits your purpose, or when you are speculating about the future, you might give a brief or extended **hypothetical example**. Here are two illustrations of *extended hypothetical examples*.

▶ Why should you get out of debt? Well, let's imagine that you have $1,000 worth of debt. If you pay only the minimum amount on a credit card with 18 percent interest, it would take you twelve years and $1,115 in interest fees to pay off the $1,000 debt.

▶ Picture a young woman—let's call her Katie—heading toward her car after working overtime. Because she's so tired, she doesn't hear the footsteps behind her until she's some distance from the building. Katie quickens her pace ….

Obviously, hypothetical examples cannot *prove* anything. They are useful for clarification because they can be tailored to fit the subject exactly. As such, hypothetical examples can be used to explain or supplement real examples, particularly if a real example is complex, a bit confusing, or doesn't quite illustrate the point you're trying to make.

Hypothetical examples do not have to be long. Here is a speech segment that uses three *brief* hypothetical examples in quick succession:

▶ What would happen if this tax law were to pass? Well, Miguel over there couldn't deduct his business lunches. Audrey wouldn't be able to depreciate her buildings. You, Tom, with kids about to start college …

As the previous example demonstrates, hypothetical examples allow you to bring the members of your audience into your speech. You'll find tips for designing your examples in Chapter **18**.

15-2c Use Appropriate Detail

When you use examples, you must decide how long or short to make each one. Examples in a speech can be kept brief when you can safely assume the audience already accepts them. To clarify an idea, you might say, "The employee benefits manager handles all of the forms of reward that are not wages—including medical insurance, dental insurance, bonuses, profit-sharing plans, and company scholarships." To prove a proposition, you could also point to familiar and accepted cases: "The next presidential election will hinge on a few swing states, including Ohio, Michigan, and Pennsylvania, much like the elections of 2008, 2012, and 2016." But, obviously, these *brief factual examples* will not be effective with listeners who have never heard of profit sharing or who know nothing of prior presidential elections. In such cases, more detail will be needed.

CHECKLIST ~ Tests of Factual Examples

- Are sufficient examples given?
- Are the examples representative?
- Are negative instances accounted for?

Dusit/Shutterstock.com

FOR YOUR BENEFIT

NEWSPRISM - THE INTERNET'S HOMEPAGE
NEWS AND OPINION
FROM LIBERAL TO CONSERVATIVE

Sites become more biased and more extreme as you move down each side and away from center.

	CENTER	
LEFT / LIBERAL	POLITICO	**RIGHT / CONSERVATIVE**

LEFT / LIBERAL	CENTER	RIGHT / CONSERVATIVE
USA TODAY		THE ECONOMIST
ABC NEWS		REAL CLEAR POLITICS
CNN		U.S NEWS & WORLD REPORT
NEWSWEEK		C. S. MONITOR
CBS NEWS		BLOOMBERG
WASHINGTON POST		FINANCIAL TIMES
NBC NEWS		FORBES
TIME		WALL STREET JOURNAL
NPR		WASHINGTON TIMES
NEW YORK TIMES		DRUDGE REPORT
MSNBC		FOX NEWS
MEDIA MATTERS		NEWSMAX
VOX	**CENTER**	NATIONAL REVIEW
SALON		BREITBART
HUFFINGTON POST	POLITIFACT	THE BLAZE
THE NATION	THE HILL	TOWNHALL
MOTHER JONES	ROLL CALL	HUMAN EVENTS
ALTERNET	NATIONAL JOURNAL	WND

LEFT / LIBERAL		**RIGHT / CONSERVATIVE**

Understanding the standpoint and bias of the supporting materials you consult is central to the development of an effective speech. Would you agree or disagree with the assessment above by Bob Seay through his website http://www.newsprism.com? What impact might the source of your support have on audience members? Why?

ESB Professional/Shutterstock.com

When a succession of quick references will not illuminate a point for your listeners, develop the example into an illustration. Though these scenarios take time to develop, they create vivid images that might make the point with more emphasis than would shorter examples.

MindTap®   SPEAKER'S WORKSHOP 15.2

1. Read or watch one of the speeches, available in Part **7** and in the MindTap for *The Speaker's Handbook*. How many examples are used in this speech? Label each as brief or extended, and as factual or hypothetical.

2. Select one of these topics:

   Teenage suicide

   Credit card fraud

   Organ transplants

   Now develop an example in each of the following categories, and briefly explain in what sort of speech situation it would be most appropriate:

   A. Brief factual

   B. Extended factual

   C. Brief hypothetical

   D. Extended hypothetical

15-3 Use Statistical Evidence

When examples are systematically collected and classified, they are reported as statistics, the source of **statistical evidence**. In the case of the literacy topic discussed earlier, it would not be feasible to discuss, by name, all the students who illustrate your point. It would simply take too much time to give enough examples to show the seriousness of the problem. This is when you turn to statistical evidence. By examining labor statistics, reviewing available data from state offices, or interviewing teachers, you could clarify and support your speech with material like this:

MindTap®   There are many excellent sources of statistical information online. For example, you can find government statistics classified by topic, state, and agency at the website https://fedstats.sites.usa.gov/. The website for the U.S. Census provides all sorts of information about the U.S. population, including statistics about ethnicity, employment, and geography. And the U.S. Bureau of Justice website provides statistical information about crime, the courts, law enforcement, and more. Visit the MindTap for *The Speaker's Handbook* and click on **Additional Resources** to access these sites.

▶ Full-time workers age 25 and over without a high school diploma had median weekly earnings of $488, compared with $668 for high school graduates (no college) and $1,193 for those holding at least a bachelor's degree (Bureau of Labor Statistics).[1]

▶ Eighty percent of Ohio inmates are high school drop outs. Approximately 30 percent of the males and 20 percent of the females are considered functionally illiterate, reading at less than a sixth-grade level (Ohio Department of Corrections).[2]

▶ Per year, 23,000 young adults drop out or complete school needing basic skills (Ohio Literacy Network).[3]

15-3a Test Accuracy of Statistical Evidence

Before you use a statistic, use the tests of who, why, when, and how.

Who Collected the Data? Investigate the qualifications and competence of the researchers. Was the work done by a professional pollster or the host of a call-in radio show? A noted scholar or a graduate student? A government task force or an advertising agency?

Why Were the Data Collected? Most people have more confidence in studies rooted in a desire to advance knowledge. Although not totally free of bias, independent pollsters, investigative journalists, scientists, and academics tend to be more objective than people committed to selling a product or promoting a cause. For example, statistics from research done by a political candidate's staff, purporting to show massive support for the candidate, may better reflect a need to demoralize the opposition than a need to show a true picture to the public.

When Were the Data Collected? Be sure your evidence is up to date. Attitudes change as swiftly as prices, and some data are obsolete by the time they are published. If you are dealing with a continuously active subject, like natural gas prices, it would be wise to consult a credible resource for the most recent data like www.nasdaq.com.

How Were the Data Collected? Find out as much as you can about the design of the research and the details of its execution. If a certain statistical finding supports an essential point of your speech, do not settle for a one-paragraph reference from Wikipedia. Track it back to the original source and learn more about the study.

CHECKLIST ~ Tests of Statistical Evidence

Ask yourself the following questions when evaluating statistical evidence used in your speech.

- [ ] Who collected the data?
- [ ] Why were the data collected?
- [ ] When were the data collected?
- [ ] How were the data collected?

First, compare definitions. You may find the title of the study promising, but a closer reading could show that the investigator defines important terms in ways that do not apply to your speech. Next, check how the cases were chosen. Subjects and examples should have been selected randomly or through some other logical and unbiased system.

Finally, evaluate the method of data collection—observation, experiment, or survey conducted by phone, mail, or personal interview. If possible, look at the actual questionnaire used. Are there leading questions or unrealistic forced choices in the interviews and questionnaires? Even if you are not an expert, you can spot bias introduced into the research method—for example, through the phrasing of directions or the way the findings are analyzed and presented.

15-3b Avoid Misleading Statistics

We know language is ambiguous, but we tend to believe that numbers make straightforward statements; there is no mystery in $2 + 2 = 4$. However, numbers *can* be just as ambiguous, with statistical pitfalls to trip the gullible.

The Fallacy of the Average   A critic once said, with tongue in cheek, that a person could stand with one foot on a block of ice and one foot in a fire and be statistically comfortable. Although the average can be a useful tool for analysis, it sometimes can obscure reality.

The *median* (the number or score that falls at the midpoint of the range of numbers or scores) or the *mode* (the most frequently occurring score or number) can be more meaningful averages to use in some cases, although they, too, can be abused. See Figure 15.1 for a graphic representation of the scanner distribution in a fictitious company. In this case, although the *mean* is 6, the *median* is 2 (scores of 0 and 1 below it; scores of 3 and 40 above it), and the *mode* is 1 (the largest number of departments, three, have this score).

The Fallacy of the Unknown Base   When speakers use percentages and proportions, they can imply that a large population has been sampled. In fact, data are sometimes reported in this manner to give credence to unscientific or skimpy evidence: "Two out of three dentists recommend this whitening toothpaste." Most listeners would see this as shorthand for "We polled 300 dentists around the country, and 200 of them recommended this toothpaste." How valid would this recommendation seem if it came to light that in reality only three were polled?

Similarly, "Of all the crimes in this county, 80 percent were committed by teenagers" seems to point to a serious problem. It certainly has more impact than "We had five burglaries this year, and four were committed by teenagers." But four instances do not make a crime wave, and 80 percent is not necessarily an epidemic.

FIGURE 15.1
Sample graph showing median, mode, and mean

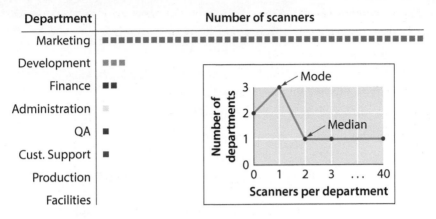

The Fallacy of the Atypical or Arbitrary Time Frame An executive of a computer circuit board company told the authors of this book that sales in February were double those of the previous month. These data could be misleading unless you know that January is always the worst month in the yearly cycle of the computer industry. If the executive had compared February to November, the month in the cycle in which the tablet and video game buying frenzy reaches its peak, then the picture would have been quite different. A more valid example to demonstrate company growth would have compared February with February of the previous year.

By choosing longer or shorter time frames, this executive could give varying spins on the company's health. If he chose November–December–January, with its downward trend, he might convince employees that this is no time to talk about raises. Or he might reassure stockholders by reporting a gradual but steady upward trend revealed by the figures from the last five Novembers.

15-3c Make Statistics Clear and Meaningful

The stereotypical dry, plodding speech is one that is overloaded with statistics. Eventually the audience becomes overloaded too, and listeners start to build a mental wall against the numbers flowing over them. When you do use statistics, round them off. Say "about fifteen hundred" instead of "one thousand four hundred eighty-nine point six."

Use comparisons to make the numbers more understandable:

▶ For the amount of money they propose to spend on this weapons system, we could provide educational grants in aid to all the needy students in the eleven western states, or triple the government funding for cancer research, or upgrade the highway system in this state and its three neighbors.

MindTap   SPEAKER'S WORKSHOP 15.3

1. What additional information would you need to have before accepting the following statistical evidence?

    A.   Studies show that over two-thirds of the total meaning a person communicates is conveyed nonverbally.

    B.   Of people who chew gum, four out of five surveyed prefer sugarless gum.

    C.   Researchers have found that the average social drinker has eight serious hangovers a year.

    D.   Dozens of cases of police harassment have been brought to my attention during my opponent's term of office.

2. Identify the use of statistical evidence as support in the speeches by Senator Bernie Sanders on January 29, 2015 available on CSPAN. Which are used to clarify and which are used to prove controversial claims? Evaluate the statistical support according to the tests discussed in this section. Find examples of how the speakers made the statistics clear and meaningful. Identify any errors the speaker made?

MindTap   For more on how to use statistics effectively, visit the MindTap for *The Speaker's Handbook* and click on **Additional Resources**, where you can access a web link that explains the basic concepts of statistics in a way that's useful to writers and public speakers.

Avoid overused comparisons. Too many dollar bills have been laid end to end and too many large objects have been improbably dumped onto football fields or placed next to the Empire State Building. Furthermore, audiences are no longer shocked to consider the "five people in this room" who will suffer some fate, or the dire toll of outside events that will be racked up "by the end of this speech" or "by the time I finish this sentence."

15-4 Draw on Testimony from Credible Authorities

Often, we call on statements from other people to get our point across. These statements, known as **testimony**, can be viewed as an outward extension of the speaker's own fact-finding. When we do not have the opportunity to verify something through our own senses, we rely on the observations of others. For instance, even if you have never had an accident due to distracted driving or never been a public safety officer, you can give a credible speech on the dangers of distracted driving by making thoughtful use of testimony.

It might be effective to share the words of a friend or colleague involved in a distracted driving incident. You can draw on eyewitnesses or on the authority of experts.

▶   Remembering his accident, Joe Jones said, "One second everything was fine and then next my bumper was buried in the back of the truck ahead of me. It all happened so fast. Until then I thought I could easily text and drive but now I won't do it. Messages will have to wait."

You can cite testimony directly or you can paraphrase it:

▶   **Direct quotation.** David Strayer, Ph.D., director of the University of Utah's Applied Cognition Lab, said, "We directly compared drunk drivers and cell phone drivers and found that cell phones were every bit as bad, if not worse, as drunk driving."[4]

▶   **Paraphrase.** Based on his study of distracted driving conditions, noted researcher David Strayer concluded that drivers are four times more likely to crash if they're talking on the phone while driving.[5]

15-4a Evaluate Credibility of Authorities

You do not have to research a controversial topic for very long before you find that there are seemingly authoritative quotations to support every side of an issue. It is easy to find citations that say almost anything; it is much more difficult to select those that provide legitimate support for your points. Test the credibility of the authorities you're considering quoting by asking whether the apparent authority has access to the necessary information, is qualified, is an expert on this subject, and is free of bias.

Does the Authority Have Access to the Necessary Information? A person does not have to be famous to be an authority. The eyewitness to an accident can tell you authoritatively what happened in the intersection. Your neighbor does not have to be a Chinese diplomat to report on her trip to Beijing. The farther removed someone is from the source, however, the less trustworthy that person's information. A quotation from the accident eyewitness is preferable to a quotation from an acquaintance recounting what the eyewitness said, but even firsthand eyewitness accounts can differ.

Ambiguous descriptions can be misleading. "My brother works for the government, and he says there's a massive conspiracy to cover up the cost overruns in the Defense Department" or "It is the opinion of a noted psychologist that the murderer is definitely insane" is testimony that loses its effect when we learn that the brother is a postal clerk and the psychologist has only read the newspaper accounts of the trial. When you use an authority, be sure that the person had firsthand experience, direct observation, or personal access to relevant facts and files.

Is the Authority Qualified to Interpret Data? Anyone can credibly describe what she or he saw. It is when a person starts making interpretations, forming opinions and conclusions, and proposing recommendations that the standards of credibility become stricter. People earn the right to be considered experts either by holding specific credentials—such as a law degree, Ph.D., or professional license—or by establishing a record of success and experience.

Is the Person Acknowledged as an Expert on This Subject? Actor William Petersen (CSI) was featured in a public service announcement on behalf of Court Appointed Special Advocates (CASA) for children. Though his character, Gil Grissom, certainly is portrayed as having concern for children, does that make Petersen a qualified expert? There are other cases in which experts' opinions have subtly stretched beyond the range of their expertise. A tax attorney may be presented as an expert on constitutional law, a social psychologist may express an opinion on the causes of schizophrenia, or a well-known chemist may receive national attention for her or his views on the efficacy of vitamin C. The opinions they express may or may not be valid, but their expertise in a related field makes them, at best, only slightly more credible than an informed layperson.

Is the Authority Figure Free of Bias and Self-Interest? It is not very surprising when the chair of the Democratic National Committee characterizes the party platform as a blueprint for justice and prosperity, or when a network spokesperson describes a new television season as "the most exciting line-up ever." Nor is it very persuasive. We give much more credence to the opinion of a political analyst or a television critic who appears to have no personal stake—ideological or financial—in the response to the opinion. What would be surprising, and highly persuasive as well, is reluctant testimony. If you can find testimony from a person speaking against his or her interests, presumably because of honesty or as a duty to a larger concept, then it certainly will be an effective addition to your presentation: "Even the National Committee chair admitted that the platform is fuzzy on foreign policy."

15-4b Don't Distort Quotations

Shortening quotations to highlight the basic thrust of the message is perfectly acceptable. What is unacceptable is editing a person's statements to such a degree that they appear to support positions other than or even opposite those espoused in the actual quotations.

CHECKLIST ~ Tests of Testimony

- Does the authority have access to the necessary information?
- Is the authority qualified to interpret data?
- Is the person acknowledged as an expert on this subject?
- Is the authority figure free of bias and self-interest?

Dusiv/Shutterstock.com

Political candidates frequently criticize their opponents by citing portions of their statements on various issues. What results is an incomplete summary of a candidate's position on an issue. For instance, if a person were to say: "About the job-retraining program, the mayor has said that it 'is a disappointment.' The president of the Chamber of Commerce stated that it 'has not fulfilled our expectations.' The chair of the Council of Unions labeled it 'a failure.'" In this instance, although the people cited may be authorities on the subject, their reservations may arise from issues unrelated to the speaker's point. For instance, each may be criticizing the funding adequacy rather than the concept of the program. The program shortcomings may be impossible to discern from cryptic quotations. It is also possible that these experts could be wrong. Listeners need to hear the *why* of the experts' conclusions along with *what* they concluded.

15-5 Cite Sources Smoothly

When you have chosen appropriate definitions, facts, examples, statistics, and testimony, you still have to marshal these supporting materials and integrate them effectively. You want to emphasize the quality of your materials, make them clear and understandable, and incorporate them appropriately in relation to the points they support.

15-5a Cite Sources of Supporting Materials

By giving credit for, or *citing* the sources of, your supporting materials, you build your own credibility by showing the range of your research. You are also providing information your listeners are almost certain to want. Very few audiences will settle for "studies show …" or "a meme I saw …" or "a friend once told …." To evaluate these statements, listeners need to know more about where the information originated.

This does not mean you are required to present regulation footnotes in oral form, citing volume and page numbers. Nor do you need to recite an authority's complete biography or necessarily explain a study's design intricacies. Although you should know the *who, why, when,* and *how* of every bit of data you use, you will probably mention only a couple of these when introducing the evidence.

MindTap° **SPEAKER'S WORKSHOP 15.4**

Evaluate the credibility of the authorities cited in the persuasive speech by Nathanael Dunlavy, available in Part **7** or visit the MindTap for *The Speaker's Handbook*. To what extent does it meet the tests discussed in this section?

MindTap®   SPEAKER'S WORKSHOP 15.5

1. Compare the ways Nathanael Dunlavy and Kayla Strickland introduce supporting materials in their speeches, available in Part **7** or through the MindTap for *The Speaker's Handbook*. Does either speaker "over-introduce" or "under-introduce" the citations? Identify examples of citation that you find most effective.

2. Review the supporting materials used in the sample speeches by Harriet Kamakil, and Kayla Strickland, available in Part **7** in *The Speaker's Handbook*. Note the presence of explanation, definition, examples, statistics, and testimony in each.

   ▶ Does each speech use a variety of methods?

   ▶ What are the two favored forms of supporting material in each speech?

How do you decide which to include? You can follow two basic approaches. First, consider the questions your audience will have. Place yourself in the listeners' place and adopt a skeptical outlook: What would you question about the data? A hostile audience might want to know whether your expert was objective; a group of social scientists might question whether the opinion poll you cite was scientifically conducted. Second, stress what is most compelling and impressive. If you have a thirty-year-old quotation from a Supreme Court justice but think the sentiment expressed is timeless, stress the *who* and not the *when*. What is the best feature of the evidence—its recency, the large size of the sample, the prestige of the journal in which it appeared, or the authority of the speaker? Look at Chapter **8** for more discussion of citing sources in your speech.

15-5b Use a Variety of Lead-Ins

Do not get into the habit of introducing all your illustrations, statistics, or data with the same phrase: "Some figures about this are … some figures about that are …." Be prepared enough that you can employ a number of lead-ins for each kind of supporting material. There are many possibilities:

▶ To support this idea …

▶ This point is verified by …

▶ _____ put it well, I think, when she said …

▶ In the words of _____ , …

▶ What causes this situation? One answer to that question was offered by _____ when he wrote in the *New York Times* …

▶ Let me tell you about a survey taken earlier this year by a Harvard psychologist ...

▶ There are several examples of this. Let me share just two ...

▶ I was immediately struck by the similarity to an experience I/he/ _____ once had ...

However, you decide to introduce a quotation, do not say "quote, unquote," or wiggle pairs of fingers in the air to approximate quotation marks. A subtle change in your voice or posture is enough to indicate to your listeners the boundaries of a direct quotation.

MindTap°   Visit the MindTap for *The Speaker's Handbook* for help with incorporating supporting materials into your speech and citing your sources.

Summary

Keep in mind the key learning outcomes from this chapter when developing supporting material.

15-1 Explain why it is important to define unfamiliar words and concepts.

▶ Words and concepts unfamiliar to your audience need to be clearly defined.

▶ Possible methods of definition include logical definition; etymological/historical, operational definitions; and definitions by negation, authority, and example.

15-2 Differentiate between factual and hypothetical examples.

▶ Factual examples come from real-world examples, whereas hypothetical are not real but could be constructed from a composite of real or plausible examples.

15-3 Demonstrate appropriate use of statistical evidence.

▶ Speakers must test the accuracy of their evidence, avoid misleading use of statistics, and ensure that any data shared is clear and understandable to the audience.

15-4 Summarize the four ways to test the credibility of authorities.

▶ When testing the credibility of authorities, ask yourself the following questions: Is the authority figure free of bias and self-interest? Is the person acknowledged as an expert on this subject? Is the authority qualified to interpret data? Does the authority have access to the necessary information? Use caution to avoid distorting the words and ideas of authorities and the information you draw into your speech.

15-5 Demonstrate how to assemble sources and cite them clearly.

▶ Boost credibility by citing sources of support clearly, sharing the most relevant aspects of who, why, when, and how for each of the sources drawn upon to support your speech.

▶ Using a variety of lead-ins will further enhance perceived credibility and help integrate those sources more effectively whether they be definitions, examples, statistics, or testimony.

Critical Thinking Questions

▶ Why is it better to use supporting materials, such as quotes, examples, statistics, and stories, from a variety of sources?

▶ When are specific examples preferable to broad generalizations in a speech?

▶ What are the tests of credibility for testimony cited in a speech?

▶ Which statistical fallacy is most common? What can you do to avoid it?

Putting It into Practice

MindTap® Locate a political or professional speech. Consider using one from *Vital Speeches of the Day*, accessible through various online sources, such as the White House's online Briefing Room. Visit the MindTap for *The Speaker's Handbook* and click on **Additional Resources** for a link to the website.

▶ What types of definitions are offered in the speech?

▶ What examples does the speaker offer?

▶ How effectively does the speaker incorporate statistics?

▶ What expert testimony does the speaker use?

▶ How does the speaker smoothly integrate the supporting statements?

16-1b People Look for Familiar Patterns

In the health care example, Person A is drawing on a pattern observed in the past—namely, that people who cannot afford a service they need will seek out that service when it becomes affordable. This is perfectly reasonable and logical; we all can think of plenty of commonsense examples.

Person B is also being logical and reasonable in linking the evidence of increased medical visits to the claim that national health care would be undesirable. This person

MindTap® SPEAKER'S WORKSHOP 16.1

1. For each of these claims, list at least three pieces of evidence you could use to support it.

   A. Smoking should be banned in all indoor public places.

   B. Bicycles are a good choice for reducing fossil fuel consumption.

   C. Drivers over the age of seventy should have to take a road test every year to renew their driver's licenses.

   After you have listed the evidence, explain how each piece of evidence supports the point.

2. Explain how the evidence in these examples can be linked to the two different claims. What logical pattern is drawn upon in each case?

Example A

Evidence: The current form of government in the United States has existed for over 200 years.

Therefore,

Claim 1: We should maintain our current form of government because *[link or reasoning]*

or

Claim 2: We should change our current form of government because *[link or reasoning]*

Example B

Evidence: Deaths from firearms have increased in the past few years.

Therefore,

Claim 1: We need even stronger gun control laws than the ones we have because *[link or reasoning]*

or

Claim 2: We should get rid of gun control laws because *[link or reasoning]*

is drawing on another observed pattern of human behavior—that people who see a resource as free and unlimited may use it inappropriately and wastefully. There is also plenty of support for this view.

The issue here is not what the facts *are*, but what the facts *mean*. For our purposes, the significance of these opposing views is to show that there are many sensible ways to interpret the same piece of evidence. A speaker who uses evidence to support a claim cannot simply present the evidence and hope it speaks for itself. The speaker must explain the relevance of the evidence and justify the link to a particular claim.

16-2 Four Main Types of Reasoning

Recall that speakers do not merely transmit information to listeners. Rather, speakers and listeners create meaning together. Therefore, for any complex and controversial topic, you need to show your audience what your evidence means and build the argument with them. This is done by spelling out your interpretation of the data and showing how this interpretation fits one of the common patterns of reasoning familiar to your listeners, including inductive, deductive, causal, and analogic reasoning, as explained next.

16-2a Inductive Reasoning

The simplest and most common kind of reasoning is induction. Induction assumes an orderly universe: a universe where we believe that much of what has happened before will happen again. We step in front of oncoming traffic because we believe from previous experiences that the cars will obey the traffic signals. Dozens of times a day, we draw inferences based on past experiences and expectations derived from those experiences. Inductive reasoning involves making an educated guess about something that is based on a subset of known factors. Figure 16.2 depicts the process of inductive reasoning.

FIGURE 16.2
Inductive reasoning draws inferences from observations

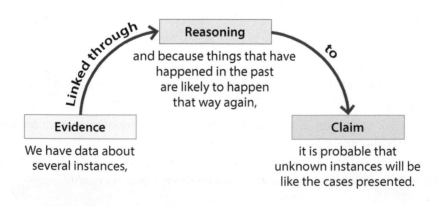

Base Inferences on Sufficient and Representative Cases **Inductive reasoning** consists of collecting enough instances to establish a pattern. Remember the logical tests in Chapter **15**. A typical line of inductive thought can be portrayed as follows:

Orchid$_1$ has no fragrance.

Orchid$_2$ has no fragrance.

Orchid$_3$ has no fragrance.

Orchid$_n$ has no fragrance.

Therefore, it is probable that all orchids have no fragrance.

The extent to which you can generalize from such observations is linked to the extent of your sampling. If you smelled only the orchids in one corner of one hothouse, you would be less able to make a general conclusion than if you had smelled orchids in different hothouses throughout the country.

By far the greatest problem in this kind of reasoning is determining how many cases to consider before drawing a conclusion. Obviously, you want to test several cases before drawing a conclusion, but how many are enough? If you use five brand-name USB flash drives and they all have problems, is that enough to say that all brand-name flash drives are defective? If a researcher finds that 132 out of 150 students surveyed encountered no problems registering for classes, is that enough to justify a conclusion about that group? At best, you can say, "It is likely that many brand-name USB flash drives are defective," and "Students will probably not encounter problems registering for classes." The conclusions drawn from induction are always *probable* rather than *absolute*. The only way you could say that *all* brand-name USB flash drives are defective would be to test every one. This would be counting, not reasoning. Reasoning, as you will recall, is defined as drawing conclusions about the unknown.

Recognize the Degree of Probability of Your Claim An inductive conclusion can fall anywhere along this continuum:

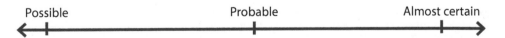

Possible   Probable   Almost certain

The degree of certainty depends on the methods used in making our observations and on the number of observations made. A conclusion like "The last two times I've gone to that restaurant, the service has been lousy—I'll bet they've changed management" would fall far to the left. Two observations is a very small number, and there are many other viable explanations for the poor service. At the other end of the continuum is a statement like "The new drug therapy cures patients of malaria." This conclusion would need to be based on a great many observations collected systematically.

CHECKLIST ~ Adequacy of Inductive Reasoning

The following questions may be helpful in considering the adequacy of your inductive reasoning:

- How many cases were examined?
- Were the cases selected fairly?
- Were the selected cases representative of the whole?
- Can contrary instances or outcomes be accounted for?
- Is the probability of the claim fair and reasonable?

How strong must this **probability** be before you can consider the conclusion of an inductive argument to be valid? A 51 percent probability, 75 percent, or 99 percent? Unlike deductive reasoning, for which there are agreed-upon tests of validity, the test of an induction varies in every case. There is no mathematical or logical answer to the question. The issue of how much is enough is more a psychological question of individual perception. Each of us would have a different threshold for how much we might be willing to bet on a coin flip. For many those odds are good enough for a dollar bet, but few would bet their life on it.

Demonstrate Your Cost–Reward Analysis   When induction is used in a public speech, the speaker's task is to convince the audience members that the conclusion arrived at is probable enough to warrant their acceptance. The so-called inductive "leap" occurs when you lead the listeners to a certain point with your data and then ask them to jump across an imaginary divide to your conclusion. Here, as in the preceding examples, the level of how much is enough is contingent on the risks and benefits perceived.

Suppose you know of a new housing rehabilitation program that has been found quite effective in pilot studies in three different communities. In urging its adoption in your city, your line of reasoning might go like this:

The program worked in Community A.

The program worked in Community B.

The program worked in Community C.

Therefore, it is probable that the program is effective and will work here.

Because these other cases were not studied systematically (e.g., with control groups, random sampling, and follow-up studies) and because there are only three cases in your sample, you cannot state your conclusion at a high level of probability.

You must recognize that the housing rehabilitation program could fail in your community. Imagine that it was possible to assign specific levels of probability and that both proponents and skeptics of the program agreed that there was about a 75 percent chance of its success. A member of your audience might well ask, "Why should we spend $650,000 for just a three-out-of-four chance we might help to stabilize our housing market?" You cannot change the 75 percent odds, but you can influence your audience's assessment of the costs and rewards. Tell them how the program, if it works, will benefit the whole community: It will increase property values, decrease crime, provide stable homes for community members, and perhaps even improve educational opportunities for families in those homes. Also minimize the costs: "I know $650,000 sounds like a lot, but it's only 85 cents per citizen." When the listeners reassess the costs and rewards, and see them as you do, the 75 percent odds may look more attractive.

Consider another example, in which the conclusion's probability is very high:

Nuclear power plant A has had no accidents.

Nuclear power plant B has had no accidents.

Nuclear power plant C has had no accidents.

Nuclear power plant *n* has had no accidents.

Therefore, it is probable that nuclear power plants are safe.

Suppose the conclusion could be granted a 95 percent level of probability. Even so, you or someone else might not feel the evidence is sufficient to make the inductive leap that nuclear power plants really are safe. In explaining your concerns to the audience, you would minimize the rewards of nuclear plants—perhaps by pointing out that most of the energy we would get can be obtained through other sources—and maximize the risks by describing just how awful a nuclear accident would be. Your argument is: "I'm not willing to subject my family to even a 5-out-of-100 chance of this sort of destruction just to have cheap electricity."

We see from these examples that no inductive argument is innately logical or illogical. In the case of the drug program, a low probability met the test of how much is enough for the speaker. In the case of the nuclear power plant, even 95 percent was not enough. The difference lies in the perception of risk and reward. The validity is negotiated between you and your audience.

16-2b Deductive Reasoning

Unlike *induction*, in which the emphasis is on collecting observable data, **deduction** consists of making verbal statements, or premises, according to formal rules. Deduction, then, involves not bringing new data into play, but rather rearranging

MindTap   SPEAKER'S WORKSHOP 16.2

1. Think of the audience for your next speech. What costs or risks would you need to minimize and what benefits would you need to maximize to establish a high probability of acceptance for these conclusions?

    A. This new treatment for herpes should be marketed.

    B. Every school bus should be equipped with seat belts.

    C. We should hire only college graduates for our sales department.

    D. You should cut aspartame out of your diet.

2. Read or watch Kayla Strickland's speech, available in Part **7** or through the MindTap for *The Speaker's Handbook*. Analyze Kayla's use of specific instances in the second subpoint in the Need step regarding the costs associated with malaria. How does she attempt to establish the degree of probability of her claim that malaria is a wide-reaching, global problem?

what you already know. A common example is the Sherlock Holmes-type English murder mystery. In the essential finale of the murder mystery, the detective patiently explains to a roomful of suspects the meaning of the details known but not assimilated by the reader:

> *Everyone who had a motive appeared to have an alibi at the time of the murder. Because people cannot be in two places at once, I deduced that the time of the murder must have been earlier than we thought. Remember the maid who discovered the body in the bedroom, saying it was as cold as ice? But the bedroom was quite warm from the fire in the fireplace. A corpse is not as cold as ice unless it has been stored in a very cold place for hours and only later returned to the bedroom. And then there were the cobwebs almost imperceptible against the corpse's silver hair. What place in this manor is both cold and cobwebby? The wine cellar. Only Peters, the butler, had a key to the wine cellar!*

Having the clues is not enough; it takes a supersleuth to recognize how the clues uniquely fit together. Figure 16.3 depicts the process of deductive reasoning.

In our everyday lives, we have that "Aha!" experience when we suddenly discover the pattern underlying disparate facts. Just as you are falling asleep, you might sit up abruptly and realize the connection between events that you had been struggling with all day. This kind of reasoning is quite different from induction, which involves gathering data. In deduction, facts that are already known are put together in a way that reveals their implications.

FIGURE 16.3
Deductive reasoning finds the patterns in what you already know

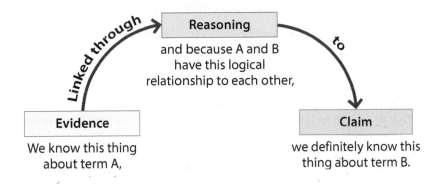

Major Premise—Minor Premise—Conclusion Because a deduction must adhere to certain rules in order to be valid, experts in deductive reasoning learn complex symbolic formulas by which they test arguments. For the purpose of this book, we need only touch on the basic concept of deduction: If we know certain things about how two terms (concepts, events, or characteristics) are related, we can discover other relationships that are logically entailed or implicated:

Term A is related in a known way to Term B.

We know certain things about B.

Therefore, we can draw certain conclusions about Term A.

To use deductive reasoning in a speech, you need to transform this into a series of steps:

Step 1: Establish that a relationship exists between two terms.

Step 2: Establish the actual condition or status of one of the terms.

Step 3: Show how a conclusion about the other term necessarily follows.

Step 1 in deduction—establishing the **major premise** or broad statement of relationship—takes many forms. It always involves an absolute relationship between two terms. Here are examples of four common relationships.

One term may be an intrinsic characteristic of the other:

▶ All ducks have webbed feet.

▶ Conflict is inherent in the collective bargaining model.

One term may be a category that includes the other:

▶ All Volkswagens are motor vehicles.

▶ The food stamp program is part of the social welfare system.

One term may be inevitably linked to the other:

▶ If you heat water to 212 degrees at sea level, then it will boil.

▶ If corporate taxes are cut, then investment will increase.

The two terms may be the opposite of or exclude each other:

▶ Either that fabric is natural or it is synthetic.

▶ Unless we crack down on drunken drivers, fatalities will rise.

When you have established one of these basic major premises, you have set up a formula that will serve as the linking device at the top of your arc of reasoning. When you move to step 2, you establish something about one of the two terms—in what logicians call the **minor premise**. A piece of evidence like "Daffy is a duck" might mean many things, or nothing, in some lines of argument. But in the context of the first major premise illustrated earlier, it is the minor premise, and the resulting, relevant implication is that Daffy has webbed feet.

Feed in the data you have, follow the rules of deductive logic, and certain **conclusions** are inevitably entailed:

▶ This blouse is made of a synthetic fiber, *so it is not made of a natural fiber.*

▶ We did not crack down on drunken drivers, *so traffic fatalities must have increased.*

The beauty of deduction lies in its certainty. If your listeners accept the premises, they *must* accept the conclusion.

This seems so attractive that you might wonder why a speaker would use any other method. Why waste energy on the probable conclusions of induction? Why not stick with deduction, in which the rules are clear and the conclusions have to be accepted? The problem with deduction is that for its conclusion to be absolute, its premises must be absolute. Unfortunately, most absolute statements of relationships are either untrue or trivial. Who really cares if ducks have webbed feet or really needs to reason about it? The things we do have to reason about, and tend to give speeches about, are complex issues of public policy, human behavior, and social values. In these domains, we rarely find acceptable statements that "*all X* is *Y*," or "if *X*, then *Y always* follows," or "either *X* or *Y* and *no other alternative.*" The requirement of having an all-or-nothing beginning premise is so restrictive that true, formal deductive reasoning is rather rare. In speaking, it is acceptable to use a slightly less rigorous form of deduction.

Probable Premises Lead to Probable Conclusions
In the if–then statement about tax cuts, does a reduction on corporate taxes absolutely *have* to result in increased investment? A more honest syllogism would be:

> It is highly probable that a cut in corporate taxes will increase investment.
>
> Congress is almost certain to cut taxes.
>
> Therefore, it is highly probable that investment will increase.

But now we have lost the tidy inevitability of deduction. The rules of logic no longer force our listeners to accept our conclusion. We are back to the same kinds of problems we face in induction—persuading the audience to weigh the probabilities as we do. Our appeal to them would be:

If you grant this premise as probable,

and

if you grant this other premise as probable,

then it is logical to grant this conclusion as probable.

When you look at deduction this way, you can take some liberties not available to the logician. You may build a deductively structured argument with premises that are not absolute, recognizing, of course, that the conclusions you derive will not be absolute, either. Each point needs to be supported sufficiently to persuade a member of the audience to say, "I'll grant that point; it's reasonable; it's probable." Thus, the degree of probability of any conclusion is a product of the degree of probability granted to each premise.

The form of a deductive argument is an elegant way to justify a conclusion, even when it has been qualified to be more realistic. It can provide an effective structure for part or all of a speech. When the conclusion you want your audience to reach can be arrived at through logical steps, seriously consider arranging your points in a deductive format.

Lay Out All Premises of a Deductive Argument One of the real advantages of structuring ideas deductively is that you must state the relationships among the concepts with which you are dealing. When you clearly state the major premise on which your argument rests, you call to your listeners' minds certain values, assumptions, or truisms. The audience can then apply these concepts when you move on to specific cases in developing your minor premise. In the following logical arguments, notice how the major premise serves in each case to direct the listeners' awareness to a statement that the speaker might otherwise have left implicit.

▶ It has always been the goal of our social welfare system to help recipients become self-sufficient.

▶ Certain current programs encourage dependency and discourage initiative.

▶ Therefore, these programs should be changed.

or

▶ A good friend is a person who helps you reach your potential.

▶ Several people in this organization have helped me strive toward my potential.

▶ Therefore, as I say good-bye, I feel as if I am leaving a number of good friends.

Sometimes, speakers have so internalized a point of view that they leave out parts of their argument that they consider obvious. When audiences and speaker

MindTap   SPEAKER'S WORKSHOP 16.3

1. What unstated assumption or absolute statement of relationship underlies each of these arguments?

    A. She must be doing a good job. She hasn't been fired.

    B. You should buy a condominium. It's cheaper than a house.

    C. Well, it's not a win for labor, so I guess management wins.

    D. I thought he had some self-respect, but now I learn he's on welfare.

2. Read the Commencement Address at Wake Forest University by Eboo Patel, available in Part **7** of this text. What type of reasoning is offered in the story about Louie Armstrong? Why do you suppose Eboo chooses to use stories as a way to offer evidence?

3. Here are some conclusions that could have been reached either inductively or deductively. Briefly lay out an inductive and a deductive argument that leads to each.

    A. Natural childbirth is best for parents and infants.

    B. More states should institute regulations protecting computer users from workplace conditions that can cause carpal tunnel syndrome and other repetitive strain injuries.

    C. The Academy Awards are rarely given to the best films.

4. Identify the basic reasoning pattern in a sample speech or two, available in Part **7** in *The Speaker's Handbook*. Are they inductive or deductive? Can you lay out the underlying argument in three or four sentences?

share common values, these assumptions may be acceptable. On controversial topics with diverse audiences, neglecting to lay out all parts of the argument is dangerous. In excellent speeches, speakers take the time to articulate and justify their premises. Consider the previous examples. The first point of each argument might have been omitted or tossed in as an aside rather than developed. By the same token, in saying, "We couldn't possibly pass this bill; it endangers free speech," you are assuming that your audience accepts your assumption that "anything that endangers the free speech is undesirable." If they do not accept those assumptions, your efforts to prove the bill's effects are wasted. If they do agree, you will not have lost much time by reiterating those points. Listeners will be more likely to remember your specifics if they have a logical framework for them.

Like the detective with the clues, your task is not merely to list the facts, but to demonstrate how they fit together and what they ultimately mean. Often, the conclusion of the speech is the place to weave together the threads of a deductive argument, as demonstrated here:

> So, I've shown that it is our goal to reach full employment and that the only available paths are through direct provision of public-sector jobs or through indirect stimulation of private-sector jobs. Because I went on to give you several reasons for rejecting the public-sector alternative, there is only one conclusion left. To create full employment, the private sector must be stimulated.

16-2c Causal Reasoning

Causal reasoning is the backbone of all speeches that deal with policy and problem solving. In most cases, if a person says, "I don't favor your policy (or program, or solution)," what that person is really saying is, "I disagree with you that X causes Y." This means you must carefully scrutinize the relationship between two events to satisfy yourself that it is causal. Then you must provide your listeners with information indicating how thoroughly you tested this relationship. Figure 16.4 depicts the causal reasoning process.

Of course, in a problem-solving or policy speech, there is rarely one lone cause. To assert that there is would be a gross oversimplification, jeopardizing the acceptance of your conclusions. Still, it helps to understand the rigorous tests you have to apply to a statement if you are to assert a pure causal relationship in it—that is, "one cause leads inevitably to one effect."

Test the Validity of Causal Relationships A causal relationship is stronger than mere correlation, coexistence, or coincidence. Two events may occur together or in sequence without one causing the other. For instance, morning sickness and weight gain often occur together, but neither causes the other; they are the result of a third condition, pregnancy. To be sure that the relationship is a causal one, apply these tests.

FIGURE 16.4
Causal reasoning links cause and effect

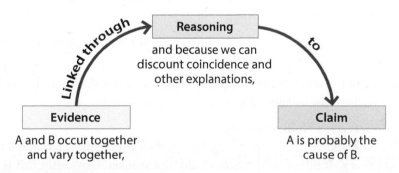

1. Do the Alleged Cause and Alleged Effect Occur Together?

To prove that a causal relationship exists, at least two formal comparisons must be made, as with a control group and an experimental group. It is not enough to show that the cause is present with the effect; you must also show that, in the absence of the alleged cause, the alleged effect does not appear:

> *If a rash appears every time you eat strawberries, and never appears when you haven't eaten strawberries, this is strong evidence that strawberries cause the rash.*

> *There are three groups of arthritis sufferers, matched in all-important characteristics such as age, sex, diet, and general health. Group A receives the drug Painaway, Group B receives a placebo, and Group C receives no treatment. Members of Group A experience dramatic relief, and there is no change in the condition of members of Group B and Group C. This supports the claim that Painaway causes a reduction in arthritis symptoms.*

To prove a causal relationship, you must show both concurrent presence and concurrent absence. Technically, all that is needed to *disprove* a suggested causal relationship is to point to a case in which the alleged cause was present without the alleged effect, or vice versa. So, if you found that your rash occurred occasionally when you had not eaten strawberries, or if you had once eaten strawberries and not gotten the rash, a pure causal relationship does not exist.

2. Do the Alleged Cause and the Alleged Effect Vary Together?

Another test of causation is to determine whether the magnitude of change in the cause matches that in the effect:

> If one bite of a strawberry gives you a small rash, and consuming many strawberries gives you a big rash, this is one more bit of evidence to suggest that strawberries cause your rash.

Don't Oversimplify Causal Relationships In the worlds of physics and chemistry, there are some clear, straightforward causal relationships:

> *An action results in an equal and opposite reaction.*

> *Adding silver nitrate solution ($AgNO_3$) to sodium chloride (NaCl) will cause silver chloride (AgCl) to precipitate.*

> *This type of relationship between cause (C) and effect (E) could be represented as* $C \rightarrow E$

However, in the areas of politics, psychology, medicine, economics, and the like, more complex patterns usually exist.

1. Some Effects Have Multiple Causes.

If smoking were the single cause of lung cancer, then every smoker would have lung cancer, and every victim of lung cancer would be a smoker. Obviously, this is not the case. Yet research does show smoking to be one causal factor contributing to lung cancer. The simple cause-and-effect tests outlined earlier cannot be the sole criteria for providing cases of multiple causation. If you speak of issues like poverty, crime, divorce, and economic recession as though they had a single direct cause, you will justifiably lose credibility with your audience.

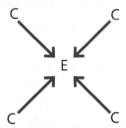

2. Some Causes Are Also Effects, and Some Effects Are Also Causes.

When we designate a cause of a certain event, we can look at the immediate cause or a more distant factor. A doctor might say that the cause of a particular death was a cerebral hemorrhage. What, though, was the cause of that? Perhaps a fractured skull, which was caused by going through a windshield, which was caused by the impact of a car with a tree, which was caused by the excessive drinking, which was preceded by worry over being unemployed, and so on:

$$C \rightarrow (E/C) \rightarrow (E/C) \rightarrow (E/C) \rightarrow E$$

In a speech, you need to discuss enough of these links to give a realistic picture and to demonstrate to your listeners that you understand the complexity of the process—without going so far back in the chain as to be absurd.

It is sometimes important to point out the cyclical nature of certain causal chains. For example, ignorance about a particular group may lead to prejudice, which in turn results in lack of contact with that group, which perpetuates ignorance. This sort of analysis is far more interesting than positing a single cause for all racial disharmony.

3. Some Effects Result from a Onetime Cause and Some from Ongoing Causes.

Effects that are labeled undesirable can be dealt with in two ways, either by treating the effect directly or by blocking the cause that produces the effect. To decide which strategy makes the most sense in a given context, you need to determine whether the cause is onetime or ongoing.

Picture a neighborhood with bare dirt for landscaping, broken windows, couches in the yards, and residents desperate for medical care. You are concerned about these symptoms and want to take some action. If you find that a tornado whipped through the area, you may push for emergency relief, intervention by the Army Corps of Engineers to clear wreckage, and loans to rebuild. However, if you learn that the area is economically depressed and that poverty is chronic, you would likely choose a different

1. Explain two ways you might disprove each of the following causal assertions, using principles discussed in this section:

   A. Supreme Court rulings on arrest procedures have allowed criminals to go free.

   B. Unfair laws have caused discrimination against women.

   C. Strokes are caused by stress.

   D. Lack of educational expenditure has produced an inferior generation of college students.

2. Explain how each of the causal statements in exercise 1 might reflect one or more of the kinds of oversimplification referred to in this section.

3. Read "Tough Truths about Plastic Pollution," by Dianna Cohen, available in Part **7**. What support does she offer for her claims? How does the speech purpose and audience affect requirements for reasoning and support?

solution—perhaps launching an educational campaign and the establishment of health clinics leading to the ability to attract businesses to the community. Assigning a solution without appropriate understanding of the causes could lead to wasteful effort and expense.

Sometimes, problems are particularly complex, making simple one-step solutions impractical. For complex issues, lay out a two-phase solution with short-range steps to deal with the symptoms supported by a long-range plan to address the underlying causes.

Explain Your Causal Claims Fully and Fairly Pure, simple causal arguments like those scientific truths cited earlier deal with absolute relationships. In this sense, they are like deductive arguments. Like deductive major premises, however, valid but nontrivial examples of absolute relationships are rare. More common are lines of reasoning that lead to probable causal claims. But probable to what degree? To the degree that your examples are sufficient and representative, and that conflicting examples are minimized or explained. With this sort of causal argument, do not overstate your claim. Say, "This is a major cause" and not "This is *the* cause." Say, "There is strong evidence of a causal link between ..." and so on.

The establishment of a probable causal claim requires the same sort of risk–benefit analysis that inductive reasoning requires. If it is highly likely that eating red meat causes cardiovascular disease, what are the risks of ignoring this link? What are the benefits of accepting it?

Also, whenever possible, explain the way the causal connection operates. Otherwise, even if you demonstrate perfect correlation between two factors, you may succeed in establishing only that one is a sign, signal, or symptom of the other. Causal reasoning tells more than *what* is connected; it tells *why* things are connected. Whenever applicable in your speech, include a brief explanation of how the cause leads to the effect. Cite expert testimony if possible or useful. The more explicit your analysis of causation, the less likely your audience is to dismiss your causal claim as mere coincidence.

16-2d Reasoning by Analogy

When we reason by analogy, we compare two things that can be placed in the same category. In the process, we assume that, because we know that A and B have a number of characteristics in common, those things we do not know about B are highly likely to resemble their counterparts that we do know about in A. Figure 16.5 depicts the process of **reasoning by analogy**.

Reasoning by analogy is a natural and powerful way to make links. People intuitively look to similar examples when they want to understand something. Suppose the president's foreign policy advisors are trying to decide whether to intervene in a foreign country's internal struggles, or a judge is pondering whether to admit expert testimony on battered wife syndrome, or you are wondering whether to take the freeway or back streets to work. In all these cases, from the most cosmic policy issues to the most mundane everyday decisions, people ask themselves "What is this like that I already know about?"

Like the other forms of reasoning we have explored, analogies can be used to support contradictory claims. For instance, some lawyer might tell a judge that the case at hand is like one in which certain evidence was admitted. Another lawyer might insist that it is more like another case in which expert testimony of a similar type was excluded. One member of your carpool will claim that this day is like other Mondays,

FIGURE 16.5
Analogy compares two things in the same category

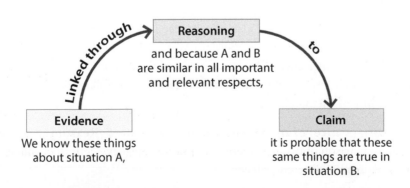

when traffic is light on the freeway. Another will point out that on other rainy days like this day there are often accidents that slow things down on the freeway. These are all reasoning by analogy. Although reasoning by analogy is so innate—or *because* it is— you need to approach it with a careful eye on the analogies you use. Several cautions are worth considering when reasoning by analogy.

Be Sure the Two Cases Are Similar   Here is the sort of unconscious analogy we all use every day. Does it pass the test?

> *Marijuana has been legalized in Colorado with positive revenue results for that state. Therefore, legalizing marijuana in your state will have similar revenue results.*

Perhaps there are similarities between Colorado and Ohio (although any state could work): Both are U.S. states, both are designed to generate operating revenue for public services, and both benefit from predictable revenue streams. It is also easy to point out differences: Colorado may have lower population, lower unemployment, and more educated residents than Ohio. No cases are identical, and simply pointing out differences does not discredit an analogy automatically. Do they differ in relevant and important ways? Historically, differences exist between people living in the Midwest, eastern, southern, or western states. Certainly all are interested in a predictable revenue stream, but the means by which they are willing to achieve stability may vary greatly. These stated differences may be important enough to lead a person to reject the conclusion that legalizing marijuana is a good way for their state to generate revenue.

When comparing cases from different geopolitical areas, be especially aware of cultural differences. The identical institutional changes might be adopted in Scandinavia, Syria, or Sri Lanka with radically different effects. Even within a national culture, microcultural differences exist. A university faculty will not respond to management practices the same way a business organization does. The innocent belief that "people are people" must be modified by our increasing awareness of the role played by gender, social class, race, sexual orientation, and numerous other factors in influencing people and shaping their experiences, even when living under externally similar conditions.

Reasoning by analogy should also be tempered by an awareness of the impact of history. Comparisons between the Vietnam War and the Iraq War have often been made, yet the very experience of Vietnam irreversibly altered U.S. perceptions of foreign policy, military strategy, and media coverage. Any war following Vietnam will be different *because* of Vietnam.

Don't Confuse Literal and Figurative Analogies   Reasoning by analogy requires a comparison of two members of the same category. *Figurative analogy* compares the members of different categories:

▶ Convincing my boss, Fred, to adopt a new procedure takes as much persistence, luck, and timing as starting my 1985 Mustang on a January morning.

▶ Fighting a war with Mexican drug lords would be like tap-dancing on quicksand.

These analogies may have stylistic impact, but they cannot support a conclusion.

The examples about school uniforms and the Vietnam War versus the Iraq War, however flawed in their logic, did make comparisons within the same categories—two state tax systems or two wars. The two examples just mentioned compare a human relationship with a human–machine relationship, and a war with a physical impossibility.

16-3 Common Reasoning Fallacies

Speakers commit **fallacies** when they use reasoning improperly, drawing unjustified conclusions. Some people do this knowingly, with dishonest intent. Others commit fallacies due to a lack of practice or skill in doing their own thinking. The good public speaker wants to avoid the appearance of either. Once you have built your speech around sound, logical arguments, go through it to detect any constructions that even hint of sloppy thinking. One glaring fallacy in your speech will diminish the potential of your other conclusions. It is not necessary to learn all the fallacies—more than 100 have been categorized—but you should be familiar with the most common ones.

A bonus of learning about these fallacies is that you can improve your critical listening skills. Not only will you be able to construct a logically sound speech, but you also will be able to detect thoughtless, sloppy, or false lines of reasoning.

1. Ad Hominem Fallacy

The **ad hominem fallacy** attacks a person based on some attribute or circumstance rather than addressing their ideas. This strategy is widely used and can be recognized by attempts to redirect the discussion away from the issues toward some personal frailty of those involved. For instance,

Of course she would say that, what would we expect from an ignorant piece of trailer trash anyway?

2. Fallacy of the Absurd Extreme (Reductio Ad Absurdum)

The **fallacy of the absurd extreme** makes a potentially sound argument appear groundless by extending it to a point at which it can be ridiculed. Often, this extension goes beyond reasonable interpretation of the original point. In challenging current methods of criminal sentencing, a speaker might say:

The average criminal is condemned to a bleak cell while top government wrongdoers lounge around in "country club" facilities. The logic is that the latter have already

been punished considerably by loss of face, prestige, and professional standing. This seems to say that punishments should be harsher on those who have the least to lose. By this reasoning, the senator who commits murder might get off with a citation and public embarrassment, while an unemployed deadbeat dad who shoplifts should be put on bread and water, with regular sessions in solitary confinement.

This kind of fallacy relies on the ridiculousness of the image it creates. Disarmed by a ludicrous example, listeners lose sight of the real issue.

3. Slippery Slope Fallacy

The **slippery slope fallacy** consists of making the false assumption that taking the first step in any direction will inevitably lead to going to dangerous lengths in that direction. The image is of someone sliding down a slope without being able to stop.

▶ If we let the government ban the sale and possession of assault rifles, banning all firearms is next.

▶ If we let the government abandon support of the arts, artistic freedom will die.

4. Circular Reasoning

Circular reasoning assumes as one of its premises the very conclusion it sets out to establish. Most of us know the hopeless feeling of trying to deal logically with such dead-end arguments as "you can't get a job in a field without experience in the field." Often, circular reasoning results from granting absolute authority to some source, and thus being blinded to the fact that others might not attribute similar authority to it, as in this example:

▶ I know that God exists. It says so repeatedly in the Bible. And everything in the Bible is true because it's the word of God.

Other instances of circular reasoning come out of definitional word games:

▶ No sane person would consider suicide, because it's insane to want to take your own life.

5. Semantic Fallacy

Semantic fallacies occur when a word's connotative meanings are misused, leading to faulty reasoning. Subtle and dangerous shifts in definition can occur in various critical parts of an argument, for instance:

The free enterprise system, which we all cherish, could not exist without competition. This bill to protect small businesses threatens our whole economic structure. There can be no true competition when one group is given special protection.

In the underlying value premise, the word *competition* is used in the general sense of a market mechanism. In claiming that the bill endangers competition, the speaker uses the term in a much narrower sense, as in "a specific contest between individuals." The semantic fallacy is especially difficult to identify and frustrating to respond to because the form of the argument appears to be valid. The problem arises from the slight change in meaning when a term is used in different contexts.

6. False Dichotomy

A **false dichotomy** is reasoning based on an *either/or* statement when the two alternatives are not really mutually exclusive or when other alternatives exist. Many speeches set up artificial choices:

> *Would you rather have a football program or a band at our school?*

This can be a false dichotomy. Even in tough economic times, most schools would allocate resources so that both can be maintained if only minimally.

Here's another example:

> *Either we stand up to naked aggression, or we lose the confidence of our allies.*

This basic premise so oversimplifies a complex issue that no conclusions can be drawn from it. Do not set up a deductive argument with a false dichotomy as its major premise.

7. Affirming the Consequent (Denying the Antecedent)

Affirming the consequent or **denying the antecedent**, occurs when a speaker assumes that, because *Y* necessarily follows *X*, the reverse is also true: that *X* necessarily follows *Y*. Political candidates so fear this kind of faulty reasoning by voters that they often publicly repudiate the endorsement of extreme groups and their supporters. They cannot count on the electorate to recognize the difference between a group endorsing a candidate and a candidate endorsing a group. Guilt by association is the most common manifestation of this fallacy.

For example:

> *Barack Obama attended the church where Reverend Jeremiah Wright is pastor. Reverend Wright supported Barack Obama. Therefore, Obama supports what Reverend Wright says as pastor.*

This is a fallacious conclusion because there is nothing in Reverend Wright's support of Barack Obama that requires Obama to fully agree with Reverend Wright. It is entirely possible that Obama has chosen to attend this church for reasons unrelated to Reverend Wright.

8. Hasty Generalization

A **hasty generalization** entails making a premature inductive "leap" based on insufficient evidence. Assumptions should be based on representative information. Making generalizations based on small samples can lead to this fallacy in reasoning. Consider the following:

> *I saw a person smoking who ran a red light this morning. Smokers are out to kill us.*

Although time may not allow you, as a speaker, to include all the data supporting your conclusions, it is especially important to have the supporting data at your fingertips so that you can respond should any accusations of hasty generalization be raised.

9. Post Hoc Fallacy

The Latin label for this fallacy—*post hoc, ergo propter hoc*—translates as "after the event, therefore because of the event." Remember just because something happens after an event doesn't mean that event caused it. To avoid this fallacy, never assume that because something happened closely after another event that the first caused the second. Test every causal hypothesis against the criteria discussed earlier in the section on causal reasoning.

16-4 Connect Evidence to Your Claim

It is not enough to have a speech that is well reasoned and free of fallacies. The reasoning process must be made clear to listeners. When speakers present only a cluster of evidence or a cluster of reasons for a claim, they are acting as if communication occurs through the simple transmission of messages. The perspective taken in this book is that communication consists of *making meaning together*. Therefore, as a speaker, you need to show listeners what makes your evidence meaningful to you.

MindTap®   SPEAKER'S WORKSHOP 16.5

For more on effective arguments and how to avoid logical fallacies, go to the MindTap for *The Speaker's Handbook* and click on **Additional Resources**.

MindTap®   Go to the MindTap for *The Speaker's Handbook* for prompts to help you ensure that your speech clearly indicates the connections between your reasoning, evidence, and claim.

16-4a Organize Points to Show Logical Relationships

Controversial claims can be found at all levels of a speech. How overall patterns of reasoning come into play is determined by how you lay out the speech. Sometimes, the thesis statement is supported by a line of reasoning, and each main point is part of the argument. For example:

Thesis statement: Prayer should not be allowed in schools because it violates the doctrine of separation of church and state, which is a central tenet of U.S. society that must be preserved.

I. The doctrine of separation of church and state is a central tenet of U.S. society that must be preserved.
   A. Why we have this doctrine
   B. Why it must be preserved

II. Prayer in the schools violates the doctrine of separation of church and state. (Develop through testimony and examples.)

Therefore: In conclusion (restate thesis).

In other cases, the thesis statement might be an "umbrella claim" that is supported by several separate and somewhat independent claims:

Thesis statement: Preschool programs such as Head Start are economically, socially, and morally justified.

The economic, social, and moral claims are separate main points where most of the reasoning of the speech will be found.

In still other cases, reasoning is necessary at specific subpoint levels in the speech to justify important claims.

There is no one way to display your lines of reasoning in a speech outline, but it is very important that you phrase points to show the connections. Do not simply group "reasons." Show reasoning.

Wrong:

I. Having a longer school day does not improve learning.
   A. They tried it at Riverdale High School, and test scores were unchanged.
   B. They tried it at Glenbrook High School, and test scores actually went down.
   C. At Creekside High School, test scores have gone up even though their school day has not been lengthened.
   D. Braeburn High School shortened their school day, and test scores did not change.

Better:

I. Having a longer school day does not improve learning.
   A. In cases in which the school day was lengthened, test scores did not improve.
      1. Unchanged at Riverdale High
      2. Went down at Glenbrook
   B. In cases in which the school day was not lengthened, test scores were not lower.
      1. Improved at Creekside
      2. No change with shorter day at Braeburn

Summary transitional statement: If there were a causal relationship between the length of the school day and learning as measured by test scores, we would logically expect that scores would be higher where the school day is longer and lower where the school day is shorter. I have just demonstrated that this is not the case. Sometimes, the opposite is true. So, you can see why I conclude that having a longer school day does not improve learning.

Remember the difference between points and support for the points. (See Chapter 11 and the introduction to Chapter 15.) Do not use sources in place of reasoning. In the first example that follows, a speaker attempts to support a causal claim by saying that experts have agreed with the claim. But the listeners do not know why these people came to the conclusion they did. In the second example, the reasoning behind the causal claim is explained, with experts used to back up specific points.

> ***Wrong:***
> I. The use of sexist language perpetuates discrimination against women.
>   A. Dr. Deborah Stone says sexist language causes problems.
>   B. Professor Lydia Sorenson says sexist language is the root of many social problems.
>   C. Linguist Chris Nupriya states that language affects behavior.
>
> ***Better:***
> I. The use of sexist language perpetuates discrimination against women.
>   A. Language shapes social perception.
>   (Cite experts and studies.)
>   B. Speech that leaves women out can lead to people overlooking them.
>   Cite experts and studies.)
>   C. If people subconsciously exclude women from certain roles, they discriminate against women.
>   (Cite experts and studies.)

16-4b Select Language That Shows Logical Relationships

In addition to setting up a speech structure that highlights your reasoning, you should give thought for selecting language that illuminates the logical linkages between your ideas. Never merely jump from one point to the next. Practice adding phrases that are specific cues to the kind of reasoning you are using as suggested in Table 16.1.

As is stated in Chapter 12, connective phrases are more important in speaking than in writing because listeners cannot look back at previous points. These cueing phrases play a crucial role in developing an oral argument. In an outline, claims are stated before their supporting reasons and evidence. This is an organizational artifact

TABLE 16.1
Language for different kinds of reasoning

STRATEGY	PHRASES AND EXAMPLES
For inductive reasoning	
Show the strength of your examples.	▶ One case that supports my claim is …
	▶ Another example that adds to this pattern is …
	▶ These statistics illustrate a widespread …
	▶ These instances are just a sample of …
	▶ Across many levels of income, the same pattern holds true. For example, …
Acknowledge the probability of your data by using qualifiers.	▶ Many …
	▶ Most …
	▶ Virtually every study in the literature …
	▶ Evidence strongly indicates …
	▶ I can say with near certainty …
	▶ From these cases, I feel quite confident in concluding …
Demonstrate costs and rewards.	▶ I'm willing to bet my tax dollars that this program will work …
	▶ I think these are good/bad odds because …
	▶ This is a gamble we can't afford to take …
	▶ The risks, though they do exist, seem minimal compared to the rewards …
	▶ Is it worth it to you to … ?
For deductive reasoning	
State your premises.	▶ I base this on a core value of mine that …
	▶ Underlying my position is …
	▶ The argument for my claim rests on one basic assumption that I hope you will agree with. It is …
	▶ Either … or …
	▶ If … then …
	▶ Only when … can …
	▶ Anyone who …
	▶ To the extent that …, then to that extent …
Spell out your reasoning.	▶ Because I've shown you *X* and *Y*, …
	▶ Therefore, …
	▶ This entails …
	▶ From this it follows that …
	▶ What this means is that …
	▶ We have no choice but to conclude that …
	▶ Based on this, I reason that …
	▶ It seems logical to conclude that …

(continued)

STRATEGY	PHRASES AND EXAMPLES
For causal reasoning	
Show how the cause and effect are related in a predictable way.	▷ In state after state where *X* happened, *Y* followed.
	▷ This is no coincidence. When *X* occurs, then *Y* occurs.
	▷ For every unit of increase in *X*, there is a proportional increase in *Y*.
Qualify your causal claims.	
	▷ There may be many causes, but the one I have identified is a major causal factor.
	▷ It is highly probable that …
	▷ In the vast majority of cases, *X* causes *Y*.
	▷ At least in middle-class white families, where most of the research has been conducted, there seems to be a strong causal link between …
	▷ Except in small family-owned companies, employee morale is greatly enhanced by …
Explain the mechanism of the cause.	▷ The reason all these experts have concluded that *X* causes *Y* is that …
	▷ I've shown you all these cases in which …. Let me explain how that happens.
For reasoning by analogy	
Stress the points of similarity.	▷ In Ecuador, as in neighboring Colombia and Peru, …
	▷ In three similar cities, the same pattern recurred.
	▷ For eight of the ten universities in our conference, adding women's sports to the athletic program has …
	▷ Likewise, …
	▷ Similarly, …
	▷ In a parallel case, …
Explain points of difference that your listeners may be concerned about.	▷ Although that case was tried in district court, the principle still applies here because …
	▷ Despite differences in size, our company can learn from this story because …
	▷ I realize that some of these instances happened a long time ago, but …
Spell out the link.	▷ If it worked in New Jersey and Idaho and Georgia, it will work in the rest of the country.
	▷ The analogy holds true. We can apply these solutions to our problems.
	▷ The groups who tried such proposals were disappointed. Let's learn from their mistakes.
	▷ Let's not wait too long to plan for earthquake safety. We put off dealing with flood control, and the results have been tragic.

and should not obscure the fact that claims are reached only at the end of a line of reasoning. However, for purposes of signposting and keeping your audience informed about the direction you are taking, it is generally a good idea to first state the claim and then explain the reasons for it. Listeners may become lost as the steps of an argument unfold, though. By the time you reach the end of your reasoning, they may forget what claim you were trying to support. Therefore, it is also generally a good idea to restate the claim after you have presented the argument.

In the following example, the speaker's thesis is the claim that marijuana should not be legalized. Each main point is a separate claim supported by a different form of reasoning. Observe how at the end of each main point the speaker summarizes her reasoning to show how it led to her claim, which she then restates. These brief statements can help audience members understand the logical relationship between evidence offered.

I. People are dangerous when they are under the influence of marijuana. (examples of accidents that were caused by people who were under the influence of marijuana)

Summary of Main Point I: These five tragic stories about innocent people who were killed by someone who was under the influence of marijuana provide us with one reason marijuana should remain illegal: People are dangerous when they use marijuana.

II. Marijuana is a highly addictive drug like cigarettes and alcohol. (testimony from doctors and other experts)

Summary of Main Point II: We all know how easy it is for some people to become addicted to nicotine and alcohol, and the problems that can result. Marijuana is very similar. It, too, can be addictive.

III. Smoking marijuana often causes people to use "harder" drugs. (statistics and testimony from drug users and doctors)

Summary of Main Point III: Therefore, even though many marijuana users do not go on to use harder drugs, many do. These experts claim that contact with criminals and experiences with "getting high" serve as significant causal factors in predicting subsequent usage of harder drugs.

IV. Marijuana use reduces intelligence.

A. Reduced number of brain cells lower intelligence.

B. Marijuana kills brain cells.

Summary of Main Point IV: Because anything that kills brain cells reduces intelligence, and because marijuana has been shown to kill brain cells, you can see that it follows logically that marijuana reduces intelligence.

Conclusion: (restatement of thesis, showing how the points are linked to it) I have shown that marijuana use puts innocent people in danger, is addictive, leads to use of hard drugs, and reduces intelligence. It seems logical that we should not legalize any practice that has these serious consequences.

MindTap   SPEAKER'S WORKSHOP 16.6

1. Identify the fallacy or fallacies in each statement:

    A. I'm surprised you health food nuts eat granola packaged in cellophane bags. Aren't you afraid the synthetic chemicals will poison the contents?

    B. Anyone who drives a foreign car doesn't care about this country anyway.

    C. It always rains on Easter. I remember it has for the last three years.

    D. Well, either you support your country, or you are critical of the government. Which is it?

    E. The jury system should be abolished. Last year a jury awarded $3 million to a woman who didn't like the nose job she got. The next month the doctor committed suicide.

2. In the marijuana outline at the end of the chapter, what kind of reasoning is being used in each of the four main points? Do you see any potential fallacies in the reasoning of the speech?

Summary

The key to effective reasoning is offering evidence linked through reasons to support claims. Sound reasoning is essential to effective speech making. Remember these key ideas:

16-1 Explain the purpose of claims, data, and warrants.

▶ Claims are statements that need to be substantiated.

▶ Data are the evidence offered to substantiate claims.

▶ Warrants are the link between a claim and the data that allows the audience to connect to understand the speaker's reasoning.

16-2 Recognize four main types of logical reasoning.

▶ Inductive reasoning draws inferences from observations; what has happened in the past will probably happen again.

▶ Deductive reasoning follows formal rules to lead to a logical conclusion based on the relationship between a major and a minor premise.

▶ Causal reasoning relies on assumptions about the relationship between two events.

▶ Speakers must be cautious to test causal relationships, avoid oversimplification, and explain causes fully and fairly.

▶ Reasoning by analogy relies on comparing a current situation to similar situations in order to decide what course of action might be best. It is imperative that cases being compared be similar in relevant ways and come from similar categories.

▶ Many speeches use these reasoning patterns in combination.

16-3 Identify several common reasoning fallacies.

▶ Common reasoning fallacies should be avoided as they lead to unjustified conclusions and can negatively affect your credibility.

▶ Possible fallacies include ad hominem attacks, fallacy of the absurd, slippery slope argument, circular reasoning, semantic fallacy, the false dichotomy, affirming the consequent, hasty generalization, and the post hoc fallacy.

16-4 Connect credible evidence to claims.

▶ By learning to link evidence to a claim through reasoning, a speaker can help *make meaning together* with an audience.

▶ Linking can be accomplished through speech organization and language choices that show logical relationships.

Critical Thinking Questions

▶ What is needed for inductive reasoning to be considered valid?

▶ What makes "absolute" deductive reasoning difficult to use?

▶ How can deductive reasoning still be effectively used?

▶ What is required to successfully use reasoning by analogy?

▶ Which reasoning fallacies described in this chapter have you committed?

Putting It into Practice

Locate a political or professional speech. Consider using a State of the Union speech, available through the American Presidency Project website. Click on **Additional Resources** to access this resource, available through the MindTap for *The Speaker's Handbook.*

1. Highlight the claims made in the speech.
2. Label the claims supported with inductive reasoning.
3. Label the claims supported with deductive reasoning.
4. Label the claims supported with causal or analogic reasoning.
5. What surprises you regarding the reasoning used in the speech you've chosen?

17

Language and Style

Choose language that makes your ideas clear and memorable.
Respect the power of language.

MindTap® Read, highlight, and take notes online.

We understand that language is the essence of thought, not a mere vessel for it. Language reflects culture and shapes our society. Our language, whether it is English or Cantonese, impacts our perceptions and shapes how we and others see and experience the world around us. Words are far more powerful than most speakers realize.

Style is a word of many meanings. A "stylish" person is one who conforms to the latest fads and fashions. A "stylized" drawing is one with the least amount of detail needed for comprehension. "Style" is the latest decorator colors or fashion, such as high-rise jeans or yoga pants, depending on the year. But in the context of speaking, **style** is simply your choice of words and the way you string them together. "Good" style involves choosing and combining those words so that your audience can easily understand and assimilate your content. Although both demand clear, appropriate, vivid, and varied language, good oral style differs from good writing style.

17-1 Oral and Written Styles Differ

Although oral style and written style use the same components, the styles are not interchangeable. Listeners expect to hear patterns that reflect the norms of conversation, if more refined. The natural-sounding speaker understands how oral style differs and talks *to* an audience rather than delivering a ten-page monologue. The ideal balance between the orality and literacy of a speech depends on the audience and the occasion. (See Chapter 1.) Sometimes, you will draw more heavily on the communicative resources of the writer. Other times, you can use the language and cadences of conversation.

There are some important ways in which oral style differs from written style. A written essay exists as a time machine: It allows a reader to return to a place where the eye had been a few seconds or many years before, or to jump ahead at will. Public speech is closely connected to time: Words are uttered and immediately start to fade. Although technology allows us to record speeches, these rebroadcasts often lose their contextual meaning when replayed. Listeners have but one contact with each word, and memory is the only instant replay. Because a listener cannot look back or ahead, oral style intentionally uses more repetition, signposting, internal summaries, and internal previews to ensure comprehension and make the organization clear. (See Chapter **12**.) Shorter sentences and words of fewer syllables are characteristic of oral style as well. Sentence fragments are more acceptable in speaking, as are contractions, perhaps even slang in some instances. Even in a formal setting, a speech will still be more informal than an essay on the same topic. Table 17.1 lists some key differences between oral and written style.

Appreciate the spoken word and take advantage of its unique features. The rhythm and meter of speech aid memory. The physical immediacy creates a bond between speakers and listeners. Attune your ear to the music of the spoken word, and use it to your advantage as you phrase your ideas. Drawing on the resources of performance—part of every effective speech to some degree—involves a feel for the power of the spoken word.

TABLE 17.1
Differences between written and oral styles

WRITTEN STYLE	ORAL STYLE
As mentioned above …	As I said a few minutes ago …
One cannot avoid individuals with this characteristic.	We can't avoid people like that.
Hypothetically, the government might …	Imagine this. Suppose Uncle Sam …
That is unlikely to result.	Well. Maybe.
Subjects were randomly assigned to either a control group or one of three experimental treatment groups. The four groups were pretested for initial attitudes toward the topic, and then posttested after each experimental group had received a persuasive message containing one of the three levels of fear appeals.	Here's how we did our research. First, we randomly assigned the subjects to four groups. Next, we gave all four groups a pretest to see what attitudes they held toward the topic. Then, three of the groups heard persuasive messages. One had a high level of fear appeals, one a medium level, and one a low level. Last, we posttested the attitudes of all four groups, including the control group that received no message.

MindTap® SPEAKER'S WORKSHOP 17.1

Notice how the rhythms and word choices vary among the speakers featured in Part **7** in *The Speaker's Handbook*. For example, speakers like Nathanael Dunlavy and Kayla Strickland, who prepared from manuscripts, display more features of written style than Eboo Patel, who uses more of a narrative style in his presentation.

17-2 Strive for Clear Language

We know that language does more than label objects, concepts, and actions. Words are acts. They do things, like promise or threaten; they can even serve to marry or excommunicate people. Because of this power, we sometimes make messages intentionally vague—perhaps to save face or build solidarity. For the most part, though, clear messages are paramount. "Bear come. We go. Now!" may not be subtle or poetic, but it certainly conveyed an important image from one early human to another. If you understand the priorities of communication, the first question you will ask yourself is, "Did my listeners understand what I was attempting to say? Did they *get the picture*?" When speaker and listeners end up with totally different mental images, something has gone awry. Perhaps the speaker has used words in nonstandard ways, or has chosen words so general that they evoke many different responses, or has buried the significant message in an avalanche of meaningless phrases.

To construct clear messages, you must do two things. First, know exactly what you want to communicate. Second, consider who the receivers of your message are and what the words are likely to mean to them.

17-2a Be Precise

To avoid fuzzy and ambiguous communication, you need to seek out the word that means precisely what you wish to convey and use it in a structure that illuminates, not obscures, its meaning. This might seem simple enough but we will soon discover even simple words carry multiple meanings.

Use the Proper Word Many words can denote the same object or idea; however, each may have a slightly different focus. Do not say a person was "indicted" for robbery if in fact you mean "arrested" (less serious) or "convicted" (more serious). Learn important distinctions and honor them.

Be careful around words that sound similar but have no similarity of meaning. *Allusion* means "a passing mention," and *illusion* means "a false perception."

TABLE 17.2
The simpler oral style

PRETENTIOUS	BETTER
I was appalled at the feculence that oozed from the typewriter of this so-called greatest living American novelist.	I was appalled at the filth that oozed from the typewriter of this so-called greatest living American novelist.
Then I butted heads with the misoneists of the planning commission.	Then I butted heads with the planning commission, which seems resistant to change.
Hear my supplication!	Hear my plea!

Some other troublesome near-homophones are *affect/effect, imminent/eminent, casual/causal,* and *aesthetic/ascetic.*

Remember that oral language is simpler than written language. Avoid using a precise word when it may seem pretentious. Table 17.2 offers some examples.

Don't Misuse Your Metaphors In attempting to convey your picture vividly, do not throw discordant images together. For example, there is a tendency in the United States to use the language of war. We have a war on poverty, a war on drugs, a war on terror, a war on women, and a war on Christmas.

Although the "war on" phrase may carry some intended clarity of purpose and effort, it can also create misunderstandings and result in a situation in which understanding and agreement are obscured. Does approaching poverty or terror from a war perspective mean that we will attack the root causes of the issue? Does it mean we will devote our last breath to defeating the enemy? After the war is over will the enemy be defeated? Who will sign the treaty? Can we be at war with terror or does war cause terror? The use of some expressions may cause more confusion than create clarity or agreement.

17-2b Use Specific and Concrete Language

The more specific and concrete your words, the less is left to your listeners' imaginations. When a speaker says, "NCAA academic standards for college athletes are ineffective," one listener may think, "Yes, they are racist"; another may think, "Yes, they are too low"; and still another may think, "Yes, they should be set by the faculty at each college." Yet all of these may be at odds with the intentions of the speaker, who perhaps feels that the standards are too high. Word choices should be both specific and concrete if shared understanding is desired. Table 17.3 gives examples of specific, concrete language.

Use abstract words such as *love, freedom, justice,* and *beauty cautiously as they* have no tangible, physical referent. These words have very different meanings among

TABLE 17.3
Specific, concrete language

DO NOT SAY	IF YOU REALLY MEAN	OR EVEN
We need to attract people.	We need to attract customers.	We need to attract grocery shoppers.
This will cause problems.	This will be expensive.	This will cost us $2,500 we don't have.
Our committee has studied it.	Our committee researched and discussed it.	Our committee read documents, heard testimony, and deliberated for several hours.

audience members. When you have no option but to use abstract words, supplement them with concrete examples:

> *What is more important to me than peace? Freedom is more important to me than peace.*
>
> *If I weren't able to travel where I wish, if I weren't able to worship as I please, meet to discuss grievances, read and write what I want, then I would struggle to regain all these things.*

17-2c Be Economical in Your Language

In the interest of clarity, express yourself with the fewest, most straightforward words that convey your meaning. Several reasons speakers might use long words, extra words, and convoluted constructions are listed in Table 17.4.

Most often, though, wordiness results from lack of discipline. Editing is not simple, and many people shy away from it. These speakers prefer a machine-gun style of word choice, repeating the message in hopes that one version of it will hit its mark. The clear speaker is more like the sharpshooter who takes careful aim and makes every word count.

TABLE 17.4
Motives for bloated language

	UNECONOMICAL	ECONOMICAL
To hide meaning, as with doublespeak	We sustained losses through friendly fire.	We shelled our own troops.
To avoid responsibility, as with the passive voice	It has been determined that your services are no longer needed.	I have decided to fire you.
To soften unpleasant messages, as with euphemism	Jesse has gone on to his reward.	Jesse died.

Wordy

Some individuals express their feeling that it is objectionable to eliminate and remove laws that serve to protect female members of the labor force. No one could really be in favor of doing away with protective laws for workers if the elimination of these laws would lead to the exploitation of the people no longer covered. The question I want to raise, however, is whether there is really any relevance to the sex of those workers who should be protected from exploitation, because wages and working conditions ought to be equitable for all employees.

Economical

There are objections to wiping out laws protecting women workers. No one would condone exploitation. But what does sex have to do with it? Working conditions and hours that are harmful to women are harmful to men; wages that are unfair for women are unfair for men.

—*Shirley Chisholm, Democratic congresswoman from New York*

17-3 Use Appropriate Language

There is no standard style to use in speaking. Different audiences and topics require different approaches. In the light of your audience analysis, you must make decisions about how formal to be, which part of your personality to project linguistically, and how deeply to descend into specialized language. Your age, status, and personality also determine what language is appropriate for you. Listeners have different expectations about the vocabulary and stylistic level of, say, a senior executive, a teenager, or a poet-in-residence.

Language is not fixed. New words and phrases are always coming into our language, and others fading out. Meanings change, as do standards of appropriateness.

17-3a Adapt Your Language to the Formality of the Occasion

Just as you dress differently for formal and casual events, so should you tailor vocabulary and usage to fit the situation. It would be a little startling if the organizer of a PTA bake sale finished an announcement in the following fashion:

This, then, is my plea to you: For the sake of our children, for the sake of our school, for the sake of our PTA, give of yourself for this culinary endeavor.

Equally inappropriate would be a CEO's annual address to stockholders that began:

Well, folks, things look kinda grim, but don't get bummed out, we'll be OK if we just hang in there.

In general, the more formal the occasion,

- ▶ the more serious the tone,
- ▶ the more subtle the humor,
- ▶ the more elaborate the sentences,
- ▶ the greater the number of figures of speech, and
- ▶ the greater the departure from everyday words.

More formal occasions include debates, presentations of policy statements, and ceremonial speeches. Less formal occasions include business conferences, roasts, rallies, and after-dinner speeches. In short, the more formal the occasion, the less you can rely on conversational language and the more you must incorporate language you'd use in writing or in a performance.

17-3b Use Jargon or Slang Carefully

Both jargon and slang can be used to create a bond with a specialized audience. At times, **jargon**—a special vocabulary used primarily within a particular group— can also allow you to get a point across more quickly. **Slang**—words and phrases that are nonstandard substitutions for more formal language—can enrich the texture of your language when used in appropriate situations. But there can be problems with using jargon and slang. You may confuse your audience with technical terms or sacrifice your credibility by using slang expressions that are offensive or out-of-date.

Notice how this excerpt from a talk on preventive maintenance is made understandable to a larger audience by substituting plain English in the second version:

Slang and Jargon Version

Let's look at how Jack could have benefited from a little PM. He burned a lot more number two than he needed to before he got around to running the rack on his Slambang. A maintenance schedule would have pointed out any problems long before the engine started smoking. Same thing with the front SQ drop-in. He wouldn't have cooked it if he had periodically checked and renewed the oil.

Plain-English Version

Let's look at how Jack could have benefited from a little preventive maintenance. He burned a lot more diesel fuel than he needed before he got around to adjusting the fuel injection system on his dump truck. A maintenance schedule would have pointed out any problems long before the engine started smoking. Same thing with the drive axle gears. They wouldn't have overheated and failed if he had periodically checked and renewed the oil.

17-3c Avoid Substandard Usage

Remember that a speaker perceived as competent by the audience will also most likely be considered credible. Although acceptable usage varies from place to place, many words and constructions are considered substandard. Speakers who consistently use *ain't* for *isn't* or who get sloppy with noun–verb agreement will find that many audience members will not seriously consider their points. Of course, you can sometimes break the rules for dramatic effect, like ending your opposition to a proposal with "Ain't *no* way!"

Where can you find a guide for what is standard? Expose yourself to models of literate and graceful usage by reading good magazines, blogs, and literature and by listening to respected public speakers and commentators on TV, radio, and podcasts. This exposure often leads to an intuitive recognition of correct usage. If you have never read or heard a respected professional say, "Alls I know is that is the nexus of the problem," then you would be wise not to say "Alls I know" yourself. Table 17.5 gives some more examples of standard versus substandard language. The "Guide to Common Pronunciation and Usage Errors" at the end of the book addresses errors in pronunciation and usage.

MindTap°   Go to the MindTap for *The Speaker's Handbook* and click on **Additional Resources**. This site's dictionary and thesaurus can help you use the right words, find more economical language, check your use of jargon and slang, and more.

17-3d Use Language That Is Respectful and Inclusive

Referring to a group or individuals by the name they prefer is a sign of respect. When changes are made, those changes are often symbolic of a new status or image. For those used to the word *Negro*, the transition to *black* in the late 1960s caused

TABLE 17.5
Substandard and standard English

SUBSTANDARD	STANDARD
Ten items or less.	Ten items or fewer.
… said to my friend and I …	… said to my friend and me …
I could care less!	I couldn't care less!
A large amount of people attended the rally.	A large number of people attended the rally.
Where'd you put it at?	Where'd you put it?
He hits the ball good.	He hits the ball well.
They couldn't hardly see what happened.	They could hardly see what happened.
I would have went there myself.	I would have gone there myself.

some problems, yet now the term seems natural. In fact, many people use it in interchangeably with the term *African American*. Today, women want to be called *women*, not *gals, girls*, or *ladies*. While it may not be possible to stay ahead of changing language use, it is expected that as the speaker you will make every effort to be sensitive to language choice. What you can do is make a reasonable effort to learn what your audience prefers. You can make a commitment to flexibility. Acknowledge that it is worth the temporary inconvenience of changing a language habit if that change is highly symbolic and important to the people involved.

A more complex stylistic issue involves the use of the generic *he–man–mankind*. Now that attention has been focused on these images, no speaker or writer can feign innocence of their impact. You may not mean to exclude females by such usage, but you should be aware that many listeners—male and female—now find "generic-he" terms grating. If you want to avoid distracting, and possibly offending, many listeners use alternatives, such as *he or she*, and replace *man* or *mankind* with *humanity, people*, or *humankind*. Sometimes, in a series of singular examples, you can provide gender balance by alternating pronouns, using *he* in one sentence and *she* in the next. If you are worried about distracting the dwindling segment of an audience offended by the current preferred usage, you can avoid the issue altogether by using plural and collective nouns instead of pronouns and by replacing words like *chairperson* with *presiding officer* and *mail person* with *letter carrier*.

MindTap® Some guidelines for the use of inclusive language can be found on the websites of various universities and publishers. Go to the MindTap for *The Speaker's Handbook* and click on **Additional Resources** for guidelines to inclusive language and gender inclusive language.

FOR YOUR BENEFIT
Not All Nonstandard Language Is Substandard

Sometimes, when people try to "standardize" the language others use, they are actually trying to change the content or to mold the identity of the speaker. Although it is important to speak in a way that allows you to be understood by your audience, women should not have to talk like men and people from New Orleans should not have to talk like they are from Connecticut. You will not feel comfortable or seem authentic if you abandon your own language style. Strive to speak so that everyone in your audience will understand you while maintaining your cultural, ethnic, and individual identity.

17-4 Use Vivid, Varied Language

You can keep your listeners attentive and interested by avoiding generic, bland, and predictable language. Your audience is much more likely to remember your message if it is filled with vivid imagery, descriptive language, and memorable phrasing. Anyone can infuse energy into a speech by utilizing the following verbal devices.

17-4a Imagery

When you describe something, put the senses and the imaginative capacities of your listeners to work. Notice the way Supreme Court Justice Ruth Bader Ginsburg vivid description of her colleague Justice Antonin Scalia:

> *I miss the challenges and the laughter he provoked, his pungent, eminently quotable opinions, so clearly stated that his words rarely slipped from the reader's grasp, the roses he brought me on my birthday, the chance to appear with him once more as supernumeraries at the opera. The Court is a paler place without him.*[1]

17-4b Stylistic Devices

Enliven your language with figures of speech and memorable arrangements of words and phrases.

Simile and Metaphor   You can add vigor to your speaking by using language that connects objects or ideas to vivid images. A **simile** makes a comparison between two things ordinarily dissimilar: "When she came in from shoveling the walk, her hands were like ice." No one would mistake a hand for a chunk of ice, but in this case they share the characteristic of extremely low temperature. A **metaphor** creates a figurative equation that implies two unlike things are the same: "Her hands were ice cubes" or "We stand in horror as our money disappears down the gluttonous maw of the federal government." Making the government a shark forms a more compelling image than "We stand in horror as the federal government operates with fiscal irresponsibility."

Personification   Objects or ideas can be brought to life by imbuing them with human qualities. We know that a room cannot really be "cheerful," that winds do not actually "whisper," and that the economy cannot possibly "limp." Nevertheless, all of these images are potent because they reflect human behavior. Here's another example:

> *And so, to all the other peoples and governments who are watching today, from the grandest capitals to the small village where my father was born, know that America is a **friend** of each nation, and every man, woman and child who seeks a future of peace and dignity.*[2]
>
> America isn't actually a person who can be a friend and yet the personification of a country is a compelling image.

Hyperbole To emphasize a point, you may deliberately overstate it in a way that is clearly fanciful and not meant to be taken literally:

▶ This paperwork will be the death of me.

▶ I thought about nothing else for the next three days.

▶ The governor has repeated this same promise to you a million times.

Repetitive Language or Structure By repeating keywords or phrases, you make your listeners feel that your points are snowballing to a certain conclusion. Use parallel structure to emphasize relationships.

Sometimes, a syntactic construction is repeated, such as the questions and brief answers in this paragraph:

> *How serious is the morale crisis? We have lost several key employees. What has caused the problem? Lack of clear upward and downward communication. How can we change things? By hiring an interpersonal and organizational communication trainer for a series of workshops.*

Notice that no phrases are repeated, but the question–answer format creates a sense of momentum.

The same phrase can begin consecutive paragraphs. For instance, a speaker can build a sense of urgency or dedication by repeating the phrase "We must act now to …" as each problem is presented.

Within a paragraph, you can achieve a similar effect by starting a series of sentences with the same words or by using a sentence as a connecting refrain.

> *You see, I was born to a teenage mother, who was born to a teenage mother. I understand. I know abandonment, and people being mean to you, and saying you're nothing and nobody, and can never be anything. I understand. Jesse Jackson is my third name. I'm adopted. When I had no name, my grandmother gave me her name; my name was Jesse Burns 'til I was twelve. So I wouldn't have a blank space, she gave me a name. To hold me over. I understand when nobody knows your name. I understand when you have no name. I understand.*

> —*Jesse Jackson, minister and civil rights activist*

Or you might end several sentences with the same words:

> *What remains? Treaties have gone. The honor of nations has gone. Liberty has gone.*

> —*David Lloyd George, former British statesman*

Additionally, for emphasis, you can repeat key words or phrases within a sentence:

> *But, in a larger sense, we can not dedicate—we can not consecrate—we can not hallow this ground.*

> —*Abraham Lincoln, sixteenth president of the United States*

Alliteration and Assonance Use of these devices involves saying the same sound in a sustained sequence. Whether it is with consonants (**alliteration**) or vowels (**assonance**), this repetition can make an idea more memorable, or at least charge it with a sense of poetry. Consider first alliteration as demonstrated here:

> *We can no longer afford to traffic in lies or fear or hate. It is the **p**oison that we must **p**urge from our **p**olitics, the wall that we must tear down before the hour grows too late. But if changing our hearts and our minds is the first critical step, we cannot stop there. It's not enough to bemoan the **p**light of the **p**oor in this country and remain unwilling to **p**ush our elected officials to **p**rovide the resources to fix our schools.*
>
> —*Barack Obama, address at Ebenezer Baptist Church*

Antithesis To contrast two ideas, you can use **antithesis**, which sometimes uses or implies word pairs like these:

▶ Not …, but …

▶ Not only …, but …

▶ Never …, unless …

Consider this example:

> *We live in a society that emphasizes military expenditures over education. We spend millions teaching young people how to kill and be killed, but we won't spend money teaching them how to live and make a living.*
>
> —*Harry Edwards, sociologist and civil rights activist*

In his acceptance of the Nobel Peace Prize, United Nations Secretary General Kofi Annan used antithesis, alliteration and assonance, and repetitive structure in one sentence:

> *Today's real borders are not between nations, but between powerful and powerless, free and fettered, privileged and humiliated.*

17-4c Use Fresh Language

The power of figurative language lies in the images stimulated in the listener's mind. After too many repetitions, the original psychological impact is lost. The phrases, "At the end of the day" and "Easy as pie," while once pleasantly descriptive, are now tired and overused.

Certain fad words attract a following. *Iconic, vanguard,* and *24/7* became overnight sensations and are used to the exclusion of many good (and fresher) synonyms. Rid your language of such phrasing. Take time to select original combinations of words and phrases that capture the image, mood, or thought you want to get across.

CHECKLIST ~ Verbal Devices to Make Your Language Vivid

- Images that appeal to the senses
- Similes and metaphors
- Personification
- Hyperbole
- Repetition of key words
- Parallel structure of key phrases
- Alliteration and assonance
- Antithesis
- Fresh language
- Varied sentence rhythms

17-4d Vary the Rhythm of Your Sentences

Although oral style is characterized by simpler, shorter phrases with fewer different words, you are not trying to breed boredom. The "sing-songiness" associated with children's rhymes can creep into a speech if you fail to pay attention to how you are stringing your sentences and phrases together. Use parallelisms and repetition but use them sparingly. Consider this plodding passage:

The association's annual convention should be user supported. The convention is attended by a core of regulars. The average association member doesn't benefit from the convention. These average members shouldn't have to bear more than their fair share.

The choppiness of this tedious passage results from the sameness of sentence length and structure. Recasting the sentences will create a more fluid and graceful paragraph:

The association's annual convention should be user supported. Who attends the convention? A core of regulars. The average association members, who don't benefit from the convention, shouldn't have to bear more than their fair share.

17-4e Use the Language Style of Your Listeners

Language is not solely the possession of speakers. Our words are shared with our listeners, drawn from a shared pool of possible statements. Speech consists not of messages sent, but of meanings jointly constructed within the context of a discourse community. Among the many possible ways to talk about a topic, the most effective way is the one that overlaps and resonates with your listeners. When you use phrases

1. Rewrite these statements in a style more appropriate to oral communication.

    A. After having removed the air filter, one can begin to investigate the origins of the problem.

    B. All clerical and administrative personnel will undergo semiannual performance appraisals designed to evaluate their competence and clarify objectives for the next appraisal period.

2. Rewrite the following sentences so that they are more concrete, economical, correct, and inclusive.

    A. It's a very unique sort of thing how Karen just makes everybody feel sort of good. She's real notorious as the most respected girl on our whole staff of salesmen.

    B. At this time I'd like to say that one point to consider is the fact that we were totally surrounded by smokers who caused us considerable irritation and distress and aggravation.

    C. Plus, I personally feel that we also face a serious crisis of psychological morale. We need to get off our duffs and sit down and talk about this epidemic that has us running on only three cylinders.

3. Read Eboo Patel's speech transcript available in Part **7**, and take special note of the rhythm of the sentences (and the use of repetition).

4. Use at least two different stylistic devices to enliven each of these phrases:

    A. A cold, rainy day

    B. An unworkable policy

    C. A delicate, intricate procedure

    D. A very stern leader

    E. A huge crowd

5. Think of fresh ways to replace these overused phrases:

    A. Like comparing apples and oranges

    B. Caught between a rock and a hard place

    C. Two steps forward and one step back

    D. Always darkest before the dawn

6. Read the speech by Donald Trump, available in Part **7** in *The Speaker's Handbook*. Identify at least two examples of stylistic devices Trump uses.

and metaphors that are comfortable for your audience, you're creating a bond that goes beyond the literal definitions of the words you use and lays the foundation for more communication. This sort of bonding is particularly important with an unfavorable audience.

In the process of bonding, be careful not to parrot phrases you do not understand, mock anyone's accent, or seem to talk down to your listeners. As a speaker, you must be yourself. But you have many facets, and without being artificial, you can choose to bring into your speech those aspects of your own language that best match your audience.

Synchronizing your language with your listeners' language involves close audience analysis. Listening to them and engaging in genuine dialogue will reveal the terms and categories they prefer. Every aspect of style can be subtly adjusted—level of formality, use of jargon or abbreviations, and selection of figures of speech and metaphors. Matching words or phrases are important because paying attention to the audience's words gives you clues about how they see the world. If you respect your listeners, you will almost subconsciously scan for terms that reveal that respect. If you do not understand them, there is the potential to offend them. For example, the board member of an orchestra who talks to the musicians about Beethoven's Ninth Symphony as a good "product" may alienate them. Or the lack of understanding may not be as dramatic: It may be simply a feeling of not really connecting, though neither speaker nor listeners can explain why.

Charly Bratt/Shutterstock.com

CHECKLIST ~ Language Use

- Is language fresh?
- Does your language style match the audience's language style?
- Is language vivid and varied?
- Is language appropriate, avoiding substandard or needless profanity?
- Is language clear?

MindTap°   **SPEAKER'S WORKSHOP 17.3**

1. Suppose you are going to speak on the topic of why a two-day strategic planning retreat is a good investment for an organization. You visit three departments to which you will be making separate presentations. Based on the following observations, how would you characterize each audience, and how might you adapt your topic and your language to establish a tone that is in sync with theirs?

   ▶ Group A uses these terms: the real go-getters, on the fast track, it's a rat race every day, pressure cooker.

   ▶ Group B uses these terms: dotting the i's and crossing the t's, getting your ducks in a row, doing your homework.

   ▶ Group C uses these terms: our family here, the team, touching base, backing each other up.

2. Find Eboo Patel's speech in Part **7** of *The Speaker's Handbook*. In the speech Wynton Marsalis is quoted as saying "The foundation of both jazz and democracy is dialogue, learning to negotiate your own agenda within the group's agenda. … You have to listen to what others have to say if you're going to make an intelligent contribution." How effective is this comparison?

Summary

Language reflects culture and shapes the perceptions of its users. How we use words determines our ability to connect with an audience and influences that audience's perception of us and our ideas.

17-1 Distinguish what makes oral style different from written style.

▶ Oral and written styles are not interchangeable. Oral style is more conversational; it requires more use of previews, signposting, summaries, and repetition. Oral style tends to use shorter, less complex sentences appropriate to the context.

17-2 Develop the ability to use clear, vivid, and varied language.

▶ Language must be clear with precise use of words, concrete language, and a sense of language economy.

▶ Language must be appropriate to the occasion, audience, and topic.

▶ Language must be vivid with imagery, stylistic devices, fresh, and varied in rhythm.

17-3 Use the appropriate language.

▶ Demonstrate awareness of and respect for the language preferences and choices an audience may have.

17-4 Use vivid and varied language for your listeners.

▶ Use vivid and varied language to keep your listeners attentive and interested.

Critical Thinking Questions

▶ Why is a choice of words considered a choice of "worlds"?

▶ When might a speaker intentionally use abstract words over more concrete language?

▶ Offer an example of a speaker who failed to effectively match language choices to the situation. How could the speaker have corrected this issue?

Putting It into Practice

Read or watch Donald Trump's "Thanksgiving Address" delivered on November 23, 2016. The text is featured in Part **7** in *The Speaker's Handbook* and video of this speech is available online.

1. As you review the speech, notice its style: oral or written.

2. Identify examples of both concrete and abstract language.

3. What instances of vivid and varied language can you identify?

4. What stylistic devices does Trump use? With what effect?

5. How does Trump adapt his language to the occasion and audience?

18

Attention and Interest

Craft your speech so that it captures your listeners' attention and retains their interest.

MindTap° **Read, highlight, and take notes online**

We can learn a great deal about what attracts interest and attention by observing nature. A rabbit will often hide unnoticed from a dog, until the dog smells the rabbit or sees it move. The rabbit blends into its surrounding through color, shape, and the learned ability to remain very still. Nature teaches us that sudden movement, drastic changes in volume or temperature, or even bright colors attract attention universally, whether we are people or animals.

As a public speaker, you can profit from understanding how to attract and maintain attention. After all, when you give a speech or presentation, your words are competing for attention with every other sight and sound in the room and with every daydream or concern in the mind of each listener. The better you understand the science of attention, the more likely you will receive the compliment most sought for and appreciated by speakers: a sincere and simple "That was an interesting speech!"

18-1 Techniques That Enliven Your Speech

A common misconception is that once you have grabbed your listeners' attention with a creative introduction, this attention is yours until you relinquish it at the end of the speech. Unfortunately, it takes more than a clever opening to keep an audience listening. People are easily distracted, and unless reengaged, their thoughts may stray every half-minute or so. When composing a speech, take every opportunity to use the attention-getting techniques in the "Attention-Getting Techniques" checklist.

People are intrigued by things that are unusual or spark their curiosity. Paradoxically, they also respond to well-known, everyday references. Most of all, as in the case of "the vital," people are attracted to material they see as connected to their own self-interest. Think of all the speeches you thought were dull or boring. Did you ever hear a complaint that a lecture was too fascinating? Attention-getting techniques can become second nature without much effort or time. Here are some examples:

Not: *A number of technologies have made business communication faster and more efficient.*

But: *About two hours ago, I received a Twitter update about a gate change for my flight this evening. I checked my e-mail messages and found that our client in Atlanta had changed the specifications for the contract we are bidding on. I sent a quick text message advising Chris of the contract change. As you all know, Chris is making his presentation in Atlanta right about now. [activity, proximity, the vital]*

CHECKLIST ~ Attention-Getting Techniques

☐ *Activity or movement*—Does your speech include appropriate movement of the speaker and a lively treatment of the content that creates a feeling of something happening?

☐ *Reality*—Does your speech include references to actual people, events, and places; being specific and concrete rather than abstract?

☐ *Proximity*—Does your speech include references to what is close at hand: people in the room, current events, local landmarks, and so on?

☐ *Familiarity*—Does your speech include the use of recognized examples, well-known phrases, and commonplace situations?

☐ *Novelty*—Does your speech include startling facts, odd turns of phrase, surprising images, and unusual combinations?

☐ *Suspense*—Does your speech include suspense through the stimulation of curiosity about what will happen next through puzzles or provocative questions?

☐ *Conflict*—Does your speech include pros and cons, opposing viewpoints, competing perspectives, or schools of thought?

☐ *Humor*—Does your speech include playful remarks, silly or exaggerated images, amusing plays on words, ironic twists of fate, entertaining stories, and the like?

☐ *"The vital"*[n]—Does your speech include references to things that are important to listeners, ranging from matters of survival to anything that saves them time, earns them money, or makes their lives more pleasant?

Not: When time is short, a good executive takes action first and then worries about causes, procedure, and policy.

But: If I told you people in the fourth and fifth rows that that chandelier's going to fall in ten seconds, what would you do? Darn right! You'd get out of the way! Later, we'd talk about why it happened, whose fault it was, and how to fix it. [proximity, novelty, suspense, reality]

Be guided by the following principles as you incorporate attention factors into your speech.

18-1a Be Specific and Use Real-Life Examples

Examples are always more interesting when they are specific and real. Never say "a person" or "one" if you can give a name. Use well-known figures, members of the audience, or hypothetical characters. And give place names, brand names, dates, and details. Notice how these paragraphs from a commencement speech by President Barack Obama, given on May 22, 2010, to the graduates of the U.S. Military Academy at West Point, create images in your mind that make tangible the vague reference to "Americans who faced times of trial":

> Here, in this peaceful part of the world, you have drilled and you have studied and come of age in the footsteps of great men and women—Americans who faced times of trial, and who even in victory could not have foreseen the America they helped to build, the world they helped to shape.
>
> George Washington was able to free a band of patriots from the rule of an empire, but he could not have foreseen his country growing to include 50 states connecting two oceans.
>
> Grant was able to save a union and see the slaves freed, but he could not have foreseen just how much his country would extend full rights and opportunities to citizens of every color.
>
> Eisenhower was able to see Germany surrender and a former enemy grow into an ally, but he could not have foreseen the Berlin Wall coming down without a shot being fired.
>
> Today it is your generation that has borne a heavy burden—soldiers, graduates of this Academy like John Meyer and Greg Ambrosia who have braved enemy fire, protected their units, carried out their missions, earned the commendation of this Army, and of a grateful nation.

18-1b Keep Your Audience Involved

If you have done a thorough audience analysis, you should be able to build many references to the audience into the speech and make use of such attention factors as proximity and familiarity. But there are always opportunities to refer to your audience once you start your speech. Be willing to throw out what you have if you can replace it with something "closer to home." Here are some techniques you might try.

Use the Names of People in the Audience Personalize supporting points with information you have learned about your audience. Before giving a speech, you may have a chance to meet a few members of your audience. It is often effective to refer to them. Why say, "Suppose a businessperson wants to obtain a loan," when you could say, "Suppose Ms. Silver's [nodding toward a listener] hardware business is expanding so rapidly that she decides to take out a loan to enlarge her store"?

Refer to the Person Who Introduced You and to Other Speakers on the Program Listen to the comments of the person who introduces you and to the content of speeches that precede yours. You might be able to return a compliment, engage in banter, or best of all, forge an intellectual link between their speech ideas and one of yours. For instance, an alert member of a speech class might include something like this:

> *So now that we have examined the causes of stress, let us look at four ways of reducing it. The first of these is physical exercise. Most people can find an activity they like. Najib was telling us about the joys of tennis. Similarly, yoga is a great way to relieve stress …*

Refer to Details in the Immediate Setting or from Common Experiences Do not use a hypothetical example if you can draw on a concrete example related to the group:

▶ And all of that expensive atom-smashing machinery was housed in a room half the size of this one.

▶ Everyone in this class knows about *situational stress*. The five of us giving speeches today are especially aware of it.

Actively Involve Your Audience Create an active role for your audience. Even though it is your show when you speak, you can still simulate a sense of interaction with your listeners. Use audience participation techniques. Ask for shows of hands if pertinent, have listeners provide examples, and ask questions of them, perhaps use response technology such as clickers or text messaging:

▶ How many people here had breakfast this morning? Ah, I see about half of you raised your hands. What did you have, Jake? Bacon and eggs? Over there? Coffee and a donut. I hear juice and toast, or cereal and yogurt. Would anyone care to hazard an answer to this question: What percentage of elementary school students go to school with no breakfast at all?

▶ Using your cell phone, respond to the following question…. Now let's look at our collective responses….

When you do not want to relinquish control or if overt audience participation is impractical, you can still keep your audience mentally involved and active. Ask rhetorical questions, have your listeners visualize examples, and ask them for nonverbal feedback and respond to it:

▶ Are there any *Family Guy* fans here? Great, I can see there are. Well, do you remember the sketch about "Excellence in Broadcasting," when Rush Limbaugh appeared?

▶ There is yet another problem with home repairs. I'll bet this has happened to everyone here.

▶ I have one colleague who always gives me feedback at the wrong time and place. Do you know people like that? Several of you are nodding. Isn't it frustrating?

▶ We can learn from our mistakes. Think of the last mistake you made. Take a minute to recall a big one. Do you have it in mind? Okay. Now I want you to think about how you felt.

18-1c Use Variety and Movement to Energize Your Speech

Change attracts attention. Sameness is dull. By changing your vocal tone, your stance or body position, and your gestures and eye gaze, you attract and maintain attention. Even visual aids can be used to create variety and add interest to your speech. Be cautious not to overdo movement or visual aids as too much can distract more than attract attention. If you become totally predictable, audience members' interest will start to wane. (For tips on vocal and physical delivery, see Chapters **25** and **26**.)

As suggested in Chapter **15**, using a variety of supporting strategies can help a speaker avoid the rut caused by relying exclusively on examples, testimony, or explanation. Draw support from many domains. Three political illustrations of one point are less interesting than a single political illustration combined with a sports example and one drawn from a popular film. Similarly, repetition of the same sentence constructions and overuse of a word or phrase should be avoided. (See Chapter **17**.)

FOR YOUR BENEFIT

Benefits

Use Clickers and Cell Phones to Engage the Audience

There are numerous technologies and cell phone applications that can be used in public speaking situations to involve audience members actively in a speech. "Clickers," which may be available through your school or organization, can be used to gather response data from audience members. Several apps, such as polleverywhere.com, smspoll.net, and Socrative.com, allow audience members to text responses directly from their personal tablets or cell phones and see aggregate responses displayed in real time. Handheld whiteboards can also be used as a low-tech alternative for quickly gathering feedback.

Whenever possible, give the speech a sense of movement. Create active images. Use verbs that have vivid connotations, and stay in the active voice as much as possible. For instance, instead of saying, "Five new businesses can be seen downtown," say, "Drive down First Street and you will find five new businesses open." If you need to point out the features of a piece of equipment, describe it in use, with "fingers flying over the keyboard" or "gears turning" or "shutters clicking" or even "electrons firing."

MindTap® Go to the MindTap for *The Speaker's Handbook* and click on **Additional Resources** for more on keeping your audience interested during your speech.

18-1d Use Humor When It Is Appropriate

Integrate humor into your speech, but make sure it is appropriate to your personality and to the situation. Humor is powerful; it is also tricky. An infusion of humor into any speech can ease tension, deflate opponents, enhance the speaker's image, and make points memorable. You need not consider yourself a humorous speaker or your speech a humorous talk to benefit from using this attention-getting technique. Developing your use of humor is not a matter of collecting random jokes and gags. What is important is the ability to spot a potentially humorous idea in your speech and craft it into a genuinely funny moment.

Look for the Humor in Your Everyday Experience The boring, frustrating, and mundane aspects of life all have their humorous elements. Take note of the everyday things that make you laugh: on your job, in your relationships, on television, and in the paper. Decide which of these humorous items have any bearing on potential speech topics. Some are merely amusing; others are both amusing and instructive. Jot them down, clip them out, or bookmark them, so that you do not find yourself saying six months later, "Now, what was the funny phrase?"

Be Selective When You Draw on Collected Humor You can definitely benefit from reading books or visiting websites on humor, but take care when using these resources. Timeliness and original twists are so important to humor that the lag time involved in publishing renders stale much of the content of such books, and if you've received the latest joke of the day, you can bet that others in your audience have as well. Better than joke books or magazine joke pages, though, are the works of genuine humorists. Review the works of Mark Twain, Will Rogers, and Robert Benchley, and contemporary columnists, essayists, and commentators such as David Sedaris, W. Kamau Bell, Jimmy Fallon, Ali Wong, Firoozeh Dumas, Jo Firestone, Steven Colbert, and Jon Stewart. They will introduce you to comic points of view that are more useful than jokes.

18-2 Convert Attention to Interest

Generating sustained *interest* in your topic is easier than capturing attention, losing it, and attempting to recapture it. When audience members become more than merely attentive, but actually interested, they begin to take a more active role. Pushing distractions aside, they put forth the effort to stay with you, even through complicated lines of thought or technical material.

When you have gained attention through the methods we've discussed, you need to use those moments to demonstrate how and why your topic is worthy of your listeners' interest.

18-2a Link Your Topic to Your Listeners' Self-Interest

Most of the time when people say, "So what?" they are really saying, "What's in it for me?" Do not assume that the benefits of your particular approach are obvious; motivate your audience to listen by spelling out the rewards. Do careful audience analysis and tap into as many of your listeners' needs and values as possible. (See Chapter **20**.) Here are some examples:

▶ If you take the time to learn the basics of car maintenance, you'll no longer be at the mercy of a mechanic. You can shop around for the most economical and reliable car care, and have the added peace of mind of knowing you'll be able to spot potentially dangerous conditions yourself.

▶ I know that many of you work in the helping professions—as teachers, social workers, counselors, and nurses. Learning to read the subtle cues of body language will help you interpret messages your clients may be unable to transmit in words.

MindTap° SPEAKER'S WORKSHOP 18.1

1. Think over the spontaneous laughs you have had in the past few days during unstructured interpersonal interactions. Can you describe what your friends or acquaintances did that amused you? Do these people have uniquely funny approaches to life or ways of responding to events? Turn this around: Can you describe what you've done to amuse your friends and acquaintances?

2. Evaluate the use of attention techniques such as novelty and surprise in the speech by Eboo Patel, available in Part **7** of *The Speaker's Handbook*.

▶ You don't have to be a vegetarian or a gourmet cook to benefit from these menu ideas. By serving just a few meatless meals a week, you can save from $30 to $100 on your monthly grocery bill and also provide a healthier diet for your family.

18-2b Incorporate Storytelling Techniques

If you ever watch *Monday Night Football,* you may have noticed that each week the announcers promote the drama of that week's game. They develop a story line that creates interest in even mundane matchups. A well-constructed story, whether it deals with traditional rivals, underdogs, comeback kids, or record-breaking leaders, commands the interest of sports fans everywhere. Likewise, storytellers who can take the confusion of everyday experience and produce a compelling narration will never have trouble attracting an audience.

A speech, even if it is an annual report, can captivate an audience if it unfolds in a narrative fashion with suspense, conflict, intriguing characterizations, lively bits of dialogue, and a moment of climax leading to the denouement. Your speech need not promise to make your listeners rich or famous if it is engaging and moves them.

MindTap® SPEAKER'S WORKSHOP 18.2

1. Identify the attention-getting factor or factors in each example:
   A. A good accountant can help you avoid paying extra taxes.
   B. You've all heard the phrase "the buck stops here."
   C. Our own accounting department has developed some new techniques.
   D. I was trembling when I went into the tax auditor's office. Could Melvin's ledgers save me or was I guilty of committing a crime?
2. Describe how you could use at least five of the attention getters described in this chapter in a speech on each of these topics:
   Autonomous vehicles
   Art frauds and forgeries
   Olympic gold
   Monuments of Washington, D.C.
3. Look at the transcript or view the speech on the MindTap for the speech by Nathanael Dunlavy available in Part **7**. Identify at least four attention factors in each.
4. Read Eboo Patel's speech, available in Part **7** in *The Speaker's Handbook.* Discuss how he transforms attention to interest.

FOR YOUR BENEFIT

Avoid Common Attention Pitfalls

Don't risk losing the goodwill of your audience by using questionable material. It is a safe bet that ethnic jokes, off-color humor, and vulgarities will offend someone in every audience. Knowledge of your listeners will also help you make a judgment about the inclusion of a slightly risqué remark or politically loaded story. Insults or ridicule—unless stylized as in a "roast"—should be avoided unless you are very sure the object of your put-down genuinely enjoys public teasing. Better to use self-effacing humor than to belittle anyone in your audience. If you aren't a good joke teller then don't tell jokes. If you haven't tested the technology and know it will work, then go without it.

ESB Professional/Shutterstock.com

Summary

Capturing the attention of your audience is important to good speech making. Great speakers maintain their audience's attention *throughout* the speech by using a variety of techniques.

18-1 Learn to create lively speech content.

▌ Attracting and maintaining audience interest requires speakers to use a variety of techniques: activity or movement, real-world examples, proximity, familiarity, novelty, suspense, conflict, humor, and an understanding of what is vital to the audience.

▌ Keeping the audience involved can be done through direct reference to the people in the audience, reference to common experiences, and even the use of technologies that engage the audience directly.

18-2 Develop strategies to convert attention to interest.

▌ Sustaining interest in a topic is essential as audience members can be easily distracted.

▌ Link your topic to audience members' interests and use strong story-telling techniques: suspense, novelty, conflict, and a story climax to maintain interest and attention.

Critical Thinking Questions

▶   What is wrong with opening your speech by saying, "Good morning, my name is …"?

▶   How can you ensure your speech will capture and maintain your audience's attention?

▶   How will you know if you are losing your audience's attention?

▶   What can you do to regain an audience's attention?

Putting It into Practice

Review the tips for keeping your audience interested on the Effective Meetings website in the Additional Resources section of the MindTap.

1.   What recommendations does the author offer to captivate a business audience?

2.   In what ways are these recommendations similar to or different from those for a classroom audience?

3.   As an audience member, what captivates your attention?

19

Credibility

Establish your credibility, both before and during your speech, by projecting competence, concern, trustworthiness, and dynamism.

MindTap® Read, highlight, and take notes online.

What is it about some speakers that make you want to accept what they say, while others make you want to reject what may be a nearly identical message? Your content and delivery determine, to a great extent, whether your listeners believe what you say. However, an independent force is at work that can doom even the best planned and practiced speeches. Beyond what you say and how you say it, your audience is influenced by who you are or, more accurately, by the person they think you are. Your **credibility** is that combination of perceived qualities that makes listeners predisposed to believe you.

19-1 Understand Credibility

For centuries, scholars have been fascinated by credibility from classical discussions of ethos to contemporary investigations of concepts like *image, personality*, and *charisma*. Aristotle observed that audiences who view a speaker as having good sense, goodwill, and good character are more likely to believe him or her. Modern social scientists have tried to isolate the characteristics that distinguish the most credible speakers from others. Their lists include competence, dynamism, intention, personality, intelligence, authoritativeness, extroversion, trustworthiness, composure, and sociability.

You can enhance your credibility, and thus the chances of meeting your speech objective, by projecting qualities of competence, dynamism, intelligence, trustworthiness, and the like. You can build your image or reputation before the speech, and you can take steps to improve your credibility as you are speaking.

Before you can work on improving your credibility, you need to see where you stand now. Is your overall credibility high or low? Which components of credibility are strongest for you? Which need to be developed? It may be very hard to gauge this alone. If possible, have some friends help you with this appraisal.

CHECKLIST ~ Assess Your Speaking Image

Are you perceived as competent?

- *Image prior to speech*: Do you have education, experience, or credentials to make you an expert on this topic? Does your audience know that?

- *Content of speech*: Have you researched broadly and deeply? Does your speech reflect this with well-documented, factual information?

- *Delivery*: Does your delivery connote competence? Do you seem to be on top of your information, well organized, and composed?

Are you perceived as concerned about your audience's welfare?

- *Image prior to speech*: If you have a history of generosity or selflessness on relevant issues, is it known? (For example, have you volunteered your time, informed yourself thoroughly, or made a sacrifice of some sort?)

- *Content of speech*: Do you stress the audience's needs and goals throughout the speech?

- *Delivery*: Is your delivery warm, unaffected, friendly, and responsive to the audience?

Are you perceived as trustworthy?

- *Image prior to speech*: Is your record one of honesty and integrity?

- *Content of speech*: Do you make an effort to be fair in presenting evidence, acknowledging the limitations of your data and opinions, and conceding those parts of opposing viewpoints that have validity?

- *Delivery*: Is your style of presentation sincere and honest, not slick or manipulative?

Are you perceived as dynamic?

- *Image prior to speech*: Is your image that of an active, assertive person, a leader rather than a follower, a doer rather than an observer?

- *Content of speech*: Does your speech have a sense of movement? Do the ideas build to a climax? Is your language lively and colorful?

- *Delivery*: Is your delivery animated, energetic, and enthusiastic?

Suggestions for improving your credibility in each of these areas are provided later in this chapter.

MindTap®   SPEAKER'S WORKSHOP 19.1

1. Use the "Assess Your Speaking Image" checklist to complete your image inventory. In a few sentences, describe your prior image as a speaker in your speech class or in a social or professional group you relate to regularly. Which is your strongest area: competence, concern, trustworthiness, or dynamism? Which is your weakest?

2. Consider how your credibility varies from topic to topic. Name three topics on which you already have high credibility and three on which you would have to work very hard to establish credibility.

3. Rate the last four U.S. presidents' credibility as high, medium, or low in each of the four areas of competence, concern, trustworthiness, and dynamism. Discuss your choices and reasons.

4. Is there a public figure you regard as competent, concerned, and trustworthy but whose image suffers due to a lack of dynamism? Can you think of a public figure for whom the opposite is true?

Benefits

FOR YOUR BENEFIT

You Are Your Own Personal Brand

It is important to take your image as a speaker seriously. Think of it as your personal "brand." Based on daily interactions, people can tell if you are serious, funny, prompt, lazy, cheerful, argumentative, intelligent, informed, and so on. Perceptions of your brand will affect the way audiences perceive your speeches. When invited to speak, thoughtfully consider what advance information to share and how it communicates about you. You may be asked for a brief biography or personal background. Construct this material carefully and provide it in advance. This might include a résumé that lists your background and achievements, news clippings, testimonials about your speaking, a list of your books and articles, a photograph if appropriate, and even an introduction to be used when you speak. You are your own brand and it is imperative that you manage that image wisely.

19-2 Build Your Credibility through Content and Delivery

As you prepare your speech outline and select your supporting evidence and examples, think about ways to communicate your competence, concern, trustworthiness, and dynamism. The following suggestions are especially relevant in the opening minutes of the speech, when the audience is forming its first impressions. (See Chapter **13**.) But many credibility boosters can be woven throughout the entire speech as well.

> MindTap®   The framework and prompts provided in the MindTap for *The Speaker's Handbook* can help you ensure your credibility as a public speaker.

1. Present Your Credentials

Most inexperienced speakers find it difficult to blow their own horns and do not do as much credibility building as they should. Do not be reluctant to provide information about your qualifications to speak. Do this even if you think your audience should remember you from the last speech you gave. For instance, you might say:

▶ In my five years as an assistant manager for Target,…

▶ The most common error I see in the twenty to thirty loan applications I look at each week is…

▶ I've had a special awareness of the barriers the physically challenged face since 2016, when my brother Dave returned from the Operation Freedom's Sentinel in Afghanistan.

Judgment and tact are important in deciding which qualifications to mention and how to work them into the speech. Our culture frowns on bragging and name-dropping; however, you can include many statements of your qualifications without seeming boastful if you play it straight and present them matter-of-factly. Include only relevant qualifications. Do not talk about well-known people you know unless it relates to the topic, and do not expound on your financial success unless the speech is specifically about making money.

2. Demonstrate a Thorough Understanding of Your Topic

To communicate a sense of expertise, let listeners know you've done your homework. Mention the nature of your research when appropriate:

▶ The three judges I interviewed all agreed on one major weakness in our court system.

▶ I read the minutes of all the committee hearings on this bill, and not one expert mentioned…

▶ There is considerable disagreement on this point in the articles I read. Several scholars say…

Use concrete examples, statistics, and testimony. Be sure you have your details straight. One obvious error early in the speech can ruin your credibility:

> *Just imagine what it would have been like for the Union soldier crouching in the trenches around Richmond, his jacket zipped up tight in a futile battle against the cold and the wet.*

The people listening to this would probably think, "If this speaker doesn't know the zipper wasn't invented until nearly 30 years after the Civil War, I wonder what other information is all wrong?"

3. Be Sure Material Is Clearly Organized

Your audience's opinion of your competence depends on their sense that you are in command of your material and know where you are headed. Listeners will view you as uninformed rather than unorganized if you wander from topic to topic or must apologetically insert, "Oh, one thing I forgot to mention when I was discussing...." Clear organization originates in the introduction (Chapter 13) and continues through the conclusion (Chapter 14) and is further enhanced with effective use of connectives (Chapter 12).

4. Present a Balanced, Objective Analysis

To demonstrate you are fair, trustworthy, and of good character, go out of your way to acknowledge the limitations of your evidence and argument, if appropriate:

▶ Now, I know there are some problems with relying on surveys, but this one was carefully conducted. It seems safe to conclude that many, if not most, working mothers are dissatisfied with the quality of child care available to them.

▶ I'm not saying television is the only cause of these problems. I realize that's an oversimplification. But I do think TV has had a pronounced effect on the imaginative thinking of the last two generations.

▶ Also, be sure to acknowledge the existence of opposing evidence and opinions:

▶ Some studies indicate that an alcoholic can return to social drinking; however,...

▶ I recognize the contributions the administration has made to social welfare programs, but it has failed in so many other areas that I still maintain it is time for a change.

Acknowledge self-interest when it exists to prevent the audience from thinking you are trying to hide something from them.

▶ It's true I'm a real estate agent and I stand to profit by having folks invest in real estate. But that's not my main reason for urging you to invest.

5. Express Your Concern for the Audience

Let audience members know your speech is offered to benefit them:

▶ I'd do anything to save your families the headaches and heartaches that go along with having a relative die without a will.

▶ Taking up cycling has added so much to my life that I'd love to see some of you share in that fun.

6. Increase Credibility with Your Delivery

Too many expert and well-prepared speakers lose effectiveness because they cannot *transmit* these qualities to their audience. Dropping cards, reading in a shaky voice, or fumbling with whatever is at hand all suggest lack of competence. An unexpressive face and voice might be interpreted as disdainfulness and detract from perceived goodwill. Hesitancy and uncertainty are sometimes mistakenly seen as shiftiness or dishonesty. Listless, monotonous, colorless speaking is the very opposite of dynamism and does little to enhance credibility; however, an overly emotional delivery can signal credibility problems, too. To be seen as a believable source of information and opinion, seek a balanced delivery that includes plenty of eye contact, natural gestures, and a dynamic tone. Additional delivery suggestions are offered in Chapters **25** and **26**.

MindTap®   Go to the MindTap for The Speaker's Handbook and click on **Additional Resources** to learn about initial, derived, and terminal credibility. Also check out **Additional Resources** for information on how to maintain credibility by correctly citing sources using a number of different style manuals.

MindTap®   **SPEAKER'S WORKSHOP 19.2**

1. Go to the MindTap for *The Speaker's Handbook* and watch Nathanael Dunlavy's speech about the 54th Regiment. How does he directly establish his credentials to speak? Which examples do you find especially effective?

2. Go to Part **7** or to the MindTap for *The Speaker's Handbook* and find an example of how Brian Sharkey and Nathanael Dunlavy explicitly establish concern for the welfare of the audience.

Summary

Credibility starts with a speaker's image (nonverbal communication) and is enhanced before and during the speech by adequate preparation and practice.

19-1 Develop an understanding of credibility.

▶ Credibility is a combination of perceived qualities that makes listeners predisposed to believe you. First, assess your credibility for a given audience. Audiences will perceive your credibility differently depending on a variety of contextual factors.

19-2 Learn to build your credibility through content and delivery.

▶ Credible speakers must not be timid about presenting their credentials, demonstrating knowledge of their topic, presenting a balanced and objective analysis, and transmitting both personal confidence and concern for the audience.

Critical Thinking Questions

▶ How might your appearance impact your perceived credibility?

▶ What can a speaker do to develop credibility before speaking?

▶ What can a speaker do to enhance credibility while speaking?

▶ What mistakes have you seen destroy a speaker's credibility?

Putting It into Practice

Review the article "Preparing American Students to Succeed in a Global Era of Change" by David Abney.[1] Go to the MindTap for *The Speaker's Handbook* to access this article through the **Additional Resources**.

1. How does the speaker connect with his audience to open the speech?
2. How effectively does the speaker present his own credentials?
3. Does the speaker demonstrate a thorough understanding of the topic? How so?
4. How does the speaker demonstrate concern for the audience?

20

Motivational Appeals

Ethically motivate your audience through appeals to emotion, needs, and values.

MindTap®   Read, highlight, and take notes online.

This handbook stresses the role of clear analysis in support of ideas, but it also emphasizes making those ideas meaningful to an audience. A good speaker is constantly aware of the humanness of the audience. To be human is to be rational, but it is more than that. Love sometimes defies logic, reverence often surpasses reason, and emotion frequently tops evidence. Understanding the humanity of your audience means presenting your case so it touches the listeners' hearts as well as their heads.

20-1 Emotional Impact of Words

Keep in mind that everything you say has the potential to trigger some sort of emotional response in your audience. Generally, you can strengthen your speech by selecting main points, supporting material, and language that engages your listeners' feelings. Positive emotions—hope, joy, pride, and love—are surefire motivators. Negative emotions like fear, envy, disgust, and contempt can also motivate, but the motivational effects of negative emotions are less predictable. Moderate levels of fear appeal can enhance persuasion, but higher levels may work against the desired effect. Some presentations feature gory films of traffic accidents, vivid visual aids showing cancerous lung tissue, or detailed descriptions of the plight of a family whose breadwinner had no insurance. These can either cause the audience to tune out the unpleasantness or appear too extreme to be statistically plausible for the listener to worry about. When adding emotion to your speech, remember the old adage, "Although some is good, more is not always better."

Devoid of Emotion

Malaria is a disease that causes a high fever and chills.[1]

Moderate Emotion

Most malaria infections cause symptoms like the flu, such as a high fever, chills, and muscle pain. Symptoms tend to come and go in cycles. One type of malaria may cause more serious problems, such as damage to the heart, lungs, kidneys, or brain. It can even be deadly.[2]

Excessive Emotion

You've been bitten and you know that while death is not immediate, you face fever, chills, and uncontrollable muscle pain that comes in waves, one more serious than the next. If you are lucky enough to live near a properly supplied hospital, you might live. That is, if you realize your symptoms are malaria and not some more benign infection. Without treatment, your brain, hearts, lungs, and kidneys are all at risk and you will likely die. In addition, you may be the cause of many other deaths in your village.

These three levels of emotion are possible for any topic. It's important to discern early on where your listeners draw the dividing lines. Try to include the optimal amount of emotional appeal—not so little that you fail to move them and not so much that you turn them off.

20-2 Appeal to Listeners' Needs

The best-known way of classifying human needs is **Maslow's hierarchy of needs**.[3] Figure 20.1 shows the hierarchy.

In this hierarchy, the lower-level needs have to be met or satisfied before an individual can become concerned with the needs on the next higher level. For instance, on the topic of physical fitness, you could appeal to your audience at any of the following levels:

▶ The effect of exercise in reducing risk of cardiovascular disease appeals to the survival need.

▶ Security might be drawn in by mentioning how physically fit people are more likely to be able to resist or evade attackers.

▶ The need for belonging can be linked to becoming trim and attractive, as well as to making friends through physical activity.

▶ Esteem needs can be tied into the current popularity of fitness and the social desirability of an active image.

▶ Fitness can be related to the need for self-actualization—the highs of exercise and the mental and physical challenge of reaching one's potential.

FIGURE 20.1
Maslow's hierarchy of needs

The significance of Maslow's hierarchy to the speaker is apparent. You must analyze your audience well enough to determine which need is most salient. Listeners whose jobs are in danger and who are struggling to feed their families do not want to hear you contrast local economic programs in terms of the implications drawn from Keynesian theory. They want to know which one will create jobs. Being absorbed with their security needs, they are not likely to respond at the self-actualization level.

It is counterproductive to aim your emotional appeals too high, and unethical to aim them too low. Suppose a speaker wants to convince colleagues to adopt a different software system from the one currently in use in that department. If the company is doing well and the colleagues are satisfactory employees, then it would be inappropriate to use a fear appeal with visions of the organization going out of business and people being tossed into the street if the new system is not adopted. The more ethical approach would be to build a case related to the colleagues' needs for efficiency, productivity, success, and prestige (esteem and self-actualization levels).

To be fair, you should respond to existing needs and not foster an artificial sense of insecurity in your listeners. Speakers who abuse their influence in this way falsely assume that the most primitive needs are the strongest. Altruism is an extremely effective motivator. In fact, it might be possible to place another pyramid beside Maslow's, illustrating the belief that every person has a basic need to *protect* others' survival, to *give* security, to *spread* love, to *build* esteem, and to *nurture* self-actualization. Appeals to the idealistic, caring sides of human nature can be equally powerful as self-oriented appeals.

MindTap®   Go to the MindTap for *The Speaker's Handbook* and click on **Additional Resources** for more on Maslow's hierarchy of needs.

20-3 Relate to Listeners' Values

Suppose in a presentation you use the argument, "and this procedure will speed up your assembly line," but you are actually unveiling only a part of the following syllogism:

> Anything that speeds up your assembly line is good.
> This procedure will speed up your assembly line.
> Therefore, this procedure is good.

You assume your listeners share increasing production speed as a value; as a result, you do not feel it is necessary to clutter your talk with the other parts of the syllogism. As it turns out, however, these particular listeners are currently satisfied with the speed of production but are more concerned with the accuracy of assembly. A little audience analysis could have alerted you to the fact, and you might have worked from the following syllogism:

> Anything that improves accuracy is good.
> This procedure improves accuracy.
> Therefore, this procedure is good.

Both arguments are logically sound, but the second is psychologically more effective because its underlying premise reflects the dominant value of the listeners.

We hold a certain value if we believe that a particular thing is either good or bad, in the broadest sense of those terms. Specifically, we *evaluate* concepts, people, objects, events, or ideas every day as we label them just or unjust, wise or foolish, beautiful or ugly, and so on. Whereas emotions and needs are considered innate (and therefore consistent across cultures, societies, and individuals), values are judgments or choices made by individuals. Looking at two people in isolation, we could predict that they both fear certain things, and both have a need for status, simply on the basis of their humanness. But we could not so easily predict whether one hates cats or the other is a passionate supporter of the free enterprise system.

20-3a Incorporate Appeals to General Values

Although values are individually chosen, the choice is rarely a totally conscious and rational one. Culture has a strong influence, shaping values through families, schools, media, and peers. Moreover, values are rarely formed in isolation; rather, they are organized and structured into related clusters. By knowing the culture of your listeners, the influences on them, and perhaps some of the other values they hold, you can make an educated guess as to how much particular values might shape their attitude toward your speech topic.

Sometimes, identifying values in your own culture can be extremely difficult; predominant values and trends often do not become clear until years later, much too late to do a speaker any good. However, paying attention to editorial writers and news commentators can help you get a clearer picture of the national mood. Many public opinion polls on specific issues like welfare, immigration, marriage rights, and privacy

FOR YOUR BENEFIT

The Universality of Values

Research has found six universal value dimensions that together capture common values affecting human behavior.[5] Consider which value dimension best represents the majority of your audience members and how appeals to values that matter to them might improve your ability to motivate their behavior.

- *Striver*: Values power, status, ambition, health and fitness, material security, courage, perseverance, public image, and wealth.
- *Fun-Seeker*: Values excitement, leisure, individuality, pleasure, enjoying life, having fun, adventure, and variety.
- *Creative*: Values open-mindedness, beauty, fulfilling work, self-esteem, creativity, self-reliance, freedom, curiosity, knowledge, wisdom, learning, internationalism, and music.
- *Devout*: Values spirituality, tradition, duty, obedience, respecting ancestors, traditional gender roles, faith, and modesty.
- *Intimate*: Values honesty, authenticity, protecting family, personal support, stable personal relationships, enduring love, romance, friendship, and sex.
- *Altruist*: Values being in tune with nature, preserving the environment, justice, social responsibility, helpfulness, equality, social tolerance, and social stability.

contain questions specifically addressed to values.[4] You can also augment your audience analysis with an awareness of trends, mainstream values caused by economic and technical trends, counterculture movements, and liberation movements.

20-3b Identify and Relate to Listeners' Core Values

If the members of a culture share common values, why do we not see lockstep agreement on every issue? Obviously, not all members of a culture give equal importance to the common values, nor is there a standard ranking of them. Values are very general, and any particular issue can touch on many values, on both the pro side and the con. Examples of this value conflict can become common around election time. Suppose there is a proposed bond issue to build an expensive performing arts complex. Stella is drawn toward approving the bond because she holds the values of a world of art, beauty, and performance. But she may also have reservations about taking on a greater tax burden because of her belief in the values of a comfortable, prosperous life and family security. Stella's resolution of this conflict will depend on how she has prioritized these values.

Because nearly every topic stirs up such value conflicts, a list of audience values will not be useful unless it is supplemented by some estimate of the relative ranking. As Figure 20.2 shows, one way to illustrate this is to imagine a series of concentric circles, with the most strongly held values at the core, and the degree of importance

FIGURE 20.2
Ranking of values

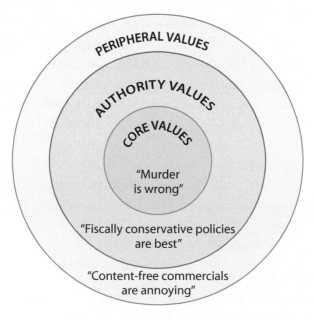

of the other values determining their distance from the center. The innermost circle contains *core values*, the ones so central to a person that to change one of them would amount to a basic alteration of that person's self-concept. The next band out from the center contains the *authority values*, the values that are influenced by and shared with groups and individuals most significant to the person. *Peripheral values* form the outer band.[6] These are the more or less incidental evaluations, easily made or changed.

MindTap   SPEAKER'S WORKSHOP 20.1

1. Which of Maslow's needs found in Figure 20.1 are appealed to in each of these examples?

    A. Following the dress-for-success formula has helped countless people advance in their careers.

    B. Every home should have an electronic alarm system.

    C. Meditation will enhance your understanding of the universe.

    D. Some of the marijuana available on the street is laced with deadly chemicals.

    E. This shampoo makes your hair more touchable.

2. Read the commemorative speech by John Lewis delivered at the dedication of the National Museum of African American History and Culture, National Mall, Washington, D.C., Sept. 24, 2016 available in Part **7**. Identify the values he appeals to and analyze which ones he seems to prioritize as core values of his listeners. Also, identify the explicit emotional appeals he makes and assess the effectiveness of those appeals.

3. Go to Part **7** to access the sample speeches. How does Dianna Cohen use emotional appeals in her persuasive speech? How does Eboo Patel use emotional appeals in his speech?

4. Of the value dimensions listed in the "For Your Benefit" box in this chapter, which one or two would you designate as your core values? Which ones do you think are most salient in the value system of the United States today? Which values do you see as having undergone the greatest change in the past few years?

5. Return to the examples in Part **1** of this activity and relate each statement to at least two of the values listed in the "For Your Benefit" box.

6. Analyze an audience you speak to regularly (speech class, professional association, study group) in terms of their probable responses to a speech on immigration.

    A. What needs could you appeal to?

    B. What core values could you appeal to?

    C. What authority values could you appeal to?

    D. What new value–issue links could you forge?

When speaking, try to make reasonable inferences about your listeners' core values and stress them in your speech or presentation. For example, suppose you have an educational innovation you want the local school system to adopt. In speaking to the school board, you might stress the values of practicality, efficiency, and local control of education. In speaking to the teachers, you might stress the more idealistic value of progress in education. Although your approach in these two cases is different, this does not mean you assume teachers are impractical or school board members care nothing about educational progress. The members of both groups probably hold each of these values. However, as a speaker, you make a decision to stress those values likely to be closer to the core in each audience.

20-3c Link Speech Issues to Listeners' Values

The *issues* of your speech are the questions that must be resolved in your listeners' minds before your speech purpose can be met. (See Chapter **6**.) Decisions about what is worth knowing, what should be done, or what touches our spirit often depend on the prior acceptance of certain values. Not only do people differ in what values they hold and how they prioritize them, but they also differ in how they perceive connections between particular values and particular issues. Even when listeners share almost identical values and priorities, it is possible for them to perceive links differently. Take two audience members who value creative freedom and efficiency, with efficiency being closer to the core. If your issue is the elimination of red-light camera intersections, one listener might link that issue to freedom from government interference and support your speech goal, whereas the other might link it to safety and efficiency and disapprove of your proposal.

It is not enough, then, to know what values your listeners hold. You must try to discover which values they see as pertinent to your topic. Often, it is necessary to point out value links that are logical but perhaps not readily apparent. As you prepare a speech, clearly develop as many *valid* links to values as you can. One of the less obvious links may be just the connection that strikes through to a core value. Table 20.1 gives some examples.

20-3d Appeal to Listeners' Sense of Community

Understandably, when people first encounter an issue, they tend to analyze it from a perspective that is close to them in time and space. They ask, "How does this affect me and my immediate circle, now and in the near future?" But one of the most powerful ways public speakers can use motivational appeals is to draw people outward and refocus their awareness on larger frames of reference.

This broader awareness is there and available to be tapped. When the U.S. public saw the devastation from Superstorm Sandy, which hit the New York and New Jersey coastline in 2012, there was an outpouring of financial support. As a speaker,

TABLE 20.1
Issues and value links

ISSUE	OBVIOUS VALUE LINKS	LESS OBVIOUS, BUT PROBABLY VALID, VALUE LINKS
Achieving equality for women and marginalized groups	Justice, fairness, compassion	Increased productivity, avoiding waste, patriotism (world image)
Buying a tablet computer	Efficiency, speed, scientific advancement, ease of use	Creativity, expressiveness, economy (in the long run)
Deregulating small business	Lack of government interference, pioneer spirit of small entrepreneur	Honesty, trust of fellow citizens, dislike of red tape and paperwork
Welcoming delegation of foreign businesspeople	International harmony, U.S. hospitality, pooling of information	Efficiency, progress, pragmatism

you can create powerful word pictures to remind listeners of their interdependence with other people and creatures, and to transport them into the past and the future. You can use your words to show people the historical and cultural meanings of endangered objects and places. You can take listeners into the future and reveal the effects of our environmental policies or our national debt on future generations. Link your speech topic to your audience's values in ways that tie into the broadest sense of community and situate the present in relation to the past and the future.

20-3e Avoid Excessive, Inappropriate Motivational Appeals

Throughout this chapter, we have promoted the effective use of appeals to the emotions, needs, and values of your audience. However, speakers also must be cautious not to overuse or misuse these appeals. A speech with too much emphasis on feelings can embarrass and offend the audience. If listeners perceive that the speaker is playing on their emotions to the exclusion of sense and logic, they can become infuriated. It is always a mistake to underestimate the intelligence of an audience. Aside from the issue of effectiveness (advertisers and politicians show us that often these appeals can be effective), there is the question of ethics. (See Chapter **3**.)

Summary

Making ideas meaningful sometimes means making ideas *human*. This is accomplished by connecting with audience members' hearts as well as their heads. Effective speakers consider the emotional impact they want to create, or avoid, and they carefully relate their ideas to the needs and values of their listeners.

20-1 Recognize the emotional impact of your words.

▶ Everything we say has the potential to trigger some emotional response. Learning to moderate emotional language is critical to effective speaking.

20-2 Develop appeals to listeners' needs.

▶ Learning to understand the needs of the audience can help a speaker improve the effectiveness of his or her message.

▶ Maslow's hierarchy of needs can help inform a speaker about which needs might be most salient to an audience and suggests that lower-level needs must be met before higher-order needs can be pursued.

20-3 Relate your speech to listeners' values.

▶ Values are the judgments or choices an individual makes about what is good or bad, right or wrong, moral or immoral.

▶ Values of audience members can include general values shared in common with others and core values that are closely tied to each individual's sense of self. Recognizing how audience members evaluate ideas you discuss can help you relate more effectively with them and perhaps impact choices they consider.

▶ Overuse or misuse of appeals to emotion, needs, or values can have a detrimental effect. When implemented ethically, appeals to emotions can have powerful effects on audience members' understanding and motivation to act. Audience members who find their emotions being toyed with may outright reject appeals.

Critical Thinking Questions

▶ What value appeals do you find most and least appealing? Why?

▶ How might understanding Maslow's hierarchy of needs help you develop a persuasive speech for your audience?

▶ What are the core, authority, and peripheral values of your anticipated audience? How could you find out?

Putting It into Practice

1. What core values or needs are targeted by your favorite TV ads?

2. Why do you think these values appeals or needs were targeted? You can find quick links to television ads at the MindTap for *The Speaker's Handbook* and clicking on **Additional Resources**.

21

Informative Strategies

For informative speaking, plan a strategy based on information processing. Use clear explanations to aid your audience's comprehension.

MindTap® Read, highlight, and take notes online.

A large part of speaking is merely explanation—stating an idea and then restating it in a way that develops or expands on the basic notion. Unfortunately, some explanations do more to confuse than to clarify. Usually, this occurs when the speaker has lost sight of which details from a complex process or idea are the most essential. It is a real challenge to select the most significant details and present them in the clearest order. How can you most economically create the mental picture that will aid your listeners' understanding? Knowledge of the way people learn can make informative speaking both easier and more effective.

MindTap® Go to the MindTap for *The Speaker's Handbook* for help preparing informative speeches.

21-1 Help Listeners Make Sense of Information

Information surrounds us in this technological age and sometimes we can feel overwhelmed by the amount and speed at which we are bombarded with information. Several strategies will help your audience make sense of the information, including providing a framework for organizing information, moving from simple to complex and familiar to unfamiliar, and helping your audience avoid information overload. Develop your speech based on an understanding of how people acquire, process, and retain information.

1. Provide an Organizational Framework

Have you ever tried to put together a jigsaw puzzle without looking at the picture on the box? What you have is a jumble of unrelated pieces. Seeing the big picture helps you realize how things should fit together. This is the same principle that makes you want to look at a map before starting off on a trip or to review the table of contents before reading a textbook. By providing your audience with a sense of the big picture early, you can improve their ability to comprehend how the pieces of your speech fit together.

2. Move from Simple to Complex

Even at the risk of temporary oversimplification, it is advisable to lay out the most basic concepts first and introduce qualifiers, exceptions, and interesting tangents later. Think of your listeners as newcomers to town who first want to learn the basic route from home to work; only after mastering that do they want to learn about alternative shortcuts and scenic detours.

3. Move from Familiar to Unfamiliar

Any group can learn about any subject if you start where its members are and move along at the proper rate. Teachers will attest that learning proceeds best when they are able to adjust the focus of their instruction to a point just beyond the current knowledge level of the learners. If the instruction duplicates what the learners already know, the material will not be challenging. If the focus is too many levels beyond them, learners will get discouraged. This principle, even more than the others, ties directly to audience analysis. A creative speaker thinks of examples and analogies that relate directly to the experiences of a particular group of listeners. Connecting listeners to new concepts through familiar concepts will bolster listeners' confidence in their ability to understand the new material.

4. Avoid Information Overload

When you speak on a topic you know a great deal about, there is a tendency to want to bring your audience up to your level immediately. However, when you share too much information in a very short time, the result is a tidal wave of facts and data that overloads the listener. The consequences of this condition—usually in this order—are anxiety, confusion, irritability, anger at the source, and finally a complete tune out of the speaker. Research suggests that the average person can comprehend no more than seven points, plus or minus two.[1] So, avoid information overload by limiting yourself to no more than five to nine points, fewer if your topic is complex. This means being selective. You are the expert, and you must pick out the important points for them.

 Go to the MindTap for *The Speaker's Handbook* and click on **Additional Resources** for information on people you might want to give an informative speech. Also check out **Additional Resources** to visit a site that provides a lot of ideas for interesting informative topics.

21-2 Explain Ideas Clearly

In addition to clear previews and summaries (Chapters **13** and **14**), you will make it much easier for your listeners to understand the points of your speech if you implement the use of organizers, emphasis cues, examples, analogies, and multiple channels, with repetition and redundancy built in. The following pages provide additional details and examples on each of these techniques.

21-2a Use Organizers

Provide your listeners with cues on how they should structure the information.

Signposts One organizer is the **signpost**. Signposts, like their physical counterparts, point the way you are going and can serve as a reminder of where you've been:

▶ *First,* I'll show you how to make a simple white sauce, and then move on to three more elaborate sauces that originate from this basic recipe.

▶ *Finally,* from this short description of one novel and three poems, you can see once again the two themes that permeate Sylvia Plath's work.

Enumeration Numbering is an obvious organizational cue.

The many steps in building an apartment complex can be grouped into these three phases:

One: Finding attractive sites with the proper zoning

Two: Negotiating for the purchase of a piece of property

Three: Contracting with architects and builders

Acronyms An **acronym** is a word formed from the first letters of a series of words and that can be pronounced like a word. For instance, *radar* is an acronym formed from *RA*dio *De*tecting *A*nd *R*anging. Other examples are *SETI*, for *S*earch for *E*xtra *T*errestrial *I*ntelligence, and *GIGO*, for *G*arbage *I*n, *G*arbage *O*ut. An acronym can make a point more memorable, as in the following example:

When you want to show empathy through nonverbal cues, remember to SOFTEN your listening style: [writes on board]

Smile

Open posture

Facial expression

Touch

Eye contact

Nodding

Slogans, Catchwords, and Memorable Phrases Like acronyms, these types of cues give your listeners a framework for remembering your points:

▶   So, look at those files in your drawer that you haven't used in a year, and assess their real value. Keep in mind Peg Bracken's advice about leftover food: "When in doubt, throw it out."

▶   Try to do something decisive with each piece of mail as you open it. Apply the "Four D's": Drop the item, Delay the item, Delegate the item, or Do the item.

21-2b Use Emphasis Cues

Emphasis when writing is easy as we can underline and highlight key points. Perhaps we add a bold font to an e-mail or note. Phrases like "this is very important," "if you don't remember anything else …," and "here's what it all comes down to…" provide emphasis in a speech much the way highlighting, underlining, or bold fonts can be used in a written document.

You can also emphasize points by vocal or physical cues. When you want an idea to stand out, speak more loudly or, occasionally, more softly. Pause intentionally before and after the important concept. You might also physically move closer to the audience or let your facial expression forecast the seriousness of a point.

21-2c Use Examples

When an audience is confused, nothing reassures them like the appearance of a concrete example. You might begin with a simple, even whimsical, example:

> A "win–win" negotiation has occurred when both parties achieve their important goals without perceiving that they have had to make a major sacrifice. Phil and Dave are roommates, and they both think the other needs to do more around the apartment. After talking about it, they agree that Dave will do all the cooking and Phil will do all the cleaning. Each thinks he got off easy.

Next, you could move to a more complex and realistic example:

> Or suppose you have a used car for sale and your neighbor wants to buy it but does not have all the cash now. You offer to carry an interest-free note due in six months if your neighbor will take care of your pets and plants for three weeks while you are on vacation. You are happy because you will receive the asking price for your car and won't have to worry about arranging for a house sitter. Your neighbor is happy because she can have the car now and doesn't have to pay finance charges on a loan.

Finally, you might give an example that is advanced enough for your audience to apply to situations they may actually encounter:

> Now, let's see how these principles apply to negotiating a new job. On this chart you will see the employer's needs and bargaining chips listed in column 1 and your prioritized needs and bargaining chips in column 2. Let's assume an original offer was made of…

Sometimes one elaborate example developed throughout a presentation can be used successfully to unify and illuminate a topic.

21-2d Use Analogies

Continually compare the known to the unknown. You might start with a simple analogy:

> *A nuclear power plant is like a steam locomotive. The fireman shovels coal into the furnace, where the heat it gives off turns the water in the boiler into steam. The steam travels through pipes to pistons, where the energy is converted and carried by driving rods to the wheels, pulling long trains of cars down the rails. Substitute a Uranium fuel rod for the coal, a turbine for the pistons, and an electrical generator for the drive wheels, and you have a nuclear power plant.*

Then you could clarify the points of dissimilarity:

> *Of course, whereas in the locomotive you'd see a grimy engineer squinting at a pressure gauge that has a pop-off valve, in the plant you'd see a large number of scientists and operators presiding over banks of sensors, controls, and computers, each with triple-redundancy safety telltales. The biggest difference, as we know, is that a lump of plutonium contains 240 million times the potential heat energy of a similarly sized lump of coal.*

To reinforce points and reach more listeners, draw analogies from many areas: sports, movies, nature, history, culture, and so on.

21-2e Use Multiple Channels

Your message will be clearer if you send it through several channels. As you describe a process with words, also use your hands, a visual aid, a chart, or a recording. Appeal to as many senses as possible to reinforce the message. A good rule to follow is this: If a point is very important or very difficult, always use at least one other channel in addition to the spoken word to communicate your message.

21-2f Use Repetition and Redundancy

People learn and remember what they hear repeatedly. If a principle is important, say it over again, in the same words or different words. Repeat it. Paraphrase it. Reinforce it. Refer back to it. Then mention it again.

MindTap®   Go to the MindTap for *The Speaker's Handbook* and click on **Additional Resources** for more informative speaking strategies.

© Dusit/Shutterstock.com

CHECKLIST ~ Helpful Strategies for Informative Speaking

- Have you provided your listeners with a framework to ensure clarity?
- Do you move from simple to complex? Do you link the familiar with the unfamiliar?
- Do you use organizers, including signposts, enumeration, acronyms, and memorable phrases?
- Have you highlighted key points with emphasis cues?
- Do you use plenty of examples—simple and complex, hypothetical and real?
- Have you considered using analogies to connect the known with the unknown?
- Do you use multiple sensory channels to communicate your message?
- Have you repeated the most important information for emphasis?

MindTap·   SPEAKER'S WORKSHOP 21.1

1. How many analogies and metaphors are used in this chapter? Do they help clarify things?

2. How might you link the familiar and the unfamiliar when speaking about these topics to these groups?

   A. A speech about nutrition to a motorcycle club

   B. A speech about developing a LinkedIn profile to help when networking for a job to a group of engineering students

3. A speech about endangered species to a group of elementary school children.

   Go to Part **7** or to your MindTap for *The Speaker's Handbook* and access the sample speeches. Analyze the speeches by Brian Sharkey and Harriet Kamakil, and identify several different informative strategies used by these speakers.

Summary

Helping your audience grasp your message is at the heart of every speaker's objective.

21-1 Explain the techniques that help listeners acquire, process, and retain information.

▶ Speakers must offer a framework for organizing information, move from the simple to the complex, from the familiar to the unfamiliar, and avoid overloading the audience.

21-2 Demonstrate ways to help listeners understand your speech.

▶ Common techniques of clear explanation, such as signposts, emphasis cues, examples, analogies, multiple message channels, and built-in redundancies, will help listeners follow and recall your informative speech.

Critical Thinking Questions

▶ How can a speaker help audience members avoid information overload?

▶ What is the speaker's concern?

▶ Which technique of explanation do you find most difficult and why?

▶ What are the dangers associated with information "underload"?

Putting It into Practice

Review a recent presidential broadcast. Go to the MindTap for *The Speaker's Handbook* and access **Additional Resources** for an archive of White House video broadcasts.

1. How does the president help listeners minimize information overload?
2. How does the president use organizers, emphasis cues, examples, analogies, and other techniques of clear explanation?

22

Persuasive Strategies

Plan a strategy based on sound logical analysis and an understanding of audience attitudes. Select and arrange your content for maximum persuasion.

MindTap Read, highlight, and take notes online.

Persuasion has in some ways taken on a bad name. Perhaps it's the fault of scurrilous profiteers willing to say anything for a buck. Perhaps it's due to political campaigns that seem to go on for years. Like it or not, persuasion is an important skill and ability required in the world and worthy of our attention. The question isn't should one persuade but how does one do it ethically? Or perhaps, what gives one person the right to try to change the attitudes or behavior of another? Answering these questions requires an understanding of how and why people change their minds.

There are many theoretical frameworks for approaching persuasion—from Aristotle's *logos, pathos*, and *ethos*; through post-World War II models of social judgment theory and consistency theories; up to the contemporary cataloging of compliance-gaining strategies or neurobiological influences on persuasion. Although an examination of these theories is out of place in a practical handbook, we touch on to several of them in the following chapter.

Regardless of which framework is used, persuasion begins with the need to clearly understand your audience and persuasive objective. By understanding the audience's attitude toward the topic either for, against, or somewhere in between, the speaker can begin to make choices and in the end organize ideas to enhance the persuasive impact of the speech.

MindTap®   Visit the MindTap for *The Speaker's Handbook* for help preparing persuasive speeches.

22-1 Clarify Your Persuasive Goals

A strong grasp of purpose is especially important in **persuasive speaking**. When you try to change people, and not simply educate or inspire them, you are more likely to run into resistance. It helps to establish a realistic target based on what your goals are—and what they are not. (See Chapter **6**.) In any persuasive speech, ask yourself if you are primarily trying to change people's minds or their actions.

Some authorities distinguish between persuasive speeches that seek to change actual behavior and those that merely try to influence beliefs and attitudes. Generally, if you want action, you should set your goals in terms of action and tell the audience what to *do*, not what to *think*. However, you can make an exception to this guideline when you will be speaking to an audience unfavorable to your position. Here, it is better to set a realistic goal of obtaining agreement with your views in order to avoid losing the audience if you ask for too much too soon.

It is also important in setting goals to think carefully about the nature and direction of the impact you seek. There is a tendency to characterize persuasion as "getting people to start doing something," such as buy a product or vote for a candidate. This persuasive goal, known as *adoption*, is only one of four. You might also try to persuade a person to stop doing something (*discontinuance*), to keep doing something (*continuance*), or to not start doing something (*deterrence*).[1]

On the general topic of physical fitness, for example, you could choose one of a number of persuasive tacks for your speech, such as persuading your audience to the following:

▶ *Adopt* a regular exercise program.

▶ *Continue* eating healthful foods.

▶ *Stop* eating junk foods.

▶ *Avoid* caffeine-based weight-loss supplements.

Technically, then, persuasion is not always geared toward change. The advocates of continuance or deterrence want to maintain the status quo from what they fear might happen. These two persuasive goals make sense only if there is some jeopardy or pressure from the opposite direction. A coach might give a persuasive speech to the booster club asking them to *continue* supporting the team. She knows that her audience has other demands on their time and money, and might choose to stop donating to the team.

22-2 Analyze Your Persuasive Goals

Inquiry precedes advocacy for both ethical and practical reasons. Before you can design a persuasive message that will achieve your goal, you need to analyze, or break down, the logical obligations you have taken on. In Chapter **6**, this process was described as finding within your thesis statement the list of questions that absolutely must be answered. In Chapter **16**, the process was discussed in terms of the kind of reasoning needed to provide a link between the evidence you have and the major claim(s) of your speech. Here, we pursue the analytical process more specifically from the direction of understanding the type of proposition you support and identifying the points at issue as you set out to prove your case.

22-2a Identify Whether You Need a Proposition of Fact, Value, or Policy

The thesis of a speech and the claim of an argument are also described as propositions—in persuasion, the speaker *proposes* something to the audience. There are three kinds of propositions: the **proposition of fact**, the **proposition of value**, and the **proposition of policy**. Determining which kind of proposition lies at the heart of your speech is essential to identifying your obligations and to planning your persuasive strategy.

Proposition of Fact It may seem that if something is a *fact,* there is no need to use persuasion to establish it, but there are issues in the factual domain that cannot be verified directly. For instance, there either is or is not life on other planets. The question is one of fact, but because we lack the means to find out, we must argue from the data we have, drawing the most logical inferences from them. Here are some other examples:

▸ E-cigarettes increase a person's cancer risk.

▸ Lack of physical activity increases a person's risk of developing type 2 diabetes.

▸ Converting to solar energy can save the average homeowner money.

Proposition of Value Persuasive speakers are often attempting to prove evaluative positions. Their goal is to judge the worth of something and to establish that it is good or bad, wise or foolish, just or unjust, ethical or unethical, beautiful or ugly, or competent or incompetent. For example:

▸ It is wrong to try to avoid jury duty.

▸ The free enterprise system is the best economic model for the working class.

▸ Tom Brady is the best NFL quarterback to ever play the game.

Proposition of Policy The most common and the most complex of the persuasive theses is the proposition of policy, which advocates a specific course of action. Here are some propositions of policy:

▶ The federal government should legalize marijuana for medical research.

▶ You should avoid consuming high-fructose corn syrup.

▶ You should send your children to a charter school.

When you undertake to prove a thesis statement that is a proposition of policy, you must be very specific about what plan or program should be adopted by what specifically empowered group or agency. Otherwise, although your thesis includes *should* or *should not*, it is really a disguised proposition of value. "Tax loopholes should be closed," for example, is only another way of saying, "The present tax system is bad." To be a proposition of policy, it must read, "Congress should change the present tax structure to reduce oil depletion allowances, home mortgage deductions, and home office deductions."

The thesis of a speech is a claim that, in turn, is supported by subpoints. (See Chapter **16**.) By the same token, notice that the types of propositions are cumulative: The proposition of value assumes certain propositions of fact, and the proposition of policy takes its direction from a proposition of value. Or, proving that something *should/should not* be done depends on proving that something is *good/bad*, which, in turn, requires establishing that something else *is/is not* the case. For instance, to establish this proposition of policy:

Our local government should/should not commence the aerial spraying of malathion to eradicate mosquitoes carrying the Zika virus.

One has to prove at least this proposition of value:

It is appropriate/inappropriate to risk some danger to human health in order to minimize the spread of the Zika virus.

To accept this proposition of value, three propositions of fact need to be established:

The effect of malathion on human health is/is not minimal or nonexistent. Malathion is/is not effective in controlling mosquitoes known to carry the Zika virus. The Zika virus carried by the mosquitoes is/is not important to contain.

Propositions of fact: IS/IS NOT

Propositions of value: GOOD/BAD

Propositions of policy: SHOULD/SHOULD NOT

MindTap®   SPEAKER'S WORKSHOP 22.1

1. Identify which of the following are propositions of fact, value, or policy:
   A. The cost of maintaining the state highway system will be immense.
   B. Pop music is simplistic and tasteless.
   C. Cats make better pets than dogs.
   D. Children should learn a foreign language before fifth grade.
2. Write a proposition of fact, value, and policy on each of these general topics:
   ▶ Immigration
   ▶ Nutrition
   ▶ Funding for college education

22-2b Use Stock Issues to Help You Analyze Your Topic

For some kinds of speeches, well-defined lists of requirements, or **stock issues**, guide speakers. Propositions of policy lend themselves to formal argumentative analysis, and so referring to a list of stock issues can be helpful. Drawing on preestablished "stock" issues can save your time and effort. For the standard argumentative problem-solving approach, there is no need to reinvent the wheel. Central to understanding stock issue analysis is the concept of burden of proof, which is drawn from the legal system and from the formal debate. It means that the individual or side that advocates change has specific responsibilities.

As an extreme example, consider all the burdens on the prosecutor in a murder case in the United States. In U.S. law, murder is defined as: the unlawful (1) killing (2) of a human being (3) with malice (4) aforethought (5).[2] We have numbered each of the five issues the prosecutor must prove. To fail on even one issue is to lose the case. That is, if the defense can show that any *one* of the conditions was not present—for instance, that there was no malice aforethought, or that the killing was not unlawful (as in self-defense)—then murder has not occurred. The burdens on the prosecutor are great, but they are publicly acknowledged and agreed to.

Stock Debate Issues In a formal debate on a proposition of policy, the speaker advocating a change must provide the audience with satisfactory answers to the following questions:

▶ Is there a compelling need for change?
▶ Is that need inherent in the very structure of the present system?
▶ Will the proposed solution meet the need presented?

▶ Is the proposed solution workable and practical?

▶ Do the advantages of the proposed solution outweigh its disadvantages?

You do not have to be a debater to use these stock issues—they serve as helpful guidelines in analyzing any persuasive topic.

Stock Issues against a Change The examples in the previous paragraph apply to persuasive speeches in which the primary objective is adoption. In a speech that argues against a policy—in which deterrence or discontinuance is the goal—this list of stock issues can be turned around. Because the burden of proof lies with the advocates of change, an opponent of change can succeed by establishing a negative answer to just one key issue.

22-3 Adjust Content for Audience

Chapter 7 asks you to analyze your listeners' possible reactions to your thesis. Based on surveys, observations, or inference, you can make some determination of their predisposition toward your topic. The following continuum classifies audiences according to that predisposition:

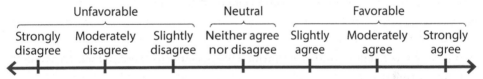

Types of audiences

Unfavorable			Neutral	Favorable		
Strongly disagree	Moderately disagree	Slightly disagree	Neither agree nor disagree	Slightly agree	Moderately agree	Strongly agree

Here are some suggestions on how to deal with such favorable, neutral, or unfavorable audiences.

MindTap **SPEAKER'S WORKSHOP 22.2**

Which stock debate issue is being addressed in each of the following points?

▶ Putting more money into the welfare program will not get at its underlying problems.

▶ Adopting a voucher system for the financing of education will allow parents to choose the educational approach that is best for their children.

▶ Violent crime has gotten out of control in our cities.

22-3a Favorable Audience

A speaker facing a favorable audience is relieved of a number of burdens. In this situation, as a speaker, you rarely need to establish credibility. Your listeners, perceiving your position as identical to theirs, approve of you and your good taste already. Furthermore, a favorable audience will not raise internal counterarguments for you to deflect or defuse. When speaking to a favorable audience, you can focus on solidifying or strengthening their attitudes, or you can cause them to move from theoretical agreement to positive action.

Use Emotional Appeals to Intensify Your Listeners' Support   The difference between intellectual agreement with and commitment to some purpose, and the difference between commitment and action are usually a function of emotional arousal. Out of the vast number of positions you might agree with, there is a much shorter list of issues that you really *care* about. These issues appeal to your most basic needs, touch on your core values, or have a personal effect on your life.

To get your speech topic on your listeners' short list, make extensive use of appeals to basic values such as patriotism, humanitarianism, and progress; to basic needs such as survival, security, and status; and to basic emotions such as fear, pity, and love. (See Chapter **20**.)

Here is one example of how a position can be intensified:

Logical Stem

It is only fair to allow groups with which we disagree to exercise their legal constitutional rights.

Emotional Intensifier

Where will it stop if we allow selective enforcement of the protection provided by the Bill of Rights? Today, the flag burners or skinheads may be denied their rights as Americans; tomorrow, it may be any of us. [appeal to fear, appeal to core value of civil liberties]

See also the examples in the appropriate sections of Chapter **20**.

When listeners agree with you but are not taking action, they probably do not feel personally involved with the subject. A major task in speaking to a favorable audience is the creation of that personal involvement in two ways. First, be very specific about how their lives are affected. Then, show them that their actions can make a difference:

▶ Your $10 check can feed a Sudanese refugee family for a week.

▶ If you can take that extra second to switch off the lights as you leave the room, you can save yourself $50 a year.

For most audiences, emotional appeals should be handled sparingly and cautiously. But for the favorable audience, you can hardly be too vivid or personalized as long as you avoid bad taste and redundancy.

Get Your Audience to Make a Public Commitment Invite your listeners to offer suggestions, sign a petition, raise their hands to volunteer, lend their names to a letterhead, or talk to others. People who have made a public commitment—oral, written, or physical—are less likely to change their minds.

Provide Several Specific Alternatives for Action Make it easy for listeners to take action by offering several specific choices. For example, to people who have shown up at a rally for a candidate, do not say, "Stop by campaign headquarters sometime." Instead, say, "I'd like everyone here either to walk a precinct or to spend an evening making phone calls. Sign-up sheets are being passed around now. If you can't help out in either of these ways, Judy will be standing at the door and can tell you about other things that need to be done to ensure our success." With a favorable audience, do not settle for urging members to do "something." If you want them to reduce their sodium intake, share with them low-sodium recipes to eat.

Present Abbreviated Arguments So Audience Members Actively Participate in the Reasoning Process Because a favorable audience often shares your values and beliefs, it is not always necessary to spell out every step of your reasoning. In fact, classical rhetorical theory suggests that **enthymemes** (compact lines of argument) are very powerful. When audience members fill in parts of the reasoning you have not spelled out—be it major premise, minor premise, or conclusion—they are actively participating in making meaning with you. Just as members of a group feel that they are bonding when they use special jargon or initials or shorthand lines of speech, favorable audience members will establish an "in-group" feeling of commitment when a speaker takes some things for granted:

▶ If we elect this candidate, it will be like returning to the Obama years. [this approach assumes that the audience will agree that the Obama years were bad]

▶ We must support this bond issue, for if it fails, there will be no raises for teachers for five years. [assuming the audience agrees that raises for teachers are desirable]

To use these brief enthymematic arguments that create audience involvement, however, you must be sure your listeners really do share your beliefs. Otherwise, the shortcut can backfire.

Prepare Your Audience to Carry Your Message to Others You can tap the potential of audience members as persuaders in their own right. Each of them may later discuss your topic with coworkers, neighbors, or friends who are neutral or hostile toward it. Give your listeners ammunition for these interactions, and make that

CHECKLIST ~ For a Favorable Audience

- [ ] Use emotional appeals to solidify agreement.
- [ ] Seek a public commitment from listeners.
- [ ] Tell your audience exactly what actions they can take.
- [ ] Give your listeners ammunition to answer opposing points.
- [ ] Create involvement by letting your listeners "fill in the blanks" in your argument.

© Dusit/Shutterstock.com

material as memorable and quotable as possible. When, in front of a favorable group, you offer examples, arguments, and statistics that support your position, your goal is not to persuade your immediate audience. Rather, you are aiming at the second generation of listeners. This second audience is a reason to avoid relying solely on the compact argument of the enthymeme.

A part of this preparation involves providing your audience with ready answers to refute standard counterarguments. This also serves to inoculate your listeners against the persuasiveness of those counterarguments. Here's an example:

> You may meet people who tell you that the administration's economic policy is designed to help the average worker. Just ask those people why the greatest tax relief goes to the rich. Have them explain to you why a person who earns $300,000 a year will have a 50 percent reduction in taxes, but a person making $18,000 a year will see a reduction of only 6 percent. They may say, "Ah, but we are creating new jobs." Ask them this....

22-3b Neutral Audience

An audience can be neutral toward your position for one of three reasons: they are *uninterested*, they are *uninformed*, or they are genuinely *undecided*.

Stress Attention Factors with an Uninterested Neutral Audience Listeners may be uninterested in a topic or position because they do not see how it affects them directly. With this sort of audience, draw on all the attention factors described in Chapter **18**, but give special emphasis to the *vital*. Their interest and attention can be gained only through concrete illustrations of the impact of your subject on their lives:

> A lot of you are probably saying, "So what? So what if somebody across the room lights up a cigarette? It's a free country, and he's inhaling the smoke, not me." Would you say, "So what?" if I told you secondhand smoke can blacken your lungs just as badly as if you smoked 2–27 cigarettes a day?

Be sure the facts and statistics you use are relevant to your listeners' experience. Sprinkle your speech with humor and human interest. Make a special effort to have a lively and animated delivery and style to stimulate your audience.

Clarify and Illuminate Your Position with an Uninformed Neutral Audience Before you can expect people to agree with you, they must have some comprehension of the issue. When they lack that essential background, you must spend a significant portion of your speech filling them in, even if it means sacrificing time better spent making points to support your position.

The main concern is clarity: Use explanation, definitions, examples, and restatement. (See Chapter **21**.) Visual aids can be helpful. Keep your language simple and your organization straightforward.

A direct persuasive appeal should be saved until the very end of the speech.

Present New Arguments that Blend Logical and Emotional Appeals for an Undecided Neutral Audience The undecided neutral audience is both interested in and informed about your topic, but these listeners find the arguments for each side equally compelling. Let them know that you understand their ambivalence. Grant the complexity of the issue, and admit that there is truth on both sides.

Offer yourself as the vehicle for reducing their ambivalence. Establish your credibility by communicating expertise and integrity. As you present the arguments for your side, emphasize any recent evidence or new interpretations that might justify a change in position. By definition, this audience finds sense in some aspects of the opposing arguments. This means you must acknowledge and respond to the main arguments against your position, using the techniques discussed at the end of this chapter. Similarly, you need to inoculate listeners against arguments they may encounter later so that they can dismiss them as having been dealt with already.

In short, a well-documented, logical presentation works best for the undecided neutral audience. Appeals to emotions, needs, and values are effective only if used sparingly and clearly interwoven with the logical argument of the speech.

22-3c Unfavorable Audience

An unfavorable audience is by no means a belligerent one—remember that *unfavorable* encompasses anything on the "disagree" side of neutral, starting with "slightly disagree." However, the more intensely the audience disagrees with you, the more its members will be predisposed to reject both you and your message. Any idiosyncrasies of appearance and style of delivery will allow them to dismiss you as someone on the lunatic fringe. A single joke that falls flat turns you into a buffoon. A stance expressed with too much conviction brands you as a fanatic.

At the same time, your audience realizes the disadvantage under which you are working. If you handle the situation with gracefully, you might earn their respect.

CHECKLIST ~ For a Neutral Audience

- Did you use a sufficient number of attention factors?
- Is your point clear and understandable?
- Did you present the most recent evidence and examples available?
- Did you send your message in multiple ways to engage the senses?
- Did you blend logical and emotional appeals?

The results can be gratifying when you approach the speech to an unfavorable audience as a challenge to your skill.

Set Realistic Goals for a Single Speech Do not try to do too much with an unfavorable audience. Attitude change takes place slowly. If most of your audience falls at the "strongly disagree" end of the continuum, do not expect your ten-minute speech to change their attitudes dramatically. Sometimes, the measure of success is that they throw eggs and not bricks. Even if it means modifying your thesis statement, set a goal that you have a reasonable chance of achieving, such as easing those who strongly disagree over to moderate disagreement, or those who moderately disagree over to neutrality. Do not make an express call for action when such action is highly unlikely. For instance, it would be self-defeating to ask an animal-rights group to support the efficiency of factory farming. Better to ask members to think about the issues you have raised, or to ask them to work together with farmers to find a compromise.

Stress Common Ground However great the difference between you and your audience on any particular issue, there are bound to be places where your opinions and experiences overlap. Ask yourself what goals and values you share with your unfavorable audience. Even an intense disagreement over, say, school busing reveals a common concern for children's education.

Finding common ground is important to every speech, but it is crucial to the speech to the unfavorable audience. Stress it in your introduction and at several points throughout the speech. Make these points of commonality the major premises from which your arguments proceed. (See Chapter **16**.) When you minimize the differences between you and your audience, you create the basis for communication to occur.

Use Sound Logic and Extensive Evidence The unfavorable audience is skeptical of your position and will reject most emotional appeals as being manipulative. Your only chance to persuade these listeners is to build an iron-clad case supported by sound, unbiased evidence. With this audience, you must clearly indicate every step of your reasoning—nothing can be taken for granted. Discuss and defend even those assumptions that seem obvious to you. Spell out the logical links and connections that hold your argument together. Do not overstate your points; be careful not to claim more than the data allow. Say, "These examples suggest …" rather than "These examples prove …"; say, "Smoking is one contributing cause of cancer," rather than "Smoking causes cancer."

Use factual and statistical evidence, and always cite your sources completely. If you mention the results of a survey, for example, tell when, where, and how it was conducted and where it was presented or published. When supporting your points with testimony, quote reluctant experts, if possible, or highly respected unaffiliated authorities. Quotations from your own partisans are hardly worth giving. (See Chapter **15**.)

Directly confront the arguments that are foremost in your listeners' minds. Do not be afraid to concede minor points that do not damage your basic case. State the remaining counterarguments fairly and answer them forcefully, but never stoop to ridicule. In fact, it has been shown to be advantageous to state your opponents' view *even more elegantly than they have*, before proceeding to refute it.

Establish a Credible Image   Despite some examples in the current media, careful establishment of good character, good sense, and goodwill is more important than in a speech to an unfavorable audience. (See Chapter **19**.) Plan every detail of your speech content and delivery to project an image of a calm, reasonable, fair, well-informed, and congenial person. The judicious use of humor can bolster this image while releasing tension and putting the issue in perspective. Direct the humor at yourself, your position, a common enemy, or the ironic aspects of the confrontation. Never direct it at your listeners and their beliefs.

Although you do not want to seem combative, you should remain firm in your position. It is fine to build rapport by stressing common ground and granting minor points, but do not waffle or be overly conciliatory. Also resist the temptation to be snide, shrill, defensive, outraged, arrogant, sarcastic, flippant, or patronizing.

Do not become defensive or frustrated by heckling or other indications that you are not getting through to the audience. (See Chapter **28**.) Remember that the attitude change is a slow process and that by maintaining your dignity and rationality you will not hurt, and may help, your cause in the long run.

CHECKLIST ~ For an Unfavorable Audience

- ☐ Are you realistic about the changes you're asking listeners to make?
- ☐ Do you emphasize common ground?
- ☐ Are you thorough in your reasoning and careful with your evidence?
- ☐ Do you build your credibility by being fair and open-minded, and by using humor carefully?

SPEAKER'S WORKSHOP 22.3

Examine Kayla Strickland's speech transcript, available in Part **7** or through the MindTap for *The Speaker's Handbook*. Do you think the speaker perceived the audience as unfavorable, neutral, or favorable? What strategic decisions reflected in the speech content justify your conclusion? Name two specific adjustments the speaker should make if presenting this speech to each of the other possible types of audiences.

22-4 Organize Points for Persuasive Impact

The speech organization patterns discussed in Chapter **10**—topical, spatial, and chronological—grow out of analysis of the speech content. Other patterns can form from retracing the reasoning that led you to your conclusion—inductively, deductively, causally, or analogically. (See Chapter **16**.) Yet another way to think about ordering points is to consider how your speech unfolds for your listeners. So, if none of the familiar formats seems strategically adequate, here are some suggestions for alternative arrangements.

22-4a Organize Using the Motivated Sequence

Developed by Alan Monroe, the **motivated sequence** is a preferred method for organizing persuasive speeches. This psychologically based format echoes and anticipates the mental stages through which your listeners progress as they hear your speech. Note that it includes the speech introduction and conclusion, unlike the sample outlines in the organization chapters in Part **3**.

Attention: The speaker must first motivate the audience to listen to the speech.

Need: Listeners must become aware of a compelling, personalized problem.

Satisfaction: The course of action advocated must be shown to alleviate the problem.

Visualization: Psychologically, it is important that the audience have a vivid picture of the benefits of agreeing with the speaker or the evils of alternatives.

Action: The speech should end with an overt call for the listeners to act.

Here is an example of a speech that follows the motivated sequence:

Thesis statement: We need a light-rail system in our county to reduce excessive commuter traffic congestion.

Attention

Introduction: I was on my way to work, having left home earlier than usual so I could be there in plenty of time for my first important presentation. I heard screeching brakes. It turned out to be only a fender bender a quarter-mile ahead of me. Nevertheless, I sat in my car, and sat, and sat, while my mood progressed from irritation to outrage to despair. I arrived at work an hour and a half late, just as the meeting was breaking up.

Need

I. Excessive reliance on automobile transportation to the county's major employment areas is causing severe problems.
    A. Major traffic jams
    B. Pollution
    C. Stress to commuters

Satisfaction

II. A light-rail system should be constructed to alleviate these problems.
    A. Definition of light-rail
    B. Proposed route
    C. Proposed funding

Visualization

III. The new system would be a vast improvement.
    A. Scenario with the light-rail system
    B. Scenario without the light-rail system

Action

Conclusion: Support the county initiative for a light-rail system. Urge your friends to vote for it. Write to members of the county board of supervisors on this issue. Ask your employer to commit to providing free shuttle service from the proposed light-rail station to your place of business.

This organization is rather similar to a standard problem–solution speech, but the presence of the visualization step makes all the difference. Instead of merely providing a logical need satisfaction in main point II, this speaker has added another psychologically powerful step in main point III. Two detailed narratives drive home the case for the listeners. The actual wording of the speech might go something like this:

If this proposal is adopted, picture yourself parking at a spacious parking lot, dropping your child off at the child-care facility right at the light-rail station, and settling back in your comfortable seat. You can enjoy a cup of coffee, read your favorite newsfeed, review materials for your first meeting, and arrive at work relaxed.

But, if this proposal is not adopted, picture your commute lasting longer and longer until you are spending nearly one working day a week driving to and from work. The smallest incident will cause gridlock. The pollution will become worse. Your stress-related health problems, such as high blood pressure and headaches, will increase.

It is essential that the attention step be engaging and that the action step be concrete. This does not preclude using the other parts of introductions and conclusions discussed in Chapters **13** and **14** if they enhance clarity.

MindTap®   Visit the MindTap for *The Speaker's Handbook* and click on **Additional Resources** for more on Monroe's motivated sequence.

22-4b Organize through a Comparison of Advantages

Sometimes, your persuasive task boils down to convincing an audience to choose between two alternatives. It may be that the need to do something is acknowledged or that the choice is *go* or *no go*. In any event, your job is to show the comparative advantage of one choice over the other, which more or less dictates that you organize your speech around a sequence of head-to-head comparisons of the components of each proposal. You might have to compare energy policy based on conservation to energy policy based on expanding access to fossil fuel, or compare cost benefits for the long term and the short term. You are not compelled to say that one is perfect and the other awful. Rather, you strive to tip the scale toward your position. That is why a recurrent and highly effective phrase in comparative advantage persuasive arguments is "on balance."

22-5 Deal with Opposing Arguments

When time is limited, it is hard to decide whether to present only your own side of an issue or to bring up and refute opposing arguments. In the first instance, you run the risk of appearing to have a weak position. In the second, you sacrifice time to develop your own arguments, and there is always the chance you will introduce a point against your case that would not have occurred to your audience otherwise.

Generally, it is a good idea to address counterarguments. On widely debated topics, these ideas will already be on listeners' minds, and they expect a response. Even on less familiar subjects with which you may have the first word, you probably won't have the last. At the end of a straightforward "pro" speech, your audience may agree with you. But if listeners become aware of powerful opposing arguments a few hours or days later, they may discredit your entire position. Speakers often inoculate their audiences by presenting a few counterarguments and answering them. Then, when these points are brought up later, the listeners will say, "Oh, yes, I was warned about this." Inoculation has created "antibodies" to resist the opposing position.

FOR YOUR BENEFIT

Place Strongest Points First or Last

Be aware that people will remember best what you say first (the **primacy** principle) and what you say last (the **recency** principle). In light of this, arranging your arguments either from weakest to strongest (climactic) or from strongest to weakest (anticlimactic) will be more effective than placing your best points in the middle (pyramidal).

The research on which one is stronger—primacy or recency—is far from conclusive. It's best to consider the importance of your topic to your listeners, their attitude toward it, and your credibility. Also, remember that previews and summaries are essential in developing any complex argument. If you use these, your listeners will hear all your most significant points both first and last.

22-5a Address Opposing Arguments Directly

If opposing positions are known, it is both ethical and prudent to address those positions directly with relevant arguments. Studies have shown that when people form opinions based on issue-relevant arguments, as opposed to peripheral cues, they feel more strongly about that issue, are more likely to act upon their feelings, and are more resistant to counter persuasion.[3]

If you choose to respond to a point, you may follow these steps of refutation:

1. State the opposing view fairly and concisely.
2. State your position on that argument.
3. Document and develop your own position.
4. Summarize the impact of your argument and show how the two positions compare.

Here is a distilled example:

1. Many people argue that flexible work schedules lead to reduced productivity.
2. I challenge the underlying assumption that most people work only for money and will do as little as possible. Employees who are treated like responsible partners take pride in their work and are dependable and productive.
3. There are several research studies that support my point of view: [speaker introduces and explains the studies].
4. So these examples refute the position that flextime will lead to decreased productivity. I have shown you how that argument is based on a false assumption about why people work.

Effective refutation can take various forms. In a speech against capital punishment, a speaker might follow the points supporting the thesis with this main point:

IV. Arguments in favor of capital punishment do not justify its continuation.
   A. It is argued that capital punishment deters crime; the facts do not support this.
   B. It is argued that it is very costly to provide life sentences for serious offenders; this is true, but expenditure of money is not a justification for collective murder.
   C. It is argued that dangerous criminals are released on parole and endanger lives; this may be a problem, but we can respond with stricter parole policies rather than execution.

Note that counterarguments may be handled in different ways. Point A is denied directly. Point B is conceded but labeled unimportant. Point C is partly conceded and then analyzed in a different light. Responding to a counterargument does not mean utterly obliterating it. You may concede it, minimize it, dismiss it as irrelevant, or attack the supporting evidence or underlying premise. Even if you grant the existence of a problem, you can differ from your audience on the best solution.

22-5b Answer Counterarguments after Developing Your Position

Pro-to-con order is almost always more effective than con-to-pro. The only exception to this rule is when you know audience members are so preoccupied with an opposing position that they may not listen to you. In that case, respond to the audience's opposing point first.

MindTap   **SPEAKER'S WORKSHOP 22.4**

1. Go to Part **7** or to your Mind Tap for *The Speaker's Handbook* and access the sample speeches. In her speech, Kayla Strickland uses vivid imagery in her visualization step to help her audience imagine the impact of ending malaria. Select another of the sample speeches and create an explicit visualization step by developing two or more scenarios of what would happen if change is or is not adopted. Explain how this addition could improve the persuasive impact of the speech.

2. Read Eboo Patel's speech "The Only Shame Is In Stagnation" and describe how he chooses to refute a counterargument directly. Eboo's speech is available in Part **7** in *The Speaker's Handbook*.

Summary

Persuasion begins with the need to clearly understand your audience and persuasive objective. By understanding the audience's attitude toward the topic, the speaker can begin to make choices that will enhance the persuasive impact of the speech.

22-1 Clarify your persuasive goal.

▶ Whether our purpose is to influence attitudes and beliefs or change behaviors, the first step must establish a clear persuasive goal keeping in mind that adoption, continuance, discontinuance, and deterrence are all legitimate persuasive goals.

22-2 Analyze your persuasive goal.

▶ Inquiry must precede advocacy, so first we must understand what is involved in the persuasive goal—researching it fully, thinking about it analytically, and examining the best evidence on both sides.

▶ Persuasion can include propositions of fact, value, and policy.

▶ Stock issues are a helpful tool to use when analyzing a persuasive topic.

22-3 Decide when to adjust content based on your audience.

▶ Persuasive strategies work best when matched to the needs and attitudes of the audience.

▶ Adjust your content and strategies based on audience attitudes.

22-4 Organize your points for persuasive impact.

▶ Organize your points for optimal impact with the strongest points first or last, and consider dealing with opposing views.

▶ Useful strategies for organizing ideas persuasively include Monroe's motivated sequence, problem–solution, and comparison of advantages.

22-5 Summarize how to deal with opposing arguments.

▶ Directly address opposing arguments by refuting opposing positions with credible evidence or testimony.

▶ The pro-to-con order is almost always more effective when answering counterarguments.

Critical Thinking Questions

▶ How should a speaker's audience analysis influence the persuasive strategies he or she employs?

▶ How would an audience in favor of the speaker's position influence the speaker's call to action?

▶ How would an audience in opposition to the speaker's position influence the speaker's organization of ideas?

Putting It into Practice

What strategies or concerns do the following situations suggest? If you were the speaker, how would you develop your speech in each situation?

1. You are trying to persuade a group of high school students to take AP math and science courses.

2. You are trying to persuade the finance committee of a local nonprofit to invest $1,000 in software to help manage the volunteers efficiently.

3. You are trying to persuade a local school board to hire an additional English as a second language (ESL) teacher to serve the needs of a growing group of immigrant families.

29 Answering Questions

29-1 Demonstrate an ability to plan ahead and manage audience questions effectively.

Checklists

The Natural Theory of Delivery

A face-to-face speech puts heavy demands on speakers and listeners. However, "keynote handouts" have not replaced keynote speeches at conventions, nor have text messages usurped the role of conference presentations. This is because information transmission is but a small part of the total communicative event. People meet in public spaces to seek understanding, develop dialogue, and affirm their sense of community. The combination of voice, body, and personality—as well as on-the-spot chemistry—makes speech a vital form of communication. It is exciting to listen to a good speaker.

By *good speaker,* we mean someone who has something to say, organizes it well, and presents it well. Too often, when people describe a speaker as good or poor, the reference is to the speaker's delivery only. It seems that an audience will listen avidly to a well-delivered speech even if, at the end, they discover there was little substance in it. Few people afford the same consideration to a poorly delivered speech, no matter how exciting or important the content.

As we explained in Chapter **1,** borrowing too directly from the performance-related repertoire of the actor can be inappropriate because theatrical acting and giving a speech are fundamentally different. As an actor, you assume the role of someone else, speak words written by another person, and strive to perform each line as directed and rehearsed. As a speaker, you present your own personality, speak your own words, and try to adapt to the response you receive. Thus, public speaking is far more like conversation than like acting.

We all have had more practice communicating than performing. The natural theory of delivery is based on the assumption that we communicate well many hours of every day without consciously thinking about speech mechanics. When we are intensely involved in conversation, we do not stop to think, "Now I'll furrow my brow and point my finger." Changes in our voice and actions just happen naturally when we are wrapped up in communicating a message. If we are similarly wrapped up in the content of our speech, delivery should take care of itself. The single most important delivery goal for any speaker is to internalize this conception of speech as conversation. Once we feel the sense of interaction with an audience—the sort of give-and-take experienced in other conversations—our enjoyment of speaking will increase along with our confidence and skill.

Part 5 of this handbook looks at presentation skills by using a natural theory of delivery focusing on an extemporaneous style. Extemporaneous speeches are practiced in advance, with natural vocal inflection, purposeful physical expression, and supportive visual aids adapted to the speech situation. They might also include opportunity for questions and answers.

23

Modes of Delivery

Select a mode of delivery that is appropriate to your topic, audience, and occasion.

MindTap®   Read, highlight, and take notes online.

We advocate an extemporaneous delivery style following a *natural theory of delivery*, which emphasizes speech as an interaction of ideas, as opposed to speech as a memorized performance like an actor. However, this does not deny the performance aspects of a public speech. It does claim that the performance will be most effective when conceptualized as amplified conversation, rather than as a whole new kind of speaking.

Perhaps you have observed a speaker present stiffly and mechanically, then heave a sigh of relief and ask for questions. As if by magic you observe a great transformation! In the question-and-answer period, while clarifying points, the speaker exhibits more facial expression, more variety of tone, and more natural body language. It was as if the speaker thought, "I'm through with my speech. Now I can really talk to these people." The delivery became much more "listenable" as the speaker's attitude toward the situation shifted from performance to interaction.

23-1 Know the Four Modes of Delivery

As we've seen, each speech is a unique blend of conversation, writing, and performance. While there are four distinct modes of delivery, it is common to use more than one mode in a given speech. Whether your speech is mostly *extemporaneous* (given from brief notes), *impromptu* (off-the-cuff), *manuscript* (written out and read), or *memorized* word-for-word, be aware that no speech is purely one mode. Even in an extemporaneous speech, for example, it is often advisable to write out the introduction and conclusion and to commit them mostly to memory. And any speaker who accepts questions or encounters hecklers must be prepared to offer some impromptu retorts.

23-2 Use Four Modes of Delivery

Extemporaneous speaking is the most common mode of delivery and the one you should use in all but a few special cases. This mode is sometimes confused with impromptu speaking. Although it shares some aspects of spontaneity with the impromptu, the extemporaneous mode is considerably more structured. In the **extemporaneous** mode, you prepare extensively, constructing the progression of ideas with the aid of an outline, planning your content thoroughly, and practicing until you are comfortable and conversational. But you never commit yourself to a rigid, exact sequence of words.

Preparing a set of ideas rather than a set of verbatim paragraphs is the only practical and realistic method for most teachers, business managers, trial lawyers, salespersons, and others engaged in speaking for hours at a time or for large portions of the day. But even for the occasional public speaker, the extemporaneous mode, once mastered, offers a sense of power and confidence. You will sound more natural and conversational if you phrase your sentences as you go along. Your mind will be on your ideas and on your audience's reaction to them—you are less likely to go blank than if you are focusing on recalling certain words. You will also find extemporaneous speaking allows the most flexibility to adjust to an audience. If you find your listeners nodding knowledgeably at points you thought would be confusing and in need of clarification, you can drop your extensive examples and move on. Conversely, you can spend more time on points at of unexpected resistance or confusion.

23-2a Prepare an Extemporaneous Speech

1. Begin with a *fully* developed outline. Follow the recommendations in Chapters **9**, **10**, and **11** to arrange your material in a logical and effective manner.

2. *Condense your full-sentence outline into a keyword or key-phrase outline.* The full-sentence outline is a tool to ensure that you develop your speech content adequately and logically. The full-sentence outline is not the written version of the words you will use in your speech, however. The declarative sentences that characterize a full-sentence outline are written English, not spoken English, and if you follow them too closely as you develop the wording of your speech, the result may be dull and lifeless. In other words, you may find your expressiveness being limited by what you see on the page. For this reason, we suggest you reduce the full-sentence outline to a **keyword or key-phrase outline**—those words and phrases that convey essential ideas or information. For instance, Main Point IV of the full-sentence outline in Chapter **11** is "During World War II and after, women were used as a dispensable and secondary source of labor." This could be reduced to "WWII—dispensable labor." An outline constructed of such phrases retains the structure derived from the full-sentence outline while enabling you to improvise as you proceed through step 3.

3. *Word the speech.* Working from your keyword outline, practice putting your ideas into words. Listen to yourself carefully to detect a clumsy sentence or an exciting turn of phrase. The second time through, some of the clumsy phrases will have disappeared (and some of the exciting ones, maybe) as you play with sentence structure, rhythms, and so forth. Third time, fourth time, fifth time through—your topic is becoming more and more familiar, giving you the freedom to relax and to allow yourself to experiment with construction. You will also discover that no one way of expressing a set of thoughts is necessarily better than another: You have said the same thing five times, differently each time, but each of the last three ways works equally well.

4. *Convert your keyword outline to speech notes.* See Chapter **24** for directions on how to transfer your content to a format that provides easy visual cues to which you can refer while you are speaking.

MindTap®   Go to the MindTap for *The Speaker's Handbook* for help with outlining your speech.

23-2b Prepare an Impromptu Speech

No one should set out to give an important speech in the **impromptu** mode— on-the-spot delivery without notes or prior preparation. Those good speakers who seem to be able to speak fluently on the spur of the moment are usually speaking extemporaneously, stringing together practiced "bits" to fit the subjects that have been dropped into their laps. Just as you should not let apprehension about speaking lead you to avoiding preparation, do not assume being spontaneous is possible without prior preparation.

Keep Your Composure Do not apologize. Knowing the situation is truly a surprise, the audience will understand minor difficulties. You should have realistic expectations of yourself and not fall apart if you fail to deliver a polished presentation. Speak slowly and confidently. Remind yourself that you speak all the time without extensive preparation. In any casual conversation, not only are you speaking, but you are also planning what to say next. You do mental composition *all the time*. Do not let the stress of a speaking situation make you forget that!

By maintaining your composure, you can take full advantage of the few minutes' lead time often afforded speakers walking into a speaking situation. Use the time to do accelerated speech preparation. However short the period, the steps should be the same: pick a theme, an organizational pattern, and a beginning and ending sentence. The more you use these steps, the more easily and quickly they come.

Pick a Theme Quickly list several possible approaches to the topic. Do it mentally, or if time permits, with pencil and paper. By thinking beyond the most obvious approach, you may discover a way to link your topic to a subject you are conversant with.

Select an Organizational Framework Of course, you will not have time to prepare an extensive outline, but that doesn't mean you are justified in bouncing erratically from point to point. You can hook your topic to a simple framework like one of the following:

▶ Past–present–future

▶ Pros and cons

▶ Problems and prospects

▶ Concentric rings, with main points progressing from immediate concerns to universal concerns (e.g., in the home, in the school, in the community; or locally, regionally, nationally, internationally)

▶ Domains, developing the different spheres touched by the topic (e.g., political, social, or economic spheres; or practical, theoretical, or moral implications)

After you have divided your topic along the lines of one of these frameworks, find one means of support or development for each idea, such as an explanation, example, story, fact, or statistic.

If time permits, make a rudimentary outline. Even a few keywords on a napkin can reassure you and keep you on track once you have started to speak.

Plan Your First and Last Sentences The beginning and ending are the most difficult parts of any speech, and this is especially true in impromptu speaking. Even the simplest attention getter can propel you through that awkward first moment. When you know what your concluding sentence is, you avoid the panicky search for an ending when you run out of steam. By planning introductory and concluding sentences, you avoid the aimless rambling so characteristic of impromptu speaking.

23-2c Prepare a Manuscript Speech

There is a widespread misconception that **manuscript speaking** is the easiest and safest mode of delivery. ("I'm not an experienced speaker, so I'm going to read my speech.") This is no excuse for avoiding the extemporaneous mode. A bad manuscript speech is much worse than a bad extemporaneous speech. Stilted phrasing, monotonous vocal delivery, and lack of eye contact are all dangerous pitfalls confronting an inexperienced manuscript-style speaker.

Prepare an Easily Readable Manuscript Do not let the fact that you are writing out a manuscript lure you away from the tenets of good organization and composition. Work from a full-sentence outline. (See Chapter **11**.) Remember that the sentences of the outline are meant to be logical guides, not the actual wording of the speech.

FOR YOUR BENEFIT

Impromptu Speaking

Several scenarios can lead to impromptu speaking.

▶ *No excuse*: A lazy or overconfident speaker may decide to "wing it" even though there has been plenty of time to prepare. The resulting shoddy word choice, lack of organization, repetition, generalities, and unsupported assertions will be a monumental waste of the audience's time.

▶ *Should have seen it coming*: Many impromptu speeches could have been extemporaneous if the speaker had analyzed the requirements and potentials of the situation. The best man at a wedding who has not prepared a toast is guilty of failing to understand his responsibilities.

▶ *Legitimately unexpected*: There are some instances in which a speaker has no idea that he or she will have to speak. Perhaps a question that will require a quick impromptu response will arise in a business meeting.

To get from the outline to the manuscript, "talk" the speech out and onto the paper. You need to check your composition against your ear more than your eye. As you write, and rewrite, keep saying it aloud, listening for the rhythms of oral style. (See Chapter 17.) A digital voice recorder or voice recorder software is helpful here, most smart phones have a record feature. Listen to yourself and identify the stiff, unwieldy phrases that need revision. To get a second opinion, have a friend listen.

When you have settled on the final version of your speech, produce the copy from which you will read, following these guidelines:

▶ Don't write it out by hand; print it, triple-spaced, with large fonts and wide margins.

▶ Use capital and lowercase letters in standard sentence format. Text written in all capitals is more difficult to read.

▶ Print it on heavy paper. Avoid lightweight, crinkly or flimsy paper.

▶ Make sure the letters are dark and legible.

Figure 23.1 gives an example of a manuscript page prepared along these lines. Note that the speaker has included marginal notations to help him find his place and has marked up the text to indicate areas for emphasis.

MindTap In some speaking situations, you will read your speech from a teleprompter or similar machine, rather than your manuscript. To practice using a web-based teleprompter, click on **Additional Resources** through the MindTap for The Speaker's Handbook. Apps are also available for portable electronic phones and the iPad.

FIGURE 23.1
Easy-to-follow manuscript

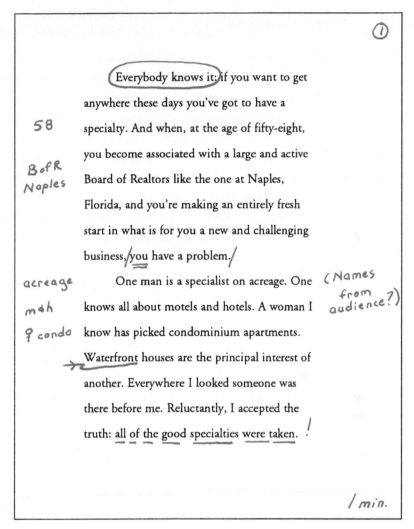

Become Familiar with Your Manuscript   The two biggest problems in delivering a manuscript speech are a lack of conversational inflection and a lack of eye contact. Even though every word is written out, you should not sight-read. Practice reading your manuscript out loud often enough to become comfortable with it. Do not memorize the words, but become familiar with the concepts and language, including the flow and rhythm. If you follow the hints for composing in the oral style, you will avoid slipping into a singsongy cadence or gasping for breath after long sentences.

The printed, easy-to-follow page, as shown in Figure 23.1, is essential to maintaining good eye contact during a manuscript speech. The spaces and visual cuing

FOR YOUR BENEFIT

When to Use a Manuscript

Limit your use of manuscripts to the following three situations:

▶ *The time allotted is specific and inflexible.* This is mostly the case in the broadcast media, such as a radio show or online audio program.

▶ *The wording is extremely critical.* There are occasions when slight differences in phrasing are unacceptable. Poor word choices can have severe consequences. The most visible examples are the public statements made by world leaders during a crisis. Could the lack of precision in speaking lead to lawsuits?

▶ *The style is extremely important.* There are special occasions when precision is required. Perhaps an occasion calls for language to be more compact, elevated, witty, or elegant than your everyday speech.

ESB Professional/Shutterstock.com

make you less likely to lose your place while looking at the audience regularly. Only through sustained eye contact can you create connections, build credibility, and gather feedback. An occasional quick glance up from the page will not provide you with much information about what is going on in the audience, and such jerky movements can be distracting to listeners. If you have practiced your speech enough, you will be comfortable raising your head and engaging the audience with unhurried looks.

Never read your first or last few sentences or your punch lines. Have them memorized so that you can begin and end your speech making eye contact with your audience.

23-2d Prepare a Memorized Speech

By definition, giving a **memorized** speech entails a manuscript speech—without the manuscript. The only times you should give a memorized speech, therefore, are the same as discussed in the previous section, with the added limitations that the speech should be a short one and the situation inappropriate for reading. These occasions are most often ceremonial: giving a toast, presenting a plaque, or accepting an honor.

Memorize the Speech Structure First Learn a few keywords that help you internalize the sequence of ideas. For example, if you are presenting an award to your company's salesperson of the year, you might learn this outline for your brief speech:

I. Selection process for the award

II. Chris Welch's sales record for this year

III. Chris's qualities as a successful salesperson

Or even more simply:

▶ Process

▶ Record

▶ Qualities

Read Speech Aloud Several Times; Then Learn in Paragraph by Paragraph Always keep your mind on the meaning. Do not try to learn sentences in isolation, but rather work on whole paragraphs at a time, reinforcing their logical and conceptual unity.

As You Practice, Visualize Giving the Speech Avoid thinking of your speech as lines of text in a social vacuum. You do not want to be startled and lose your concentration when you realize you are actually facing a roomful of people.

Avoid Trance-Like Delivery Once again, be comfortably familiar with your material so that you can maintain eye contact and establish a rapport with your audience, instead of having your eyes glaze over and your voice and body tighten with concentration. Your audience should sense your presence and connection to the moment. If you happen to forget your lines, the best strategy is to speak along the general lines of the point you know you were trying to make, so you can collect your thoughts and connect back into what you have memorized.

MindTap **SPEAKER'S WORKSHOP 23.1**

Go to the MindTap for *The Speaker's Handbook* to access the interactive videos and watch the speeches by Nathanael Dunlavy and Kayla Strickland. Classify each speaker's delivery mode as extemporaneous, impromptu, manuscript, or memorized. Did any of these speakers blend more than one mode? The speeches are also available in Part **7**.

MindTap®   Go to the MindTap for The Speaker's Handbook and click on **Additional Resources** to visit a site that concisely reviews the four modes of delivery.

Summary

23-1 Differentiate among the four modes of delivery.

▶ The four main speech delivery modes are extemporaneous, impromptu, manuscript, and memorized.

▶ Although most speeches should be delivered extemporaneously, even an extemporaneous speech might incorporate impromptu and memorized modes.

23-2 Demonstrate an ability to speak following the four modes of delivery.

▶ Use a four-step process to develop an effective extemporaneous style. Start with a full-sentence outline, practice the speech aloud to develop the wording of the speech, and develop a keyword outline.

▶ When speaking impromptu, it is important to keep your composure, pick a theme, select an organizational frame, and carefully plan your first and last sentences.

▶ Use a manuscript only if necessary, and then be sure to prepare an easy-to-read manuscript and become familiar with the manuscript to maximize eye contact and natural vocal qualities.

▶ Memorizing a speech requires considerable preparation because it involves memorizing the speech structure and each portion of the speech. Break the speech into logical parts to make memorization easier. Visualize yourself delivering the speech in a natural conversational way and avoid becoming robotic or trance-like in delivery.

Critical Thinking Questions

▶ Which delivery style is most conducive to developing a conversation with the audience?

▶ How are the impromptu, manuscript, and memorized styles useful to an extemporaneous delivery?

▶ What are the disadvantages of extemporaneous speaking?

Putting It into Practice

MindTap® Go to the MindTap for *The Speaker's Handbook* and click on **Additional Resources** to locate the speeches listed below. Determine the style of delivery employed in each speech.

1. Sheryl Sandberg's TedX presentation on Women Leaders
2. James Winston's 2013 Heisman Trophy acceptance speech
3. Michael Bloomberg's address in support of religious tolerance and the New York City mosque
4. Andre Agassi's farewell to tennis address at the U.S. Open
5. Robert Kennedy's "Remarks on the Assassination of Martin Luther King, Jr." What are the advantages and disadvantages of each style?

Practice Sessions

Use practice sessions to help compose and polish your speech. Allow time for three stages of practice.

S tart practicing your speech aloud well before your presentation. This enables you to finalize your points, get feedback, and polish your delivery. Individual differences and situational constraints will determine how much practice time is necessary. Novice speakers will benefit from five to seven run-throughs; more experienced speakers will find two to three rehearsals sufficient.

24-1 Make Improvements through Practice Sessions

It is not necessarily true that more is better. In the case of your speech or report, too much practice may make your delivery stale, and you run the risk of becoming bored with your topic. Most new speakers err in the opposite direction, however, and the result is even more disastrous. To avoid falling into either of these traps, you should plan your practice sessions, write down a timetable of steps and phases, and adhere to it. We recommend three stages of practice: early, middle, and final.

Your speech is not going to be lifeless between these sessions. The creative process, as outlined in Chapter 5, will continue, and the practice timetable should not be so rushed that the periods of incubation between sessions are squeezed out. Doing a stand-up, full-scale practice once in the morning and once in the evening for three days is immeasurably better than running through the speech six times in a row. With your practice sessions spread out, you are more likely to benefit from the illumination and refinement that follow incubation.

There is no one timetable that works for all speeches. Table 24.1 shows possible timetables for three speeches in which the advance notice is different for each. This can be used as a guide to help you create a schedule unique to your circumstances. A practice timetable can also be influenced by personal differences in speaking ability. For instance, an experienced speaker giving a classroom speech may not need three practices a day—one may suffice. Adapt your timetable based on an honest evaluation of your speaking skills.

24-1a Use Early Sessions to Develop Your Outline

During these early developmental sessions, you transform your outline of ideas into a speech by adding the elements of language and delivery to the logical framework erected by your outline. Begin by internalizing your outline. Read it over a number of times, becoming familiar with the flow of the logic. Sit at your desk or a table and talk

TABLE 24.1
Practice schedules for different types of speeches

	MAJOR POLICY ADDRESS	CLASSROOM SPEECH	ROUTINE ORAL REPORT IN BUSINESS MEETING
Commitment made to speak	Several weeks before	Ten days before	Twenty-four hours before
Preliminary analysis, research, and outline completed	One week before	Four days before	Evening before
Early practice sessions (development)	One to two weeks before: Discuss ideas with colleagues. Five to six days before: Talk through speech once a day.	Four to ten days before: Talk about speech with friends. Four days before: Read outline several times; practice aloud twice.	Afternoon or evening before: Talk through basic ideas with friends or colleagues. Evening before: Practice aloud one to three times.
Middle practice sessions (feedback)	Four days before: Video record speech, review with advisors, repeat.	Three days before: Give speech to friendly critic, receive feedback, practice aloud once more.	Morning of meeting: Give report to colleague if possible.
Final practice sessions (refinement)	Three days before: Practice aloud each day; read notes or outline each day. Day of speech: Practice aloud once; review notes just before speaking.	Two days before: Practice aloud one to three times each day; read outline and notes several times. Day of speech: Practice aloud once; review notes just before speaking.	Day of presentation: Practice aloud once; review notes just before leaving for meeting.

your way through the outline. Try to explain the ideas to yourself—part thinking, part talking it out, and part note taking.

At this point, pick a quiet spot and start to put together the speech as it will actually be given. Stand up and give the speech out loud in your speaking voice. Include everything. Do not say to yourself, after making a point, "and then I'll give a few examples"—actually give them. You want to discover awkward phrases and poor word choices sooner rather than later. Visualize the speech situation and mentally put yourself there. Do not think, "This is a practice session." Instead, make it real—envision the faces out there and talk to them. At this point, do not worry about refining your gestures and vocal inflection.

Sometime during this stage, you will have made the first draft of your speech notes, which are discussed later in this chapter. Do not carve them in stone. Things will change as you tinker with the wording.

24-1b Use Middle Sessions to Get Feedback

After you have become comfortable with your material but before doing the final polishing, seek feedback on your speech. This is usually sometime in the middle of your timetable. If you solicit feedback on content, style, and delivery before you have finished shaping your basic speech, you will miss getting help on those parts that have not yet been crystallized. If the feedback comes too late in the schedule, you will not have time to incorporate the useful information you have received.

Practice in Front of Others and Ask for Their Feedback Seek a variety of responses from others—colleagues, family members, and friends. If possible, move beyond your support group and find critics who are representative of your potential audience. If you are going to speak to a high school audience, for instance, ask your teenage cousin to listen to a practice session. As you rehearse your speech, imagine you are in front of your actual audience, and skip the nervous clowning and friendly informality. Do not leave things out and say, "You've heard this story." Tell the story. *Most importantly, do not talk about your speech. Give your speech aloud from start to finish.*

Ask for honest feedback on content and delivery, but do not necessarily take any single person's comments as the last word. He or she has quirks and prejudices just like everyone else. A group of people is preferable because it gives you a sampling of responses.

You should not ask, "How'd you like my speech?" Answers like "It was nice" or "I thought it was okay" certainly do not help you much. Lead your critics with a few questions and seek clarification of their answers. Here are some specific questions you can ask:

- "What did you see as the single most important thing I was trying to say?"
- "What were the main ideas I was trying to get across?"

Get answers to these two questions before moving on to finer points of development and delivery. If your audience cannot come up with your thesis sentence and main points, then you must look at your structure again. You are speaking for a specific purpose, and everything else is insignificant if your reason for speaking is not being understood. If you are satisfied that your purpose is clear, then you can ask questions along these lines:

▶ "Did my ideas flow in a logical sequence?"

▶ "Did the speech hold your attention? What parts were boring? Confusing?"

▶ "Did I prove my points?"

▶ "Did my introduction show you where I was going?"

▶ "Did the conclusion tie the speech together?"

▶ "Did I sound natural?"

▶ "Did I have any distracting mannerisms?"

Record Your Practice Session and Analyze Your Performance   A video is the next best thing to a human critic. You might use a video camera, smart phone, or tablet to record your speech. If you are taking classes, your school may have equipment for this purpose available through the library or the Communication lab. Some speech consultants will offer to record your speech and review it with you.

When you view your performance on playback, try to get outside yourself and see the image as that of a stranger. Become the audience and ask yourself the same questions raised previously. You might not believe it when a friend tells you that you start every other sentence with "I mean" and you are always playing with your hair, but the evidence is inescapable when you review a recording. A hazard to avoid here is being too self-critical. Seeing yourself on video can be devastating if you notice only the aspects that need improvement. Look also for things you are doing right. Do not get caught up in examining physical attributes—worrying about the shape of your nose, or the fact that your ears stick out, or that your recorded voice sounds strange to you. This is where it can be helpful to watch the recording with a friend or coach who can give you a more balanced perspective.

If recording equipment is not available, an audio recorder can be useful for feedback on content, pacing, voice, and so on. Occasionally, you may want to use an audio recorder earlier in the schedule, especially if you are blocked creatively. The recording can help you remember good ideas and possible wordings, and hearing your own ideas and phrasings will complement talking your ideas out with friends.

Practice in Front of a Mirror No More Than One Time   Practicing in front of a mirror often does more harm than good. Other feedback methods *delay* the feedback: first you speak, and then you assess the details of your presentation. With a mirror, however, you are compelled to divide your attention between what you are saying and how you are saying it. If you have no other way to check on the visual impact of your posture, gestures, and facial expressions, it may be worthwhile to practice before a mirror just once. But focus on giving the whole speech. Avoid starting and stopping your delivery, and use the mirror as a guide to the amount of eye contact you are currently able to make.

24-1c Use Final Sessions for Refinements

By this time, you should be committed to a basic version of your speech while maintaining the flexibility of the extemporaneous mode. You should not be making radical changes.

Make the Final Practice Sessions as Realistic as Possible If you are going to use visual aids, they should be ready early enough that you can include them in your final practice sessions. The same holds true for the final draft of your note cards. Check yourself against your time limit. Practice your speech, standing up, at the rate and volume you will be using at your presentation. Speaking with rudimentary mechanical amplification to a large audience, for example, will use more breath than will the conversational volume used in early practice. You need to boom out your speech unabashedly in the final practice sessions if that is what it will take to be heard when you actually give the speech. Continue reading through your notes and outline, but do not think of these activities as a substitute for the formal practice sessions.

24-2 Prepare Speaking Notes

You should not confuse speaking notes with your speech outline, as they serve different functions. An outline is used to ensure the speech has a logical organization. **Speech notes** (also called **speaker's notes**), in contrast, are used as an aid while you are actually speaking.

Like your outline and wording, your notes can go through several drafts. Work on them, doodle on them, and then copy them over. The physical act of copying over your notes is an excellent way to firm up your speech in your mind.

24-2a Include Keywords, Phrases, and Material to Be Cited Directly

Unlike your outline—in which points must be parallel, mutually exclusive, and in full sentences—speech notes do not have a regulation format. A point can be represented by a word, a sentence fragment, or a complete sentence or two. What goes into your notes depends on what you find you need during practice. For example, perhaps one point of your speech, which in your outline was developed to the second level of

FIGURE 24.1
Speech notes

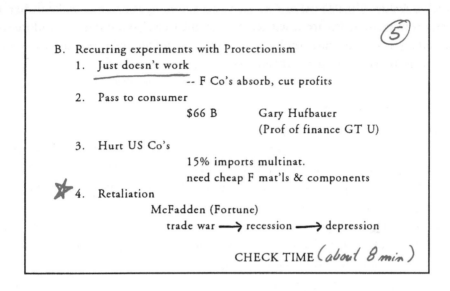

subordination, with all its accompanying A's and B's and 1's and 2's, is one with which you are so familiar that it can be represented in speech notes resembling those in Figure 24.1.

While practicing, you may also find that you want more than just a keyword reminder to get through an important but tongue-twisting sentence, or to ensure you remember an especially eloquent turn of phrase that has a delicate rhythm. Your notes may also contain material that you will be citing exactly as written out, such as long quotations or complicated statistics.

Keep in mind, however, that your notes should remain *notes*. If you make them too extensive and detailed, you risk moving out of the extemporaneous mode and into the realm of the manuscript speech. Your notes should be referred to, *never read*.

24-2b Prepare Speech Notes in a Format That Aids Delivery

Your speaking can occur in many contexts (see Part **6**), and these will dictate to some degree the format your notes take. The invited speaker at a world affairs forum may use 4 × 6-inch cards. An attorney in court does not look out of place referring to a legal pad while speaking. A project manager can glance at the PowerPoint note page on her laptop screen covering the content of her slides. For all of these instances, however, our earlier advice on preparing speech notes still applies.

In addition, formatting guidelines apply to notes in any layout. The words and phrases should be large, well spaced, and uncluttered. There should be a lot of visual cues—large card numbers, underlining, indenting, stars, highlighting, and different colors—all for the purpose of making it easy to find what you want at a glance. Speech notes should also include written cues for choices you will make during the speech. Time notations are essential. You might write at one point, "If more than eight minutes, skip to [card 6/point 4/slide 10]." You might use a special color to mark optional sections of the speech. Examples highlighted in yellow could mean: "Include this if the audience seems uncertain about my point. Otherwise, omit it."

Preparing Speech Notes on Note Cards   Many speakers prefer to put their notes on 4 × 6-inch cards. As opposed to a large, flimsy 8½ × 11-inch sheet of paper, a few medium-sized note cards in your hand will not distract your listeners as you gesture and move about. Do not be coy about using your notes—refer to them honestly. A surreptitious peek at protectively cupped hands will not fool your listeners into believing that you are speaking without aids.

Do not go to the other extreme and get lost in your notes. You should be able to look down, see what is next, and then talk about it. If you find yourself burying your nose in your notes, you have not prepared them correctly.

Preparing Speech Notes with Presentation Software   Presentation software gives you the option of entering notes to accompany the digital slides you create. You can even include the precise data or a short quotation. Adjust the font so that it is easily readable, and feel free to mark up the output with the other visual cues, as illustrated in Figure 24.1. Trim excess paper and staple or glue the sheets to your note cards. Chapter **27** provides additional suggestions for preparing and practicing with presentation aids.

24-3 Adjust Speech to Fit into Time Limit

As discussed in Chapter **6**, you must limit your topic according to the time allowed. Often, you cannot tell for sure how much time your speech will take until you have gotten well into the practice sessions. In extemporaneous practice, your speech time will vary as you work with the form of your ideas and the style and rhythm of your speaking. This again is where envisioning audience response is helpful. Most first-time speakers practice at a speaking rate faster than the one they find necessary for clarity during the speech itself. The more realistic your practice, the less likely you are to overestimate or underestimate your time.

To clock your speech, do not glue your eyes to the sweep hand of your watch or the changing digits on your watch or cell phone. Merely note the time when you begin and when you finish. Time watching can induce unnatural behavior, such as speaking at twice your normal rate for the last minute if you think you are running long, or, in the opposite case, slowing your delivery to a tired shuffle. There are more sensible

CHECKLIST ~ Formatting Guidelines for Speech Notes

- [ ] Are your note cards clearly written using brief words or phrases in large well-spaced fonts?
- [ ] Do you include visual cues (large card numbers, underlining, indenting, stars, highlighting, and different colors) to make it easy for you to find what you need at a glance?
- [ ] Have you added time notations to keep on track (for instance: "> 8 minutes, skip to conclusion")?
- [ ] Are your optional speech sections marked clearly (consider color-coded highlighting to signify importance)?

Dusit/Shutterstock.com

ways to address problems of length. The first step is to time the parts of your speech, perhaps by having a helper jot down the times of your main points on your outline as you practice or doing it yourself with an audio recorder.

Look at the relative proportions of your introduction, body, and conclusion. Generally, the body should make up 75 percent of your speech. Does an extended story make the introduction too long? Look, too, at the relative proportions of your main points. Are you spending half your time on only the first main point? Is it worth it?

If Your Speech Is Too Long:

1. Consider cutting out an entire main point. (Adjust your thesis accordingly.)
2. Eliminate redundant supporting evidence and examples. (But save the ones cut; you might be able to use them for the question-and-answer period.)
3. Turn some of your illustrations into examples; instead of telling the whole story, toss off a one-liner that encapsulates it.
4. Eliminate long stories, jokes, and narrations unless they are absolutely essential.
5. Instead of explaining technical or detailed information, use handouts or visual aids.
6. Polish and tighten your language and phrasing. Speak simply.

If Your Speech Is Too Short:

1. Consider whether some important ideas are not sufficiently developed in relation to the other points.
2. See if you are too concise for your own good. Remember that the spoken word needs repetition, embellishment, and illustration to bring home your message to every member of the audience.
3. Make sure you have proved all your points. Double-check your evidence to make sure you have not assumed too much or made some logical leaps that are not justified.
4. Do more research. You may have given up too soon on your research.

In a speech class, there may be penalties for not reaching a minimum time limit. In most other settings, no one is going to be awfully upset if you take only fifteen out of the twenty minutes you have been given. However, taking forty minutes when you have been allotted twenty can disrupt the schedules of many people.

The experienced speaker always knows the duration of each element of the speech. Even if the first clocking run-throughs show that the speech meets the time requirements, it still helps to have a point-by-point time breakdown. This knowledge makes it easier to adapt to changes that might crop up in the speech situation itself. (See Chapter **28**.)

When you reach that point in your practicing at which the speech consistently comes out the same length, mark the cumulative times of the parts in your notes. For example, you might print "2 min" at the bottom right of your notes on the introduction, "4 min" after the first main point, "6 min" after the second, and so on. (See Figure 24.1.)

Here, as examples, are two plausible scenarios in which knowing the timing of the elements of your speech will help you adapt without panic:

First Situation
You planned to spend five minutes on your first main point. Feedback from the audience convinces you to use eight minutes to make certain they are getting it. You decide to drop anecdotes from your second and third points to make up the three minutes.

Second Situation
You are on a program that is running late but can't go over time because of scheduling conflicts. The moderator asks you to trim your presentation from 30 minutes to 10 minutes. You begin doing mental arithmetic, subtracting combinations of points until you arrive at a plausible shortened version of the speech.

Some people have internal clocks that are accurate enough that they do not need external cues. If yours is not that well developed (and most people's are not), feel free to take off your watch and lay it where you can see it, use your cell phone's clock feature, or have a colleague in the audience give you prearranged time signals. However, avoid excessive reliance on the clock. Become comfortable with your presentation by practicing and timing your speech.

24-4 Avoid Common Practice Pitfalls

Many students make the mistake that working on their speech or visual aids is the same as practicing the speech itself. It is necessary to understand that there is a difference between preparing the speech and actually practicing it. Follow these steps to avoid the common practice pitfalls.

1. "Mental" Rather Than Oral Practice

Sitting and thinking about your speech, or reading over your outline or notes, is no substitute for rehearsing the speech aloud. Oral practice is essential to get comfortable with phrasing and to check your timing. Do not let your speaking anxiety (Chapter 4) lead you to put off practicing orally until the last moment. Instead, replace negative messages with positive, affirming statements and visualize yourself being successful.

2. Too Many Critics

Some speakers seek feedback from everyone they know, and most of these people are happy to oblige. Although it is good to get a variety of opinions, it can be confusing to receive contradictory advice: "Make it longer." "Make it shorter." "You seem too serious." "You seem too casual." It is *your* speech; after receiving comments from a few people whose judgment you trust, decide what advice to take, and move on to finalizing your speech.

3. Over-Preparation

This is rare, but some speakers rehearse their speech so much that it becomes mechanical. As noted in Chapter 1, by drawing too heavily on writing or performing or both,

FOR YOUR BENEFIT

Getting Effective Feedback

With a little planning, you can increase your chances of getting focused and useful feedback.

▶ **Form a Feedback Support Group**

Although you can get feedback from a number of sources, the best way is to establish an ongoing relationship with people who have similar goals. In a speech class, this may be a group of classmates who meet to discuss ideas and practice speeches. Consider joining a local Toastmasters club to gain valuable practice and support. The most effective speakers routinely test their messages with others throughout the phases of development.

▶ **Set Guidelines for Feedback**

Any group of speakers should establish some ground rules for commenting on each other's speeches, such as offering specific rather than general feedback. See Chapter 2 for a discussion of constructive feedback. Often, the speakers lead these discussions, asking for comments with respect to organization, delivery, message clarity, or other areas of concern.

CHECKLIST ~ Practical Practice

- Have you used the three stages of practice, including early, middle, and final practice sessions?
- Have you practiced aloud while timing your speech?
- Have you practiced relaxation and positive visualization techniques?
- Do you have your speaking notes (note cards)?
- Have you allowed for a practice run-through in the venue space on the day of your speech, including use of visual aids and/or microphone?
- Have you adjusted your speech to fit the time available?
- Did you use feedback to make adjustments appropriate to your audience or context?
- Do you have everything you need to speak, including speaker notes, visual aids, and location and room of your presentation?
- Have you considered possible contingencies (e.g., power cord, backup visual aids, and bottle of water)?

Dusit/Shutterstock.com

speakers can lose all sense of the original meaning of the words and ignore audience reactions. When speaking, do you notice the audience members' facial expressions and are you able to respond to them? You should.

4. Self-Consciousness Rather Than Audience Consciousness

Except for a few middle practice sessions in which you receive feedback from others or from recordings, try to keep your attention off yourself as a speaker and on your message and the audience response you desire. Remember to visualize *them* when you practice. Again, don't let the performer upstage the conversationalist.

MindTap°   Go to the MindTap for *The Speaker's Handbook* and click on **Additional Resources** for tips on how to practice a speech.

Summary

Adequate practice is paramount to successful public speaking.

24-1 Demonstrate the ability to make improvements through practice sessions.

▶ Using beginning, middle, and final practice sessions over several days will lead to reduced anxiety and a conversational style comforting to both audience and speaker.

▶ Proper planning for practice sessions can offer the additional benefits of illumination and refinement that follow from incubation.

24-2 Understand how to prepare your speaking notes.

▶ Recognize that your speech outline is not the same as your speaking notes.

▶ Include keywords, phrases, and any quotes or direct paraphrase you need help remembering. Keep your notes brief to avoid reading.

▶ Prepare notes in a format that will aid your delivery, including the use of small note cards, a large font, color coding, time notations, and other visual cues to help enhance delivery.

24-3 Adjust your speech to fit into time limit.

▶ Plan your practice to include timed practice sessions. Adjust your speech by cutting lesser points or secondary support if your speech is long or by embellishing important ideas if your speech is too short.

24-4 Understand how to avoid common practice pitfalls.

▶ Common practice pitfalls can be avoided by practicing aloud a few times over multiple days with a limited number of critics while maintaining an audience focus.

Critical Thinking Questions

▶ Why is practicing "in your head" a mistake?

▶ How might technology aid the practice phase of speech preparation?

▶ What is your best strategy for effective practice?

Putting It into Practice

Review several online or published articles on speech preparation. Use your favorite online search tool or library database to locate appropriate articles.

1. What do the articles have in common?

2. Where do the articles differ? Why?

3. What advice do you find most helpful? Why?

25

Vocal Delivery

Speak clearly, correctly, and conversationally. Vary your vocal delivery for interest and emphasis.

MindTap®   Read, highlight, and take notes online.

A s important as preparation, organization, content, and style are, the essence of the speech is still your spoken words. What a waste of time and brain-power if what you have to say cannot be heard or understood by your audience. You must be aware of the mechanics of transmitting sound: articulation, breath control, projection, and so on. At the same time, your most important goal is to develop a style of vocal delivery that sounds natural and conversational. The "ora-tor," who overdramatizes his speech with trilling *r*'s and shuddering pauses, creates distractions and reduces opportunities to create mutual understanding. Except for the stylized chants of the auctioneer and revival minister, most public speech should sound like private speech, adjusted only to fit the size of the audience in the room.

25-1 The Four Aspects of Voice

Your voice is your instrument. It is a tool through which you can influence others and be heard. Although we certainly communicate in ways beyond just our voice, how we use our voice has a dramatic impact on how audience members will perceive and later recall your message. How loudly, quickly, clearly, and properly you speak all affect your ability to be heard, understood, and remembered by your listeners.

25-1a Speak Loudly

For the inexperienced speaker, just about *any* volume level will sound too loud. This is understandable. There are few occasions for speaking above a conversational level, and even on such occasions, like yelling at a football game, we rarely care if we are being understood. But when giving a speech you'll need to be heard—and understood— by the entire audience, and the only way to feel more comfortable speaking loud is by practicing. In the early stages of practice, you may have to ignore how loud your voice seems to you and get feedback from a friend or recording device set some distance away.

What you are aiming for is a louder voice that retains the rhythms and inflections of your normal conversation. You want to be loud, but not be yelling like a drill instructor. As you practice, you will discover that this requires more air for each phrase. You will need to develop breath control to keep your breathing pauses in normal patterns. Think of yourself as spreading or pushing your voice to the far corners of the room. You will then begin to do things that naturally aid projection, such as keeping your head up and opening your mouth wide.

25-1b Speak at an Average Rate

The average rate of speaking is around 150 words per minute. To check your rate, time yourself for three or four minutes as you read a magazine or newspaper article aloud in a natural, conversational manner. Next, count the number of words in the passage and divide by the number of minutes you read. If you speak more than 200 words per minute or fewer than 100 words per minute, you may not be fully understandable to your audience. Extremely fast speakers expect listeners to decode and process information more rapidly than is their custom. Plodding speakers, who seem to avoid phrases and slowly lay out each word as if it were unrelated to any other, keep listeners in a state of bored suspension as they wait for the words to gel into some sort of context. Generally, when giving a speech, plan to speak a little more slowly than you do in daily conversation. To be sure you have timed the speech realistically, practice at the rate and volume you will actually use.

25-1c Enunciate Your Words

When speaking, either publicly or privately, people rarely enunciate *every* sound in *every* word. The phrase "jeetyet?" can be deciphered as "did you eat yet?" by a friend who has a context for the remark. In public speaking settings, much information can be lost due to the audiences' distance from the speaker and distracting noises. So, it is important to work on crisp, precise articulation. Use your tongue, teeth, and lips to pronounce every sound. Be sure you say "government" rather than "goverment" and "hundred" rather than "hunnerd." Do not mumble, run words together, or swallow whole phrases.

You can enunciate properly and still sound natural. It merely takes some practice incorporating precision into your normal conversation. Some people, in a misguided attempt to sound more formal or "literate" during a speech, will overarticulate words or take on exaggerated mannerisms or pronunciations. The result is quite the opposite of what they wish. Rather than sounding well educated, they come across as patronizing, melodramatic, and a little silly. Do not say "thee" in a place where "thuh" is natural when pronouncing *the*. Do not use "would not" where "wouldn't" feels right. (Just be sure to say "wouldn't" rather than "wunt.")

25-1d Make Adjustments for an Accent

Proper speech is quite relative. If you have an accent unfamiliar to your audience, you may be concerned about being understood. There is no need to eliminate or hide your accent. Your manner of speaking is part of your personality. The differences can add interest and charm to your presentation. However, to ensure that your audience understands you, follow these suggestions:

1. Don't start out with the most important material. Use your introduction to let the audience adjust to the pronunciations and patterns of emphasis that differ from their own. Usually, this will take just a minute or so.

2. Speak more slowly and distinctly than you do in daily conversation.

3. Be very alert to audience feedback. If you see confused faces, repeat ideas slowly. Unclear vocabulary or mispronunciation of one key word may mystify your listeners for just a moment. Try several synonyms for important words.

4. Consider using more visual presentation aids and gestures with key phrases.

   If you are a nonnative speaker of English, you may also find these two simple tips will help people understand you:

1. Prolong your vowel sounds. In contrast to many other languages, spoken American English carries more meaning in vowels than consonants. It will sound odd to you, but make a conscious effort to extend your vowels.

2. Blend the end of one word into the beginning of the next so that each phrase sounds like one long word. This reduces the perceived choppiness of much accented English.

MindTap° Nonnative English speakers aren't the only ones who must consider their accents. If you're a native English speaker who must speak to an audience of nonnative English speakers, or if you have a strong regional accent, you also must ensure that you're understood. For tips on communicating effectively with nonnative English speakers, go to the MindTap for *The Speaker's Handbook* and click on **Additional Resources**.

25-2 Use Vocal Variety to Communicate Effectively

Speakers who have clear speaking voices devoid of vocal tics waste these good qualities if they speak hypnotically, with no variation in pitch, rate, or volume. Such change and movement of the voice—what's referred to as **vocal variety**—are intrinsically more

FOR YOUR BENEFIT

Benefits

Your Voice; Your Brand

Your way of speaking reveals your ethnic and cultural heritage, as well as your personality. Your "voiceprint" is as distinctive as your fingerprints. In a multicultural society, the sounds of everyday speech are always changing to include new voices. As you develop your public speaking skills, stay attuned to your distinctive sound. Understand that variations in voice make listening to a speaker interesting. Accents, as long as they are not too hard to follow, actually increase audience members' interest and attention.

interesting than an unchanging or monotone voice. In Chapters **17** and **18**, we stress the importance of variety in word choices and examples in maintaining a high level of audience attention. Vocal variety is equally important, and the need for it goes beyond a mere desire for novelty. Your voice should not simply transmit words; it should underscore and reinforce your message. Suppose your speech on air pollution contained these two sentences:

▸ When the pollution levels are high, my hair feels gritty, and I have to wash it more often.

▸ Every time pollution reaches the alert level in our city, more people with chronic respiratory problems die.

Delivering these sentences in the same tone of voice could imply that they are of equal importance. Changes in pace and emphasis show your audience what is significant and can signal humor, seriousness, irony, and a range of emotions.

25-2a Vary Your Pitch

Speaking in a monotone says to an audience: "I have little interest in the subject or confidence in my ability to interest others in it." A listless vocal performance will negate any dynamism that ordinarily would spring from your word choice and content. Do not be afraid to use the full range of your voice.

Varied inflection, or **pitch**, implies a high energy level and self-confidence, and generally aids your credibility. The pitch you use for the delivery of a word or phrase can underscore its meaning or imply its opposite. For instance, it is common to indicate disagreement with an assertion or a statement merely by raising the tone of our voice at the end of the statement signaling a question. Try it. Vocalize the following sentence: "You do love me." As you say it emphasize the word "do" by raising your voice. Now say it again, this time raises your voice at the end of the statement. It will sound like a question. This vocal adjustment creates a powerful difference in meaning.

25-2b Vary Your Speaking Pace

The average pace of your delivery should be geared toward comfortable listening. However, changes in **rate** at different times during the speech can be effective in creating interest by establishing moods or adding emphasis. Speaking slowly can make you seem thoughtful and deliberate, and it can also impart a sense of drama. Similarly, an extended pause at the end of a sentence signals to your audience that you consider what you just said important and worth some thought. Rapid delivery shows excitement and activity. A climactic effect is achieved by presenting a series of ideas or examples at a rapid clip, as in the following example:

> *[slow] Since we adopted this management system, [fast] absenteeism is down, productivity is up, morale is up, sales are up, profits are up.*

This example also demonstrates that the shift in rate (in this case, slow to fast) is as important to creating a climactic effect as the rate itself.

The following passage shows what a fast-to-slow shift can achieve. If you read it aloud, you would speak more quickly through the first sentence, but you would read the second sentence very slowly.

> *In the next hour they looked in her room, checked the tree house, went over to the playground, called several of her friends, drove around the block, asked all the neighbors. No one—had seen—Emily—since—she—got off—the school bus.*

The accelerating pace of the first sentence communicates mild concern turning to frantic worry, which leads to the climactic moment of fear contained in the measured delivery of the last sentence.

25-2c Vary Your Volume

You should speak loudly enough that you can drop your voice for effect and still be audible to the listeners in the far corners. At the same time, you should hold some **volume** or loudness in reserve so that you can raise your voice for emphasis. Consider two examples.

Notice how a drop in volume can attract interest by evoking an air of confidentiality:

> *I was having an awful week. Few prospects, no sales. It was hard on a young, eager guy just out of school. On the other hand, I never saw old Jones without a customer at his side or a signed contract in his hand. I guess he saw my hangdog look and took pity on me, because he walked over and said, "Smith, you've got the makings of a great salesman, but you're doing one thing wrong." [in a softer voice] Now, this is what he said…*

MindTap°   SPEAKER'S WORKSHOP 25.1

1. Locate a video online by a nonnative speaker (consider Americanrhetoric.com or YouTube.com) and analyze the speech delivery using the guidelines for nonnative speakers.

2. Go to the interactive videos in the MindTap for *The Speaker's Handbook* and analyze the presentations of Harriet Kamakil and Nathanael Dunlavy. Identify the ways they reinforce the meaning of their ideas through the use of voice.

And notice here how raising one's voice can add emphasis:

The city council has approved yet another check-cashing service. The university is using our streets for its parking lot. The state parole board dumps its parolees downtown. Prostitutes from miles around converge each night on Second Street. [in a louder voice] Do you want to know what's coming next?

25-3 Use Standard Pronunciation

Speakers are often unaware of habitual mispronunciations. Yet an educated audience is likely to dismiss any speaker, no matter how important his or her message, when they misuse words or pronounce them incorrectly. There can be few things more damaging to a speaker's credibility than attempting to quote a well-known speaker and butchering the pronunciation of the person's name. It's worth the effort to identify such areas of unconscious incompetence (see Chapter 1) and address them.

25-3a Identify Words You Habitually Mispronounce

Some differences in the ways people pronounce words are inevitable and cause no problem for public speakers. A person from New England might say, "I went to a pahty," a Pennsylvanian may have "cot a cold," and a Texan may tell you to come "ovah heah." Unless they have strong biases against some part of the country, listeners rarely make negative inferences about the speaker on the basis of regional pronunciations like these. If, however, a person says "warsh" instead of "wash" or "ax" instead of "ask," many listeners will consider this deficient and draw conscious or subconscious conclusions about the speaker's educational level, competence, and intelligence. This sort of linguistic snobbery can be unfair, but it is easier to change some pronunciations than to change everyone else's attitudes.

TABLE 25.1
Pronunciation errors

WORD	PROPER PRONUNCIATION	IMPROPER PRONUNCIATION
Ask	Ask	ax
Get	Get	git
Just	Just	jist
Across	a cross	a crost
Nuclear	nu clee ar	nu cyou lar
Perspiration	pers pir a tion	press pir a tion
Strict	Strict	strick
Escape	es cape	ex cape
Compulsory	com pul sory	com pul so rary
Recognize	rec og nize	reck a nize
Library	li brar y	li berry
Mischievous	mis che vous	mis chee vious
Theater	*thee* a ter	thee *a* ter
Picture	pic tchure	pit chure
Surprise	sur prise	sup prise
Comparable	*com* per able	com *pare* able
Larynx	lar inks	lar nix
Relevant	rel a vant	rev a lant
Drowned	Drowned	drown ded
et cetera	et cet era	ek cet era
February	feb roo ary	feb you ary
Temperature	temp per achure	temp achure

Look over the list in Table 25.1 and see if you make any of these pronunciation errors. If you find one or two words that you mispronounce, you can easily work on correcting them. If you find five or more, you may need more extensive help in the form of coaching or coursework. Due to factors in your background or perhaps a lazy ear for the finer distinctions of speech, you probably are also mispronouncing several other words and impairing your effectiveness in communicating with certain groups of people. Here, too, feedback from your practice audience can alert you to errors of which you were unaware.

MindTap° To see additional words that are commonly mispronounced, go to the MindTap for *The Speaker's Handbook* and click on **Additional Resources**.

25-3b Check the Pronunciation of Unfamiliar Words

Your vocabulary can include words you frequently see and understand yet rarely speak or hear spoken. Without exposure and feedback, you might develop your own way of mentally pronouncing such a word that involves a mistake like adding a sound or reversing sounds. If you give a whole speech about the Elector*i*al College (instead of Electoral), your listeners might wonder just how knowledgeable you really are. Or they may be confused or amused if you constantly refer to the need for a counselor to listen "emp*h*atically" when you think you are saying "empathically," a word that means something entirely different. Check words you encounter in research, but do not use regularly, to be sure you are using them correctly.

Place names are always an area for careful investigation. Looking at the word *Beaulieu*, you might expect to say it "Bowl yew." However, the village by that name in Britain is pronounced "Byew lee." Similarly, *Leicester* is "Lester." The Cairo in Egypt we call "Kie row"; the Cairo in Illinois is "Kay row." Houston Street in New York City is "How ston," but Texans have "Hyew ston." The city in Peru is called "Leema," but in Ohio the name is pronounced "Lyma," like the lima bean.

Minor differences in pronunciation can also be troublesome. "Apricot" or "ayp-ricot"? "Har rass" or "*har* rass"? Which pronunciation of Vietnam, Peking, or Caribbean? A dictionary is not much help when there are several correct pronunciations or changing ones, or when words become more or less anglicized, or when unusual proper names like Lupita Nyong'o spring upon the scene. It has been said that the arbiters of the most current acceptable pronunciation are the anchors of national news programs. You are usually safe to follow their lead or that of other such models as the most articulate and respected leaders of your community.

Refer to these sources for questions of pronunciation:

▌ Eva Easton's Authentic American Pronunciation website. To access her site, go to the MindTap for *The Speaker's Handbook* and click on **Additional Resources**.

▌ Jean Yates, *Pronounce It Perfectly in English with Audio CDs*. Hauppauge, NY: Barrons Educational Series, 2013.

25-4 Identify Distracting Vocal Characteristics

Your reason for speaking is undermined when your listeners begin to pay less attention to what you are saying and more to how you are saying it: "That's the fifteenth time she's said 'actually'" or "Why doesn't he clear his throat?" Your voice and speech style should illuminate your ideas not impede them.

Distracting speech habits are difficult to identify and even more difficult to change. Vocal mannerisms become so familiar to you and your closest friends that they are often overlooked, but they can be blatant to a new audience. Follow the suggestions in Chapter **24** for receiving feedback. Use video or audio recordings and feedback from knowledgeable friends to get some objective perspectives on your performance. When you isolate a problem, do not view it as simply a public speaking problem. An overused phrase and a shrill voice reduce your daily communication effectiveness. Resolve to correct problems gradually and permanently by modifying your everyday speaking habits.

25-4a Determine Voice Quality Problems

The resonant, musical voice you view as an ideal may be beyond your reach, but there is, of course, no one perfect voice for effective speaking. Rather, there is a range of pleasing voices. Although the quality and timbre of your voice are determined to a great extent by your larynx and by the size and shape of your nasal cavities, you can find yourself within that range unless you are hampered by one of the following problems.

Harshness, Hoarseness, or Stridency These qualities are caused by constriction of the throat or by tension in or damage to the vocal folds. The voice may sound husky, rough, or shrill and so give an impression of anger or gruffness.

Breathiness, Thinness, or Weakness These qualities are caused by having an inadequate air stream, by releasing excessive air, or by speaking in an unnaturally high falsetto. The result is a soft, childish-sounding voice that lacks authority and power.

Nasality and Denasality Incorrect flow of air through the nasal passages creates these problems. With nasality, too much air escapes through the nose; with denasality, too little air escapes. These problems primarily affect *m, n,* and *ng* sounds, and produce either whiny or stuffed-up qualities.

25-4b Identify Articulation Problems

Many people have speech problems that are not severe enough to be considered disabling, but that are still sufficiently distracting to impede good communication. Stutterers are certainly aware of their condition, but people with lesser problems are usually not conscious of their misarticulations.

Listen closely to your speech for irregularities in **articulation**—the way you produce consonant sounds or blends of consonants. Many articulation errors take the form of *substitutions*, such as "*th*olution" for "solution" or "*dese*" for "*these*." Also common are sound *distortions*: the slushing, hissing, or whistling *s* or the lazy *l* or *r*. If you discover any of these errors, notice whether they occur every time you make the sound or only in the initial, middle, or final positions in a word. For instance, a lazy *r* may show up in the middle but not the initial position: you can say "*r*abbit," but "tu*r*key" comes out as "tuw-key." Also, consonant sounds that you produce well in isolation may tend to be distorted in consonant blends: That same *r* sound may give you trouble only in *cr*, *gr*, or *dr* combinations. In severe cases, it may be necessary to see a speech thera-pist to learn how to form these sounds and properly articulate words.

The real distraction caused by these misarticulations is not the minor aural irri-tation it may arouse in your listeners. Rather, these speech problems can create a con-tradictory message that harms your credibility. An audience listening to a speaker who says "wange of pothibilities" will experience conflict between the competence con-veyed by the words and what may seem like a lack of maturity due to the way those words are pronounced. Similarly, sound distortions can produce an image of slop-piness that conflicts with an otherwise crisp and concise presentation. Consider the image discord created by the accountant who presents precise facts while slushing his *s*'s in phrases like "the projections for the next fishcal year sheem to shupport our pre-diction of sholid growth potential." It may seem unfair to associate certain articulation errors with a lack of maturity, but there is a subconscious tendency of listeners to do so.

25-4c Identify Irrelevant Sounds and Phrases

Don't be afraid to pause between sentences or thoughts when you speak, but avoid filling those pauses with distracting, meaningless sounds and phrases known as **vocalized pauses**. When a speaker is nervous, a one-second pause can seem like a ten-second stretch of dead air, and the temptation to fill it with something can be great. Consider these questions:

▶ Do you use vocalized pauses: "uh," "um," and "err"?

▶ Do you fill pauses with other nonspeech sounds: lip smacking, tongue clicking, throat clearing, and sniffing your nose?

▶ Do you subconsciously insert a giggle after every sentence?

▶ Do you repeat to excess certain words or phrases in nonsensical places?

In the last case, repetition of certain phrases may have originated in requests for feedback. The coherent question "Do you know what I mean?" following a complicated idea turns into "y'know" tossed in whenever the speaker feels uncertain. From there, it is a short step to using it as a pause-filler. Other irrelevant repetitions may develop when individuals feel their communication is less than clear. Tacking on "or whatever" at the end of every sentence is an example.

Check your speech for the use of these words and phrases:

▶ *okay?*	▶ *and so on and so forth*
▶ *y'know*	▶ *et cetera*
▶ *see*	▶ *in other words*
▶ *like*	▶ *so to speak*
▶ *I mean*	▶ *you might say*
▶ *and stuff like that*	▶ *right?*

25-4d Identify Repetitious Patterns of Inflection

While growing up and listening to other people, you learned very early that there are logical and natural places in sentences to vary the pitch of your voice. For instance, in English, your voice usually goes higher in pitch at the end of a question or deepens for an emphatic statement. In normal conversation, we use a variety of inflections without having to think about it. In public speaking, however, there can be a tendency to deliver every sentence with the same inflectional pattern regardless of the sentence's meaning or grammatical structure. This happens when the speaker is not thinking about the content of the speech, is nervous, is reading from a manuscript, or is recalling a memorized text. A singsongy, hypnotic pattern of *inflection* can easily lead to drooping eyelids in the audience. Review a recording of your speech for vocalized pauses or repetitious inflection.

25-4e Use a Self-Improvement Program or Get Professional Help

When you identify a problem and your motivation to correct it is strong, the next step is to determine how best to rectify it.

Self-Improvement In some cases, you may devise a simple plan of action, as Demosthenes did in ancient Greece when he was troubled by problems of articulation and enunciation. His solution was to practice being understood while speaking over the roar of the ocean with his mouth full of pebbles. That may seem a bit ridiculous today; we can be thankful that there are other resources to tap. Books and recordings are available that provide exercises in breathing and projection. Some exercises, such as tongue twisters, make apparent the muscle groups used to produce certain sounds properly. You can start with resources such as these:

▶   MindTap゚   J. Goldes, *The Dialect Coach.* To access his website, go to the MindTap for *The Speaker's Handbook* and click on **Additional Resources**.

▶   Lyle V. Mayer, *Fundamentals of Voice and Articulation*, 15th Edition. New York: McGraw Hill, 2013.

For a deeply ingrained habit, you may choose to map out a program of behavior modification. This approach, which has been quite successful in helping people to lose weight or to quit smoking, is based on the premise that habits developed gradually are best eliminated gradually. New behaviors are substituted for old ones, and the new behaviors are rewarded. For many, the result of a changed habit is a sufficient reward. But there's nothing wrong with rewarding yourself with something more tangible (a new shirt, a movie with a friend, etc.) if it will help you stay on track and reach your goal.

CHECKLIST ~ Assessing and Modifying Vocal Behavior

- [ ] Have you identified any articulation problems?
- [ ] Have you identified distracting vocalized pauses or other filler words or phrases?
- [ ] Have you identified and adjusted repetition inflection or pauses using a recording?
- [ ] Have you considered a self-improvement plan?
- [ ] Do you have persistent challenges that might benefit from professional assistance of a speech therapist or coach?

Dusit/Shutterstock.com

Professional Help Some problems of vocal delivery are difficult to diagnose or solve without professional help. In seeking help, consider the nature and seriousness of your vocal problem, as well as the time and money you are able to commit. Then consult the appropriate professional from the following list:

- *Speech therapists* are the best source of help for fairly serious or persistent articulation and voice problems.

- *Voice coaches* may be affiliated with theater, radio, or television. They can help you improve voice quality, diction, and pronunciation. If you also want to work on regionalisms or accents and want to develop greater variety and expressiveness, consider a course in voice and diction or oral interpretation. An acting or improve class will help in these areas and improve your physical movement.

- *Public speaking teachers* and *consultants* can provide help with voice, articulation, emphasis, and expressiveness within the context of public speaking. Usually, work on speech vocal delivery is integrated with the development of speech content.

Summary

25-1 Explain the four elements of voice.

- Speak loudly enough to be heard and understood.
- Speak at an average rate.
- Enunciate your words completely.
- Adjust for an accent that may be unfamiliar to your audience.

25-2 Demonstrate an ability to use vocal variety to communicate effectively.

▶ Vary pitch, rate, and volume to improve understanding and add interest to your speech.

25-3 Demonstrate an ability to use standard pronunciation.

▶ Use standard pronunciation with both familiar and unfamiliar terms to avoid misunderstandings and loss of credibility.

25-4 Identify distracting vocal characteristics.

▶ Voice quality issues include hoarseness, breathiness, nasality, articulation issues, and vocalized pauses.

▶ It is incumbent on the speaker to make adjustments to ensure message clarity.

▶ Self-improvement programs and professional help are good ways to improve vocal delivery issues.

Critical Thinking Questions

▶ What is the danger of speaking too quickly or too slowly?

▶ Should a person eliminate his or her accent in order to be understood more effectively? Why not?

▶ How might vocal variety make a speech more "listenable"?

▶ What options are available for individuals interested in improving their voice or diction?

Putting It into Practice

MindTap® Go to the MindTap for *The Speaker's Handbook* and click on **Additional Resources** to read Candace M. Coleman's article, "Improving Vocal Variety."

1. To what degree do you believe you use a wide vocal range when speaking with friends?

2. How does your vocal range change when you give a speech?

3. What aspects of your delivery could be more varied when you present in front of a group?

26

Physical Delivery

Use physical delivery to project confidence and add interest to your speech.

MindTap®   Read, highlight, and take notes online.

M uch of how your listeners respond to you is a result of what they see rather than what they hear. The words may be confident, but shaking knees and fidgeting fingers tell another story. Slouching posture and a grim expression can reveal the lie in "I'm so happy to be here!" When practicing and delivering your speech, be aware of the visual image you are creating. As with vocal delivery, the goal of physical delivery is to be natural and to avoid anything that would contradict your verbal message.

26-1 Project Confidence through Physical Delivery

It is important to realize that your speech really starts before you start speaking. The moment the attention shifts to you—whether you are sitting at the head table or in the first row of seats, or standing to the side of the boardroom—you need to begin to develop a rapport and prepare your audience to listen to you by your physical presence. For the most part, audiences want to like you and want to listen. However, audiences can sense a speaker's anxiety and will, in turn, feel anxious. Your listeners will relax when they see that you know what you are doing, which will in turn help them to better follow your speech.

Perhaps you have witnessed speakers who start talking halfway up from their seats, continue talking while walking to the podium, and only then look toward the audience. As the speaker, when you become the center of attention, stand up and, if necessary, move confidently to the position from which you will speak, pause to make eye contact with your audience members, and only then begin to speak.

26-1a Project Confidence through Your Appearance

What kinds of first impressions do people have of you? Are they initially intimidated by you because you are big and brawny? Do people dismiss you because you look ten years younger than you are? Obviously, you cannot trade in your body, but if such impressions get in the way of your speech goals, you can try to compensate. Correct false impressions, especially in the opening minutes of your presentation, by using speech content and all those physical characteristics you can control.

As you get ready for a particular speech, consider what your hairstyle, grooming, clothing, and accessories might communicate to your audience. You do not need, nor do you necessarily want, to mimic the dress of your audience. Regardless of differences in sense of style, however, you should show that you took care in preparing, that you consider the event important enough to expend some energy in trying to look good. Don't make the mistake of looking like you just rolled off your friend's couch.

Ideally, your clothes should match your personality and your remarks. Your appearance should not distract the audience from your message. Be aware of regional, cultural, and occupational norms. In some parts of the country, and in certain professional or social settings, jeans and a sport jacket may be considered formal enough for a presentation. When in doubt, though, lean toward conservative business attire. "Business casual" may be acceptable in a college speech class. There is no need to be drab, but remember that your audience could be distracted by loud colors, busy patterns, showy jewelry or piercings, unorthodox combinations of apparel, and any clothing they consider too revealing. Tattoos, while increasingly acceptable, can be distracting to some audience members. Avoid anything that will divert attention from your primary message.

26-1b Project Confidence by Eliminating Distracting Mannerisms

Distracting mannerisms fall into two categories: those you have all the time (pushing your glasses up on your nose, tucking your hair behind your ear, and cracking your knuckles) and those you have only when giving a speech (noisily fanning and squaring up your note cards, rocking back and forth on your heels, and tapping your pencil on the lectern). These are physical equivalents of saying "um ... y'know ... um ... y'know." Few acts are inherently distracting—it is the repetition of some act that becomes distracting. As with vocal mannerisms, you may be unaware of the frequency of the act until someone points it out. Thus, the first step toward eliminating the problem is to become consciously aware of it. Use the practice techniques laid out in Chapters 2 and 24 to get feedback on your delivery; then work to reduce the frequency of any distracting mannerisms by adapting the behavior modification techniques described in Chapter 25.

26-1c Project Confidence through a Relaxed, Alert Posture

As a general rule, you should stand when speaking. This focuses audience attention on you and gives you a better view of your listeners. There are exceptions, of course. In an intimate setting, such as a circle of a few people, you might choose to remain seated while you speak. As a member of a panel discussion, you may feel constrained to use a lectern if other panelists do so; however, it is permissible to stand away from the lectern or desk for your portion of the presentation even if other panel members don't. It is best to learn to be comfortable speaking without a lectern—with your weight evenly distributed, your notes grasped casually in one hand at waist level, and no props of any kind for support. Appropriate variations might include leaning forward to show deep involvement or sitting on the edge of a desk or table to signal the shift to an informal mood. However, avoid draping yourself across the lectern, slouching, standing with hands at your hips, elbows extended, or rocking back and forth, as these positions are incompatible with the energetic and composed image of a polished public speaker. You should also avoid an overly rigid stance. Be especially careful not to lock your knees, as you risk becoming light-headed or even fainting.

26-2 Add Interest through Physical Delivery

Have you seen a speaker stand motionless, arms and legs locked stiff, head down, and eyes on the podium? Sitting through the speech is painful, listless, and boring. It doesn't have to be that way. You've probably also seen a speaker who, through physical delivery, captured an audience's interest and attention. Physical delivery can be used to add interest through movement, gestures, eye contact, and facial expression. Learning how to add interest through physical delivery is essential to effective public speaking.

26-2a Add Interest through Purposeful, Relevant Movements

You can give a perfectly good and proper speech standing behind a podium. However, most speeches can be aided by movement at appropriate times. Taking a few steps to the left or right or moving closer to your listeners can add variety and emphasis to your speech. You also establish contact with the segment of the audience that you move toward. If you sense you've lost the attention of one portion of an audience, sometimes movement toward them can regain their attention. Moreover, physical movement during a speech is a constructive way to release tension.

Make your movements purposeful. Pacing nervously around the room is distracting, as are the tentative dance steps of the speaker who cannot really decide whether to move or not. This speaker shuffles, rocks from side to side, and seems to stay in constant motion. If you are going to move, be decisive. Take at least two or three normal paces diagonally or directly forward. When you stop, keep your body orientation and eye contact toward the most concentrated part of your audience.

The timing of your movement can reinforce your ideas. Generally, it is best to remain in one place while explaining complex material or when delivering your most emotional examples or powerful arguments. Physical movement works best at transitional points, where it signals a change in content, mood, or form. A moving transition literally combines physical movement with a transitional statement such as those described in Chapter **12**.

MindTap®   Visit the MindTap for *The Speaker's Handbook* and click on **Additional Resources** to read more about physical movement during speech delivery.

26-2b Add Interest through Natural Gestures

Many people have trouble figuring out what to do with their hands while speaking. The solution is actually quite simple. We should use our hands while speaking exactly as we do in normal conversation. For some people, using their hands in this manner means hardly using them at all. For others, it means gesturing a great deal. Whether you gesture a little or a lot, you do it to describe, point out, enumerate, emphasize, implore, and so on.

There is no need to plan what gestures go with your speech. If you are absorbed with your topic and with communicating it to your listeners, your gestures will emerge spontaneously at the appropriate points. But this will happen only if your hands are free to move. Too many speakers immobilize their hands completely, out of both the panicky need to cling to something and the desire to prevent uncontrolled movement.

Do not lock yourself into any of these gesture-inhibiting stances:

▶ *The bear hug*: Arms across the chest—one of the most common ways of getting a grip on yourself

▶ *Ten-hut!*: Arms stiff, wrists nailed to hips

▶ *The flesh wound*: One arm hanging useless at the side, the other hand serving as a tourniquet above or below the elbow

▶ *The firing squad*: Legs slightly spread, hands clasped behind back

▶ *The choirboy/girl*: Hands clasped at waist level, with fingers entwined

▶ *The supplicant*: Same as the choir, but higher, at chest level

▶ *The fig leaf*: Demurely crossed hands, strategically placed

Actually, all of these are perfectly acceptable *transitory* postures. The problem with them lies not in the position of the limbs, but in the temptation to leave them there, statue-like, while you concentrate on what is coming out of your mouth. As you become more involved in your message and the audience's response to it, your natural gestures will come back to you. When these natural impulses collide with the unnatural posture you have locked yourself into, the results can be bizarre.

So, what *do* you do with your hands? First, do nothing distracting such as nervously shredding note cards, drumming on the table, scratching, or making other kinds of unproductive hand movements:

▶ *The Lady Macbeth:* Hands wrung compulsively and continuously to wash out the "stain" of having to speak

▶ *Happy pockets:* Keys, change, and other pocket contents set to jingling by restless hands, the sound competing with the speaker's voice

Second, do nothing contrived—no rehearsed gestures. A hand can be at your side, holding cards at waist level, resting lightly on the other, *gently* grasping the lectern, or casually resting in a pocket (no change-jingling). What matters most is that your arms, wrists, and fingers are relaxed so that your hands can move naturally as the occasion arises.

26-2c Add Interest through Strong Eye Contact

Be familiar enough with your material that you can look at as many members of your audience as possible, as often as possible. In an American culture, looking into another's face connotes openness and interest, whereas looking away or down is interpreted as a sign of insincerity or shiftiness. People would much rather look at your face than the top of your head. Moreover, it can distract them from what you are saying if you stare fixedly out the window or up at the ceiling. After a while, listeners' attention begins to shift in those directions, and they wonder if cue cards are taped to the rafters or if a major crime is in progress outside. But more essentially, maintaining eye contact allows you to read your listeners' faces to get feedback on how your message is being received. Faking eye contact by looking between heads or just over the heads of the people in the back row misses the whole point.

FOR YOUR BENEFIT

Simply Smile

The one expression that has the same meaning in every culture is the smile. Most public speakers underuse or misuse this powerful tool. A constant, fixed, jaw-aching grin is as bad as a deadpan expression. A smile at a sad or serious moment is inappropriate. However, remind yourself to smile genuinely whenever it can reinforce your message. Before you say anything, begin your speech with direct eye contact and a smile to your audience. It is one of the easiest ways to establish rapport, show your goodwill, and put you and your audience at ease.

MindTap®   SPEAKER'S WORKSHOP 26.1

MindTap® Visit the MindTap for *The Speaker's Handbook* to access the interactive videos for this book. Analyze the physical delivery of these speakers in terms of appearance, gestures, movement, and facial expression: Brian Sharkey and Nathanael Dunlavy. What aspects of their delivery do you find particularly effective or ineffective?

At the beginning of your speech, find a few listeners who are responding supportively with nods and positive facial expressions. Look at them and use their support to help you through this initially uncomfortable phase. As soon as you start to feel more confident, however, broaden your eye contact to include everyone.

Actually look into the eyes of the individual audience members, and hold that contact for at least three seconds. Do not skim across rows of faces. Move your eye contact throughout the room. Do not fall into a head-bobbing pattern: left, center, right, center, left…. Have a friend or colleague observe and tell you if you scan mechanically or if you have a tendency to neglect any one segment of the audience.

In any speech, even a manuscript speech, you should have eye contact 85 percent of the time, looking down only to read technical material or to refer briefly to your notes. Most important, be sure to maintain eye contact throughout your introduction and conclusion and during the most telling points and pivotal arguments.

26-2d Add Interest through Facial Expression to Reflect Tone

Do not let the tension of a speaking situation force you into a deadpan face. Your natural facial expressions serve as one more channel for effective communication. Generally, changes in facial expression precede and forecast shifts in tone or mood. Replacing your cheerful countenance with a concerned frown can be a better transition than using that old cliché "but seriously, folks."

You should not plan a series of mugs, smiles, and grimaces—all you need to do is exaggerate slightly those expressions that arise normally. The subtle nuances that work in face-to-face contact will not reach the back row.

Summary

26-1 Demonstrate how to project confidence through physical delivery.

▶ Project confidence and support; enhance, rather than distract from, your message.

▶ When you practice, be aware of what messages you may be sending via dress and adornments, movement, and gestures.

▶ Eliminate or reduce distracting mannerisms; focus on natural delivery.

26-2 Discuss how to add interest through physical delivery.

▶ Physical delivery should add interest through purposeful, relevant movement.

▶ As you practice your speech, be aware of what messages you may be sending via eye contact and facial expression.

▶ Match your facial expression to the mode or tone of the speech.

Critical Thinking Questions

▶ How does physical delivery affect speaker credibility?

▶ How can movement be used to enhance audience members' comprehension of a speech?

▶ What impact does eye contact have on audience attention and later retention? How?

▶ What might you do physically that could be distracting to your audience? What do other speakers do that most distracts you?

Putting It into Practice

MindTap® Visit the MindTap for *The Speaker's Handbook* and click on **Additional Resources** to watch former Governor Jennifer Granholm's speech on globalism and the economy at the University of California, Berkeley, in January 2014.

1. What does the speaker do physically to enhance the verbal message?
2. What does the speaker do physically that detracts from the verbal message?
3. What would you recommend the speaker do differently?

Presentation Aids

Use presentation aids appropriately and effectively to support your message.

MindTap® Read, highlight, and take notes online.

D
epending on circumstances and context, presentation aids may help you be more effective in communicating your message. A **presentation aid** is an object or entity that adds another communicative dimension beyond your vocal content and physical delivery. Generally, presentation aids are visual, but they can be aural (audio only) or audiovisual, depending on the need and available resources. Also depending on the need or the context, the aids could be *discrete* or *continuous*.

Aids that are independent of each other are considered discrete. For example, a speaker may supplement a talk on competing in triathlons by bringing in a triathlon bicycle, presenting posters with charts and diagrams showing training schedules and choices for swimming and running gear, and even showing short video clips of techniques used to make the transitions from swimming to cycling and from cycling to running. Each visual aid type, including the bike, the posters, and the video, is a discreet visual.

Continuous presentation aids are an integrated sequence of similar items produced by the same technology. An example of a continuous aid is the pervasive PowerPoint presentation of digital slides that capture in text every point and subpoint of the speech. A slide show of Frank Lloyd Wright's architecture would also be a continuous aid. These two aids are supplemental "streams" of images that form a continuous backdrop to the speech. A continuous aid need not necessarily be electronic, though. A series of posters on an easel or a string of flip chart pages also fit the "continuous" definition. The electronic forms of continuous aids, however, do present challenges that the others do not. These challenges are addressed in this chapter.

You may use both discrete and continuous aids in the same speech. In a speech about triathlons, the triathlon bike might be a useful prop, even if the predominant aid is a projected PowerPoint presentation. Keep in mind, there are challenges to using multiple aids.

MindTap®   Go to the MindTap for *The Speaker's Handbook* for prompts that will help you effectively integrate presentation aids into your speech.

27-1 Plan Your Use of Presentation Aids

The first step is to consider your speaking goals and decide whether aids will help you achieve those goals. (See Part **6**.) Then you can move to deciding what form the aids will take and what tools you'll use to create and present them.

There are places in a speech where a visual or audio presentation aid can help you make a point more clearly and quickly than if you used your spoken words alone. Conversely, poorly used or overused aids can obscure your ideas and drag down your speech. Keep in mind that the aids should support your message; they should not *be* your message. Overreliance on presentation aids cuts into speech time better spent on analysis or development of points and ideas. In addition, sometimes speakers fall into the trap of spending more time preparing the aids than the speech itself.

Another consideration is the context. In some settings, such as the business world, speakers are expected to have a projected slide show regardless of the usefulness of such an aid to their particular subject. In other settings, such as a graduation speech, the expectation is that there will not be any aids. Determining this sort of information is an important part of the speech planning process.

27-1a Decide If a Presentation Aid Is Appropriate

The need for a visual aid should arise from an analysis of your material as you weigh the best ways to make your points and pursue your speech goals. Do you have complex data to compare? Well, there's a possible subject for an aid. Do you need to intensify an emotional point? Another aid possibility. Is there a recurring theme in your speech? Yet another aid possibility.

The two most obvious reasons for using presentation aids are to explain an unfamiliar, complex, or technical idea, and to reinforce a particular message. The approach you use for doing these things will vary to some degree, depending on whether you use discrete or continuous aids. A geneticist might find it useful to have a wire-frame model of the DNA double helix when talking about how that remarkable molecule duplicates itself. Speakers wishing to impress upon their audience the importance of stiffer drunk-driving penalties may choose to reinforce a recitation of traffic fatality percentages with a pie chart that demonstrates the overwhelming predominance of drunk driving over other causes of traffic deaths. To help the audience understand the differences between blues-rock, grunge, and power metal guitar styles, another speaker may choose to play three short audio clips from Cream, Pearl Jam, and Dragon Force demonstrating the stylistic differences.

27-1b Determine the Type That Best Suits Your Purpose

If you've concluded that presentation aids of some sort would be useful in your speech, the issue to consider is what the venue permits. Begin by investigating the physical environment of your speaking space. Does the room include projection technology and audio capabilities? Is the room small or large? Is the room bright or dark? Can the lights be adjusted? Will the room be noisy or quiet? Are electrical outlets available? Knowing the physical limitations allows you to decide what visual aids will work best. You also need to consider how much time you have to prepare your aids, how much time you will have to share your aids, how portable are they, what technology is available to you for creating the aids, and how visible (or audible) will the aids be for you to utilize them.

A Multitude of Approaches   After thinking about your needs, you may decide you need only a small amount of text, along with a few graphs and images to clarify your points. There are many possible approaches to producing these aids: You can make posters and prepare a flip chart, PowerPoint, Prezi, or Google slides. Or, you may wish to add impact to a particular point. You could choose to handle this with text, image, sound, a stirring quotation, a photograph, or an audio clip that brings the point to life. For example, to supplement one point in a speech on hurricanes and hurricane preparedness, you could display the slogan "Run from the water; hide from the wind," or project a photograph of the devastation of New Orleans by Hurricane Katrina, or play an audio clip of the visceral screech of hurricane-force winds.

From another angle, consider how many items or images you want to show. If there are just a few, it may be simpler to create a poster or model than to go to the effort of creating a two-slide presentation, which requires a computer, projector, and screen, in a slightly darkened room.

Presentation Software   We have already mentioned Microsoft's PowerPoint in the introduction to this chapter and elsewhere. Other popular **presentation software** packages include Keynote from Apple and Impress presentations from OpenOffice, Google Slides, and Prezi. Once you've made the decision to use presentation software, you must decide what physical form the output will take. With the same file, you can have the slides enlarged, printed, and mounted as posters, or the simplest way using a connected computer and projector.

27-1c Decide on the Best Way to Represent an Object or a Concept Visually

Let's look at three ways of representing something with a *visual* presentation aid. One of them will work best for the information you're imparting.

The Object or a Physical Reproduction of It   While explaining the simplicity of a new lens-to-camera attachment system, a speaker can put force behind his or her words by using the actual camera and lens to show the ease of coupling. With a large audience, however, this sort of demonstration might not work if the equipment is too small to be seen clearly. In this case, the speaker might use larger-than-life-size models to make sure the message is clear. Other considerations arise when deciding between an object and its reproduction. In many cases, using a model is preferred over the real object due to size or safety limitations.

Pictorial Reproductions   **Pictorial reproductions** can include photographs, sketches, plans, pictures, slides, overhead transparencies, computer animations, film clips, and videotapes. These are amenable to use in both discrete and continuous forms of aids. If the mechanical device that makes the lens-to-camera coupling so easy is itself complex, the speaker might use an exploded three-quarter view schematic drawing to show the interaction of all the pieces. The speaker wishing to show an aspect of the human musculature might prefer a large graphic representation of the human heart. Again, object and audience sizes are important factors in determining which aids to use, and which technology would best serve to prepare and present them.

Pictorial Symbols   **Pictorial symbols** are used with more abstract concepts and can include graphs, charts, diagrams, maps, and lists of important words and phrases. When speaking on the declining state of the economy, setting fire to a handful of dollar bills will probably get an audience's attention, but it will not be as useful as a line graph showing the buying power of the dollar over the past two decades. An aerial photograph of San Jose will not be as appropriate in a speech on local politics as a map showing City Council District boundaries. If a speaker wants to highlight a motto, inspirational phrase, or name of a product, then suitably lettered posters can help. Figure 27.1 shows some common pictorial symbols.

Each kind of chart or graph is best suited for a particular kind of information. For instance, in general, **line graphs** are better for showing trends than **bar graphs**, and **pie charts** are better for showing relationships of parts to a whole than line graphs. Table 27.1 describes the best use of each type, along with some examples, to help you select which might work for the data you wish to present. Be aware that using the wrong type of graph may convey information or implications that are not really present in your data. Figure 27.2 shows automakers with at least one million cars produced in 2014 using two different graphs, one ineffective, the other effective. The line graph

FIGURE 27.1
Pictorial symbols (A–E)

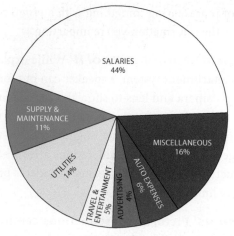

(A) Pie Graph

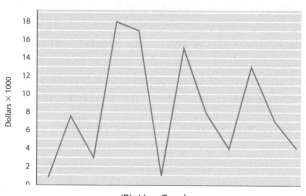

(B) Line Graph

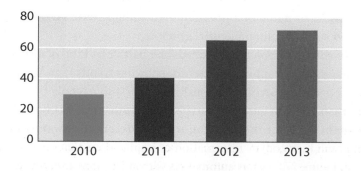

(C) Bar Graph

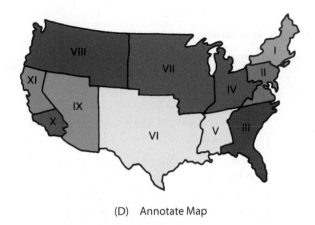

(D)   Annotate Map

(E) Displayed Slogan or Memorable Phrase

is the wrong one to use for this information because the connected dots imply some trend or direction among the totals that does not exist. The bar graph allows the viewer to see the totals and make comparisons without confusion.

27-2 Make Aids Clear and Manageable

With a plan in place for supplementing your speech with presentation materials, the next step is to create them with an eye toward clarity, effect, and ease of use.

27-2a Make Sure the Audience Can See and Hear Your Aids

The nature of the place in which you will be speaking and the size of the audience determine to a great extent the form your aids may take. It helps to look over the facility in advance, if possible. Stand at the back of the room and envision the scene. Screens for projected presentations, slides, and video should be large enough for the size of the room, and projectors should have focal lengths great enough to fill the screen.

TABLE 27.1
Using charts, graphs, and tables

TYPE	BEST USE, WITH EXAMPLES
Bar graph/ pictogram	Show comparisons, especially differences in quantity or frequency. ▸ Interest rates at different banks ▸ Number of users for different computer applications ▸ Sales by region
Line graph	Illuminate trends or changes over time, or to show how one thing is affected by another. ▸ New subscribers to a service, per year, over past five years ▸ Heart rate affected by level of exercise ▸ Number of injury accidents per month, in past year
Pie chart	Illustrate relationships between parts and the whole, relative proportions, or percentages. ▸ Project costs by department ▸ Registered voters by party affiliation ▸ World production of heroin, by continent
Flowchart	Demonstrate a process or a series of related decisions or actions. ▸ Steps to troubleshoot and fix a problem ▸ Flow of information through an organization ▸ Instructions for assembling a computer
Table/grid	Report large amounts of data in one place (table) or to juxtapose and compare discrete elements (grid). ▸ Actuarial table of male and female life expectancy ▸ Rubella infections by age and location ▸ Comparison checklist of features among different products

If you are showing a video, make sure that the image can be seen by people in the back row. Check that your sound equipment is adequate for the size of the room and the ambient noise of the environment.

If you already have a rough mock-up or draft of one of your discrete aids, like a poster or a model, place it where you expect it to be when you speak, and walk around the space. Can you see it clearly from all points, or do you need to enlarge it? Can you make out the lines on the chart, read the captions, and distinguish the model parts? If the room is too large for a poster, flip chart, or **whiteboard** to be effective, consider digital projector and presentation software. At the other end of the scale, reduce any aid that is too large for the size of the room or too unwieldy to manage easily.

FIGURE 27.2
(A) Ineffective and (B) effective choice of graph to match data type

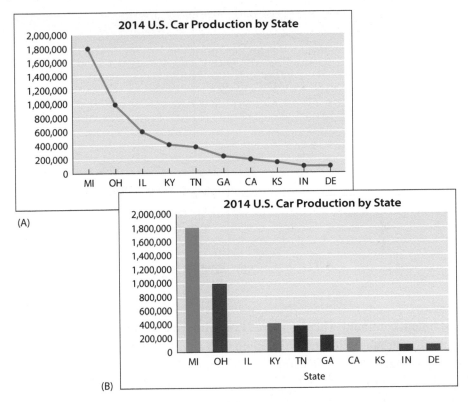

(A)

(B)

27-2b Keep Visual Aids Simple and Clear

Do not design overly elaborate visual aids. They should contain just enough detail to allow your listeners to distinguish one part easily from another. Look at the two cutaway drawings of a car engine in Figure 27.3. If you want to demonstrate the ignition system, the one on the right will be the better one to use. It provides information on where the ignition system is in relation to the rest of the car's engine, without forcing the audience to try to distinguish it from the fuel system, the cooling system, the air conditioning system, and so on. Similarly, do not crowd maps, charts, graphs, models, and photographs with so much data that your audience is confused about which part you are referring to. For instance, you should have one map showing only City Council Districts and another showing only County Supervisory Districts in the city. Avoid having so many lines on a line graph that audience members are at risk of taking a "wrong turn" while attempting to distinguish lines. With photographs, try to find one that shows the object in isolation or in sharp focus in relation to other objects. Keep the wording on any visual aid simple and familiar. Use no more words than necessary to label parts and ideas.

FIGURE 27.3
(A) Overelaborate versus (B) clear visual aid

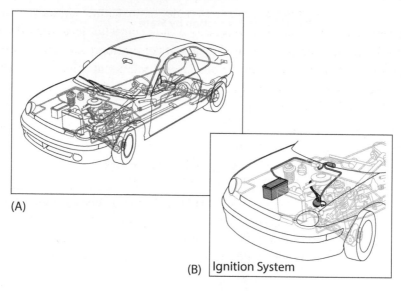

(A)

(B) Ignition System

Maintain continuity when you spread your information out. If you use a pie chart for your first aid, any following aids dealing with similar or related information should also be pie charts. If you are using flip charts, a whiteboard, or some other hand-lettered means, print in clear block letters. Use color to delineate different aspects of the object or symbol. A large model heart with bright blue, red, and yellow parts may not look totally realistic, but audience members will find it a lot easier to keep the parts separate in their minds as they follow the explanation.

MindTap°   To read more about infographics and see Fast Company's Infographic of the Day, visit the MindTap for *The Speaker's Handbook* and click on **Additional Resources**. Fast Company is an online business magazine that focuses on innovation in technology, ethical economics, leadership, and design.

27-2c Design Visual Aids for Maximum Audience Impact

The design and form of your visual aids can enhance your credibility, add humor, provide information beyond the data presented, or simply maintain the interest of your listeners. A professional-looking aid can lend a polished air to a speech. Properly used, a computer will help you create crisp and clear aids. But a computer is not the only choice: Art supply stores stock transfer letters, stencils, and colored plastic in various geometric forms—all sorts of simple graphic materials that even the inartistic can use to produce a neat and attractive visual aid.

For whatever type of visual presentation aid, basic, natural colors are best to use unless a certain color is popularly associated with the object or idea being depicted. In other words, avoid fluorescent color choices. Of course, there are standard uses, like green for forests, blue for water, and so on. Keep in mind that color choices should be easy on the eye if you want people to look at the visuals. Include the use of contrasting colors between foreground and background.

Along this line, you can construct your visual aids in a manner that underscores the theme of your speech. For instance, instead of using bar graphs to indicate yearly differences in logging revenues, substitute pictogram tree outlines with the proper relative dimensions. (Be careful here—if you go by relative height alone, the relative volume of the objects will be out of scale, and the graphic will be misleading.) Or compare rows of objects—houses, barrels, stick figures with dunce caps—where each object represents a certain number of housing starts, gallons of oil, or failing students. Infographics have become increasingly popular in recent years because they communicate a great deal of information with minimal text.

CHECKLIST ~ Design Suggestions for Effective Slides

- *Use simple typefaces.* Do not mix more than two typefaces. Stay with block style fonts such as Verdana and Tahoma. Avoid ornate type, and stay away from decorative modifications that add visual "noise."

- *Use uppercase and lowercase letters in the titles and text.* Sentences printed exclusively in capital letters are harder to read.

- *Maintain "open space."* Do not crowd information on one slide. Keep the information simple; use your spoken words to provide details.

- *Maintain visual continuity.* Settle on a design theme and use it on each slide. Use the same border or background on all slides.

- MindTap® *Seek color legibility.* Use high-contrast foreground and background colors. Background colors should be cooler (dark blue and green tones) and easy on the eye. To check the adequacy of your color choices for your presentation slides, visit the MindTap for *The Speaker's Handbook* and click on **Additional Resources**.

- *Obey the 3 × 5 rule.* No more than three lines with five words per line.

- *Use images more than text.* Pictures, charts, and graphs have more impact than text-heavy slides.

27-3 Blend Your Aids Smoothly into the Speech

Whether discrete or continuous, handheld or projected, still image or streaming video, seen or heard, your presentation aids should be a seamless part of your speech, not an interruption. Choosing appropriate aids that supplement and augment your points will go a long way toward easing this blending. Beyond the structural appropriateness of the aid or aids you select, there are a few simple things you can do to smooth your aids' introduction.

1. Practice with Your Aids

Your aids should be prepared early enough that you can practice with them several times. (See Chapter **24**.) This will alert you to any changes that might be necessary. Become comfortable with them so that you do not fumble around during the presentation. Remember to spend twice as much time practicing with your aids as you spend developing them. This strategy will help you keep your aids simple and ensure you spend substantial time practicing with them.

2. Have Your Aid Ready to Go

For audio aids, have the audio recording cued to the appropriate spot so you have only to press a button. If you are projecting from a computer, have the program ready and the file(s) open and ready to go. It is essential that you practice with this type of aid in advance to ensure proper sequencing and volume levels.

3. Maintain Eye Contact

Be so familiar with your material that you can look at your listeners while explaining a visual aid. Often, a speaker makes the mistake of turning away from the audience and speaking to the projection screen or wall. Doing so communicates a lack of concern for the listener and is a sure way to lose your audience. In addition, how will you know if your audience understands if you are looking at the visual aid?

4. Keep Talking While Using Visual Aids

Avoid long pauses when demonstrating a process. If there is some complexity, or if many steps are needed to produce your desired result, you might take a hint from cooking shows and prepare a series of aids to demonstrate the various phases, thereby eliminating the periods when both you and the audience are waiting. For example, a speaker could say, "Then you apply glue to the two blocks, press them together like this, and let the bond dry. Here are some that have already dried. Now, I'll show you the next step…." When you cannot avoid a time lag introduced by some process, have a planned digression—some bit of history related to the process, perhaps—ready to fill the gap.

5. Don't Let Aids Become a Distraction

Keep individual visual aids turned off or hidden from your audience until you are ready to reveal them. Remove or recover them immediately after they have served their purpose. If you are using an overhead projector or similar device, turn it off whenever you can to eliminate the cooling fan noise. For a continuous visual aid like a PowerPoint presentation of charts and graphs that support particular points, use a blank slide between each content slide. When you have finished addressing the point related to one of the content slides, reveal a blank slide until it is time to advance to the next content slide. If you use a flip chart, use every other sheet when you are preparing it—this gives you the same effect as the blank slide.

Refrain from passing objects around the room, as that will cause a ripple of inattention. This rule is flexible, especially when you are dealing with an unusual object and a small audience, but still it is probably best to share the item with an audience at the time it is discussed in the speech. Consider using a document camera (Elmo is one brand) if available; otherwise, share the object after the speech. By the same token, handouts should be distributed after the presentation. You want the audience to listen now and read later. (Of course, there are some contexts, primarily business, where this is not necessarily the norm. See Chapter **32**.)

Finally, presentation aids are most distracting when you are clumsy with them. Be sure that your charts are in the right order, your models are set up, and your equipment is working.

27-4 Use Presentation Software Wisely

Presentation software can be both good and bad for a speaker. On the one hand, it is possible to create slides and handouts that are consistent and attractive. On the other, it is all too tempting to narrate your outline rather than give a speech. There is perhaps nothing worse than listening to a speaker read every word they've prepared on a slide series.

27-4a Keep Your Text Slides Simple

The templates that come with the presentation software application are designed to keep your slides simple. That is, if you use the typefaces in the sizes that come as the default, it will be difficult for you to clutter up a slide with too many words and ideas. This is good; avoid the temptation to finesse your way around the constraints of the type size. Instead, look for better ways to organize your material and pare down your language to the minimum. (See Chapters **9** and **10**.) This doesn't mean that all templates are equally appropriate for your speech. Remember the 3 × 5 rule mentioned in the "Design Suggestions for Effective Slides" checklist.

FOR YOUR BENEFIT

Video Clips: To Use or Not to Use

Video clips are a popular strategy to jazz up a speech. Unfortunately, incorporating video is more difficult than most speakers realize. Numerous problems can occur, including video and audio problems, video loading or streaming issues, video that doesn't fit the speaker's need, and other technical problems. In many cases, speakers misuse this tool thinking that showing the video will somehow make up for a lack of delivery skill or content. In reality, video cannot respond to the audience as effectively as even a moderately effective speaker.

If you decide, you must use video, as with any visual aid, the recommendations mentioned in this chapter would all still apply. A few additional tips may also be useful.

1. Keep your video segment use short and to the point. In a five- to six-minute speech, any use of video should be less than twenty seconds and should directly support a main point of your speech.

2. Have the video segment cued and ready to view. That means incorporating the video into your PowerPoint presentation at the point you want to have the audience begin viewing with the sound levels verified. Avoid showing opening commercials or other materials that would distract the audience from your intended point.

3. Direct your audience's attention prior to starting the video. If you wish to talk while the video is playing, then mute the audio.

4. Control your video; don't be controlled by it. Know how to start and stop it, and adjust its volume and screen size prior to using the video. Audiences have little patience with speakers who have not properly practiced with their visual aid.

5. Have a contingency plan ready in case the video segment doesn't work.

You can use animation effects, moving images, or "builds" to expose certain elements of a slide in a particular order for dramatic effect or to keep the focus on the most immediate point. Use this capability with restraint, as the impact diminishes with overuse. Similarly, exercise restraint with the sound effects that come with the package—"zoop"-ing sounds may be interesting for the first slide, but will become an annoying distraction to your audience. Put simply, just because you can doesn't mean you should.

MindTap® To read in-depth debates about the pros and cons of using PowerPoint, visit the MindTap for *The Speaker's Handbook* and click on **Additional Resources**.

27-4b Maintain Consistency

Used properly, presentation software can help you maintain a consistent look throughout your slides. Although templates work for keeping the type consistent, the program's settings for color schemes, slide backgrounds and patterns, and so on, work to keep other elements consistent. Even with this help, though, you need to review your slides to make sure no discrepancies have crept in. Look at the captions. Are they all in burgundy 14-point bold Helvetica? Or has one somehow ended up in green 14-point Arial Narrow? How about the placement of elements? Click through the slide show quickly to see if elements seem to jump from place to place. Also, check other features, like transition effects and builds, for consistency. Sometimes these may get mixed up, so that you end up with most slides using a "fade to black" transition and a few using a "wipe right," creating an unnecessary distraction.

27-4c Use Clip Art Sparingly

Given the widespread availability of high-quality photo images, the use of clip art has become passé. Images in different styles (one line drawing of a person followed by a low-resolution bitmap image, then a sharp PostScript image) aren't professional. Even stock images, such as businesspeople standing around a table or the ubiquitous business handshake, create an unremarkable message.

MindTap® Keeping in mind all the cautions you've been reading here about using images during your speeches, visit the MindTap for *The Speaker's Handbook* and click on **Additional Resources** for access to a comprehensive image search engine. The link provides a list of resources for copyright-free and public domain images.

27-4d Don't Become Secondary to Your Slides

It is a common scene in conference and convention settings: One or two large screens dominate in a room holding dozens or hundreds of people; dwarfed by the screens, a speaker is partially hidden behind a bank of computer monitors, hunched over in the dim light, clicking away at the mouse while talking into the body mike, and often commenting on some glitch with the system. Obvious problems here are lack of connection with the audience because of the darkened room and the speaker focusing more on the machine than the audience, confinement of the speaker to the space behind a barrier, and the "aid" becoming an impediment.

If you are in a situation in which this sort of projection will be used, take steps to counteract the potential difficulties. Enlist a colleague or friend to operate the computer so that you are free to move around and to make eye contact with the audience. If you cannot avoid operating the equipment, or if you must compensate for dim lighting, use vocal variety to counterbalance immobility and lack of visibility. (See Chapter **25**.) If possible, use the slides for key illustrations and points only, leaving the screen blank the rest of the time.

Consider the use of infographics or network visualizations as a way to present large amounts of information graphically. See Figure 27.4 for a sample infographic. Numerous tools are available to assist in creating compelling and professional looking graphics. Consider tools including Canva (https://www.canva.com/create/infographics/), Pictochart (https://piktochart.com/), or infogr.am (https://infogr.am/). Remember to apply the checklist for effective slides to any graphic or visualization you use or create.

FIGURE 27.4
Sample infographic

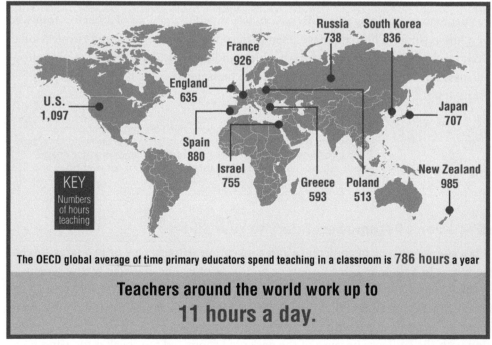

MindTap®   SPEAKER'S WORKSHOP 27.1

1. Suggest three different forms of discrete presentation aids that might be used for speeches on each of these topics:
   A. Bicycle lanes and bike safety
   B. Understanding how to apply for a college scholarship
   C. The cause and effects of a freshwater algae bloom
   D. Death penalty costs compared to life imprisonment
2. Visit the MindTap for *The Speaker's Handbook* to access the interactive videos for this book. Evaluate Kayla Strickland's speech by focusing on both the content of her presentation aids and her use of those aids.

Summary

Although proper use of presentation aids won't guarantee speech success, misuse of presentation aids alone can doom a speech. What, if any, aids should be used is determined by the goals of the speech and the appropriateness of available aids to the speaking situation.

27-1 Plan your use of presentation aids.

▶ Decide if an aid will help to explain complex material or reinforce a message.
▶ Determine the type of aid to suit your purpose.
▶ Select the best way to represent an object or idea.

27-2 Develop clear and manageable aids.

▶ Aids must be accessible to the audience: clearly visible and set to play at an audible level.
▶ Keep aids simple and clear for maximum audience impact.

27-3 Organize your aids so they blend smoothly into your speech.

▶ Practice speaking with the aids.
▶ Maintain eye contact and, if necessary, explain the visual aids being used; visuals should not become a distraction.

27-4 Use presentation software wisely.

▶ Use with the goal of maintaining simplicity, consistency, and control.

Critical Thinking Questions

▶ What are the benefits and drawbacks of using a poster, object, model, infographic, presentation software, or video as a visual aid?

▶ What presentation aids would improve the speech you are currently developing?

▶ What advantages and disadvantages do presentation aids offer the speaker? The audience?

Putting It into Practice

MindTap° Visit the MindTap for *The Speaker's Handbook* and click on **Additional Resources** to access the article, "Audiences and the Misuse of PowerPoint".

1. Why do so many business speakers rely on PowerPoint?

2. What mistakes mentioned in the article do you encounter most often?

3. What does the article suggestion to help avoid those errors?

28

Adapting to the Speech Situation

Your actual speech may be quite different from the one you initially envisioned. Be prepared to take advantage of the good variations and to cope with the bad ones.

MindTap® Read, highlight, and take notes online.

W hat do you do if twenty people show up for your speech when you were told there would be 300 people in the audience? What if your expected favorable audience turns out to be unfavorable? How will you handle distractions or hecklers during your speech? To cope with these turns of events, you must resist the temptation to proceed as planned. Instead, your preparation will now be valuable in a new way, because the actual creation of the speech occurs now, as you talk. So as you prepare for any speech, you can avoid some unpleasant shocks if you spend some time thinking about the contingencies you might face.

28-1 Prepare for and Adapt to Audience Distractions

The give-and-take between speaker and listeners is one thing that makes giving a good speech more than merely reading aloud. A speaker can present the same report twelve times without becoming boring and flat, simply by experiencing the excitement of interacting with a different audience each time. The changes and adaptations sustain the vigor of the speech. Adaptation is not a new skill you must laboriously learn; it is nothing but a more structured version of the mood sensing and monitoring you do all the time in ordinary conversation. Table 28.1 summarizes common guidelines for various kinds of audiences.

TABLE 28.1
Guidelines for adapting to various audiences

If your audience seems bored or restless	1. Use more humor and novelty.
	2. Use more concrete examples.
	3. Make more direct references to the audience.
	4. Invite direct participation—ask listeners to give examples or to raise their hands in agreement.
	5. Cut out or simplify technical descriptions and statistics.
	6. Make your delivery more animated.
	7. Make a physical change—walk around the lectern and sit on a desk.
	8. Cut it short—especially if the program is running late, cut out subpoints, drive home your thesis, and stop.
If you are not getting the agreement you expected	1. Stress common ground.
	2. Spend extra time establishing your credibility.
	3. Modify your goal; do not try to do so much.
	4. Appeal to your listeners' sense of fair play: "Whether you agree with me or not, I'm sure you will hear me out."
If your audience is less informed than you expected	1. Check your perceptions with questions such as, "How many of you know the difference between fission and fusion?"
	2. Use more supporting materials that are geared toward clarification: definitions, explanations, examples, restatements, and analogies comparing the unknown to the known.
	3. Delete the more technical materials.
If your audience is more informed than you expected	1. Condense your basic material and call it a review: "As most of you know …"
	2. Use some of the more technical information you encountered in your research.
	3. Introduce the issues that you see as unresolved aspects of the topic.
	4. Cut the speech short and invite discussion of your topic.
If your audience is more heterogeneous than you expected	1. Gear supporting material and language to the "typical" audience member, by gender or age, for example.
	2. Add materials that acknowledge the range of listeners, but do not change the main thrust of your speech. For example, mention a television show that children in the audience can relate to.

28-1a Take Steps to Prevent Distractions

"If something can go wrong, it will" seems to be especially true when it comes to public speaking. This truth is magnified whenever technology is utilized. Here are some suggestions on how to mitigate the effect of Murphy's law.

Check for Possible Sources of Distraction Arrive early and examine the room where you will speak. Make whatever changes are necessary to ensure that attention will be focused on you and your message. For instance, if the room has windows, you

MindTap SPEAKER'S WORKSHOP 28.1

Visit the MindTap for *The Speaker's Handbook* to access the interactive videos for this book. Watch the speech by Eboo Patel at the Commencement ceremony of Wake Forest University. What distractions does a commencement speaker face? How does the speaker overcome possible distractions in his introduction? What more might you do if this were your speech?

may have to draw the blinds or modify the seating arrangement to prevent outside traffic or sunlight from distracting your listeners. Remove or cover any disturbing objects or posters. The chairs should be arranged to suit your type of presentation. Test the acoustics to see if you need to close windows against outside noise or if you require amplification to ensure you will be heard. Now, and not after being introduced, is the time to check the sound level of your microphone. If you are using a computer, make sure it is compatible with the projection system. Inevitably, there will be some sources of distraction that cannot be controlled. You won't be able to have air traffic rerouted, but you might be able to close the door to busy hallway outside your room while you speak.

Ignore Low-Level Distractions The first rule of dealing with distractions is that you yourself must not become or seem distracted. When all heads turn as a late-comer enters through the door behind you, do not legitimize the interruption by turning your head also. Do not appear to be flustered when a light bulb starts to flicker overhead—simply speak a little louder, become a bit more animated, or add some extra attention-getting devices such as humor or storytelling.

Incorporate Moderate Distractions into Your Speech One frequently told story is of the politician whose campaign speech was interrupted by a crying baby. "I can't blame that youngster," he remarked. "She's just thinking about four more years of this administration." In another instance, a speaker had to pause when a waiter dropped a tray of dishes. He continued with, "That's about how the intercollegiate athletics department came crashing down when the scholarship scandal hit the press. Guess who got elected to pick up the pieces?" Your audience will appreciate your ability to incorporate the unexpected into your planned remarks.

Confront Interruptions Quickly Your job is to give the speech—not to close doors, answer telephones, adjust the thermostat, and so on. But if no one else takes care of a problem, then you must interrupt your speech to deal with it so that everyone can quickly return to the business at hand. Sometimes, you do not have to stop speaking to handle a problem: "... which would justify that course of action. Would someone please unlock that door? There are people wanting to get in. For my second point, I would like you to consider ..."

Other times, circumstances may require that you stop speaking while certain actions are taken by you or members of the audience. After you are satisfied with the result of that action, summarize your most recent point prior to the interruption and then move on. For instance, if some medical emergency interrupted your speech, you might say: "Thank you for handling that so competently. Now, as you will remember, I was just a moment ago talking about ..."

28-1b Adapt to Audience Distractions

The worst distraction a speaker can face is the intentional interrupter. The problem can range from the tipsy listener who can't keep quiet to the resentful person who is attempting to undermine your speech. Generally, respond to such disruptions by progressing through the steps described in the previous section: ignore; if you cannot, incorporate; if you must, confront.

Always keep your credibility with the audience in mind, and remember that you do not want to do anything that will interfere with achieving your speech purpose. You never want to lose your composure, dignity, or temper; you do not ever want to sink to the heckler's level.

The Verbal Heckler   If you start justifying yourself to a heckler, you have lost control of the situation and have given the heckler control. Do not become defensive. For example, do not defend yourself against name-calling: "You're a crook!" or "You don't care about the environment." Do not waste time with denials. Deal with the substance, not with the accusations.

▶ *Establish a tone of reasonableness.* Make it clear you are not opposed to dialogue, even if the heckler is disregarding the polite convention that gives the floor to you. Give the heckler the benefit of the doubt in terms of sincerity.

▶ *Appeal to fair play.* Say, "I base my opinions about China on my three months of travel there. Please hear me out while I describe those experiences. Then we'll listen to your objections."

▶ *Build on common ground.* Say, "We both want the best schooling for our children. If we didn't think it was vitally important, neither of us would be here."

▶ *Suggest continuing the conversation later.* The conversation could be short or long but later out of respect for the other audience members.

Never seem to shut out the heckler or the heckler's point of view completely. You want the audience to view you as a reasonable person. If you believe that the heckler is sincere but has a vastly oversimplified analysis of a complex issue, you should communicate that to your listeners.

In the course of being polite, you do not want your audience to think that you enjoy the disruption. There comes a time when you have to cut the person off and get on with the speech.

▶ *Enough is enough.* If the heckler has not been mollified or deflated by your reasonableness, then you can say something like "I think you've made your point. Now, I really must ask you to sit-down and let me continue my speech." Even if the heckler does not, this will give the audience permission to tell the person to shut up or give security permission to remove the person.

▶ *The zinger.* As a last resort, it is sometimes appropriate to flatten a heckler with a pithy and pointed comeback. Effective use of the "zinger" depends on your ability to think of a wise and witty retort and your correct reading of the audience. Perhaps something in the vein of "I'd love to help you out, but I don't know which way you came in." If your listeners are irritated with the heckler, they will welcome your initiative. If you have misjudged their mood, however, you risk seeming petty or nasty.

The Nonverbal Heckler You will run into these hecklers more frequently than verbal hecklers. Rolling their eyes, fidgeting, sighing, whispering, and passing notes—these are the nonverbal heckler's trademarks. They do not quite have the nerve to heckle you out loud, but they want you to know that they disagree or are bored. If you focus on their behavior, your self-confidence may start to erode. These people can absorb all your attention, diminishing your ability to attend effectively to the rest of the audience.

By and large, the way to deal with the nonverbal heckler is to ignore the person. Sometimes, you might have to cut off eye contact completely with that section of the audience. Instead, make eye contact with the people who are displaying positive signs, and avoid allowing your eyes to drift back to the heckler.

If you find it difficult to ignore the heckler, you may want to try one of the following strategies:

1. If you know the heckler by name, throw the name, in a complimentary sense, into the speech. This may either get the heckler's interest or embarrass the person into being polite.

2. If you are sufficiently self-assured, maintain eye contact with the nonverbal heckler until the person defers.

If the heckling is an ongoing problem—in a class, say, or in a series of business meetings—you might want to talk to this person privately before or after the regular meeting and ask for feedback. He or she may be gratified enough by the attention to modify the behavior.

You should avoid, however, projecting your own interpretations too freely onto the audience. Often, teachers have been surprised when the student who has been sitting in class all year with crossed arms and a sour expression comes up at the end and says, "This was the best class I've ever had." The frown may be the result of a headache, indigestion, or merely concentration. Do not leap to conclusions about the nonverbal messages your audience is sending you.

Summary

Despite preparation and practice, sometimes the speaking situation isn't quite what we expect. In these instances, it is essential that we use our skills to adapt to the actual speaking situation.

28-1 Prepare for and adapt to audience distractions.

▌ Check the room and equipment prior to your presentation.

▌ Consider possible distractions and plan for them.

▌ Ignore low-level distractions and try to incorporate larger distractions into your remarks.

▌ Minimize disruptions and refocus listeners if necessary by providing a brief recap prior to moving forward.

▌ Hecklers, though distracting, can positively influence your speaking goal. The key is to be calm but firm in your response.

Critical Thinking Questions

▌ What are examples of preventable speaking distractions?

▌ What are examples of unpreventable speaking distractions?

▌ Which of the various audiences described in Table 28.1 presents the most difficulty for you? What can be done to overcome these difficulties?

Putting It into Practice

MindTap®   Visit the MindTap for *The Speaker's Handbook* and click on **Additional Resources** to read the article by John Kinde titled "Speaking of Nightmares."

1. Which of Kinde's nightmare situations have you encountered?

2. How might preparation help avoid nightmares like these?

3. What would you do in situations like this?

Answering Questions

Use the question and answer period to ensure that as many people as possible understood your message. Prepare fully, answer questions directly, and maintain control of the interaction.

MindTap®   **Read, highlight, and take notes online.**

The question and answer period is a great opportunity to further the goals of your speech. During your speech, you attempted to address the needs of your audience, and now you can see how close you came. From your listeners' questions, you can learn what points are unclear or what arguments and objections they have. Do not approach the question and answer period as if facing a firing squad. Communicate an eagerness to interact with your listeners and to hear their ideas on your topic. Express your enthusiasm through reactions such as "I'm glad you brought that up," "That's a good question," and "That's an interesting question. Allow me to think about this for a moment."

29-1 Plan Ahead to Respond Effectively

Even though your speech is over, don't forget to use your delivery skills. Maintain eye contact and avoid fidgeting or mumbling. Keep in mind the importance of the **question and answer period** throughout the stages of preparing your speech. Anticipate the audience questions that will likely arise from each of your points. One aid to this is to have the friends who listen to your practice sessions ask you questions afterward. Rehearse aloud possible answers to the most complicated and difficult ones in the same way that you prepare the "planned" portion of your speech.

Ideally, your research has been so extensive that you have much more material than you were able to use given the time constraints of your speech. Rather than simply forgetting about this extra material, continue to review it so you are familiar enough with it should you need to use it in response to questions.

Think of possible applications of particularly effective evidence. For instance, for a speech on women in the labor force (see Chapter **11**), you decide not to use an interesting story you found about a female Japanese worker because your speech concentrates on conditions in the United States. However, the day before the speech you go over the details of the story, so you can tell it accurately should any of the audience question you about how your observations may relate to women in other cultures. The statistics used in the speech relating income differences between men and women in city government jobs may be challenged by some in the audience, so put together a backup note card that (1) explains the sampling frame for the survey, (2) breaks down the statistics by occupation group, and (3) lists comparable statistics for eight other major cities.

29-1a Answer Questions Directly

Do not worry if there are not any questions immediately, or if there are long pauses between questions at first. It usually takes your listeners a moment to collect their thoughts. In some cases, you can start the ball rolling yourself by asking a question of the audience. "What additional differences in the treatment of women have you noticed?" can generate counterquestions. Be sure to respond in a straightforward way to questions that are asked of you.

Always include a one-sentence, direct answer in your response to a question. For emphasis, place this sentence first or last in your response to a question, as in these examples:

First

Yes, I do oppose building nuclear power plants, at least until several safety questions are answered satisfactorily. My reasons include ...

Or Last

... so, because of all these serious problems I see, my answer to your question would be *yes, I do oppose building new nuclear power plants at this time.*

Do not try to bluff your way through an answer for which you don't have a solid response. Rather, admit you do not know. If you have some idea where the answer might be found, suggest one or two sources to the questioner. Ask other audience members to help you out by volunteering what they know. Or you might promise to look it up if the listener wants to get in touch with you later.

29-1b Manage Process and People

The purpose of a question and answer period is to clarify issues for the entire audience. When individual audience members attempt to use this time for a detailed consultation on a specialized problem or to get on their favorite soapbox, you have an obligation as speaker to bring the interaction back to its true course. This can be done by thinking in advance about how you manage the people and the process.

Manage Process Call on questioners in the order they sought recognition and maintain eye contact while the question is being asked. It is acceptable to limit individuals to one question and one request, and that the question be asked in a simple, straightforward way. In some instances, questions can be screened by facilitators in the room to ensure the appropriateness of questions. If you are not sure you understand the question, paraphrase it according to your own interpretation and ask the questioner if it is accurate. When both of you are satisfied, restate or paraphrase it for the entire audience and direct the answer to them.

Manage People Be prepared to keep control of the people asking questions as well as the process by dealing in a firm and tactful manner with several types of distracting questioners. This skill will require the above-mentioned planning and a willingness to trust your ability to use impromptu delivery for situations and issues that you may never have encountered.

▶ **The Person Who Wants to Give a Speech**

This person may agree or disagree with you, or may have a favorite ax to grind that is only loosely related to your topic. It soon becomes obvious that this person has no real question to ask you but rather is taking advantage of an assembled audience to rant. It is rarely effective to ask, "What is your question?" The person will just say, "Don't you agree that ..." and take off for another five minutes. You have to jump in at the end of a sentence, manufacture a question somewhat related to the person's ramblings, answer it, and recognize another questioner on the opposite side of the room: "So, you're saying there is so much inefficiency in government that you wonder how this or any other problem can be solved? That is a tough question to answer, but I am hopeful that the recent reorganization of our agency will permit us to be successful in our efforts. Next question over there?"

▶ **The Person Who Wants to Have an Extended Dialogue**

This person might start out with a genuine question, but refuse to relinquish the floor when you respond. Rather, he or she counters with follow-up questions, comments on your answer, or opens new lines of discussion. Sometimes, this sort of person wants free professional advice or therapy and does not mind seeking it in public. Other times, the person simply finds you and your ideas fascinating and wants to converse at length, as though you were both guests at a cocktail party. The best way to deal with this sort of person is to end the exchange firmly but with a compliment or invitation: "Thank you, you've given me quite a number of interesting insights here. Maybe you can come up and talk to me about them some more later."

▶ **The Person Who Wants to Pick a Fight**

Intellectual confrontation and probing, penetrating questions are to be expected, and even welcomed, from audience members who disagree with you. But sometimes questioners become inappropriately argumentative and mount hostile, personal attacks against a speaker. It becomes obvious they are not really seeking an answer to a question, but are trying to destroy your credibility. Do not let them succeed by becoming angry or by defending yourself against generalized name-calling. (See Chapter **28**.) Pick out the part of such a person's diatribe that contains the kernel of a question, paraphrase it, and answer it calmly and reasonably.

Q: What about all this poisonous junk that you greed-crazed despoilers dump into our rivers to kill our children and whole species of animals?

A: The questioner has brought up the valid and difficult subject of toxic waste disposal. What is our company doing about it? Well …

In short, respond to these disruptive people diplomatically. Remember that, unlike hecklers, their participation has been invited. Do not take cheap shots or direct humor at them to shut them off. Likewise, when you are taken aback by incomprehensible questions or questions that demonstrate gross ignorance or misinformation, you should react positively. Avoid language that embarrasses the questioner or points out errors:

Not: Well, as I said in my speech …

But: Let me go over these statistics more carefully …

Not: You've totally confused fission and fusion!

But: Many of those problems relate to nuclear fission. The fusion reaction is quite different. It works like this …

Try to find ways to dignify bad questions and turn them into good ones. Keep in mind that some questioners may be nervous or confused. Your efforts to put them at ease will earn you an audience's goodwill.

Summary

Answering questions during or after a speech takes skill and tact.

29-1 Demonstrate an ability to plan ahead and manage audience questions effectively.

▶ Planning and preparation improve your success when responding to audience questions. Anticipate possible questions and plan your responses in advance.

▶ Practice responses aloud as you would the rest of your speech.

▶ Invite and respond to questions calmly in the order they are raised.

▶ Ensure that your responses are clear, and manage questioners with care by respecting their inquiry. Restate queries so that the whole audience can hear what was asked and respond honestly.

▶ Avoid the traps of self-indulgent questioners by controlling the question and answer session with professionalism.

Critical Thinking Questions

▶ How might managing a person with a personal agenda be similar to and different from managing a heckler (Chapter **28**)?

▶ What communicative resources (Chapter **1**) are important to answering questions?

▶ What is essential in responding to any question asked by your audience?

Putting It into Practice

MindTap° Review the question and answer session with John Ferriola, COO of Nucor, on the company's No Layoff Practice. You can watch the session by visiting the MindTap for *The Speaker's Handbook* and clicking on **Additional Resources**.

1. What does John Ferriola do well?
2. Based on information from this chapter, what could he do better?
3. What skills would you need to develop in order to achieve this level of success?

Adapting to Speaking Contexts

This handbook emphasizes meanings rather than messages. What is important to a speaker is not what is said but what meaning is created through the process of speaking. Any message or text takes on meaning from the circumstances that surround it—from the context. (See Chapter 1.) Speakers and listeners rely on the context to make sense of messages, and knowing the rules and customs of a given speaking occasion reduces the uncertainty felt, offers some guidelines for engagement, and helps to minimize fear.

Learn all you can about the contexts in which you will speak: general expectations, specific formats, and unspoken norms for speakers and listeners. The chapters that follow address some broad contextual categories. The purpose in offering these preliminary suggestions is not to prepare you fully for these demanding forms of speaking. Rather, this sampling of some specialized kinds of speech events illustrates how the basic principles of all public speaking events—preparation, organization, development, and presentation—have universal transferability. If you are invited to participate in a panel discussion or present a workshop, you don't start from scratch. In these cases, and all others, your task is to learn enough about a given context—its special demands and expectations—to make appropriate adjustments to the basics. A clear sense of purpose and an attention to audience analysis will set you up to make good decisions as you adapt your speaking skills to a wide variety of contexts.

30

Analyzing Speech Contexts

Become familiar with the variety of contexts in which you will speak.

MindTap® Read, highlight, and take notes online.

The skills and recommendations discussed throughout this handbook are necessarily general. They become useful to you when you are able to tailor them to the demands and expectations of a particular context. Just as there are genres of literature—fiction, nonfiction, and poetry—there are familiar categories or **contexts** of speaking. A person with excellent generic speaking skills may still be at a loss if a situation requires knowledge of a particular situation. For example, it does a concerned citizen no good to prepare a compelling, persuasive argument if he or she cannot penetrate the rules of parliamentary procedure to gain recognition to speak at a Local Government Council meeting.

30-1 Analyze the Context

You will save time and work more efficiently if you think carefully about the overall context of your speech before you even begin to plan it. You can do this by starting with some familiar, fundamental questions: who, where, what, when, why, and how?

▶ *Whom* will you be speaking to? And *where* will you be speaking? It's virtually impossible to begin designing a speech without some sense of the situation you will be entering. The people gathered in a particular place, or linked electronically, constitute the audience that will help define the meaning of your speech. As soon as you identify them, use Chapter **7** to guide your more detailed audience analysis.

▶ *What* will you speak about? Topic selection is rarely completely under your control or completely out of your control. In every case, an early determination must be made to map out the content you will address.

▶ Then, and only then, can you begin to gather materials and organize, develop, and craft them into an effective speech.

▶ *When* will you be speaking? Both the calendar and the clock have much to do with your overall approach to the speech. Be realistic about how soon you need to have the speech ready and how long you will be talking. This information is necessary to manage your preparation time (Chapter **5**) and to practice your speech (Chapter **24**).

▶ *Why* are you giving the speech? You always have some reason for speaking. Maybe you were invited to speak at some event, assigned to speak in a class, or have sought an opportunity to address a particular audience. Additionally, you have some purpose for speaking. In this handbook, we classify general speaking purposes as to persuade, to inform, to invite, and to evoke, but most situations involve a blend of these goals. Chapter **6** goes into more depth about how to identify these purposes and how to refine them into specific objectives and thesis statements.

▶ *How* will you be presenting the speech? From the outset, decide whether your speech will be extemporaneous (carefully planned and outlined but not recited word for word), delivered from a written manuscript, memorized, or impromptu ("off the cuff"). The decision will influence how you prepare, following the guidelines for each mode of delivery as presented in Chapter **23**.

30-1a Identify Formats Associated with Speaking Context

When one conducts a training workshop, delivers a sermon, or participates in a debate, there are some well-known, albeit general, expectations about the shape that speech will take. In other cases, there are more specific formats speakers typically follow. Examples of some workplace, civic, and ceremonial formats are found in Chapters **32**, **33**, and **34**. Whenever such standard formats exist, it is your responsibility to learn about them and to adhere to them.

If you are not given a particular format to follow, your first research task should be to seek out models and exemplars to study. How do social workers present case reports at staff meetings? What is included in a progress report on an engineering project? What topics have been covered as keynote addresses to the organization you will address? What protocols are required for the promotion ceremony? There may be a set of written guidelines to follow. If not, ask for manuscripts, outlines, and recordings of previous presentations, or interview members of the organization about what is expected. If possible, sit in as an observer on presentations of the type you will be making. Make note of the steps that are followed, the kinds of arguments and evidence that are accepted, and the style and tone that are common; generate a template for your presentation from these observations.

30-1b Analyze the Dimensions of the Speaking Situation

In addition to finding out the essential information about a speech situation and researching existing formats, speakers benefit by thinking about the factors that define every context for speaking. These dimensions might be arrayed along several continua

MindTap°   SPEAKER'S WORKSHOP 30.1

Read the speeches by John Lewis and Eboo Patel available in Part **7** in *The Speaker's Handbook*. How do you characterize the context in which each speech was given? What norms and expectations accompany each of these contexts? Give at least one specific example from each speech that indicates the speaker was aware of the demands of the context.

such as public/private, formal/informal, monologic/dialogic, or the divergent aspects associated with power, participants, audience, and culture. Locate where your speaking situation falls within each category.

Contexts Can Be Public or Private   A context is established in part by the venue or domain in which speaking occurs. One set of expectations accompanies a meeting in a legislative hall, in a large city square, or in a sports arena. Quite different expectations come into play if a speech about the same topic takes place in a private office or in a living room. Your audience analysis should help to clarify this issue.

Contexts Can Be Formal or Informal   Some contexts carry the expectation of a high level of formality—dressy attire, use of titles, respectful forms of address, dignified word choice, and rules of order. The informality of other contexts is signaled by casual dress, use of first names, colloquial speech forms, and loose use of rules. All public speaking is rule-bound to some extent, but there is tremendous variation in how explicit those rules are. Some contexts have very rigid rules about who may speak, for how long, and on what topic. In a formal parliamentary meeting, a speaker must receive recognition and then link the discourse to a particular motion. Contrast this to a meeting of a small task force, in which participants can seize the floor at any time and change subjects at will. Highly rule-bound contexts tend to also have formal expectations for dress, titles, and word choice. It may be helpful to plan to observe the group you hope to speak to in order to learn the level of formality to expect.

Contexts Can Be Monologic or Dialogic   Contexts are also defined by the role of the participants. In monologic situations, the primary speaker dominates the event, taking primary responsibility for what is talked about. In dialogic situations, other participants can direct both the topic and the form of the interaction. As with all the other continua, many situations fall between the extremes or blend the norms. At a public lecture, for example, the expectation is that the audience will listen to the main speaker without interruption until the question and answer period begins. Then, the norms of dialogic speech take precedence, and it is considered inappropriate for the speaker to give another speech. An invitational speech follows a more dialogic format as does a question and answer session after a speech, although perhaps to a lesser extent.

Monologic   Dialogic

Contexts Vary Depending on Who Holds the Power Power differences between speakers and listeners inevitably influence context. Sometimes, the power resides with the listeners: Bosses control paychecks, teachers assign grades, and judges make rulings. Whether motivated by common sense, self-preservation, or genuine respect, speakers usually show a degree of restraint in addressing those in higher power positions. At other times, power resides with the speaker. Here, the expectations differ: Often, the speaker doesn't deny the power but chooses to downplay it to avoid creating psychological distance between speaker and listeners.

Power resides with speaker   Power resides with listeners

Contexts Differ Depending on Relationship of Participants The context of a speech differs according to the relationship among the participants. When an established group comes together, speeches typically include in-group jokes, use of shorthand expressions, and references to shared history. Well established groups do not need time to build a sense of community or purpose; whereas, individuals gathering for the first or only time may need to spend time getting to know one another and understand their purpose.

Existing community   One-time assembly

Contexts Differ Depending on the Nature of Immediate or Extended Audience Most often, a speech is intended for those who are present. However, there are occasions when everyone understands that the real context of the speech involves a much wider audience that will read it, hear it broadcast, or see it televised or webcast. Even speeches intended for immediate audiences can be recorded and rebroadcast with or without the speaker's knowledge or permission.

Immediate audience   Extended audience

←——————|————————————————————————————————|——————→

Contexts Vary According to Culture Mastering the marketing presentation in a U.S. business context will not prepare someone to give a similar presentation in Japan. Knowing about different cultural norms and expectations also helps listeners to be respectful of international guests. A faculty member from Europe, invited to share her research with colleagues at a U.S. university, was shocked and offended to find that many of them had brought their lunches and were eating during what she perceived to be a formal presentation.

These dimensions illustrate the uniqueness and complexity of speech contexts. A speaker could be right on target in analyzing most of the relevant factors, but misreading just one—say, the expected level of formality—could jeopardize effectiveness. Do not hesitate to thoroughly inquire about contextual issues brought up here during the audience analysis phase of your planning for a new speaking situation. Moreover, if you are in charge of an event, be sure that invitations and announcements communicate shared expectations. People don't appreciate a one-hour "open discussion" on a topic that turns out to be a fifty-five-minute monologue.

The chapters that follow offer some preliminary suggestions for four kinds of contexts: the educational, the business and professional, the social and ceremonial, and the civic and political. However, even these generalizations need to be adapted and combined for each specific event. For example, a retirement dinner within a company would combine the expectations of workplace communication and social communication.

MindTap   **SPEAKER'S WORKSHOP 30.2**

1. Classify the following events along the seven dimensions of context:
    ▷ Pep rally
    ▷ Union meeting
    ▷ Opening statement in a courtroom
    ▷ Business advance/retreat
    ▷ Rehearsal dinner for a wedding party
    ▷ Neighborhood crime watch meeting
    ▷ A live television interview with first responder at the scene of an auto accident
2. What are other dimensions along which speaking contexts may vary?

Summary

Analyzing your speech context involves considering the basics of context.

30-1 Analyze the context of your speaking situation.

▶ Ask yourself who the audience is, what your topic will be, when you will be speaking, why you are giving the speech, and how you will present it.

▶ Different speaking contexts invite varied speaking formats. Whether you are given a particular format to follow or not, your first task should be to seek out and study exemplars to ensure your presentation matches your audience's expectations.

▶ Next, analyze the speaking situation by considering the seven-dimensional continua: public to private sphere; formal to informal demeanor; monologic to dialogic format; speaker-focused to listener-focused power; existing to one-time assembly; immediate to extended audience; and culture differences.

Critical Thinking Questions

▶ How does context influence the communication skills required to speak? In what way might culture influence context? Where might you learn common cultural expectations?

▶ What dimensions best describe the speaking situation you most often face?

31

Educational Context

Become familiar with the educational context.

MindTap® Read, highlight, and take notes online.

lthough it is common to contrast academic life with the "real world," the classroom speaking context is a real one in all important respects. Classroom presentations involve real people who are involved in the mutual creation of meaning with significant consequences. Speakers are challenged to analyze the expectations and requirements of each educational context. To adapt the recommendations from other sections of this book, begin by determining why an oral assignment is being used in a particular classroom.

31-1 Develop Speaking Skills in Context

Academic speech classes, presentation skills training programs, speech contests, and Toastmasters-type groups are contexts in which the presentation of a public speech is the primary activity rather than a means to some other end. In these situations, the assignment is typically designed around the skills students need to develop, practice, and demonstrate. You may be required to give a speech to inform, invite, persuade, invoke emotion, or include a variety of types of supporting material or specific forms of reasoning.

To succeed in these contexts, it is important to learn exactly what each assignment requires and to accomplish each objective. Try to select topics that relate to and engage your listeners. You might anticipate or request a recording of your presentation for later review. Take full advantage of this rare speaking opportunity to receive detailed feedback on both the impact of your message and the technical aspects of your presentation. Review your video recording if one is available and look for areas to improve your speech structure, content, and delivery. Reflect on your successes and strengthen any areas of weakness.

31-1a Practice for Professional Contexts

Most introductory speech classes teach analysis, research, organization, and delivery—skills that apply across contexts. However, in advanced academic classes and in organizational training programs, you will have opportunities to learn how those generic speaking skills are modified in various contexts. In presenting a literary critique, a social science research report, an engineering design review, a health care plan for a patient, or a training program for employees (see Chapter **32**), you must master a new set of conventions. Speaking assignments are designed to simulate situations you will face in career settings. Audience members may be asked to role-play colleagues, customers, or clients. Outside experts are sometimes invited to presentations to provide a sense of realism and offer feedback. It is particularly important in these projects to get detailed information about the purpose of your presentation and the expectations of your audience members. See Chapter **32** for guidelines about various professional presentations and reports.

Although we always encourage you to "be yourself," assignments of this sort invite you to project yourself into a new persona. If you aspire to be a chemist, a journalist, or a physical therapist, the classroom setting provides a safe environment to explore how you will communicate in this role. Step up to class assignments and try on the conventions, speaking style, and even the attire that will be expected in the new contexts you will face later.

31-1b Master Subject Matter

In contrast to situations in which learners speak for the purpose of improving speech skills, the most common use of oral assignments in educational contexts is as a means to a broader end. Educators in almost every field have found that oral reports, debates, and group presentations are powerful ways to explore and master subject matter. When student presenters know they have to talk about ideas in public, they are forced to engage material deeply to synthesize points and make them clear to others. In essence, they learn more completely. Members of classroom audiences often find that peer presentations help reinforce course content, possibly because their classmates explain things in more accessible ways than professors sometimes do. Instructors find oral presentations to be one important way to assess student learning, a way that is sometimes superior to papers or exams in showing how fully students understand course material and how creatively they can apply it.

For these assignments, success depends on taking the extra time, after studying the topic and doing research, to follow the principles of effective speaking. For example, don't assume that the oral presentation consists of reading an academic paper. (See Chapter **17**.) Clarify the expectations and time limits and then plan and rehearse a lively, well-organized presentation that engages the audience and boosts your credibility. Guidelines for debates can be found in Chapter **34**. Guidelines for team presentations are in Chapter **32**, and suggestions about how to prepare for a group presentation are in Chapter **34**.

31-1c Follow Guidelines for Educational Presentations

▶ *Understand the instructor's purpose in assigning an oral presentation.* You will prepare somewhat differently if the goal is to improve your speaking skill, simulate a professional context, or enhance your grasp of the subject matter.

▶ *Understand exactly what "deliverables" will accompany the presentation.* This will vary with each class and might be an outline, a paper, a set of slides, or an analysis of your group process.

▶ *Understand the criteria that will be used in evaluating the assignment and how the various components will be weighted.* This may be very different in a history or business class than in your public speaking class. Ask your instructor if a grading rubric is available to clarify the criteria.

▶ *Understand the format and time limits of the assignment.* For example, is the question and answer period to be included as part of the presentation?

▶ *Practice as thoroughly as you would for any other speech.* Try to use the extemporaneous mode rather than reading from a manuscript. Practice with your presentation aids. If the assignment involves a group project, insist on a formal run-through with your team members.

▶ *Take time to debrief after your presentation.* What did you learn about the subject matter, about speaking in this context, or about working cooperatively?

MindTap®   To see sample educational presentation guidelines, visit the MindTap for *The Speaker's Handbook* and click on **Additional Resources**. These guidelines are for presentations made by members of the youth organization 4-H, but they can be applied to any speech in an educational context.

Summary

The classroom context challenges the speaker to master both content and delivery in a somewhat artificial environment. Nevertheless, it requires real people to make real presentations with real audiences based on specific assignment expectations.

31-1 Develop speaking skills in an educational context.

▶ Clarify the oral assignment criteria and focus on the skills being developed for each assignment.

▶ Consider various contexts that might be appropriate within the educational setting and how skills might be applied.

▶ Remember that sometimes presentation formats are used as much to demonstrate content mastery as to develop communication skills.

▶ Following the guidelines for educational presentations will provide a useful process equally beneficial in other contexts.

Critical Thinking Questions

▶ What makes classroom speaking different from speaking in other contexts? What makes it similar?

▶ How should you prepare for a classroom speech given by a team?

▶ How might preparing to pitch a business plan in a business class be different than a presentation on wound care in a nursing lab?

▶ What audience behaviors might you expect when listening to a classroom speech?

32

Workplace Context

Become familiar with the workplace context.

MindTap® Read, highlight, and take notes online.

Generally, presentations in business and professional settings are expected to be efficient and clear. A routine report to a work group typically does not begin with an attention-getter, rather it features a detailed, logical orientation to situate the topic within the organization's multiple tasks. Visual aids (including handouts) are considered central to professional presentations, in part so that technical details will be available for examination and reference without having to spend a great deal of time reviewing them orally. (See Chapter **27**.) Because it is assumed that goals are shared within organizations, listeners may ask each other tough questions and play devil's advocate. In a team environment, internal communication is a way to test ideas, so they can be improved upon before costly investments are made. Of course, organizational communication must include a healthy dose of team building, and sales and marketing presentations to people outside the organization will involve a very different set of expectations. Although we use the term *workplace*, the recommendations in this chapter apply to situations beyond paid employment settings. Communicators in many kinds of unpaid volunteer work are expected to meet the same standards of professionalism as those in a more traditional work setting.

The following sections cover training sessions, **project proposals**, project status reports, employment interviews, and team presentations. Typical presentations in a business and professional context also include sales interviews, marketing presentations, technical presentations, and business reports.

32-1 Use Informative Speech Strategies in Training Sessions

Examples of **training presentations** include workshops for new employees on proper techniques for handling hazardous materials, training sessions for an organizational customer on the use of a new product, and health education classes for people who have recently been diagnosed with a medical condition.

Making information clear and usable is the centerpiece of training. (To review informative strategies, see Chapter **21**.) However, one key difference between training and informative speaking is that training is typically expected to produce some verifiable skills in the participants. Having a strong informative message is not enough. To get people to change their behavior, you need persuasive skills of motivation as well. Review the model of skill learning in Chapter **1** and use it as a guide for planning a skill-related training program.

32-1a Conduct a Needs Analysis

It's essential for trainers to discover exactly what trainees already know and what they need to learn. A needs analysis is an extension of the same sort of careful analysis you do in preparing a speech; the process is essentially a kind of audience analysis. (See Chapter **7**.) However, often trainers need to satisfy two different audiences: the organizational decision makers who requested the training and the training participants. Trainers should use multiple sources of information, such as interviews, observations, and questionnaires, to identify the various perceived needs of organization members and to set up clear expectations for what training will cover.

In planning the training, you should use the needs analysis to identify the training objectives, or the behavioral outcomes, you are aiming for. (See Chapter **6**.) You should ask yourself, "What should participants be able to do after the training that they can't do now?"

32-1b Design a Varied, Engaging Program

As the leader of the training session, you should follow all the principles of effective organization, maintain attention through content of consequence, and have a dynamic yet conversational and professional delivery style. (For more on leadership roles, see Chapter **35**.)

But keep in mind that a training program is not a speech! To ensure learning, participants need to be actively involved. A good workshop or training program always includes discussions *and* opportunities for practice. It is usually a mix of activities, such as group exercises, analysis of case studies, role-playing, brainstorming, and sharing. Selecting and facilitating such activities builds on your speaking skills, but usually requires additional preparation in training techniques. Besides enrolling in Train-the-Trainer programs, you will find it useful to observe effective trainers in action and to work with a more experienced cotrainer at first.

Another expectation of a training program is that visual and presentation aids will be used extensively in training, and that they will be clear, useful, and professional. Pay particular attention to the suggestions in Chapter 27.

32-1c Develop an Organized Plan and Realistic Agenda

The training should follow principles of organizing any presentation (see Chapters 10 and 12), with a logical progression of content, coherent groupings, and effective transitions between points. However, because you are involving the participants, you will not have complete control of the timing. You may have planned for ten minutes of questions after your first "mini-lecture" and find that there is only one brief question. Later, an activity you had thought would require about fifteen minutes ignites the group, and they spend twice that long discussing it. Sometimes, you may need to rethink an activity on the spot, dropping some planned components and making smooth transitions between the newly arranged pieces. At other times, you will need to wrap up a difficult discussion skillfully and move on.

To maintain your credibility as a trainer, avoid seeming rushed or bothered by the inevitable adjustments to your agenda.

Not: *I had two more really great activities planned, but now I guess we don't have time for them.*

But: *You've brought up most of the key points I wanted us to consider in this discussion. For a little more depth on [subject x] and [subject y], look over these pages in the printed materials you received.*

Not: *Well, this framework has seven components, but I only have time to cover three of them.*

But: *You see from this slide that this is a robust theory with several components. For our purposes in this workshop, we will be discussing three of them.*

32-1d Establish a Clear Training Objective

Begin by explaining the importance of the training material to be covered and then be specific about the objectives: When this workshop is over, the participants will be able to [do these particular things]. It is customary for the participants to introduce themselves and to state their goals for the training early in the process. In dealing with busy adults, it's always a good idea to give a detailed agenda of what is to come and to be specific about timelines and breaks. You will also need to establish your credibility on the topic and establish rapport. People learn better when they like and trust the instructor.

32-1e Save Time for a Two-Part Conclusion

The wrap-up of a training program differs from a simple conclusion in a speech. Of course, you will have provided opportunities for questions and comments throughout the session, but leave additional time for discussion during the wrap-up. In addition to a summary of what has been covered, which provides closure, it is a good idea to have participants state what has been most meaningful and useful for them, because training often includes explicit plans for the application of the concepts covered. Participants might be asked to make an action plan to use the material on the job, or they might be invited to a follow-up session to discuss how the training has influenced their work. Finally, always save time at the end of training for feedback and a written evaluation of some sort.

32-2 Develop Persuasive Project Proposals

To pursue a plan, you often have to use a project proposal to convince others your ideas are worth their time, money, and energy. The project might be a research idea, services for a possible client, a course of action to reach an institutional goal, or an innovation that you would like your organization to adopt. In each case, you are addressing the decision makers who will endorse or reject your plan.

32-2a Become Familiar with Evaluation Criteria

If you are proposing a research idea for your senior thesis, look at the standards set by the faculty. If you are applying for funds from an agency or bidding on a contract, carefully review the request for proposals (RFP) and be sure you address every single criterion. If you are making a pitch to a client or customer, find out what is important to them in deciding among competing proposals. As with any form of audience analysis, listening is key. Talk to the decision maker directly or get information from documents and experts. Whenever possible, find models of successful proposals to emulate.

32-2b State Your Proposal Clearly

After a greeting and introducing yourself and any colleagues, begin with a concise statement of the problem the proposal addresses. You will probably include a brief discussion of the background, clarifying its significance. You might mention alternative approaches that have been tried or are available. However, within the first couple of minutes, make a direct statement of your proposal. This is similar to a thesis statement. (See Chapter **6**.) Notice that the following examples all include references to the positive outcomes anticipated as a result of the proposed action.

▶ My partner and I propose the management all your public relations and advertising placement needs, *freeing you to concentrate on your business operations.*

▶ Our agency is requesting funding from your foundation to provide a pilot program that will *empower senior citizens* by teaching them how to access health care information online.

32-2c Provide a Detailed Description of Your Proposal

In the body of your presentation, explain the overall strategy and the rationale for your proposal; then provide an explanation of the steps you propose. You may also discuss timelines, costs, personnel for the project, and so on. If there are deliverables, such as product designs, prototypes, and documents, be specific in your commitments. In some cases, it may be helpful to define what deliverables are *not* included. For example, "We will deliver 6,000 widgets in bulk, but it will be up to you to provide the packaging."

Presentation aids are especially helpful in making your vision clear. Handouts can show that you have thought about specifics, while still allowing you to direct the oral presentation toward the major concepts of the proposal. (See Chapter 27.)

If there are limitations or risks, mention them briefly, but don't dwell on them. Be ready to discuss them further if there are follow-up questions.

32-2d End on a Positive Note

After a short recap of your key points, make a direct appeal for the acceptance of your proposal. (See Chapter **14**.) Once again, be sure to emphasize the benefits of your plan by linking it to the needs and values of the decision makers.

Not: *Our consulting firm has an excellent reputation and we take pride in doing exceptional work.*

But: *Adopting our plan will help you to refashion your website to better serve your customers while attracting new ones.*

32-3 Follow Guidelines for Project Status Reports

A **project status report** can be delivered to the project team for an advertising campaign, the search committee of a religious organization looking for a new minister, or the funding agency for a large government contract. Whatever the organization and the project, the following guidelines will be useful in presenting a project status report.

1.   Begin with a Statement of the Project's Status
Start your report with a very brief summary of what is being undertaken and where you are in the process. Assume that listeners are familiar with the overall project. This statement may be brief but should include a clear reminder of the reason for the project to begin with, the phases anticipated for the project, and the status of the current phase.

2.   Provide a Detailed Description of Progress
Depending on the scope of the project, the detailed description of progress can be organized within the body of the report into categories—such as task, objective, or department. For large projects, several speakers might report on different areas, such as the development, testing, documentation, and marketing of a software application.

When addressing problems, delays in the schedule, and so on, be open and direct, but always maintain a tone of confidence and optimism. Tell what you have done to rectify the situation and how you have made adjustments to minimize impact on the total project.

▶ While we are waiting for the replacement parts to be delivered, we have shifted three production engineers to work on packaging.

▶ Recent server problems at the university library have curtailed access for students. This has had an impact on my ability to see the appropriate research, but I have approached the County Library System and expect to get an account there so that I can log into the necessary databases.

3. End by Assessing Project Status

End with a realistic assessment of the status of the project. If changes in budget or timelines are inevitable, state them directly. If you have proposals to overcome problems or to make improvements, declare them here. If things are going great, don't be bashful about saying so! Allow plenty of time to answer questions. Welcome them and respond directly and as nondefensively as possible. (See Chapter **29**.)

32-4 Observe Guidelines for Team Presentations

Often, teams form within an organization to present information on products, processes, or decisions to internal and external audiences. Usually, the information to be presented is complex enough to require an interdepartmental approach. This means that, in addition to good speaking skills, success depends upon planning, coordination, and teamwork.

32-4a Establish an Overall Preparation Plan

In the workplace, everyone is already over tasked, so it is crucial at the beginning of a project to make a plan that ensures people's time is used efficiently. This responsibility falls to the project manager, who should initiate the first planning session well before the date of the **team presentation**. Although each situation will be different, in most cases this means weeks not days before the presentation is due. The following checklist can assist with planning key team tasks for group presentations.

32-4b Create an Outline of Speakers' Responsibilities

We have all heard group presentations in which the speakers contradicted each other, overlapped in content, left out key points, jumbled the order of ideas, and even squabbled publicly about the order and coverage of points. To provide coherent content and project a professional image, each team member must think of the presentation as one "macro-speech" rather than as a series of individual "micro" presentations, and each must have a clear sense of how each piece relates to that whole.

CHECKLIST ~ Key Tasks for Group Planning

☐ Have you clarified the purpose, including identifying who the stakeholders are, what their expectations are, and what constitutes success? (See Chapters **6** and **22**.)

☐ Have team members agreed on the core message, the equivalent of the thesis statement, which will serve as a touchstone against which all content will be evaluated? (See Chapter **6**.)

☐ Has the work been divided among team members according to their skills?

☐ Have you established a timeline, making sure to cover intermediate milestones and practice sessions?

© Dusit/Shutterstock.com

Before an outline is created, the group will have engaged in brainstorming and preliminary decision making. When the topic is narrowed and focused, someone needs to create a detailed outline of the presentation, complete with an introduction and a conclusion, transitions, time limits for each segment, and a list of visual support and equipment needed.

In this process of decision making and outline crafting, the group should answer the questions:

▶ *How will the presentation be introduced?* Whether done by the team leader or the first speaker, the introduction should cover introduction basics: Make the audience want to listen, tell them what will be covered, and introduce the team members.

▶ *What are the main points of the presentation?* Each segment must connect directly to the overall objective. As with a speech, it is a good idea to have only a few key ideas and, generally, a few speakers. However simple or complex the organization, there needs to be agreement on the goal of each part of the presentation and on the time allotted for it.

▶ *How will transitions be handled?* Listeners need to be reminded of the road map for the presentation. The transition from segment to segment can be handled by a group leader acting as an emcee of sorts, or each speaker can be charged with building a bridge to the next. In either case, it is important to review the principles of transitions (see Chapter **12**) and to go beyond "Here's Johnny" and offer a statement like, "Once the basic design is completed, it needs to be tested. Here is where John Carlton's testing group comes in."

▶ *How will the presentation be concluded?* Again, the group leader or the final presenter can review and integrate the material. The important point is to plan a wrap-up that ties things together and ends on a positive note. (See Chapter **14**.)

▶ *How will questions be handled?* A long or technical presentation might have a question and answer period after each segment. Otherwise, time needs to be provided for questions at the end. Decide who will field questions or how they will direct them to the appropriate person. Remember, sometimes content experts who did not participate in the main presentation are available as resources during the question and answer period. (See Chapter **29**.)

32-4c Agree on Unifying Elements

Potential customers or clients are greatly reassured if the organization seems to be functioning as a coordinated team. Projecting the impression of unity, mutual respect, and teamwork should be one of the goals of any team presentation. Having a clearly organized presentation is the most important way to make this point; however, there are a few additional ways a team can show they are "on the same page."

▶ *Make the segments parallel.* Presenters might use common phrasing for the main idea: "With our technological innovations, we will own this market space next year.... With our dedicated and knowledgeable sales force, we will own this market space next year.... With our uncompromising support, we will own this market space next year." Or presenters might use the same organization. In a cross-departmental status report, each department might follow this pattern: (1) Review the goal, (2) report on progress to date, (3) report on problems encountered, (4) identify solutions, and (5) provide a current timetable.

▶ *Use common themes and phrases.* Develop a glossary of technical terms, abbreviations, and acronyms, and get the group to agree to adhere to the "approved list" so that listeners aren't confused by different words meaning the same thing. Other integral concepts and themes can be consciously constructed in parallel language woven throughout the presentation.

▶ *Present a consistent visual message.* Slides, presentation software, and diagrams should have a common look. Agree on a template at the beginning of the process, and have a designated specialist polish and unify the visual materials.

32-4d Practice the Presentation

Practice is important for an individual talk, but it is essential for pulling together a team of speakers.

▶ *Schedule at least one early run-through.* Even if some pieces are still under construction, the goal is to get a sense of how the presentation fits together and to find opportunities to improve it.

▶ *Schedule at least one final run-through.* This will polish the transitions and familiarize the speakers with the equipment and visual aids.

▶ *Arrange for feedback after the practice.* Participants may comment on one another's content and clarity. It is also common for managers or other organizational members to sit in on practice sessions to make suggestions. For very important presentations, simulations may be staged with people role-playing potential audience members, and communication consultants may be brought in to record the rehearsal and even coach individuals on presentation skills.

▶ *Pay attention to the timing of the entire presentation, whatever the level of rehearsal.* You might also designate someone to give time signals during the actual presentation to keep the team on track. Going overtime will not be appreciated by the audience and other presenters and may ruin chances for further consideration of solid ideas.

32-4e Debrief after Each Presentation

Shortly after a presentation, whether it was successful or disappointing, the team should meet to talk candidly about what worked and what can be improved in the future. Learning from both failures and successes will distinguish winners from losers.

MindTap®   Visit the MindTap for *The Speaker's Handbook* and click on **Additional Resources** which includes tips for group work and presentations.

Summary

The workplace context includes presentations as varied as training sessions, project proposals, briefings, and team presentations. Fortunately each speaking situation follows guidelines that stem directly from the basic principles reviewed in Parts **3**, **4**, and **5** of this text.

32-1 Use informative speech strategies in training sessions.

▶ The workplace context shares some similarities with the classroom context. Speakers should learn what the audience already knows, use the principles of effective organization, offer credible support, and have a dynamic yet conversational and professional delivery style.

▶ Training involves more interactive, hands-on engagement.

▶ Visual and presentation aids are used extensively; they should be clear, useful, and professional.

▶ A clear training objective is essential.

▶ The conclusion must effectively summarize the training, address questions or comments, and afford an opportunity to assess the impact of the training.

32-2 Develop persuasive project proposals.

▶ Required additional preparation is not always part of preparing a speech.

▶ Start by becoming familiar with the criteria used to evaluate the project.

▶ Clearly state your project proposal early in the presentation.

▶ Provide a detailed description of the proposal.

▶ End by emphasizing the benefits of your project proposal linked to the needs and values of the decision makers.

32-3 Follow guidelines for project status reports.

▶ May be required for a variety of business situations; following standard guidelines will save time and effort: (1) Begin with a statement of the project's status, (2) provide a detailed description of the progress, and (3) end by assessing the project status.

32-4 Observe guidelines for team presentations.

▶   Follow established guidelines to ensure a consistent and coherent presentation; success depends upon planning, coordination, teamwork, and practice.

Critical Thinking Questions

▶   How is workplace speaking similar to giving a speech in a classroom? How is it different?

▶   Why is team practice necessary when presenting as a group?

▶   What audience behaviors might you expect when presenting a workplace speech?

▶   What mistakes have you observed most often in a workplace environment?

Putting It into Practice

Business settings require us to be concise and clear in our communication. Develop three "elevator" speeches that you could use to introduce yourself and your interests in 60 seconds or less to a businessperson at various levels of the organization you work for (or would like to work for). Consider how the speech might differ for the president, chief financial officer, or sales associate.

Social and Ceremonial Context

Become familiar with the social and ceremonial context.

Arguably, the most ancient forms of speech are those that people developed simply to affirm their connectedness. We make small talk to share our everyday experiences, and we draw together to share joy, grief, outrage, and reverence. The emphasis in social and ceremonial contexts centers on what is common between participants, and how they are united. This is not a time to mention differences or to construct consensus. Rather the assumption is that consensus exists and it should be celebrated.

Some speeches, classified in this book as **evocative**, are designed more to fill a ritualistic function than to transmit information or change behavior. This type of speech tends to follow a standard format, and as with all rituals, the familiarity of the format is part of what people like about them. Happy moments like winning an Olympic medal and sad ones, like mourning the passing of a loved one, are made more memorable or bearable when accompanied by a traditional, familiar ceremony. On these occasions certain words, gestures, and acts are expected—the Olympic athlete would undoubtedly be disappointed if the medal award ceremony and playing of the national anthem were replaced by a gift certificate presented at a pizza house get-together.

33-1 Observe Guidelines for Various Social and Ceremonial Contexts

Typical speaking situations in the social and ceremonial context include presenting an award, sharing a memorial address, proposing a toast, and accepting an award. In each case, the circumstances call for specific conventions to be followed. Pay particular attention to how you can fulfill the functions of the ceremony while keeping in mind the uniqueness of the recipient and the needs of the audience.

1. **Presenting an Award or Honor**
- Unless suspense or a surprise is part of the tradition, announce the person's name early in the speech.
- Explain how the person was selected for the honor and by whom.
- Besides listing achievements or qualities, try using a brief anecdote or description to capture some unique qualities of the person.
- If a tangible object (plaque, certificate, or Key to the City) is presented, explain what it symbolizes.

2. **Delivering a Eulogy or Memorial Address**
- Do not accept this assignment unless you feel able to keep your composure.
- Acknowledge shared feelings of sadness, loss, or remorse, but do not dwell on them.
- Highlight and celebrate the value of the one being eulogized. Some people present may have known the person only professionally, socially, long ago, or only recently. Touch on several aspects of the person's life. Do not be reluctant to share light, and even humorous, moments.
- Use phrases that bond the group together: "All of us who cared for Eleanor …" or "I see many people here who …" or " We all know how persistent she could be when she believed in an idea."
- Try to place the loss in some larger, more optimistic perspective. Themes of the continuity of life, appreciation of each moment, and growth through pain are timeless and universal. These philosophical concepts are still a source of comfort.
- Do not play on the grief of a captive audience to promote a specific religious belief, social or political cause.

3. **Giving a Toast**
- If the toast is a formal part of the event, make arrangements ahead of time so that everyone will have a beverage in hand at the proper point. Be sure that nonalcoholic beverages are available so that everyone can participate. Avoid substantial drinking prior to making the toast.
- Refine your basic idea into a short message of goodwill and memorize it.
- If no witty inspiration comes to you, and the toasts in books seem corny and contrived, then there is absolutely nothing wrong with taking a sincere thought and stating it gracefully.
- If the toast is more than a few sentences (and is more like a short speech), do not make listeners hold up their glasses the entire time. Begin your speech, and then at the end say something like, "Let's raise our glasses to our new laboratory director. Sheila, we wish you luck and success, and may all your troubles be microscopic!"

MindTap®   Visit the MindTap for *The Speaker's Handbook* and click on **Additional Resources** for tips for wedding speeches.

4. Accepting an Award or a Tribute

▶ Unless asked in advance to prepare a major acceptance speech, limit your remarks to a few sentences.

▶ Accept the honor with pride. Do not let humility and embarrassment make you seem to reject the gesture.

▶ Share the honor with those who deserve it. But do not get into an endless thank-you litany of the sort that seems to make the Academy Awards presentation run overtime.

▶ Give a gift back to the audience. Can you offer them a genuine tribute, an insight, or even a funny story related to your relationship with them?

End with a future-oriented statement about what the honor means to you.

33-2 Create a Ceremonial Speech to Match Expectations of the Audience

No matter how predictable they are, you must cover the expected bases. Do not be too creative, but at the same time, strive to make these ceremonial moments special and fresh. Above all, avoid overused phrases or expressions such as

▶ On this auspicious occasion …

▶ It is indeed an honor and a privilege …

▶ … this small token of our esteem.

Information exchange is secondary in these speeches; style becomes crucial. Because the two or three ideas you transmit will be fairly basic, you should expend your energy crafting ways to express them, polishing your language and timing. This is made easier by the fact that ceremonial speeches are usually short and rarely unexpected. Through careful planning and reasonable oral preparation, you can develop an appropriate language style to fulfill expectations while avoiding trite, overused expressions. Frequently, a memorized or partially memorized mode of delivery is best. (See Chapter **23**.) Your language should be more elevated than in everyday speech, but not so formal as to seem stiff or unnatural. Above all a solid ceremonial speech must take into account the people the speech aims to impact.

When preparing all ceremonial speeches, consider three questions.

1. *What are the needs of the person about whom I speak?* Suppose that as company president, you give a safety award each year, and so for you it is old hat. However, it is a special moment for the recipient. What can you say that he or she will remember with pride? Address the *uniqueness* of that person. Although the speech structure may be formulaic, the content should be personalized.

2. *What are the needs of the people for whom I speak?* In most ceremonial or ritualistic addresses, you are speaking on behalf of some group or community and not just for yourself. People have come together to share emotions. Yet these emotions may be unfocused.

When you deliver a thoughtful and moving speech, you symbolize the feelings of audience members, thus bonding them. You also help them gain perspective and find deeper meanings in their experiences. Early in the preparation for this sort of speech, envision yourself as a vehicle for group expression: "All of us feel such affection for Gary. What is the best way to say what each of us would like to tell him as he retires?"

3. *What are the needs of the people to whom I speak?* Recognize that ceremonial speaking often involves audiences that are quite diverse in age and background. A toast at a wedding will include three or four generations of people from two often very different family traditions. Avoid saying anything that might embarrass or shock those in attendance. Your purpose is to evoke emotion; however, that emotion should not be anger, resentment, guilt, or shame. Instead, seek to instill emotions of pride, hope, wonder, awe, surprise, joy, and love.

Summary

The social and ceremonial context requires a speaker to walk the fine line between tradition and triteness.

33-1 Demonstrate an understanding of the guidelines for various social and ceremonial contexts.

▶ Evocative speeches fill a ritualistic function and tend to follow a standard format.

▶ Ceremonial speaking situations require that specific conventions are followed.

33-2 Create a ceremonial speech to match the expectations of the audience.

▶ Use slightly more formal language style to fulfill expectations while avoiding trite, overused expressions.

▶ Ceremonial speeches address at least three distinct groups: the people **about whom** you speak, **for whom** you speak, and **to whom** you speak.

Critical Thinking Questions

▶ What makes ceremonial speaking different from speaking in other contexts?

▶ What role will audience analysis play in preparing a ceremonial speech such as a wedding toast or a eulogy?

▶ What advice would you offer a speaker concerned about crying while delivering a eulogy?

▶ What audience behaviors might you expect when listening to a ceremonial speech?

34

Civic and Political Context

Become familiar with the civic and political context.

MindTap Read, highlight, and take notes online.

Many elected officials aren't the best examples of effective communication. Yet the very existence of our democracy hinges on citizen participation in deliberate discussion regarding how resources are used. When you speak as a member of a community or a political unit, you may be entering a context in which there are conflicts of interest. Historically political and civic contexts have been characterized by explicit affirmations of respect and common ground. Notice, for example, how representatives from opposing political parties continually say things like, "My highly distinguished colleague from South Carolina …" and "The esteemed senator and I have cosponsored legislation in the past, and it is with regret that I must reluctantly disagree with her remarks." In a democratic society, we value the testing of ideas through vigorous debate and argumentation. We maintain social order by setting fairly strict rules constraining the form of speech. The ideal is that personal attacks are taboo, as are arguments from pure self-interest. We do not argue for restricted parking in the neighborhood around a university campus by saying, "The students are stupid and I am inconvenienced when they take my parking spot.." Instead, we state that the community needs to work to ensure that residents and students maintain the special character of the neighborhood and to continue to be good neighbors to one another.

Passion and eloquence are not out of place in this context. Sound argument and evidence are frequently combined with appeals to common values. Typical speaking situations in this context include public debates, community forums, legal arguments, panel discussions, political conventions, town hall talks, appearances before community agencies, rallies, and broadcast talk shows.

34-1 Develop a Presentation That Matches the Appropriate Group Format

Group formats include, among others, the symposium, panel, forum, and debate. Too often, labels for group presentations are used interchangeably and inconsistently. You may be invited to be part of a "panel" and prepare accordingly, only to discover that the organizer has actually set up a debate. Here are the definitions most commonly used by speech communication texts:

Symposium: A series of short speeches, usually informative, on various aspects of the same general topic. Audience questions often follow.

Panel: A group of experts publicly discussing a topic among themselves. Individually prepared speeches, if any, are limited to very brief opening statements.

Forum: Essentially a question and answer format. One or more experts may be questioned by a panel of other experts, journalists, and/or the audience.

Debate: A structured argument in which participants speak for or against a preannounced proposition. The proposition is worded so that one side has the burden of proof, and that same side has the benefit of speaking first and last. Speakers assume an advocacy role and attempt to persuade the audience, not each other.

However, do not assume that the person arranging the program uses the terms this way. Find out as much as possible about the program by asking questions listed in the following checklist.

34-1a Prepare as for a Speech

Do not be lulled into thinking a group presentation is merely a conversation. Even if you know your topic very well, brush up on your research, plan a general outline, and bring along notes with key facts and statistics. Prepare visual aids if appropriate. Plan an introduction and a conclusion for your formal part of the session.

Be prepared to adapt, however, in your best extemporaneous style. Because you are in a group presentation, make frequent connections to the other panelists: "Ms. Larsen has pointed out some of the reasons mental health care is so expensive" or "I won't get into the medical details. Dr. Nguyen is the expert on that." Also, unless the panelists coordinate beforehand, overlap is inevitable on related topics. When you hear your favorite example or best statistic being presented, quickly

CHECKLIST ~ Group Format Presentations

- What is the purpose of the group presentation?
- Have you confirmed the presentation format?
- Who are the immediate and extended audiences?
- How and where will the presentation be broadcast?
- How much time is allotted? How will it be divided among speakers? How will time limits be enforced?
- Will there be discussion among participants? Will there be questions from the audience? Who will facilitate that discussion?
- Who are the other speakers? What will they talk about? In what order?

© Dusit/Shutterstock.com

reorganize and substitute the backup material you wisely brought along. Review the principles in Chapter **29** for use in the question and answer exchange.

34-1b Be Aware of Your Nonverbal Communication

When you speak in a group, you should still follow the guidelines for effective delivery. Avoid rocking or slouching in your chair. Being seated does not allow you to be off-hand or overly casual. On the contrary, you may need to project a little more energy to compensate for the lack of visibility and movement.

What far too many speakers seem to overlook is that they are "on stage" during the whole presentation. While other speakers are talking, look attentive and be courteous. Consider taking notes of what others say or things you might wish to address. Above all, do not distract the audience by whispering, checking messages on your phone, or grimacing in disbelief. Do not hurt your own credibility by looking bored or by frantically paging through your notes.

The previous suggestions, combined with general speaking skills, should get you through most group situations. The public debate presents some additional challenges.

34-2 Apply the Guidelines for a Public Dialogue or Debate

Formal academic debating and competitive tournament debating require skills beyond the scope of this handbook. Excellent texts and classes are available. Any good public speaker, though, can handle informal discussions or debates—such as those held during election campaigns or at public meetings or club functions—by remembering and applying the following prescriptions.

1.   Consider the Opposing Point of View

Research both sides of the topic to see what evidence you will encounter. Look at the strongest points of your opponent's case and the weakest points of your own. This helps you anticipate the arguments and prepare for them. Acknowledge other's points as warranted during public discussion. Refute with evidence those things that your research suggests are inaccurate.

2.   Organize Your Ideas, Arguments, and Evidence

First, develop your own best case for your position, which will be your opening state-ment or constructive speech. Next, plan your challenges to the opposing position or interpretation of the situation. Finally, compile defense material, which you will prob-ably need to answer challenges to your position.

3.   Prepare Your Presentation Strategically

Pay particular attention to organizational clarity and to sound support of asser-tions. Follow the general suggestions for speaking to an unfavorable audience. (See Chapter 22.) Time is usually limited, so address only major issues during the refu-tation phase. When you refute a point, explain the argumentative impact and show what damage you have done to the underlying logical structure of your opponent's argument. If you weaken an opponent's case, drive home the point by issuing a specific challenge for the opponent to repair the damage. See Chapter 22 for guidelines about dealing with opposing arguments.

4.   Save Time for a Summary

Debates can be confusing, with points flying back and forth. So, even if you have to skip some additional specifics, use the final few minutes to focus the controversy, interpreting how it has emerged during the discussion. End with a persuasive closing statement and a clincher that capitalizes on your strongest point.

5.   Maintain a Civil Professional Demeanor

As in sports and poker games, emotions can sometimes get out of hand. Do not lose perspective: Getting the last word on every single point is less important than main-taining your long-term credibility. Even if another debater distorts or misleads, you should remain courteous and unflappable. Your tone may be vigorous, but it should never be hostile. Address your arguments to the audience, and refer to the other speaker by name, and not as "my opponent." Treat his or her arguments respectfully, and recognize the strength of ideas offered. Always assume the honesty and good intentions of the other speaker. Never say, "That's a lie"; rather, say, "I think those figures are inaccurate. Here's what I found."

MindTap   Visit the MindTap for *The Speaker's Handbook* and click on **Additional Resources** which argues that a free and open discussion is essential to the establishment and preservation of open democratic societies.

Summary

The civic and political context is our opportunity as citizens to affect community decisions. Whether the situation is a community forum, town hall discussion, rally, or debate, public speaking skills will help you to speak with confidence and impact.

34-1 Develop a presentation that matches the appropriate group format.

▶ Recognize the differences between presentation formats, such as symposiums, panels, forums, and debates. Confirm the format with presentation organizers and prepare accordingly.

▶ Prepare as if for a speech, keeping in mind the importance of clear organization; meaningful, credible content; and effective verbal and nonverbal delivery.

34-2 Apply the guidelines for a public dialogue or debate.

▶ Contribute positively by considering the opposing viewpoints and preparing in advance.

▶ Organize a clear opening statement, specific challenges you would like to introduce, and clear evidence to defend your ideas.

▶ Prepare strategically with careful organization and sound support of your assertions.

▶ Summarize to ensure listeners hear and recall your strongest points at the close of your presentation.

▶ Maintain a civil professional demeanor.

Critical Thinking Questions

▶ Why is a civil decorum important to effective deliberate discussion in a democracy?

▶ How might a lack of civility affect your credibility among your neighbors?

▶ What audience behaviors might you expect when listening to a civic or political speech?

▶ What topic do you wish you could address to elected representatives in your city or town?

35

Leadership across Contexts

Be prepared to assume leadership roles in a variety of contexts.

MindTap® Read, highlight, and take notes online.

The recommendations so far have dealt with situations in which you as an individual speaker will need to fit into an existing context. Sometimes, people will find themselves in leadership roles and in a situation to shape a context for both the speakers and the audience. In this case, the leader will be looked up to for clarification of ground rules, to introduce speakers and perhaps transition between segments in series of presentations, and possibly to facilitate some dialogue between the audience and presenters. It will be essential that the speaker be prepared to facilitate efficiently and ensure a positive communication environment.

35-1 Prepare for a Leadership Role

There are as many leadership roles as there are contexts, but we present here suggestions common to establishing a program or meeting agenda, roles, and considering contingencies.

35-1a Prepare Before You Chair a Program or Meeting

It will be necessary to complete a number of preparatory activities prior to chairing a program or meeting. Clarifying the format, coordinating the participants, and anticipating contingencies are all leadership functions necessary for proper program preparation.

The agenda ensures a clear understanding of what will occur and in what order. In some cases, the format is already set by bylaws and custom. Regardless, try to establish mechanisms whereby all potential agenda items are submitted to you well in advance.

Too often, business meetings and banquets are thrown off schedule by the surprise request for a "brief announcement"—which turns into a speech followed by a debate. It is your responsibility to manage the communication so that the group's goals are met efficiently. Be firm in sticking to the agenda and moving the proceedings along.

Generally, an **agenda** should follow a consistent order. Take care of old business before new business, time for routine reports, and opportunity for announcements. The agenda will vary depending on the type of meeting being conducted. A project status meeting, banquet, parliamentary session, or club meeting will all likely have previous meeting agendas to guide your development. Consider asking past leaders or officers for samples.

35-1b Articulate the Agenda and Roles to All Participants

It is considered professional to communicate expectations, including an agenda with specific meeting outcomes identified ahead of time, stating what will be discussed, who is responsible for leading the discussion, and the amount of time anticipated for the discussion. Give a *written* copy of the agenda to all participants in a formal business meeting in advance of the meeting. Confirm how and when they will participate: "I'll call on

CHECKLIST ~ Key Tasks for Moderating a Forum, Panel, or Debate

- Are the format and ground rules clear to all participants in advance?
- Do the speakers know who the other speakers will be and what they will cover?
- Have you planned an introduction that will engage and motivate the audience to listen? (See Chapter **13**.)
- Have you planned a *brief* transition between each segment of the presentation?
- Can you strictly enforce time limits? Have you emphasized the importance of timeliness to speakers before the program, and arranged an unobtrusive signal for when the time is almost up?
- Are you prepared to politely but unapologetically interrupt a speaker who goes way over time?
- Have you planned for possible contingencies?
- Will you be able to moderate discussion aspects of the session, keeping the participation balanced? Can you interrupt politely and move the discussion along if one participant begins to take over the discussion?
- Have you planned a way to wrap up the parts of the presentation with a conclusion? (See Chapter **14**.) The logical closure should be an extemporaneous summary of the points that have actually emerged.

© Dusit/Shutterstock.com

you for the treasurer's report right away. Save your idea for fund-raising, though, and introduce it under new business." For a decision-making session, let every participant know what to expect so each can come prepared with the right information and some prior thoughts. For an informal program such as a banquet, you might not write out the agenda, but you should still apprise each person of your plan: "Right after the ventriloquist performs, I'll introduce you for the presentation of the Scholarship Award."

35-1c Be Prepared for Contingencies

As chair of any event or session, you are a coordinator, facilitator, and host. You are not the "star"; you are there to serve the group by helping members meet their goals efficiently and pleasantly. To this end, prepare by visualizing the event that you will chair. Anticipate any issues that might arise. Will the group need information for its discussion? Perhaps you should bring minutes, policies, reports, and data for reference. Prepare handouts, slides, or charts to put key information before the group. Consider the comfort and convenience of those assembled. At a business meeting, are there writing materials, name tags, refreshments, and scheduled breaks? At a banquet or public program, oversee or delegate even small details such as seating arrangements, water at the speakers' table, and audiovisual equipment.

Carefully plan your opening and closing statements. Try to develop coherent, and even graceful, transitions to bridge the parts of the program so that you do not fall back on "moving right along" or "last, but not least."

35-2 Create a Positive Communication Environment

Beyond the logistical concerns of agenda setting and troubleshooting, an effective leader can shape a context that helps a group meet its goals for communicating by creating a positive environment for communication.

CHECKLIST ~ Key Tasks for Emceeing a Ceremony or Banquet

- Have you planned opening remarks that establish an appropriate mood? Whether the occasion is a solemn one, a celebration, or a regular monthly luncheon, the emcee should make guests feel welcome and set the tone for the events to follow.
- Can you make gracious and concise introductions?
- Will you be able to direct audience response by asking listeners to hold their applause or by signaling for it through your phrasing and inflection?

As the person who speaks first and from a position of leadership, you can let a group know about a situation by the way you present yourself, the tone you take, and the level of formality you assume. Participants appreciate a leader's ability to set communication ground rules and norms and respond promptly to violations.

35-2a Set Communication Ground Rules

Sometimes it is necessary to be more explicit about the way communication will proceed. In these cases, a leader should *metacommunicate*, or talk about talking. For example, you might say:

▶ At our meetings, we agree to seek the floor by raising a hand and letting the speaker call on people.

▶ Because of the sensitive nature of our topic, we request that you not use names or identifying information when you share examples from your organization.

▶ So that more people have time to participate, we request that you keep questions and comments brief.

▶ This morning, we will be discussing only the problems that have brought us together and the causes we can identify. After lunch, we will get into possible solutions. If we start to jump ahead of ourselves, I will remind you to hold the thought until later.

MindTap®   SPEAKER'S WORKSHOP 35.1

Under what circumstances can a group rely on implicit understandings of communicative norms and rules? When are members likely to need more explicit discussions and metacommunication?

If you were leading a communicative event, what would you do in each of the following situations?

1. One person engages in angry refutation and personal attacks on the invited primary speaker.

2. Three individuals in the back of the room continue to whisper and carry on private conversations that distract the group.

3. In a general discussion of a social issue, one participant reveals very personal information and becomes extremely emotional.

4. At a business meeting, an employee connects observations to general market climate to advocate for the election of a specific political candidate.

MindTap®   To read about the importance of listening as a leader, visit the MindTap for *The Speaker's Handbook* and click on **Additional Resources**.

35-2b Respond Promptly to Violations of Rules and Norms

Remind the entire group of the ground rules: "Remember, we agreed not to make any personal attacks in this discussion." If there have not been explicit ground rules, ask the group if it wishes to set some: "I notice that we've covered only two points on our agenda. Because we have to finish by four o'clock, would the group like to set a policy of limiting discussion to ten minutes per point, and then we can return to discuss any in more depth once we've covered everything?"

If you must single out an individual, try to do so with a compliment: "Tony, You have so many experiences to share that you have already given us a great deal to think about. Now we need to move on to the next area of discussion."

MindTap® Visit the MindTap for *The Speaker's Handbook* and click on **Additional Resources** to see helpful links about leadership.

Summary

35-1 Prepare for a leadership role.

▶ A well-designed agenda and a confident leader guiding a group through that agenda are essential to an efficient project status meeting, banquet, or parliamentary session.

▶ Articulate the agenda and roles to all participants.

▶ Develop contingency plans.

35-2 Create a positive communication environment.

▶ By carefully preparing an agenda based on the objectives and traditions of a group and modeling appropriate communication while setting and enforcing ground rules, a leader can create a positive team environment.

▶ Set communication ground rules.

▶ Deal promptly with violations of rules and norms.

Critical Thinking Questions

▶ Why is an agenda so vital to effective meetings?

▶ How might you redirect meeting participants who have gotten off track?

▶ How does an effective leader positively influence the climate of a business meeting?

Because There's No Substitute for a Concrete Example

We stress the power of examples in Chapters **15**, **18**, and **21**, and we rely on them throughout this handbook, because, no matter how clearly a general concept or precept is explained, an example almost always aids understanding. This part of *The Speaker's Handbook* presents sample speech outlines and transcripts so that you have a handy collection of complete sample speeches. These speeches are also annotated; you'll find our comments in the margin next to each speech, along with arrows and highlighting that ensure you will know which section of the speech we are discussing. Videos of many of these speeches are also available through the MindTap for *The Speaker's Handbook.* MindTap˙ The MindTap icon next to a speech title indicates instances in which the video is available either directly in MindTap or when a link to the video is provided in MindTap. For some videos, Interactive Video Activities are also available.

The sample speeches in this part of the handbook and their corresponding videos, referenced throughout the text (primarily in the Speaker's Workshop boxes), give you numerous opportunities to see different models of how the principles you encounter throughout the book are put to use. The term *model* should not be taken to suggest either that all these speeches are perfect or that you should try to imitate exactly what you see. Instead, these speeches show you the many different ways in which the task of speaking can be approached. Even those sample speeches you admire may not fit your speaking personality, but you will probably get a few good ideas from each speech. Finally, though we have included speeches that we think are good exemplars of the principles from this text, not one is perfect. You can take comfort in noticing how a speaker might have a stiff delivery or lack effective transitions yet still have a successful overall presentation.

Speeches by Student Speakers

The student speeches are drawn from two main situations: classroom assignments and forensics competition. Most of the speeches were originally given extemporaneously by the speakers in their classrooms, and then recorded for this book. These speeches include **Brian Sharkey's** speech about Native American code talkers, **Harriet Kamakil's** speech about the Maasai people of Africa, **Nathanael Dunlavy's** speech about the 54th Massachusetts Volunteer Infantry Regiment, **Stephen Garrett's** invitational speech about a new drug being used to treat posttraumatic stress, **Kayla Strickland's** speech about malaria nets, and **Adam Parrish's** speech about cyberbullying. Not every speech has a video, and in some cases, as indicated, a student other than the original speaker delivered the speech for the video.

It is interesting to notice the small differences in manuscripts (what one planned to say) and the transcripts (what one actually said). Observing this difference should assure you that outlines and manuscripts are important tools for various kinds of speech preparation, but they need not constrict the speaker's spontaneity at the moment of speaking.

Speeches by Public Figures

Speeches in this second group were given by people in the public eye: two elected officials, a past U.S. president, the current U.S. president, a visual artist and activist, and an executive director of an interfaith organization. I have chosen these speeches for their brevity, political speeches tend to be long, for their importance, and for the broad spectrum of perspectives they represent.

Speeches by Student Speakers

Native American Code Talkers

Please take a look at the words on the screen behind me. By the end of my speech today, their true meaning will make sense.

During World War II, one group of soldiers was credited with having a large part in defeating the Japanese in the Pacific Theater. Because of these men, the Japanese never discovered the true meaning of the communications sent by the U.S. Marines during the war. These men were the Navajo code talkers.

In researching this topic, I found a lot of great resources dedicated to these incredible men. Most of the information I'm going to share with you today came from http://history .navy.mil and http://bingaman.senate.gov. Today I'd like to share with you how the U.S. Marines came to use the Navajo as code talkers, the development of the code, and why the code talkers were such valuable assets to the Marines in World War II.

Let's start today by looking at the how the Marines started using the Navajo as code talkers. The idea of using the Navajo to encode messages came about because the Japanese had decoded every code the United States had tried to use. The U.S. military saw a need to find an unbreakable code.

Notice the use of "dot-gov" and "dot-mil" websites as sources. For this speech, these sources are more credible than "dot-com" sites, which might have been more easily accessible to Brian.

Notice Brian's clear preview of the main points he intends to cover.

[1]Used with permission.

The idea of actually using the Navajo language came from Philip Johnston. He was the son of missionaries who worked with the Navajo, and at the time he was one of the very few non-Navajos who could speak the language fluently. Soon after the Japanese attacked Pearl Harbor, he presented his idea to his superiors, and in May of 1942 the first 29 recruits showed up at Camp Pendleton for boot camp.

Now that we know how the Navajo came to be used as code talkers, we can examine the code they developed. The code they used was developed by those first 29 recruits, and one way the code talkers passed on information was by using unrelated Navajo words. One way to demonstrate this method is found at http://history.navy.mil. The words tsah, wol-la-chee, ahkeh-di-glini, and tsah-ah-dzoh translate to the English words needle, ant, victor, and yucca. The receiver of the code would take the first letter of each English word and put them together to form words. So in this case, the *n* from *needle*, the *a* from *ant*, the *v* from *victor*, and the *y* from *yucca* come together to spell *Navy*.

The developers also came up with ways to transfer often-used military terms that did not exist in the Navajo language. For example, the word *lo-tso* translates to *whale*, which the developers assigned to the term *battleship*. Another example is *dah-he-tih-hi*, which translates to *hummingbird*, which in turn was equated with the term *fighter plane*. According to Alexander Molnar, Jr., at http://history.navy.mil, the developers did this for over 450 words.

Last, now that we know how the Navajo came to be used as code talkers and how they developed the code, we can understand why the code was so effective and why the Navajo were such valuable assets to the Marines. During fighting in the Pacific Theater in World War II, the Japanese proved themselves to be very good code breakers. However, the Navajo code was the only one they were unable to break. The Navajo code was unbreakable because of the language it was based on. The language is an unwritten language, with no alphabet or symbols, and is only spoken in the American Southwest. It is an extremely complex language that is totally unintelligible to

Brian practiced pronouncing these foreign-looking and foreign-sounding terms so that he wouldn't negatively impact his credibility by struggling with them in front of the audience.

Here, and throughout his speech, he enhances his credibility by citing the sources of the information he uses.

anyone who has not had immense exposure to it. According to Molnar, at the time of World War II, fewer than 30 non-Navajos worldwide could understand the language.

One particular occasion that the Navajo showed themselves to be invaluable was during the battle for Iwo Jima. I've got a map here that shows the island of Iwo Jima in the middle, Guam down at the bottom, and Japan at the top. Iwo Jima was important to the United States because Japanese fighters were based on airfields there, and they routinely attacked U.S. bombers on their runs to Japan. In order for the bombers to get to their targets, the Marines had to take the island and shut down the Japanese airfields. According to the website bingaman.senate.gov, in the first 48 hours of battle for Iwo Jima, six code talkers sent and received more than 800 messages without error. Afterward, Major Howard Connor was quoted as saying, "Were it not for the Navajo, the Marines would have never taken Iwo Jima."

Hopefully now you all understand a little better the important role the Navajo had in fighting World War II. Today I shared how the Navajo came to be used as code talkers, how they developed the unbreakable code, and how they were invaluable to the U.S. Marines, specifically in the battle for Iwo Jima.

To illustrate just how effective the code was, I'd like to leave you with a story of a Navajo soldier who was captured by the Japanese. He was not trained as a code talker, and when he could not decipher what the intercepted codes meant, his captors tortured him. Upon meeting a code talker after the war, he is quoted as saying, "I never figured out what you guys who got me into all that trouble were saying."

On that note, take a look at the screen for six Navajo words and their translations. I made my own code here, using the same method the code talkers did. *(Brian shows six Navajo words and their English translations.)* There are the Navajo words and their English translations. Take the first letters of the English words, and—there you go. *(He reveals his hidden message: THE END.)*

The Maasai Initiation Ceremony

MindTap°   *Informative Speech by Harriet Kamakil[2]*

In the old days, warriors were like gods, and women and men wanted to be the parent of a warrior. Everything else would be taken care of as a result: When a poor family had a warrior in the family, they ceased to be poor. The warriors would go on raids and bring cattle back. The warriors would defend the family against all odds. So who exactly are the Maasai, you may ask? Where exactly do they live in Kenya? And what does it take to be a Maasai warrior? That's what I will be talking about with you today.

To start with, I'll show you a map of the place where they are located in Kenya. The Maasai live right across the Serengeti Plain. There are some who live in Kenya, and some who live down in Tanzania, so they are spread out—there are the Kenyan Maasais and the Tanzanian Maasais.

So, does anybody know what initiation is? I know that initiation means inducting new people. For example, if you want to be inducted into any secret society, you probably have to go through an initiation. The Maasais make a very big deal out of the initiation ceremony, which actually involves circumcision, and that's what I'm going to talk to you about today.

Before the circumcision takes place, the first thing adults in the family do is talk to the initiate about the family's honor, which is very important to the Maasai, because everybody in the community knows everybody else. So when you're going to your circumcision, your father sits down with you and tells you, "Do not let your family down." Your family tells you that you cannot flinch during the circumcision and that you are required to look in one direction during the entire time and not flinch, no matter what. Otherwise, you will be seen as a coward, and that's a bad thing.

[2]Used with permission.

Notice Harriet's use of questions to preview her main points. Although her questions do preview the content of her speech, a more concise declarative statement would have made the main points clearer.

Harriet uses the chronological pattern to organize her speech, which is an effective way to inform her audience of an unfamiliar process. Notice her clear signposts throughout the speech: "before the circumcision takes place," "three days before the circumcision," "on the eve of the circumcision," "on the day of the circumcision," and "after the circumcision."

Some people get very, very scared, and they may decide they don't want to go through with the ritual, but then they will be held down and forcibly circumcised. But if that happens, your chances of getting into a leadership position will never happen—everybody would say you are a coward, and no one would want to marry you, and your family name would be soiled.

Three days before the circumcision, the warriors-to-be are required to discard all their possessions—their spears, their knives, their necklaces, their clothing. Even their heads are shaved. Anything that you had before, you're supposed to get rid of it, because the Maasai look at this point in your life like being baptized—all the things from your childhood are put aside, and the ceremony will make you a new man. Also, three days before the ceremony you get the knife that will be used to circumcise you, and you sharpen it yourself. You protect it from people who may have ill will and want to make the knife blunt so that it won't work on the day of the circumcision.

On the eve of the circumcision, the warriors-to-be are insulted by their families—your family is afraid that you'll flinch and cause them to lose honor, so they insult you and try to see whether they can break you. Then, on the day of the circumcision, you are insulted by other warriors who have already been circumcised. There are two reasons for this. First, if you start crying or if your spirit is not strong, it will show at this point. Second, as Tepilit Ole Saitoti wrote in his book about his own initiation as a Maasai warrior, you get so annoyed that you resolve not to flinch, just to show them what you can do. The insults make you stronger.

On the day of the circumcision, somebody comes in and takes you to out by the river, and ice cold water is poured on your head—you know, your head is now shaved, so the cold water just flows over your body. Then the circumciser comes up with a knife, and before he makes the cut, he announces "One cut!" so you know what's coming. So in the end you won't say, "I was caught unawares, so that's why I flinched." He says "one cut," and then you are prepared for when the knife actually comes. And then he does it.

Harriet's comparison of the preparation phase of the initiation to baptism helps connect an unknown to something most of her audience members understand.

Notice the descriptive language Harriet uses to paint a clear picture for her audience.

If you do not flinch, it's a wonderful thing. There's all this celebration—you drink beer, you dance. White paint is splashed on your face—that's symbolic. You're given cattle by your father and your relatives. Cows are a big deal in Maasailand. That's how you pay your dowry if you ever get married, and now that you're circumcised, you go from being a boy to a man, and hopefully you'll be getting married soon. After the circumcision, you are given all these presents, and the biggest present the family can give you is cows. Ole Saitoti was given 14 cows, and the community was very happy for him.

It takes about two weeks for the wound to heal. After the circumcision, your blood is not supposed to get to the ground, so you're supposed to sit on your bed and let the blood keep flowing on your bed so that it doesn't get to the ground. Now, Ole Saitoti didn't know that he was supposed to squeeze the organs so that all the blood could come out—they forgot to tell him that for some reason. So it got infected and was very painful, until someone told him that that's what you're supposed to do. It takes about 2 weeks to heal. Then, the man is a warrior.

(Harriet holds up a small African statue.) This is a Maasai warrior. When you go to Kenya, these are everywhere because the warriors are so revered. That's his spear, and this is his shield, which he uses to protect himself. When he's going to war, this is how a Maasai warrior would look. I also have some photos so you'll know what the Maasai look like—these are Maasai warriors.

Today I have informed you about the Maasai people of Kenya, and some of them are also in Tanzania. I've told you about the initiation ceremony and what it takes to be a Maasai warrior. I will complete with a quote by Ole Saitoti: "When a society respects the individual and displays confidence in him the way the Maasai do their warriors, the individual can grow to his fullest potential."

The 54th Massachusetts

MindTap°

It was eighth grade history class, and I hated, absolutely hated, history. But as another boring week began, I heard what was music to my ears: "Class, this week we're going to watch a movie." The movie was called *Glory*. It was about the Civil War and the raising of the first black regiment from the Northeast.

Notice how Nathanael's attention-getter device draws his audience in immediately to the topic.

Every year in the month of February, our country celebrates Black History Month. We recognize the efforts of such African Americans as Harriet Tubman, Booker T. Washington, and Martin Luther King, Jr. However, today I will not be speaking on such notable names as these, but on quite the contrary. I'll be speaking about what review author Jeff Shannon calls a noble, yet little known, episode of history: the 54th Massachusetts. After watching *Glory*, I became intrigued with the Civil War and began doing research on it, specifically the events surrounding the 54th Massachusetts. It all began on January 1, 1863, when Abraham Lincoln signed the Emancipation Proclamation, allowing for the first time in this nation's history the opportunity for men of color to sign up and fight for their country. Today, I'll be discussing the formation of the 54th Massachusetts, the racial difficulties they faced, and the Battle of Fort Wagner. Let's begin with the formation of the troops.

This is the thesis for the speech. Clear and specific, it leaves no question as to what the remainder of the speech will cover.

In March 1863, the regiment simply known as the 54th was formed in Readville, Massachusetts. The man who would be colonel and in charge of the men was Robert Gould Shaw, the 25-year-old son of a prominent Boston abolitionist family. Although he was young, he was already a veteran of the battlefield. Civil War historian William James notes that from the time Shaw accepted the preferred command, he lived but for one object, and that was to establish the honor of the 54th Massachusetts. On May 28, 1863, a parade honoring the men

Notice the smooth transitions between main points, here and at the end of the next paragraph.

[3]Used with permission.

Cengage Learning, Inc.

cheered them on as they left Boston to fight for the Union. With the men trained, suited up, and ready for battle, next I'll be discussing the racial difficulties the men faced.

The 54th was comprised mostly of free men who had never been slaves or had to face the types of racial prejudices that were to come. First, according to Civil War author and lecturer Kathy Dahl of BitsofBlueandGray.com, instead of the promised Army wage of $13 a month, because they were black troops, they would receive $10 a month—minus $3 for clothing. Then, despite intense training and fighting readiness, the regiment was only ordered to do basic manual labor. Then in June 1863, Shaw was given orders to have his men burn and loot a small town in Georgia. Shaw saw this as a Satanic action, and in a letter to his wife he writes, "I fear that such actions will hurt the reputation of black troops and those connected with them." Performing only manual labor with little pay and the possible disgrace brought upon them with the burning of the town, this will take us to the last point: the Battle of Fort Wagner.

On July 16, 1863, the men of the 54th saw action and were successful in their attempts. That night, under the secrecy of darkness and in a torrent of rain, the 54th trudged through mud and hazardous terrain for 8 hours, and on the morning of July 18, Colonel Shaw accepted the honor of leading his troops in the assault on Fort Wagner. The fort was to be taken by bayonet in hand-to-hand combat. At dusk, Shaw and his men began their assault. In front of the fort was a moat followed by a 30-foot wall of sand. Confederate fire opened. Nearly blinded by gun smoke and fire, Shaw led his men up to the top of the hill. With a final charge of: "Forward, 54th!" Colonel Shaw was shot through the heart, falling face down into the fort.

William Carney, a member of the regiment, saw that the flag bearer had been shot and lay dead in the moat. Carney climbs down the hill, races into the moat, grasps the flag, and begins his ascent back to the top. In the process, Carney is shot through the leg, the shoulder, the arm, and in the head. With orders to retreat, Carney clutches onto the flag, gets on his hands and knees, and crawls back down the hill, which is now covered with the bodies of fallen comrades, and flees

The use of description and action words makes this a very exciting passage. Notice in the video Nathanael's use of voice to convey the difficulty and bravery faced by William Carney.

some 500 yards to safety. Before collapsing, his only words were, "Boys, I only did my duty; the flag never touched the ground." The next day, the body of Colonel Shaw and 300 of his men were thrown into a sandy ditch and buried. Thirty years later, William Carney would become the first African American in this nation's history to be awarded the Congressional Medal of Honor and become the public symbol of the many unsung heroes of the 54th Massachusetts. Because of the efforts of the 54th, more black troops were enlisted, and President Lincoln credited the raising up of African American troops as helping to secure the final victory.

In conclusion, we have covered the formation of the 54th Massachusetts, the racial difficulties they faced, and the Battle of Fort Wagner. There have been many years removed since that eighth grade history class, but the images of those brave men serve as constant reminders that although their names may remain ambiguous, their place in our nation's history lasts forever. The courage and legacy of the 54th is encapsulated best in the words of an unknown author that read: "Glory was not to be found in victory, but in their willingness to keep fighting for what they believed in."

> Nathanael returns the audience to his opening lines to create closure and signal the end of the speech.

Treatment for PTSD

Invitational Speech by Stephen Garrett[4]

Invitational Speech Outline

Purpose: To invite

Specific purpose: To invite my audience consider the implications of an experimental treatment for Post-Traumatic Stress Disorder

Thesis: In this speech I will invite you to weigh the advantages of an experimental treatment called propranolol as well as some disadvantages of using propranolol and finally consider your opinions on the treatment.

[4]Used with permission.

Introduction

I. Attention : Joe saw the horrifying events of active combat during his time in the Army. No matter how hard he tried he couldn't leave behind the memories—like the horrifying sight of Gary, a close friend, who was blown-up by a land-mine. Even after Joe returned to civilian life, these images haunted him. Scenes from battle would run repeatedly through his mind and disrupt his focus on work. The smell of diesel, or loud noises like a backfiring engine would startle him. Joe was almost entirely unable to relax and sleep at night.

II. Reveal topic: According to the VA Healthcare, 2.7 Million Veterans of the Iraq and Afghanistan Theatre, just like Joe, suffer from Post-Traumatic Stress Disorder. I became interested in possible treatment when I heard about Propranolol being used as an experimental drug in my Psychology class.

III. Credibility: I found several studies being conducted around the world. I gathered information from Texas A&M University, 60 Minutes, and The Atlantic. IV.

IV. Preview: Now that I have researched about this topic I will share with you my findings and ask you to weigh the advantages of an experimental treatment called propranolol as well as some disadvantages of using propranolol and finally consider your own opinions on the treatment.

Body

I. Propranolol, an experimental drug has been used successfully in treating PTSD.

   A. Texas A&M University reported on findings that a common drug may help dampen fears. "Patients with PTSD have trouble learning to suppress fearful memories of their traumas," says Stephen Maren, professor of psychology at Texas A&M University. Propranolol, the drug used in the study, is a beta blocker that is also used to treat angina, irregular heartbeat, and other heart conditions."

   B. The Atlantic reported on a study conducted by Dr. Roger Pitman, a Harvard psychiatrist who directs the PTSD and Psychophysiology Laboratory at the Massachusetts General Hospital reported in Biological Psychiatry that "patients treated with propranolol in the emergency room hours after a physical trauma, like an auto accident, were much less likely to show physical reactions to recalling their experience three months later. Here the treatment appeared to reduce the formation of new memories."

C. In a report by 60 Minutes, one of the first subject in one of these studies was Kathleen Logue, a paralegal, who had been knocked down in the middle of a busy Boston street by a bicyclist. Three months after her treatment she showed no signs of PTSD, whereas many who received a placebo still suffered from symptoms. The findings show promising results at preventing PTSD from setting in when administered to patients shortly after the incident. This could drastically change the statistics not only for military personnel but also civilian Emergency Rooms.

Transition: While it may seem like a medical miracle to finally have a cure for PTSD, there are also some potential hazards to the use of propranolol.

II. There are also serious negative implications.

A. In the same report by 60 Minutes, after receiving funding for a large scale study by the National Institutes of Health, the President's Committee on BioEthics condemned the study saying, "Our memories make us who we are….rewriting memories pharmacologically risks undermining our true identity." They argue that changing a person's memory is in effect the same as changing the person themselves.

B. David Magnus, Ph. D, Director of Stanford University's Center for Biomedical Ethics, says he worries it won't just be trauma victims trying to dull painful memories. He points out that drug companies would want as many people as possible to be diagnosed with this condition and would be looking for the widest possible use of the drug. "If I embarrass myself at a party Friday night and can take a pill, then I'm not going to have to avoid making a fool of myself at parties."

C. Magnus claims that our breakups, relationships and although sometimes painful experiences teach us and make us who we are. People will no longer have to face up to their fears and can use this treatment as a "crutch."

Transition: Now that we have considered both advantages and disadvantages to the use of propranolol, I would like to hear your thoughts.

III. Dialogue/discussion:
   A. Question 1: What are some other implications of using a drug like this to suppress memories?
   B. Question 2: What kinds of issues would be faced if people found a way to use this drug as a "crutch?"
   C. Question 3: What factors do you think should determine whether experimental treatments are allowed?

Transition: I know there are many more questions that we could discuss, but I would like to thank all of you for your thoughts in this discussion.

Conclusion

I. Summary: We have examined some advantages of propranolol, disadvantages of propranolol, and we have considered some of the deeper philosophical questions, and discussed some additional benefits and potential risks of using propranolol.

II. Closing: Hopefully you will never have to suffer through a traumatic episode, but if you ever do find yourself in a situation where you need to decide if a treatment like this is right for you, I hope our discussion will help you decide what is best for you.

References

Department of Veterans Affairs, Veterans Health Administration, Office of Public Health, Post-Deployment Health Group. Report on Health Care Utilization among

OEF/OIF/OND Veterans FY2002-FY2014 (n.d.): n. pag. Jan. 2015. Web. 18 Oct. 2016. <http://www.publichealth .va.gov/docs/epidemiology/healthcare-utilization-repo rt-fy2014-qtr4.pdf>.

Henton, Lesley, Texas A&M. "Common Drug May Help PTSD Patients Dampen Fear—Futurity." Futurity. Texas A & M University (13 July 2015). Web. 20 Oct. 2016. <http://www.futurity.org/blood-pressure-drug-ptsd -fear-957702/>.

Lavine, Robert. "Ending the Nightmares: How Drug Treatment Could Finally Stop PTSD." The Atlantic. Atlantic Media Company, n.d. Web. 20 Oct. 2016. <http:// www.theatlantic.com/health/archive/2012/02/ending -the-nightmares-how-drug-treatment-could-finally -stop-ptsd/252079/>.

60 Minutes. N.p., 2010. Web. 20 Oct. 2016. <https://www .youtube.com/watch?v=qeQBrMkVzHU>

Bite Back

Persuasive Speech by Kayla Strickland[5]
Organized with Monroe's Motivated Sequence

General purpose: To persuade

Specific purpose: To persuade my audience to get involved in the fight to end malaria.

Thesis statement: Malaria, a disease that stunts economic growth, education, health care, and productivity, and takes thousands of lives every day, can be stopped and reversed within our lifetime.

I.   Introduction

Attention: It's just a mosquito, right? To us it is, but to half the world it is also fever, vomiting, aches, jaundice, anemia.

Notice how Kayla uses the description of malaria's side effects to draw her audience in prior to revealing her speech topic.

[5]Used with permission.

It is seizures, comas, lung inflammation, cardiovascular collapse, kidney failure, paralysis. It is speech impediments. It is still-births and maternal deaths and low birth-weight babies. It is blindness. It is deafness. It is malaria.

Reveal topic: The disease is caused by a little parasite from the genus *Plasmodium* that is carried from human to human via mosquitoes. It invades and ruptures red blood cells, reproducing rapidly, and every day this process takes thousands of lives and stunts economic growth, child development, and health care productivity.

Credibility: You've most likely heard of malaria as a distant problem—something that affects Africa and poor people in jungles. But what if I told you that this disease actually has global implications that affect you and me? And what if I also told you that we have the ability to stop this disease and reverse the negative effects it has on economics, education, health care, and life expectancy?

Preview: Today I would like to talk about why malaria is a problem, what can be done to fight it, and what the benefits of ending malaria would be.

Transition: We have the ability to deaden malaria's sting. This is a reality. But today it is not yet accomplished, so let me share with you some other realities.

II. Need step

    A. Malaria has killed a million people just this past year, according to estimates by the Centers for Disease Control and Prevention.

        1. The disease has it out for the most vulnerable members of society—pregnant women, children, and groups living in conflict areas.

        2. The Roll Back Malaria Partnership (RBM)—made up of representatives from the World Bank, the World Health Organization (WHO), and UNICEF, among others—points out that nearly a third of malarial deaths occur in areas racked with the stresses of war, food shortages, displacement, and civil unrest.

Many students struggle a bit with Monroe's motivated sequence, but notice how Kayla previews her points clearly, identifying that she will address the problem (need), the solution (satisfaction), and the benefits (visualization).

B. You are probably beginning to see that lives are not the only cost of malaria.

   1. RBM reports that malaria costs Africa US$12 billion each year.

      a. Some causes are productivity losses due to illness-related absences from work, and diminished foreign investment and tourism.

      b. The same report stated that the cost on poor families for prevention and treatment of malaria is around a fourth of their annual income.

      c. Poverty keeps communities sick, and sickness keeps communities in poverty.

   2. Malaria also overloads the health care infrastructure in affected countries.

      a. The disease renders the infrastructure less efficient to tackle other health concerns like HIV/AIDS and tuberculosis.

      b. The *Global Strategy and Booster Program*, published by the World Bank, estimates that malaria consumes close to 40 percent of all public spending on health in Africa.

      c. Up to half of the beds in African hospitals are occupied by malaria victims.

   3. You can imagine that when most of these beds are filled by children, education and child development are hampered.

      a. Kids who stick through the horrible malarial pains and fevers are likely to experience recurrent episodes.

         i. They can be left with severe brain damage and physical impairments like paralysis, deafness, and blindness.

         ii. These afflictions negatively affect their ability in school and inhibit them from adding to the prosperity of their communities.

      b. These many costs of a mosquito bite suggest that malaria is a wide-reaching, global problem.

Notice the use of language. Kayla is very descriptive here, helping her American audience understand the physical and economic impact that malaria has on people throughout the world.

Transition: So now let's talk about what can be done to fight it.

III. Satisfaction step

A. There are many methods of malaria prevention.
1. These methods range from insecticide sprays to antimalarial drugs.
2. An efficient combination of them is the only way that malaria can be stopped.

B. But there is no time to cover all of the methods here, so I would just like to introduce one: the simple bed net.
1. The progression of malaria is dependent on continued contact between humans and mosquitoes.
2. Bed nets sever this contact for $10 apiece.
3. Improved technology allows nets to be treated with insecticides as they are manufactured, weaving a chemical barrier into the physical one.
    a. This means that they prevent infection and kill mosquitoes at the same time.
    b. These insecticide-treated nets, called ITNs, are a tried and true method of malaria prevention.
    c. A 2007 WHO report on ITNs said that they have been shown to avert around half of malaria cases and to reduce deaths in children under five by nearly 20 percent.

Kayla was given only eight minutes to complete her speech. Notice how she avoided becoming bogged down in issues and strategies that were not part of her primary objective.

Transition: We see that malaria is a global problem. We see a simple, proven solution to the problem. Now let's see the benefits of ending malaria.

IV. Visualization step

A. The UN (United Nations), along with many international organizations, set eight international development goals to be met by 2015.
1. These are known as the Millennium Development Goals (MDGs).
2. Addressing the problem of malaria has the potential to impact six of these eight goals.
    a. Eradicate extreme poverty and hunger.
    b. Achieve universal primary education.

Notice how Kayla uses the transition to *review* previous points and *preview* the next phase of her appeal.

      c. Reduce child mortality rates.

      d. Improve maternal health.

      e. Combat HIV/AIDS, malaria, and other diseases.

      f. Develop a global partnership for development.

  3. Poverty is a worldwide problem, so any actions that take steps against it, like those laid out by the MDGs, offer rewarding returns on our investments.

 B. Imagine economic productivity restored in Sub-Saharan Africa.

  1. The weight of poverty will be a little less crushing.

      a. Men and women can remain at work instead of in hospitals or at home looking after sick children.

      b. They can grow their crops, raise their livestock, build their trades.

      c. Poor families will no longer have to make a decision between buying antimalarial pills or food.

  2. Trade and tourism will increase.

  3. Government funds will no longer be sucked dry by mosquitoes.

  4. The health care infrastructure will be freed up to take on other issues like HIV/AIDS and TB.

  5. Children will stay in school.

      a. Their futures will not be clouded by the uncertainty and fear that a mosquito's pinprick used to bring.

      b. The minds of future generations will be free to excel and contribute to their families, their communities, their countries, and the entire world.

Transition: In conclusion, I've told you how malaria affects us, showed a way of fighting it, and revealed the benefits that we would see by being rid of it.

The visualization step should help audience members envision how the solution helps and motivate them to become involved. Does Kayla accomplish her objective? Could she do it another way?

V. Action step

Summary: So what can you do to take your bite out of malaria?

Call for action: Buy a net. Ten dollars will provide the funds for a treated net, its distribution, and education for the happy owner. I bought one through biteback.net. Roll Back Malaria recommends Malaria No More and Nothing But Nets.

You may be saying, "One net? What will that accomplish?" Consider the African proverb: "If you think you're too small to make a difference, try sleeping in a closed room with a mosquito." Just take a look at the benefits we've been over, and you can see that a simple bed net is probably one of the best investments you could ever make.

Closing: The mosquito will always be a nuisance, but it doesn't have to be a killer.

> Notice the very specific call to action and Kayla's willingness to take this step herself.

> A nice clincher that effectively ties back to her opening. Watch Kayla's speech on your MindTap for other examples of her effective use of language.

References

Centers for Disease Control and Prevention (CDC). "Disease," (February 12, 2010) www.cdc.gov/malaria/about/disease.html (accessed November 11, 2010).

Centers for Disease Control and Prevention (CDC). "Malaria Facts," (February 12, 2010) www.cdc.gov/malaria/about/facts.html (accessed November 11, 2010).

Roll Back Malaria Partnership. "Looking Forward: Roll Back Malaria," (2004) www.rollbackmalaria.org/docs/rbm_brochure.pdf (accessed November 11, 2010).

The World Bank. *Rolling Back Malaria: The World Bank Global Strategy and Booster Program*, (2005): 15.

World Health Organization. "Insecticide-Treated Mosquito Nets: A WHO Position Statement," *Global Malaria Programme* (2007) www.who.int/malaria/publications/atoz/itnspospaperfinal.pdf (accessed November 11, 2010).

United Nations. *United Nations Millennium Development Goals*, (2010) www.un.org/millenniumgoals/index.shtml (accessed November 11, 2010).

Together, We Can Stop Cyber-Bullying

Persuasive Speech by Adam Parrish[6]

MindTap°

General purpose: To persuade
Specific purpose: To persuade my audience to do their part to stop cyber-bullying.
Thesis statement: Cyber-bullying is a devastating form of abuse that must be confronted and stopped.

Introduction

I. "I'll miss just being around her." "I didn't want to believe it." "It's such a sad thing." These quotes are from the friends and family of 15-year-old Phoebe Prince, who, on January 14, 2010, committed suicide by hanging herself. Why did this senseless act occur? The answer is simple: Phoebe Prince was bullied to death.

II. Many of us know someone who has been bullied in school. Perhaps they were teased in the parking lot or in the locker room. In the past, bullying occurred primarily in and around schools. However, with the advent of new communication technologies such as cell phones with text messaging capability, instant messaging, e-mails, blogs, and social networking sites, bullies can now follow their victims anywhere, even into their own bedrooms. Using electronic communications to tease, harass, threaten, and intimidate another person is called cyber-bullying.

Here Adam entices his listeners to pay attention by offering relevant information we all can relate to. He then clarifies his topic with a concise definition.

III. As a tutor and mentor to young students, I have witnessed cyber-bullying firsthand, and by examining current research, I believe I understand the problem, its causes, and how we can help end cyber-bullying.

IV. Cyber-bullying is a devastating form of abuse that must be confronted and stopped.

V. Today, we will examine the widespread and harmful nature of cyber-bullying, discover how and why it persists,

Notice the clarity of Adam's preview. With it, his listeners know the nature of his main points and how they will be ordered.

[6]Used with permission.

and propose some simple solutions that we must engage in to thwart cyber-bullies and comfort their victims.

Transition: Let's begin by tackling the problem head on.

Body

I. Cyber-bullying is a pervasive and dangerous behavior. Many of us have read rude, insensitive, or nasty statements posted about us or someone we care about on social networking sites like MySpace and Facebook. Whether or not those comments were actually intended to hurt another person's feelings, they are perfect examples of cyber-bullying.

    A. Cyber-bullying takes place all over the world through a wide array of electronic media.

        1. According to an article in the winter 2005 edition of *Reclaiming Children and Youth*, 57 percent of American middle school students have experienced instances of cyber-bullying ranging from hurtful comments to threats of physical violence (Keith & Martin, 2005).

        2. Females are just as likely as males to engage in cyber-bullying, although women are 10 percent more likely to be victimized (Li, 2007).

        3. While the number of students who are targets of cyber-bullies decreases as students age, data from the Youth Internet Safety Survey indicate that the instances of American high school students being cyber-bullied increased nearly 50 percent from 2000 to 2005 (Ybarra, Mitchell, Wolak, & Finkelhor, 2006).

        4. Quing Li (2007), a researcher of computer-mediated communication, noted that Internet and cell phone technologies have been used by bullies to harass, torment, and threaten young people in North America, Europe, and Asia.

        5. A particularly disturbing incident occurred in Dallas, Texas, where an overweight student with multiple sclerosis was targeted on a school's social

Notice how Adam uses a host of supporting evidence to support his claim that cyber-bullying is a pervasive and dangerous problem.

networking page. One message read, "I guess I'll have to wait until you kill yourself, which I hope is not long from now, or I'll have to wait until your disease kills you" (Keith & Martin, 2005, p. 226).

Transition: Clearly, cyber-bullying is a widespread problem. What is most disturbing about cyber-bullying, however, is its effects upon victims, bystanders, and perhaps even upon the bullies themselves.

B. Cyber-bullying can lead to traumatic physical and psychological injuries upon its victims.
   1. According to a 2007 article in the *Journal of Adolescent Health*, 36 percent of the victims of cyber-bullies are also harassed by their attackers in school (Ybarra, Diener-West, & Leaf, 2007).
   2. For example, the Dallas student with MS had eggs thrown at her car and a bottle of acid thrown at her house (Keith & Martin, 2005).
   3. Ybarra et al. (2007) reported that victims of cyber-bullying experience such severe emotional distress that they often exhibit behavioral problems such as poor grades, skipping school, and receiving detentions and suspensions.
   4. Smith et al. (2008) suggested that even a few instances of cyber-bullying can have these long-lasting and heartbreaking results.
   5. What is even more alarming is that victims of cyber-bullying are significantly more likely to carry weapons to school as a result of feeling threatened (Ybarra et al., 2007). Obviously, this could lead to violent, and perhaps even deadly, outcomes for bullies, victims, and even bystanders.

Again, more support is offered to bolster the claim that cyber-bullying can lead to physical and psychological injuries.

Transition: Now that we realize the devastating nature, scope, and effects of cyber-bullying, let's look at its causes.

I. Cyber-bullying is perpetuated because victims and bystanders do not report their abusers to authorities. Think back to a time when you may have seen a friend or loved one being harassed online. Did you report the bully to the network administrator or other authorities? Did you console the victim? I know I didn't. If you are like me, we may unknowingly be enabling future instances of cyber-bullying.

A. Cyber-bullies are cowards who attack their victims anonymously.

    1. Ybarra et al. (2007) discovered that 13 percent of cyber-bullying victims did not know who was tormenting them.

    2. This is an important statistic because, as Keith and Martin (2005) point out, traditional bullying takes place face-to-face and often ends when students leave school. However, today, students are subjected to bullying in their own homes.

    3. Perhaps the anonymous nature of cyber-attacks partially explains why Li (2007) found that nearly 76 percent of victims of cyber-bullying and 75 percent of bystanders never reported instances of bullying to adults.

B. Victims and bystanders who do not report attacks from cyber-bullies can unintentionally enable bullies.

    1. According to DeNies, Donaldson, and Netter of *ABCNews.com* (2010), several of Phoebe Prince's classmates were aware that she was being harassed but did not inform the school's administration.

    2. Li (2007) suggested that victims and bystanders often do not believe that adults will actually intervene to stop cyber-bullying.

    3. However, *ABCNews.com* (2010) reports that 41 states have laws against bullying in schools and 23 of those states target cyber-bullying specifically.

Transition: Now that we realize that victims of cyber-bullies desperately need the help of witnesses and bystanders to report their attacks, we should arm ourselves with the information necessary to provide that assistance.

I. Cyber-bullying must be confronted on national, local, and personal levels. Think about the next time you see a friend or loved one being tormented or harassed online. What would you be willing to do to help?

    A. There should be a comprehensive national law confronting cyber-bullying in schools. Certain statutes currently in state laws should be amalgamated to create the strongest protections for victims and the most effective punishments for bullies as possible.

        1. According to Limber and Small's (2003) article titled, "State Laws and Policies to Address Bullying in Schools," Georgia law requires faculty and staff to be trained on the nature of bullying and what actions to take if they see students being bullied.

        2. Furthermore, Connecticut law *requires* school employees to report bullying as part of their hiring contract (Limber & Small, 2003). Washington takes this a step further, by protecting employees from any legal action if a reported bully is proven to be innocent (Limber & Small, 2003).

        3. When it comes to protecting victims, West Virginia law demands that schools must ensure that a bullied student does not receive additional abuse at the hands of his or her bully (Limber & Small, 2003).

        4. Legislating punishment for bullies is difficult. As Limber and Small (2003) noted, zero-tolerance polices often perpetuate violence because at-risk youth (bullies) are removed from all of the benefits of school, which might help make them less abusive.

        5. A comprehensive anti-cyber-bullying law should incorporate the best aspects of these state laws and find a way to punish bullies that is both punitive and has the ability to rehabilitate abusers.

    B. Local communities must organize and mobilize to attack the problem of cyber-bullying.

        1. According to Greene (2006), communities need to support bullying prevention programs by

conducting a school-based bullying survey for individual school districts. We can't know how to best protect victims in our community without knowing how they are affected by the problem.

2. It is critical to know this information as Greene noted; only 3 percent of teachers in the United States perceive bullying to be a problem in their schools (Greene, 2006).

3. Local school districts should create a coordinating committee made up of "administrators, teachers, students, parents, school staff, and community partners" to gather bullying data and rally support to confront the problem (Greene, 2006, p. 73).

4. Even if your local school district is unable or unwilling to mobilize behind this dire cause, there are some important actions you can take personally to safeguard those you love against cyber-bullying.

C. Take note of these warning signs that might indicate a friend or loved one is a victim of a cyber-bully. If you see a friend or loved one exhibiting these signs, your decision to get involved could be the difference between life and death.

1. Victims of cyber-bullies often use electronic communication more frequently than do people who are not being bullied.

2. Victims of cyber-bullies have mood swings and difficulty sleeping (Keith & Martin, 2005).

3. Victims of cyber-bullies seem depressed and/or become anxious (Keith & Martin, 2005).

4. Victims of cyber-bullies become withdrawn from social activities and fall behind in scholastic responsibilities (Keith & Martin, 2005).

5. According to Raskauskas and Stoltz (2007), witnesses of cyber-bullying should inform victims to take the attacks seriously, especially if the bullies threaten violence.

6. Tell victims to report their attacks to police or other authority figures (Raskaukas & Stoltz, 2007).

Here, the speech turns from a speech of public policy to a speech of personal policy. Adam asks his audience to take action to support the bullied.

7. Tell victims to block harmful messages by blocking e-mail accounts and cell phone numbers (Raskaukas & Stoltz, 2007).
8. Tell victims to save copies of attacks and provide them to authorities (Raskaukas & Stoltz, 2007).
9. If you personally know the bully and feel safe confronting him or her, do so! As Raskaukas and Stoltz (2007) noted, bullies will often back down when confronted by peers.
10. By being a good friend and by giving good advice, you can help a victim report his or her attacks from cyber-bullies and take a major step toward eliminating this horrendous problem.

Transition: So, you see, we are not helpless to stop the cyber-bullying problem as long as we make the choice NOT to ignore it.

Conclusion

I. Cyber-bullying is a devastating form of abuse that must be reported to authorities.
II. Cyber-bullying is a worldwide problem perpetuated by the silence of both victims and bystanders. By paying attention to certain warning signs, we can empower ourselves to console victims and report their abusers.
III. Today, I'm imploring you to do your part to help stop cyber-bullying. I know that you agree that stopping cyber-bullying must be a priority. First, although other states have cyber-bullying laws in place, ours does not. So I'm asking you to sign this petition that I will forward to our district's state legislators. We need to make our voices heard that we want specific laws passed to stop this horrific problem and to punish those caught doing it. Second, I'm also asking you to be vigilant in noticing signs of cyber-bullying and then taking action. Look for signs that your friend, brother, sister, cousin, boyfriend, girlfriend, or loved one might be a victim of cyber-bullying and then get involved to help stop it!

Phoebe Prince showed the warning signs, and she did not deserve to die so senselessly. None of us would ever

Recognize the speaker's use of multiple levels of action and a blend of both logical and emotional appeals.

want to say, "I'll miss just being around her." "I didn't want to believe it." "It's such a sad thing." about our own friends or family members. We must work to ensure that victims are supported and bullies are confronted nationally, locally, and personally. I know that if we stand together and refuse to be silent, we can and will stop cyber-bullying.

References

Greene, M. B. (2006). Bullying in Schools: A Plea for Measure of Human Rights. *Journal of Social Issues, 62*(1), 63–79.

Keith, S., & Martin, M. (2005). Cyber-bullying: Creating a Culture of Respect in the Cyber World. *Reclaiming Children and Youth, 13*(4), 224–228.

Li, Q. (2007). New Bottle of Old Wine: A Research of Cyberbullying in Schools. *Computers in Human Behavior, 23*, 1777–1791.

Limber, S. P., & Small, M. A. (2003). State Laws and Policies to Address Bullying in Schools. *School Psychology Review, 32*(3), 445–455.

DeNies, Y., Donaldson, S., & Netter, S. (2010, January 28). Mean Girls: Cyberbullying Blamed for Teen Suicides. Retrieved from http://abcnews.go.com/GMA/Parenting /girls-teen-suicide-calls-attention-cyberbullying/sto ry?id=9685026.

Raskauskas, J., & Stoltz, A. D. (2007). "Involvement in Traditional and Electronic Bullying Among Adolescents." *Developmental Psychology, 43*(3), 564–575.

Smith, P. K., Mahdavi, J., Carvalho, M., Fisher, S. Russel, S., & Tippett, N. (2008). "Cyberbullying: It's Nature and Impact in Secondary School Pupils. *Journal of Child Psychology and Psychiatry, 49*(4), 374–385.

Ybarra, M. L., Diener-West, M., & Leaf, P. J. (2007). Examining the Overlap in Internet harassment and School Bullying: Implications for School Intervention. *Journal of Adolescent Health, 41*, S42–S50.

Ybarra, M. L., Mitchell, K. J., Wolak, J., & Finkelhor, D. (2006). Examining Characteristics and Associated Distress Related to Internet Harassment: Findings from the Second Youth Internet Safety Survey. *Pediatrics, 118*, 1169–1177.

Speeches by Public Figures

Senate Floor Speech on Civility in the Senate

Speech by Marco Rubio,[7] February 7, 2017

Visit the MindTap for *The Speaker's Handbook* and click on **Additional Resources** to watch a video of this speech.

MindTap®

Senator Rubio: And the reason I ask that, Mr. President, is the following: Look, I think we all feel very passionate about the issues before us. I have not been here as long as Senator Leahy, whose service here is quite distinguished and a long period of time, and I truly do understand the passions people bring to this body. I'd feel to think—I'd like to think that I too am passionate about the issues before us and I think this is an important moment.

It's late. I doubt very many people are paying attention. I wish they would though because I think what's a question here is perhaps one of the very reasons why I ran for this body to begin with. And maybe it's because of my background and where I'm surrounded by people that have lost freedoms in places where they're not allowed to speak. One of the great traditions of our nation is the ability to come forward and have debates. But the founders and the framers and those who established this institution and guided it for over two centuries understood that that debate was impossible if in fact matters became of a personal nature.

[7]Used with permission.

And let me begin by saying that I don't believe that that was necessarily the intention here, although that was perhaps the way it turned out. But I think it's important for us to understand why that matters so much.

I want people to think about our politics here today in America because I'm telling you guys I don't know of a single nation in the history of the world that's been able to solve its problems when half the people in a country absolutely hate the other half of people in that country. This is the most important country in the world. And this body cannot function if people are offending one another, and that's why those rules are in place.

I was not here when Secretary Clinton was nominated as a member of this body at the time. But I can tell you that I am just barely old enough to know that some very nasty things have been written and said about Secretary Clinton. And I think the Senate should be very proud that during her nomination to be Secretary of State, despite the fact that I imagine many people were not excited about the fact that she would be Secretary of State, to my recollection, and perhaps I'm incorrect, not a single one of those horrible things that have been written or said about her, some of which actually did accuse her of wrongdoing, were ever uttered on the floor of the Senate.

I happen to remember in 2004 when—when then-Senator Kerry ran for President. Some pretty strong things were written and said about him. I was here for that vote when he was nominated and confirmed to be Secretary of State. And I don't recall a single statement being written into the record about the things that had been said about him.

And I want everybody to understand at the end of the night, this is not a partisan issue. It really is not. I can tell you this with full confidence: If one of my colleagues on this side of the aisle had done that, I would—I would like to think that I would have been one of the people objecting—and here's why.

Turn on the news and watch these parliaments around the world where people throw chairs at each other, and punches, and ask yourself how does that make you feel about those countries? Doesn't give you a lot of confidence about those countries. Now I'm not arguing that we're anywhere near that here tonight, but we're flirting with it. We're flirting with it in this body and we are flirting with it in this country. We have become a society incapable of having debates anymore.

In this country, if you watch the big policy debates that are going on in America, no one ever stops to say, "I think you're wrong, I understand your point of view—I get it. You have some valid points, but let me tell you why I think my view is better." I don't hear that anymore. Here's what I hear, almost automatically—and let me be fair, from both sides of these debates. Immediately, immediately, as soon as you offer an idea, the other side jumps and says, "The reason why you say that is because you don't care about poor people." "Because you only care about rich people." Because you're this, or you're that or you're the other. And I'm just telling you guys, we have—we are reaching a point in this Republic where we're not going to be able to solve the simplest of issues because everyone is putting themselves in a corner where everyone hates everybody.

Now I don't pretend to say that I have—am not myself from time to time in heated debates outside of this forum; been guilty of perhaps of hyperbole, and for those—I'm not proud of. But I gotta tell you I think what's at stake here tonight, and as we debate moving forward, is not simply some rule but the ability of the most important nation on earth to debate in a productive and respectful way the pressing issues before us. And I just hope we understand that because I have tremendous respect for the other chamber and I understand that it was designed to be different.

But one of the reasons why I chose to run for the Senate, and quite frankly to run for reelection, is because I believe that I serve with 99 other men and women who deeply love their country, who have different points of view, who represent men and women who have different views from the men and women that I may represent on a given issue, and who are here to advocate for their points of view—and never impugning their motives.

One of the things I take great pride in—and I tell this to people all the time—is the one thing you learn about the Senate is whether you agree with them or not, you understand why every single one of those other 99 people are here—because they're intelligent people; they're smart people; they're hardworking people; they believe in what they're saying, and they....articulate it in a very passionate and effective way. And I understand when I see my colleagues stand up and say something I don't agree with, I try to tell myself, "Look I don't understand why they stand for that but I know why they are doing it; because they represent people who believe that."

And I am so grateful that God has allowed me to be born and to live and to raise my family in a—in a nation where people with such different points of view are able to debate those things in a way that doesn't lead to war, that doesn't lead to overthrows, that doesn't lead to violence.

And you may take that for granted. I'm telling you that right now, all around the world tonight, there are people that if they stood up here and said the things that we say about the—the President or others in authority, you go to jail. And I'm not saying that's where we are headed as a nation. I'm just saying don't ever take that for granted.

And the lynchpin of that is this institution. The lynchpin of that debate is the ability of this institution, through unlimited debate and the decorum necessary for that debate, to be able to conduct itself in that manner.

And so, I know that tonight is probably a made-for-TV moment for some people. This has nothing to do with censoring the words of some of the great heroes. I have extraordinary admiration for the men and women who led the civil rights effort in this country. And I am self-conscious enough....or understanding to know that many of the things that have been possible for so many people in this country in the 21st century were made possible by the sacrifices and the work of those in that movement that came before us.

This has to do with the fundamental reality—and that is that this body cannot carry out its work if it is not able to conduct debates in a way that is respectful of one another, especially those of us who are in this chamber together. And I also understand this: that if the Senate ceases to work, if we reach a point where this institution, given everything else that's going on in politics today, where you are basically allowed to say just about anything. For I have seen over the last year and half things said about people, about issues, about institutions in our republic, that I never thought I would see—ever.

Ever.

If we lose this body's ability to conduct debate in a dignified manner, and I mean this with no disrespect towards anyone else—I don't believe anyone else came on this floor here tonight saying, "I'm going to be disrespectful on purpose and....turn this into a circus." But I'm just telling you that if this body loses the ability to have those sorts of debate, then where in this country is that going to happen? What other forum in this nation is that going to be possible?

And so, I would just hope everybody would stop and think about that. I know I've only been here six years so I don't have a deep reservoir of Senate history to rely on. But I know this: If this body is incapable of having those debates, there will be no place in this country where those debates can occur. And I—I think every single one of us, to our great shame, will live to regret it.

https://www.americanrhetoric.com/speeches
/marcorubiosenatecivility.htm

Dedication of the National Museum of African American History and Culture

Speech by President George W. Bush,[8] September 16, 2016

Thank you all. (*To Laura.*) Thank you, darling. (*Laughter*) Laura has been very much engaged in this museum for a long time. She sits on the board. And we're honored to be here. My first reaction is I hope all of our fellow citizens come and look at this place. It is fabulous.

Mr. President and first lady, vice president, chief justice, [Smithsonian Secretary] David [Skorton], thank you very

[8]Used with permission.

much. The board. I do want to give a shout out to [museum director] Lonnie [Bunch]. It's really important to understand this project would not and could not have happened without his drive, his energy and his optimism.

As Laura mentioned, 15 years ago, members from both parties—Congressman John Lewis and Sam Brownback, then-senator from Kansas—informed me that they were about to introduce legislation creating a new museum to share the stories and celebrate the achievements of African Americans. You know, it would be fair to say that the Congress and I did not always see eye to eye. If you know what I mean, Mr. President. (*Laughter*) But this is one issue where we strongly agreed. I was honored to sign the bill authorizing the construction of this national treasure. And I'm pleased it now stands where it has always belonged, on the National Mall.

This museum is an important addition to our country for many reasons. Here are three. First, it shows our commitment to truth. A great nation does not hide its history. It faces its flaws and corrects them. This museum tells the truth that a country founded on the promise of liberty held millions in chains. That the price of our union was America's original sin.

From the beginning, some spoke to truth. John Adams, who called slavery an "evil of colossal magnitude," their voices were not heeded, and often not heard. But they were always known to a power greater than any on earth, one who loves his children and meant them to be free.

Second, this museum shows America's capacity to change. For centuries, slavery and segregation seemed permanent. Permanent parts of our national life. But not to Nat Turner or Frederick Douglass; Harriet Tubman; Rosa Parks; or Martin Luther King, Jr. All answered cruelty with courage and hope.

In a society governed by the people, no wrong lasts forever. After struggle and sacrifice, the American people, acting through the most democratic of means, amended the constitution that originally treated slaves as three-fifths of a person, to guarantee equal protection of the laws. After a decade of struggle, civil rights acts and voting rights act were finally enacted. Even today, the journey toward justice is still not complete. But this museum will inspire us to go farther and get there faster.

And finally, the museum showcases the talent of some of our finest Americans. The galleries celebrate not only African American equality, but African American greatness. I cannot help but note that a huge influence in my teenage years is honored here, the great Chuck Berry. (*Laughter*) Or my baseball idol growing up in far West Texas, the great Willie Mays. And of course, something I never really mastered, the ability to give a good speech, but Thurgood Marshall sure could. And some of you may know I'm a fledgling painter, a struggling artist. (*Laughter*) I have a new appreciation for the artists whose brilliant works are displayed here, people like Robert Duncanson, Henry Ossawa Tanner, Charles Henry Alston.

Our country is better and more vibrant because of their contributions and the contributions of millions of African Americans. No telling of American history is neither complete nor accurate without acknowledging them.

The lesson in this museum is that all Americans share a past and a future by staying true to our principles, righting injustice, and encouraging the empowerment of all. We will be an even greater nation for generations to come. I congratulate all those who played a role in creating this wonderful museum. May God bless us all.

Time to Restore the Bonds between Citizens

Speech by President Donald Trump,[9] January 2017

We are very blessed to call this nation our home. And that is what America is: it is our home. It's where we raise our families, care for our loved ones, look out for our neighbors, and live out our dreams. It is my prayer, that on this Thanksgiving, we begin to heal our divisions and move forward as one country, strengthened by a shared purpose and very, very

What effect does the use of President Abraham Lincoln's words have on the audience here?

[9]Donald Trump, "Time to Restore the Bonds between Citizens." *Vital Speeches of the Day* 2017, 83 (1): 8. Retrieved from EBSCO*host* Academic Search Complete database on February 25, 2017.

common resolve. In declaring this national holiday, President Lincoln called upon Americans to speak with "one voice and one heart." That's just what we have to do. We have just finished a long and bruising political campaign. Emotions are raw and tensions just don't heal overnight.

It doesn't go quickly, unfortunately, but we have before us the chance now to make history together to bring real change to Washington, real safety to our cities, and real prosperity to our communities, including our inner cities. So important to me, and so important to our country. But to succeed, we must enlist the effort of our entire nation.

This historic political campaign is now over. Now begins a great national campaign to rebuild our country and to restore the full promise of America for all of our people. I am asking you to join me in this effort. It is time to restore the bonds of trust between citizens. Because when America is unified, there is nothing beyond our reach, and I mean absolutely nothing.

Let us give thanks for all that we have, and let us boldly face the exciting new frontiers that lie ahead.

Thank you. God bless you and God bless America.

> Why might this reference be appropriate? Could it be seen as inappropriate?

Tough Truths about Plastic Pollution

Persuasive Speech by Dianna Cohen,[10] Artist and Co-Founder of the Plastic Pollution Coalition, April, 2010

MindTap   Visit the MindTap for *The Speaker's Handbook* and click on **Additional Resources** to watch a video of this speech.

I'm a visual artist, and I'm also one of the co-founders of the Plastic Pollution Coalition. I've been working with plastic bags, which I cut up and sew back together as my primary

[10]Dianna Cohen, "Tough Truths about Plastic Pollution," speech delivered at TED Talks (April 2010). Retrieved from www.ted.com/talks/dianna_cohen_tough_truths_about_plastic_pollution.html. Used by permission of the author.

material for my artwork for the last 20 years. I turn them into two- and three-dimensional pieces and sculptures and installations. Upon working with the plastic, after about the first 8 years, some of my work started to fissure and break down into smaller little bits of plastic. And I thought, "Great. It's ephemeral just like us."

Upon educating myself a little further about plastics, I actually realized this was a bad thing. It's a bad thing that plastic breaks down into smaller little bits, because it's always still plastic. And what we're finding is that a lot of it is in the marine environment. I then, in the last few years, learned about the Pacific garbage patch and the gyre. And my initial reaction—and I think this is a lot of people's first reaction to learning about it—is, "Oh my God! We've got to go out there and clean this thing up." So I actually developed a proposal to go out with a cargo ship and two decommissioned fishing trawlers, a crane, a chipping machine, and a cold-molding machine. And my intention was to go out to the gyre, raise awareness about this issue, and begin to pick up the plastic, chip it into little bits and cold mold it into bricks that could potentially be used as building materials in underdeveloped communities.

I began talking with people who actually had been out to the gyre and were studying the plastic problem in the marine environment. And upon doing so, I realized actually that cleaning it up would be a very small drop in the bucket, relative to how much is being generated every day around the world, and that actually I needed to back up and look at the bigger picture. And the bigger picture is: We need to find a way to turn off the faucet. We need to cut the spigot of single-use and disposable plastics, which are entering the marine environment every day on a global scale.

So in looking at that, I also realized that I was really angry. I wasn't just concerned about plastic that you're trying to imagine out in the middle of the Pacific Ocean—of which I have learned there are now 11 gyres, potentially, of plastic in five major oceans in the world. It's not just that gyre of plastic that I'm concerned about; it's the gyre of plastic in the supermarket. I'd go to the supermarket, and all of my food is packaged in plastic. All of my beverages are packaged in plastic, even at the health food market. I'm also concerned about the plastic in

Notice how Dianna Cohen builds in her explanation of the problem.

Sometimes helping audience members see a problem in a new way is essential to a speaker's ability to persuade. Does Cohen effectively connect the Pacific gyre to the gyre in your supermarket?

the refrigerator, and I'm concerned about the plastic and the toxins that leach from plastic into us and into our bodies.

So I came together with a group of other people who were all looking at this issue, and we created the Plastic Pollution Coalition. We have many initiatives that we're working on, but some of them are very basic. One is, if 80 to 90 percent of what we're finding in the ocean—of the marine debris that we're finding in the ocean—is plastic, then why don't we call it what it is. It's plastic pollution. Recycling. Everybody kind of ends their books about being sustainable and greening with the idea of recycling. You put something in a bin, and you don't have to think about it again. What is the reality of that? In the United States, less than 7 percent of our plastics are recycled. And if you really look into it, particularly when it comes to plastic bottles, most of it is only downcycled, or incinerated, or shipped to China. It is downcycled and turned into lesser things. While a glass bottle can be a glass bottle again, or can be used again, a plastic bottle can never be a plastic bottle again. So this is a big issue for us.

Another thing that we're looking at and asking people to think about is we've added a fourth R onto the front of the Reduce, Reuse, Recycle three R's, and that is Refuse.

Whenever possible, refuse single-use and disposable plastics. Alternatives exist. Some of them are very old-school. I myself am now collecting these cool Pyrex containers and using those instead of Glad and Tupperware containers to store food in. And I know that I am doing a service to myself and my family. It's very easy to pick up a stainless-steel bottle, or a glass bottle, if you're traveling and you've forgotten to bring your stainless-steel bottle and fill that up with water, or filtered water, versus purchasing plastic bottled water.

I guess what I want to say to everybody here—and I know that you guys know a lot about this issue—is that this is a huge problem in the oceans, but this is a problem that we've created as consumers and we can solve. We can solve this by raising awareness of the issue and teaching people to choose alternatives. So whenever possible, choose alternatives to single-use plastics. We can cut the stem—tide the stem of this into our oceans, and in doing so, save our oceans, save our planet, save ourselves.

This is Cohen's solution. It is a novel solution in that it builds off the familiar, but it adds a new "R" to the Reduce, Reuse, Recycle catch-phrase, creating a new expectation.

How effectively does Cohen help her audience visualize the benefits of supporting her solution? What more could she do?

This appears to be the call to action. Is it effective?

The Only Shame Is in Stagnation

Wake Forest University Commencement Address May 18, 2016 by Eboo Patel, Executive Director of Interfaith Youth Core[11]

In the early part of the 20th century, a group of esteemed scholars gathered in Boston to take up an urgent question: Would the United States ever make a unique contribution to music? Could there be, out there somewhere, an American Bach?

They looked far and wide in the places that they knew, they searched for faces that they might recognize, they listened deeply in the idioms in which they were familiar. And they came away disappointed.

The jazz critic Gary Giddins shakes his head as he recounts the tale. If these so-called experts had simply taken a train south from Boston to New York City and stepped in to the Roseland Ballroom on a Thursday night, they would have experienced the American Bach, Dante and Shakespeare all rolled into one: Louie Armstrong.

Born to a 16-year-old girl who sometimes worked as a prostitute, raised in a New Orleans neighborhood so violent it was known as the Battlefield, sent to a juvenile detention facility at eleven for firing a gun into the street—let's just say that this was not the profile that the aforementioned experts had in mind.

And yet, Louie Armstrong virtually invented American music. Duke Ellington said Louie Armstrong was so good he wanted him on every instrument. Wynton Marsalis commented that the only way to describe his sound was to say there was light in it. Ken Burns wrote that Louie Armstrong is to American music what Einstein is to physics, Freud is to medicine and the Wright Brothers are to travel. As for himself, Armstrong liked to say that his purpose was to blow his horn so beautifully Angel Gabriel would come out of the clouds.

I love the image of the black, working-class patrons of nightclubs in Harlem and Bronzeville swinging to the genius

Notice the speaker's use of questions to get the audience thinking.

How might the reference to Louie Armstrong both surprise and excite the Wake Forest University audience including graduates and their family members?

What is the effective use of Eboo Patel's narrative? What can a story do that other forms of support fail to do as well?

[11]Eboo Patel, The Only Shame Is in Stagnation *Wake Forest University Commencement Address May 18, 2016*

of Louie Armstrong while the academic elite wrung their hands in stuffy boardrooms wondering whether such a figure existed. Reminds me that there's more than one definition of being educated. And if I'm honest with myself, reminds me that my pedigree is more likely to place me in a stuffy boardroom wringing my hands than in a Harlem nightclub swinging to the next American genius.

And as of today, yours does too.

And so allow me to speak to you about the burden that is customarily placed on the education you received at this fine institution. The burden of certainty. Of knowing. Of believing that you leave here with a set definition of what treasure or genius or success looks like, and a clear road map for how to find it. It's a view that understands an elite education as a classical music score. You've done the hard work of putting the notes on the page, now all you have to do is play them—go to the right grad program, get the right first job, and presto, the music of the good life.

Who can blame anyone for wanting this? The world feels so insecure. If you work this hard and pay this much, the least you can expect is certainty, right?

Well, I have good news and bad news. The bad news is that the world is even more insecure than you've been led to believe. You may end up not liking the sound of the symphony that you spent your education putting on the page. And anything you can write down and follow, a machine is likely to be able to play better, or faster, or at least cheaper.

All of this makes your Wake Forest education even more valuable. (This, by the way, is the good news.) There are things machines can't do, only humans can. These include telling stories, offering comfort, building teams, framing problems, inspiring others. The people most ready to do these very human things are the ones who carry liberal arts thinking deep in their bones. People who have a healthy suspicion of sameness and a knack for finding ideas on the margins and integrating them into the center. People who can take things apart and put them together again, on the fly, in ensemble. In other words, people who have absorbed the music so fully, they can improvise.

Wynton Marsallis says that he plays both classical music and jazz, and jazz is much harder. Not only do you have to

> What impact does Eboo Patel's use of imagery have on the audience? In what way is this metaphor effective for describing the educational process as a person transitions from student to graduate?

know the notes and instrument cold, you have to listen to what other people are doing, and create as you go along.

Louie Armstrong was a master. When his sheet music fell off the stand in a recording session, he didn't stop the tape, he just sang a string of rhythmic nonsense, inventing on the spot a whole new dimension to jazz music: Scat.

There are a lot of missteps when you're improvising. You try this, it doesn't sound so good. You try that, it comes out worse. There's no shame in those kind of mistakes. Having a failed company or two is a badge of honor in Silicon Valley. The only shame is in stagnation, or not doing the work.

Ask anybody you admire about what they hoped would happen in their lives that didn't, and you get a glimpse into the most interesting part of their story. When I was in high school, I was hell-bent on playing varsity basketball. I worked and worked and worked—left hand layups, mid-range jumpers. I was devastated when I didn't make the cut. But I had to find something to do with my time, so I joined speech team. Let's just say that my basketball prowess was unlikely to get me to Wake Forest.

I'm not telling you to throw away the road map you've sketched for your life. I'm just saying that your liberal arts education has given you the eyes to read the road signs along the way, and the ability to change direction when the original plan goes sideways. There is something to be said for reaching the milestones you set for yourself. There's a lot more involved in re-charting your course when you miss them.

This isn't just how careers are made, it's also how countries are built. You are at a jazz age in your lives and we are at a new jazz age as a nation. Wynton Marsalis says that "The foundation of both jazz and democracy is dialogue, learning to negotiate your own agenda within the group's agenda.... You have to listen to what others have to say if you're going to make an intelligent contribution."

In doing this, we have to pay special attention to those who are different, unfamiliar, strange. As Marsalis puts it, to "invest energy in people who are not like us ... invest in them to keep the whole system working."

Remember those highly educated experts I mentioned at the beginning—the ones so focused on finding the American Bach that they missed Louie Armstrong? Well, there was

---

Is the comparison of democracy to jazz effective? In what way does the use of a comparison allow Eboo to communicate effectively with his audience?

another set of people who displayed a wider sense of won-der. The Karnofskys, a Jewish family from Russia, owned a junk wagon and hired young Louie Armstrong to blow the tin horn when the wagon entered a new neighborhood. They took Louie into their home, made sure he had a good meal at the end of every night, invited him to join in the singing of Jewish lullabies around their dinner table.

Something about that tin horn, those Russian Jewish melodies, that extra bit of love, turned something in young Louie Armstrong. When he saw a cornet in a corner store, he asked the Karnofskys for a $5 advance to buy it. He put the instrument to his lips, and lo and behold, songs came out. The early notes of American music.

Louie Armstrong wore a Star of David until he died out of gratitude for the role the Karnofskys played in his life.

Think about that. A Russian Jewish family who owned a junk wagon nurtured the musical genius of a black teenage prostitute's son from a New Orleans ghetto.

That's not just the history of the American songbook. That's the essence of the American story.

> Notice how the speaker returns the listeners to the opening hook. The atten-tion-getting technique cap-tures us further as we learn "the rest of the story." The resulting surprise ending leads listeners to rethink what they thought they knew about this legendary American Jazz icon and per-haps what it means to be fully American.

This is a Great Achievement

Speech delivered at the Dedication of the National Museum of African American History and Culture, National Mall, Washington, D.C., September 24, 2016 by Congressman John Lewis[12]

MindTap®   Visit the MindTap for *The Speaker's Handbook* and click on **Additional Resources** to watch a video of this speech.

President and Mrs. Obama; Vice President Biden; Dr. Jill Biden; President and Mrs. Bush, President Clinton, Mr. Chief Justice, and members of the Board of Regents, to the Museum Advisory Council; Secretary David Skorton; and Dr. Lonnie

> Notice the formality of the opening. Special occasion speeches often open with neces-sary recognition

[12]John Lewis, "This Is a Great Achievement." *Vital Speeches of the Day* 2016, 82 (11): 348. Retrieved from EBSCO*host* Academic Search Complete databse on February 26, 2017.

Bunch. To the leadership of the United States Congress and all of my colleagues in both the house and senate; in memory of the late Rep. Mickey Leland of Texas; the architects of this incredible building; and to all of the staff of the White House, the federal agencies, the Congress, the Smithsonian, who pushed and pulled together to make this moment happen; and to all of the construction companies and their crews; I say thank you.

of dignitaries, elected officials, or other attendees of note.

Thank you for all you did to help lead our society to this magnificent day. As long as there is a United States of America, now there will be a National Museum of African American History and Culture. This was a great achievement. I tell you, I feel like singing the song, the Mahalia Jackson song, from the March on Washington over 50 years ago: "How we got over; how we got over." There were some who said it couldn't happen, who said, "you can't do it." But we did it. We did it.

We are gathered here today to dedicate a building, but this place is more than a building. It is a dream come true.

The purpose of the speech is simply this: to dedicate.

You and I. Each and every one of us were caught up in a seed of light. We were a vision born in the minds of black Civil War veterans and their supporters. They met right here in Washington, D.C., in 1916, exactly 100 years ago at the Nineteenth Street Baptist Church, still in existence today. Oh say, oh say: See what a dream can do. Roll up the sleeves of those veterans or touch the rubble on their backs—you might find the wounds of shackles and whips. Most could not read the Declaration of Independence or write their own names. But in their hearts—burning, enduring vision of true democracy that no threat or death could ever erase.

Notice the powerful imagery used. Through thought word choice listeners can envision the images and even feel the wounds.

They understood the meaning of their contribution. They set a possibility in motion, passing down through the ages from heart to heart and breath to breath. That we are giving birth today to this museum is a testament to the dignity of the dispossessed in every corner of the globe who yearn for freedom. It is a song to the scholars and scribes; scientists and teachers; to the revolutionaries, and the voices of protest; to the ministers in the office of peace. It is a story of life, the story of our lives, wrapped up in a beautiful golden crown of grace.

Notice here the parallel sentence structure.

I can hear the distant voice of ancestors whispering by the night fire: "Steal away, steal away home, ain't got long to stay here." A big bold choir shouting, "I woke up this morning with my mind stayed on freedom." All of the voices roaming, for centuries, have finally found a home here in this great monument to our pain, our suffering, and our victory.

When I was a little child growing up in rural Alabama, a short walk to the cotton fields, but hundreds of miles from Washington, from the Washington Monument or the Lincoln Memorial, my teachers would tell us to cut out of pictures of great African Americans for Carter G. Woodson's Negro History Week, now called African American History Month. I became inspired by the stories of George Washington Carver, Jackie Robinson, Rosa Parks, and so many others whose life and work would be enshrined in this museum.

As these doors open, it is my hope that each and every person who visits this beautiful museum will walk away deeply inspired, filled with a greater respect for the dignity and the worth of every human being and a stronger commitment to the ideals of justice, equality and true democracy. Thank you.

Notice the use of the inclusive pronoun "our" which Congressman John Lewis is particularly qualified to use here as a member of the original 13 Freedom Riders having survived a bus bombing and brutal beating during his march across the Edmund Pettus Bridge near Selma, Alabama.

Guide to Common Pronunciation and Usage Errors

This last part of the handbook provides a Guide to Common Pronunciation and Usage Errors; it is followed by a Glossary of Key Terms. Both resources are intended to be references—compilations of specific information that you may choose to consult as needed.

We created the Guide to Common Pronunciation and Usage Errors for both native and nonnative speakers of English. Many English words are used and pronounced incorrectly every day, and often we encounter them courtesy of popular media. Because we tend to think that media figures must know how to say things correctly, and because we hear incorrect forms over and over, we sometimes even adjust our usual way—which had been the correct way—of saying things to the incorrect ways that are so prevalent. If you're going to give a public presentation, you may want to play it safe and check this guide to ensure that you are understood and are perceived to be as credible as possible.

If you are uncertain about the pronunciation of words not included in this guide, then you might want to visit the Merriam-Webster website, which provides audio pronunciations for about 105,000 English words. Other online dictionaries also provide audio pronunciation, and you can find guides to English usage online as well. One good source is Paul Brians' *Common Errors in English Usage*, a site sponsored by Washington State University.

MindTap® For audio pronunciations of words and guides to English visit the MindTap and click on **Additional Resources**.

The Glossary of Key Terms pulls together all of the words and phrases that appear in **bold** throughout the chapters. Here, those "key," or essential, terms are presented with definitions of each. Even though we define most terms in the context of using them in the chapters, you may find this alphabetical compilation helpful. A few of the words we use while discussing communication concepts and precepts throughout the book are rather exotic—for example, *enthymeme* and *assonance*. Possibly as challenging are the words that are used in a specialized way when related to communication theory: *rhetoric*, *style*, and *credibility* are not new words, but the way they are used in everyday conversation may be somewhat different from the way they are used in the context of helping you to prepare and deliver a public speech. We hope you'll consult the glossary for clarification as often as you need to.

Guide to Common Pronunciation and Usage Errors

For a speaker, pronunciation and usage errors are impediments to intelligibility and credibility. Well-reasoned points and lively descriptions can lose their impact if a mispronounced or misused word lands with a clunk to interrupt the concentration and attention of your listeners. Here we list just a few of the common errors that can crop up; references at the end describe many more usage and word-choice snares to which you should be alert. You can find pronunciation references in Chapter **25**.

Problems in Pronunciation

WORD	PROPER	IMPROPER
across	*a cross*	*a crost*
athlete	*ath leet*	*a thuh leet*
comparable	*COM per able*	*com PARE able*
compulsory	*com pul sory*	*com pul so rary*
drowned	*drowned*	*drown ded*
err	*ur*	*air*
escape	*es cape*	*ex cape*
et cetera	*et cet era*	*ek cet era*
February	*feb roo ary*	*feb you ary*
get	*get*	*git*
just	*just*	*jist*
larynx	*lar inks*	*lar nix*
library	*li brar y*	*li berry*
mischievous	*mis che vous*	*mis chee vious*
nuclear	*nu clee ar*	*nu cyou lar*
perspiration	*pers pir a tion*	*press pir a tion*
picture	*pic tchure*	*pit chure*
recognize	*rec og nize*	*reck a nize*

relevant	rel a vant	rev a lant
strict	strict	strick
surprise	sur prise	sup prise
temperature	temp per achure	temp achure
theatre	THEE a ter	thee A ter

Word-Choice Errors

WRONG USE	COMMENTS
adverse/averse	
"I would be adverse to adopting this plan."	Because the speaker is talking about an aversion to something, the proper adjective is "averse." When describing feelings, use "averse"; when describing things, use "adverse"—for example, "Without restructuring, we shall end up working in adverse conditions."
affect/effect	
"The affect of the plan could be very beneficial."	Usually "affect" is a verb. Properly, this sentence should use "effect" in its sense of "result."
bi/semi	
"Under this plan, paychecks will be distributed bimonthly on the first and fifteenth."	"Bi" means "every two" and "semi" means "twice a," so in this case it should be "distributed semimonthly on the first and fifteenth."
comprise/compose	
"Let's look at the three actions that comprise this plan."	A whole comprises its parts, so this sentence is backward; "compose" or "constitute" would be correct. For "comprise" to be correct, the sentence should read: "The plan comprises three actions; let's look at them now." Also, "is comprised of" is not correct.
disinterested/uninterested	
"Some of you may be disinterested in the workings of this plan."	"Disinterested" means having no stake in the outcome or being neutral, as in "a disinterested third party will judge the results." If you instead mean "lack of interest," then use "uninterested."
flaunt/flout	
"One thing about this plan is that it makes it less easy for users to flaunt our guidelines."	"Flaunt" means to show off; "flout" means to treat with disregard or scorn. These words are not interchangeable.
i.e./e.g.	
"Some parts of this plan, i.e., restructuring, won't take place immediately."	This choice is wrong at two levels. First, "i.e." is an abbreviation of the Latin *id est*, meaning "that is." It does not mean "for example"—that role is taken by "e.g.," from the Latin *exempli gratia*. Second, a speaker should not use these abbreviations orally and instead use plain English "that is" and "for example."

(continued)

WRONG USE	COMMENTS
imply/infer	
"I'm not inferring this plan will solve everything."	"Imply" means to *suggest* something that has not been stated explicitly, and "infer" means to *draw a conclusion* from something not stated explicitly. So, correct use would be either "I'm not implying this plan will solve everything," or something like, "You might have inferred that I think this plan will solve everything, but that is not the case."
ironic/coincidental	
"It's ironic that, after working on this plan, Alexis and I discovered we both changed our original expositions."	Irony is more than mere coincidence. Irony requires that there be some incongruity rising from a result that was different from the one expected. So, unless the speaker and Alexis had both vowed repeatedly that they were going to be steadfast in their original positions, it would be more accurate to say: "Coincidentally, Alexis and I discovered we both changed our original positions after working on this plan."
less/fewer	
"There are less opponents to this plan than supporters."	If something can be counted in discrete units it should be modified by "fewer," not by "less." So, "there are fewer opponents" is correct. Note that changing to "there is less opposition than support" makes the usage correct, too.
nonplussed/nonchalant	
"The opponents of this plan seem remarkably nonplussed in their calm acceptance of the status quo."	When one is nonplussed, one is bewildered or perplexed, not "nonchalant" or "calm."
tortuous/torturous	
"The torturous logic of the opponents of this plan is hard to fathom."	Because the speaker means "twisted or complex"—not "painful"—in this context, "tortuous" is the correct choice.

Some Grammar and Usage Problems

WRONG USE	COMMENTS
Dangling/misplaced modifier	
"Having failed twice before, I wouldn't support any more attempts by the Baker committee to come up with a plan."	As constructed, this sentence makes the speaker the one who has failed twice. To be grammatically correct, and certainly less confusing, the sentence could be: "Having failed twice before, the Baker committee won't get my support for any more attempts to come up with a plan" or "I wouldn't support any more attempts by the Baker committee to come up with a plan because they have failed twice before."

Misuse of pronouns in the subjective case

"The composition of the Baker committee came as a surprise to Alexis and I."	"I" is a subjective pronoun and so is reserved for use as the *subject* of a sentence: "Alexis and I were surprised by the composition of the Baker committee." For a sentence in which the speaker is the *object* of the verb, the objective case is appropriate: "The composition of the Baker committee came as a surprise to Alexis and me." A preposition (to, by, from, etc.) is usually a dead giveaway to use the objective case of a pronoun.

Misuse of reflexive pronoun

"The people who looked over the plan were David, Carla, and myself."	"Myself" is the reflexive form of the pronoun, and the reflexive ordinarily is used only where the object of a sentence is the same as the subject ("I overworked myself on this project"), as an object of a preposition that refers to the subject ("I worked on this project by myself"), or to emphasize the subject ("Although others helped with the research, I wrote the plan myself"). The sentence in this case should use the objective case for the pronoun: "The people who looked over the plan were David, Carla, and me." Be alert to the misuse of other reflexive pronouns like "himself," "herself," "yourself," and "themselves."

Subject–verb disagreement

"The source of these failures are to be found in the incomplete research done."	"Of these failures" is a phrase that modifies the singular subject of the sentence, "source," and the fact that the noun in the phrase is plural has no effect on the verb. Because the subject is singular, the verb should also be singular: "The source of these failures is to be found in … "

Glossary of Key Terms

A

acronym A device to aid in memory based on creating a word from the first letters of a phrase.

ad hominem fallacy An error in reasoning that consists of attacking a person identified with a position instead of refuting the position itself.

affirming the consequent The most common form of the faulty reversal of an if–then statement. A person reasons that because *X* necessarily follows *Y*, the opposite is also true. Just because "if there is a rainbow, it is raining," it does not mean that every time it is raining there is a rainbow.

agenda A specific predetermined plan for the conduct of a meeting or a group event. It provides structure for groups and helps minimize conflict over what will be discussed, in what sequence, and, perhaps, for how long.

alliteration A stylistic device that consists of the repetition of a consonant sound. "Big, brutal bullies" will be more memorable and have more impact than "large, mean bullies."

antithesis A stylistic device that consists of two contrasting ideas set up in opposition.

articulation The ability to produce the sounds of speech correctly so that words are understandable.

assonance A stylistic device that consists of the repetition of a vowel sound. "People are dreaming of pie in the sky, by and by" repeats the long "I" sound and is likely to have an impact.

attention getter The opening one or two sentences of a speech introduction designed to immediately engage the listeners' interest.

B

bar graphs A format for displaying data that compares related items by having them represented by bars of different lengths or heights.

C

causal reasoning The justification for an argument claiming that one thing is the direct result of another. A causal claim should not be confused with mere coincidence or correlation.

cause–effect pattern A way of organizing speech points that begins by discussing the origins of a situation and moves to discussing the consequences that follow those conditions.

central idea A more informal designation for the thesis of a speech. Even if one's major point is not fully developed into a subject–predicate assertion as required for a thesis sentence, this core idea provides a touchstone for developing the speech.

chronological pattern A way of organizing the points of a speech that follows a time order; it might be historical or it might follow steps in a process, for example.

circular reasoning An error in reasoning that occurs when a speaker assumes the truth of the conclusion and uses that as the starting point for developing an argument, instead of building a case for the conclusion by creating a valid line of reasoning.

claim A proposition that a speaker advances as a conclusion. The claim might be the thesis of the speech, a main point, or a subpoint. Typically, a claim is a controversial statement that does not earn automatic acceptance but needs to be proven by the development of an argument.

clearinghouse question An open-ended question asked near the end of an interview segment that allows the interviewee to offer any additional information that may be useful to the interviewer.

clincher The closing sentence of a speech conclusion that gives a sense of finality and has a powerful impact. A carefully thought-out clincher replaces the "trailing off" phenomenon that can ruin a good speech.

cognitive restructuring A treatment for communication apprehension that involves discovering the underlying statements that are driving one's fear, analyzing the logic of these, and replacing them with more realistic statements. Regularly repeating the more realistic statements can eventually restructure the way you think about speaking.

concept mapping An organizational technique for marshaling ideas. Before a speaker settles on main points, it is often helpful to use circle diagrams or movable components to pull similar ideas together and show how clusters relate to one another.

conclusion The final section of a speech, which generally restates the thesis and main points and often attempts to establish logical and psychological closure for the speech.

context The features that surround the core message of a speech and shape its meaning. General contextual features involve time, space, degree of formality, and the like. Specific contexts such as the workplace or the political sphere have sets of norms and expectations that shape speaking in those settings.

coordinate points Points of equal importance that cannot be nested under one another. For example, points I, II, and III are coordinate to each other. Points A, B, and C under each of these are also coordinate to one another.

credibility The perception that a certain speaker is believable, over and above the logical message and the emotional impact. The persuasive power of credibility comes from being able to project qualities such as competence, trustworthiness, concern, and dynamism. Other things being equal, speakers perceived as having these qualities will be more persuasive.

D

data Verifiable information often in numerical form, such as statistics used in a speech to support a specific point or line of reasoning.

deduction A form of reasoning that demonstrates how the relationships among established premises lead to a necessary conclusion.

definition by authority Explaining the meaning of a word by calling on an expert in the field or by some authoritative ruling, such as in a court.

definition by example Explaining the meaning of a word by giving familiar instances of the concept.

definition by negation Explaining the meaning of a word by contrasting it to its opposite or telling what it is not.

denying the antecedent A form of faulty reasoning that is related to but less common than affirming the consequent. It assumes that, because *X* necessarily follows from *Y*, the absence of *Y* means the absence of *X*. However, there may be other causes for *Y*. (If a major premise states "if and only if *Y* is present, *X* will be present," then denying the antecedent is not fallacious.)

E

enhanced conversation A way of thinking about public speaking that encourages speakers to rely heavily on the same resources they use daily in conversation but to amplify these, project them more enthusiastically, and pay a bit more attention to crafting details of style and organization.

enthymemes The classical term for the more informal, conversational, often shortened form that reasoning takes in actual persuasion. For example, a complete logical syllogism might state: "Anything our president does is in the national interest. This policy is initiated by our president. This policy is in the national interest." An enthymeme would be shorter and more natural sounding, such as: "Of course this is in the national interest; the president introduced it." Enthymemes are harder to dissect and analyze. However, they can be powerful in that they call on the listeners to "fill in the blanks" and thus involve them in making the case.

etymological definition A way of explaining the meaning of a term by looking at the historical roots of the word or at its linguistic origins.

evocative A speech with the purpose of evoking is designed to call forth an emotion or shared feeling. This is sometimes called the speech to entertain, but evocative speaking is a broader term that can include arousing feelings of sympathy or grief as well as feelings of happiness or amusement.

extemporaneous A mode of delivery that consists of preparing the organization of a speech and becoming familiar with the structure and some of the phrases where language is important but not writing out or memorizing the speech. It is delivered in a conversational manner from general notes. This is the most common form of delivery.

F

factual examples Specific instances used to illustrate a more general point. Brief examples are used when the audience is assumed to be familiar with the case, such as "it hurts about as much as a pinprick." Extended examples are used when the audience is not familiar with the case, so more details are required to make the point, such as "let me tell you about my Uncle George's experience…."

fallacies Errors in reasoning that make a particular argument or position invalid.

fallacy of the absurd extreme An error in reasoning that makes a potentially sound argument appear groundless by extending it to a point where it can be easily ridiculed.

false dichotomy An error of reasoning that results from assuming that there are only two clear-cut alternatives in a situation when there are, in fact, many intermediate alternatives.

full-sentence outline A detailed logical plan for a speech that states each main point and at least the first level of subpoints in complete subject–predicate sentences. This attention to detail provides a test to be sure that every part of the speech is logically related to each other. The outline is an important planning tool but it is not the same as a speech manuscript or as speaking notes.

G

Gantt A project management tool (named for its developer Henry Laurence Gantt) used to establish the timeline of a project by offering a visual representation of when each task occurs and how long it will take.

H

hasty generalization An error in inductive reasoning that results from making a premature inductive leap and basing a generalization on insufficient data.

historical definition Explaining the meaning of a term by tracing how it has been used in the past, perhaps showing how the meaning has evolved.

holistic listening Listening to another person in an open, nonjudgmental way—not just analyzing his or her points but trying to take in all the verbal and nonverbal cues, silences, and omissions to get some sense of the full message that is available to be interpreted.

hypothetical example A plausible story created by the speaker to illustrate a point. As with factual examples, these may be either brief or extended. In contrast to factual examples, though, hypothetical examples can be used only to clarify a point, not to prove it.

I

impromptu A mode of speaking that does not allow for any formal preparation but requires the speaker to speak "off the cuff." Impromptu speaking can still draw on many of the principles of other kinds of speaking, such as having a clear first and last sentence, involving the audience, and using lots of examples.

inductive reasoning A pattern of reasoning that consists of combining a series of specific observations that lead to a probable general conclusion.

internal preview At some point after the first point has been developed, a speaker forecasts the remaining points to be covered.

internal summary At some point before the last point is developed, a speaker restates the points that have been covered so far.

introduction The opening section of a speech that serves to get attention and orient the audience before beginning to develop the first main point.

J

jargon Informal or technical terms that relate to a particular activity or group; the use of jargon sets apart the practitioners or group members.

K

keyword or key-phrase outline A preliminary organizational tool that consists of just words and phrases to be used. It is more developed than brainstorming tools like concept mapping but less elaborate than a topic outline or a full-sentence outline.

L

line graphs A format for displaying data that uses points connected by lines to indicate changes over time or distance.

listening A complex and active process of receiving, processing, and evaluating an oral message. It includes the reception of stimuli, their organization into usable chunks of sound, the identification of comprehensible words or phrases, and the interpretation of meanings.

logical definition The most common and precise way of defining terms, which begins by placing the term in its broad category (genus), and then listing the qualities that differentiate the term from all other members of that category (species).

logical orientation A section of the introduction that provides the intellectual framework for the speech, often stating the thesis sentence and previewing the main points.

M

main points Primary ideas, those that are central and indispensable to the development of the thesis.

major premise The basic assumption that underlies a line of deductive argument. If the argument is laid out as a formal syllogism, then the major premise is the first statement and it lays out an absolute relationship such as either/or, if/then, or the classic "all men are mortal."

manuscript speaking A mode of delivery that involves writing out a speech fully (in the oral style preferably) and then practicing it until it is familiar and sounds conversational when delivered.

Maslow's hierarchy of needs   A systematic arrangement of human needs based on the assumption that people will give priority to more basic needs and fill these at a minimal level before attending to higher needs. The hierarchy proceeds from security needs to belongingness needs to esteem needs to self-actualization needs.

meaning   The complex mutual understanding of communication co-created by senders and receivers within a given social, contextual, and contingent situation.

memorized   A mode of delivery that involves writing out a speech fully (in the oral style preferably) and then practicing it until it can be delivered word for word from memory.

metaphor   A stylistic device that uses language as if there were an identity between two things that belong to different categories—for example, "my job is a nightmare."

minor premise   The part of a deductive argument that introduces some data about the actual state of affairs into the reasoning. In an either/or or if/then syllogism, for example, it asserts that one of the alternatives is or is not true. In a categorical syllogism, the minor premise places a specific case into a general category, as in "Socrates is a man."

motivated sequence   An organizer for persuasion that echoes the mental stages through which listeners progress as they hear a speech.

mutuality of concern   A give-and-take between a speaker and a listener that develops over time into a meaningful exchange of ideas.

operational definition   A way of explaining the meaning of a term by explaining how it works or what it does.

P

persuasive speaking   Speech that has the purpose of changing behavior or attitudes of the listeners.

PERT   A project management tool used to organize a project by visually establishing the required order of steps needed to complete the task. PERT stands for Program Evaluation and Review Technique.

pictorial reproductions   Presentation aids that use a visual depiction (e.g., a photograph, sketch, or video) of an object in two dimensions.

pictorial symbols   Presentation aids that consist of representations of abstract concepts.

pie chart   A format for displaying data that compares related items by having them represented by pie segments, all of which add up to 100 percent of some category.

pitch   How high or low a speaker's voice is. It is helpful to find a pitch that is natural and also to vary one's pitch.

post hoc fallacy   The error in reasoning that results from assuming that, because one event followed another event, it is caused by that event. The tests of causation must be met or the relationship might be coincidental or correlational.

presentation aid   An object or thing that adds another communication dimension beyond a speaker's content and delivery.

presentation software   Computer software specialized for creating presentation aids.

preview   An organization tool that gives listeners a road map of what is to follow: "Today I will cover these three points."

primacy   The persuasive effect that sometimes comes from placing a point first or early in a speech to give it greater impact or make it memorable.

primary audience outcome   The most important result that a speaker wants to achieve, phrased in terms of what the audience will actually do after the speech.

probability   The condition that exists when a conclusion is likely to be true but cannot be established with absolute certainty. In psychological and social matters, most claims are discussed in terms of some degree of probability. When speakers try to persuade listeners on these topics, the task is to show the likelihood of certain costs and benefits coming about so that the "odds" favor the speaker's position.

problem–solution pattern   A way of arranging the main points of a speech that begins with creating an awareness of some issue requiring change and then moves to explaining what should be done to remedy the concerns raised.

project proposal   A kind of workplace presentation in which a speaker or a group provides a plan that should be undertaken and then gives the rationale for this approach. These presentations can range from a research proposal to a sales presentation to a proposal for undertaking some technical project.

project status report A kind of workplace presentation that updates listeners of the progress being made on a project that is already under way. This sort of interim report serves to reassure colleagues or customers about what is being done, to alert them to any problems encountered, and to seek feedback.

proposition of fact A claim that something is or is not true.

proposition of policy A claim that a certain course of action should or should not be adopted.

proposition of value A claim that something is good or bad (in the broadest sense).

public speaking A communication setting in which one person has primary control and direction of the resources of communication. It may happen in a formal or informal setting, but it involves preparation and the focus is on the speaker for much of the time.

Q

question and answer period A time allotted after the conclusion of the main speech in which audience members can ask for clarification or elaboration on the speaker's position.

R

rate The speed or pace at which one speaks. Ideally, rate must be fast enough to hold attention, slow enough to be understood, and varied to emphasize meaning.

reasoning by analogy A form of reasoning in which people can draw conclusions about unknown events based on what is known about similar events.

recency The persuasive effect that sometimes comes from placing a point last or late in a speech to give it greater impact or make it memorable.

refutation A structured challenge to an opposing point of view that consists of showing exactly how the evidence and reasoning are faulty. One can refute a point in a debate where another speaker is present or refute a position that is widely held in society and that audience members may have heard about.

rhetoric The art of finding the available means of persuasion in any given situation. The emphasis is on the thoughtful decisions speakers make in adapting their points to audiences. This classical use contrasts with some contemporary suggestions that "mere rhetoric" is superficial or tricky persuasion.

S

secondary orality Sound-based communication that, unlike the primary orality of preliterate cultures, is based in literacy and finds its outlet in electronic media.

semantic fallacy An error in reasoning that occurs when a word is used in different senses in different parts of the argument.

signposts Organizational techniques that keep the listener informed about how the speech is unfolding. They tell what has been covered, what remains to be covered, and when changes in direction are occurring.

simile A stylistic device that compares two things from different categories, such as "managing a group of scientists is like herding cats."

slang Nonstandard words and expressions.

slippery slope fallacy An error in reasoning that claims the first step in some direction must result in going to dangerous lengths in that direction.

spatial pattern A way of organizing the main points of a speech according to some relationship in space. This might be by geographical regions or by rooms in a museum, for example.

speech or speaker's notes These are working notes designed for quick reference and easy readability during a speech. They are not the same as a manuscript or a full-sentence outline, but they contain keywords, phrases, organizational cues, and perhaps some specific details that must be cited exactly.

statistical evidence Data that have been systematically collected and coded in numerical form so that speakers can capture a broad number of cases or make formal comparative statements.

stock issues A set of standardized questions to which a speaker can refer in order to be sure that a proposition has been fully established. These can be the basis of building a strong persuasive case or they can be points of refutation for a speaker who opposes a proposition. The stock issues vary in context—such as the legal context, where each kind of charge raises particular points of controversy—but in a general policy proposition the stock issues are: Is there a need? Is the need inherent to the current system? Does the proposal meet the need? Is the proposal workable? Does the plan have disadvantages that outweigh the advantages?

style The use of language to make speech effective. Style consists of being clear and concise and also of using various devices to enhance the impact of language.

subordinate points The lesser points that fall beneath main points of a speech—either to elaborate on the main points or to support them.

superordinate points An item of superior rank, standing, or status to another item.

supporting materials The parts of a speech that expand on or prove the claims made in main points or subpoints. These examples, definitions, statistics, and testimony serve as the actual building blocks of a speech.

T

team presentation A speech given by a small group of presenters who have worked collaboratively to prepare a unified statement and to make sure that all the requirements of an effective speech are present. Presumably, the presenters all bring some special expertise or perspective to the presentation.

testimony A form of supporting material that reports the experience or opinions of another person. The testimony is most helpful when the person cited either is an expert or has direct experience with the topic.

text A message captured in words. Thus, all the nonverbal, psychological, and cultural factors that

surround this core message and help shape its meaning are called the context.

topic outline An outline that identifies the points to be covered and the relationships among them but that may not spell out all of the logical connections that would be present in a full-sentence outline.

topical pattern A way of organizing the main points of a speech that grows naturally out of what is being talked about and is not arranged according to sequential, spatial, or logical rules.

training presentation A form of informative speaking that is in an extended and focused format. Associated with the workplace, it will often take the form of a series of workshops or seminars in which the goal is to help people learn a rather specific set of skills or body of knowledge.

V

vocal variety Altering the tone and pitch of one's voice to provide for interest and emphasis. It's the opposite of a monotone.

vocalized pauses Filler phrases such as "um," "er," "y'know," and "like" that break the fluency of speaking and can be distracting to listeners.

volume The loudness (or softness) with which one speaks.

W

warrant The part of an argument that links the evidence to the claim. Because the same data can be used to prove multiple (even opposite) points, a speaker must show explicitly the reasoning that links data to a particular conclusion.

whiteboard A board with an erasable shiny surface for making temporary markings, such as drawings or words.

Notes

Chapter 1

1. Daniel J. Boorstin, "Dissent, Dissension, and the News," in *The Decline of Radicalism: Reflections on America Today* (New York: Random House, 1960). Retrieved from the Columbia World of Quotations, http://www.bartleby.com/66/80/7780.html, on June 28, 2008.

2. J. William Fulbright, Speech to the American Newspaper Publishers Association, April 28, 1966. Retrieved from the Columbia World of Quotations, http://www.bartleby.com/66/56/24156.html, on June 28, 2008.

3. W. J. Ong, *Rhetoric, Romance, and Technology: Studies in the Interaction of Expression and Culture* (Ithaca, NY: Cornell University Press, 1971).

4. Marshall McLuhan, *Understanding Media: The Extensions of Man* (New York: McGraw-Hill Book Co., 1964).

5. Claude E. Shannon and Warren Weaver, *The Mathematical Theory of Communication* (Urbana, IL: University of Illinois Press, 1949).

6. Sonja K. Foss and Cindy L. Griffin, "Beyond Persuasion: A Proposal for an Invitational Rhetoric," *Communication Monographs, 62* (March 1995): 2–18.

7. Patrik Jonsson, "Shirley Sherrod: Does She Have a Case against Andrew Breitbart?" *Christian Science Monitor*, July 29, 2010. Retrieved from EBSCO*host* Academic Search Complete database on August 2, 2010.

Chapter 3

1. Adapted from Alfred McClung Lee and Elizabeth Briant Lee, *The Fine Art of Propaganda* (New York: Harcourt and Institute for Propaganda Analysis, 1939), 23–24.

Chapter 4

1. H. Thomson, "What Is the Function of Mirror Neurons?" *New Scientist, 205*(2754), (2010): 28–29. Retrieved from EBSCO*host* Academic Search Complete database on May 9, 2011.

2. V. Cunningham, M. Lefkoe, and L. Sechrest, "Eliminating Fears: An Intervention That Permanently Eliminates the Fear of Public Speaking," *Clinical Psychology & Psychotherapy, 13*(3), (2006): 183–193, doi:10.1002/cpp.487.

Chapter 5

1. Based on Catherine Patrick, *What Is Creative Thinking?* (New York: Philosophical Library, 1955), 1–48. Patrick's work is based on G. Wallas, *The Art of Thought* (New York: Harcourt, Brace, 1926). This theory has been further advanced by Sébastien Hélie and Ron Sun, "Incubation, Insight, and Creative Problem Solving: A Unified Theory and a Connectionist Model," *Psychological Review, 117*(3), (2010): 994–1024. Retrieved from EBSCO*host* Academic Search Complete database on September 12, 2010.

Chapter 6

1. Arne Duncan, "The Quiet Revolution," *Vital Speeches of the Day, 76*(10), (October 2010): 455–459. Retrieved from EBSCO*host* Academic Search Complete database on December 3, 2010.

2. Hillary Rodham Clinton, "Women's Progress Is Human Progress," *Vital Speeches of the Day, 76*(5), (May 2010): 199–203. Retrieved from EBSCO*host* Academic Search Complete database on December 3, 2010.

3. Muhtar Kent, "Are We Ready for Tomorrow, Today?" *Vital Speeches of the Day, 76*(3), (March 2010): 117–121. Retrieved from EBSCO*host* Academic Search Complete database on December 3, 2010.

4. Barack Obama, "Educated Citizens in a Changing World," *Vital Speeches of the Day, 76*(8), (August 2010): 364–366. Retrieved from EBSCO*host* Academic Search Complete database on December 3, 2010.

5. John M. McCardell Jr., "From Tentative Twig to Mighty Branch," *Vital Speeches of the Day, 76*(11), (November 2010): 492–495. Retrieved from EBSCO*host* Academic Search Complete database on December 3, 2010.

Chapter 7

1. Izzy Gesell, "How to Lead When the Generation Gap Becomes Your Everyday Reality," *Journal for Quality & Participation, 32*(4), (January 2010): 21–24. Retrieved from EBSCOhost Academic Search Complete database on December 5, 2010.

2. Sidney Lowe and Susie Skarl, "Talkin' 'bout My Generation," *College & Research Libraries News, 70*(7), (July): 400–403. Retrieved from http://crln.acrl.org/content/70/7/400.full.pdf+html on December 5, 2010.

3. Definition of "ethnicity" from the *American Heritage New Dictionary of Cultural Literacy*, 3rd ed. (Boston: Houghton Mifflin Co., 2005). Retrieved from Dictionary.com, http://dictionary.reference.com/browse/ethnicity, on August 3, 2008.

4. Barack Obama '08, "Meet the Candidate." Retrieved from http://www.barackobama.com/learn/meet_barack.php on May 25, 2008.

Chapter 12

1. Barack Obama, "The World That America Seeks," *Vital Speeches of the Day, 76*(11), (November 2010): 508–512. Retrieved from EBSCOhost Academic Search Complete database on December 10, 2010.

Chapter 13

1. Kayla Strickland, "Malaria." Personal outline for Effective Public Speaking class at Sinclair Community College (November 2010).

2. Robert M. Gates, "What Must Change in the U.S. Military," *Vital Speeches of the Day, 76*(7), (July 2010): 310–314. Retrieved from EBSCOhost Academic Search Complete database on December 10, 2010.

3. Lisa Kudrow, "The Biology Major Who Became a Friend," *Vital Speeches of the Day, 76*(8), (August 2010): 367–370. Retrieved from EBSCOhost Academic Search Complete database on December 10, 2010.

4. Glenn Beck, "It Is Still Morning in America," *Vital Speeches of the Day, 76*(4), (April 2010): 167–173. Retrieved from EBSCOhost Academic Search Complete database on December 10, 2010.

5. Dan Brutto, "Globalization 4.0 and the New Logistics," *Vital Speeches of the Day, 76*(11), (November 2010): 512–514. Retrieved from EBSCOhost Academic Search Complete database on December 11, 2010.

6. Carol W. Kinsley, "What Is Community Service Learning?" *Vital Speeches of the Day, 61*(2), (November 1, 1994): 40–42.

Chapter 14

1. Kayla Strickland, "Malaria." Personal outline for Effective Public Speaking class at Sinclair Community College (November 2010).

2. Peter M. Gerhart, "The Future of the Legal Profession," *Vital Speeches of the Day, 60*(11), (March 15, 1994): 347–352.

Chapter 15

1. Bureau of Labor Statistics, "Usual Weekly Earnings of Wage and Salary Workers News Release." Retrieved from http://www.bls.gov/news.release/archives/wkyeng_07162009.htm on December 12, 2010.

2. Department of Rehabilitation and Correction, "Frequently Asked Questions." Retrieved from http://www.drc.ohio.gov/web/FAQ.htm on December 12, 2010.

3. Ohio Literacy Network, "Donate." Retrieved from http://www.ohioliteracynetwork.org/donate.html on December 12, 2010.

4. Laura Walter, "EHS Today: Why We Need to Hang Up on Our Distracted Driving Addiction," LexisNexis® Academic & Library Solutions, June 1, 2010, p. 35. Retrieved from http://www.lexisnexis.com.sinclair.ohionet.org/hottopics/lnacademic on December 13, 2010.

5. Regina Brett, "Making Your Car a No-Phone Zone," *Cleveland Plain Dealer*, Metro Final edition, May 2, 2010, p. B1. Retrieved from http://www.lexisnexis.com.sinclair.ohionet.org/hottopics/lnacademic on December 13, 2010.

Chapter 16

1. David Zarefsky, "Argumentation," in *Encyclopedia of Rhetoric*, edited by Thomas Sloan, October 2001, Oxford University Press. Retrieved from http://rave.ohiolink.edu/ebooks/ebc/t223 on May 22, 2011.

Chapter 17

1. Michael E. Eidenmuller, "Personification," American Rhetoric: Rhetorical Figures in Sound. Retrieved from http://www.american-rhetoric.com/speeches/bobbyjindallouisiana-govvictory.htm on May 22, 2011.

2. The Ebenezer Sermon "The Daily Dish," *The Atlantic* (n.d.). Retrieved from http://www.theatlantic.com/daily-dish/archive/2008/01/the-ebenezer-sermon/221010 on March 15, 2014.

Chapter 18

1. Kathleen German, Bruce E. Gronbeck, Douglas Ehninger, and Alan H. Monroe, *Principles of Speech Communication*, 17th ed. (New York: Allyn and Bacon, 2010).

Chapter 19

1. David Abney, "Preparing American Students to Succeed in a Global Era of Change," *Vital Speeches of the Day, 74*(4), (April 2008): 178–181. Retrieved from EBSCO*host* Academic Search Complete database on December 11, 2010.

Chapter 20

1. "Malaria—Topic Overview: What Is Malaria?" WebMD website, http://www.webmd.com/a-to-z-guides/malaria-topic-overview.

2. "Malaria—Topic Overview: What Are the Symptoms of Malaria?" WebMD website, http://www.webmd.com/a-to-z-guides/malaria-topic-overview.

3. Abraham Maslow, *Motivation and Personality*, 2nd ed. (New York: Harper & Row, 1970), 35–58.

4. One resource for poll information is the Inter-University Consortium for Political and Social Research (ICPSR) databank in Ann Arbor, MI (www.icpsr.umich.edu). Another resource for poll information is the Roper Center for Public Opinion Research, http://www.ropercenter.uconn.edu/about_roper.html.

5. Simeon Chow and Sarit Amir, "The Universality of Values: Implications for Global Advertising Strategy." *Journal of Advertising Research, 46*(3), (September 2006): 301–314. Retrieved from EBSCOhost Academic Communication & Mass Media Search Complete database on December 14, 2010.

6. This approach to values is adapted from Milton Rokeach's method of classifying beliefs by their centrality. Rokeach, in collaboration with Richard Bonier and others, *The Open and Closed Mind* (New York: Basic Books, 1960).

Chapter 21

1. Nelson Cowan, Troy D. Johnson, and J. Scott Saults, "Capacity Limits in List Item Recognition: Evidence from Proactive Interference," *Memory, 13*(3/4), (2005): 293–299. Retrieved from Academic Search Complete, EBSCOhost on September 26, 2008.

Chapter 22

1. Wallace C. Fotheringham, *Perspectives on Persuasion* (Boston: Allyn & Bacon, 1966), 32.

2. United States Code: Title 18,1111. Murder | LII/Legal Information Institute. Retrieved from http://www.law.cornell.edu/uscode/uscode18/usc_sec_18_00001111—-000-.html on February 16, 2010.

3. Richard E. Petty and John T. Cacioppo, *Communication and Persuasion: Central and Peripheral Routes to Attitude Change* (New York: Springer-Verlag, 1986), 5.

Index

In this index f indicates figures t indicates tables.

FIGURES AND TABLES

FIGURES

TABLES